GUARD YOUR HEART

FOR IT IS THE WELLSPRING OF LIFE

366 Daily Devotionals

By David Meengs

Guard Your Heart, For It is the Wellspring of Life
By David Meengs
English

Copyright 2016

©Biblical Counseling Worldwide

All Scripture quotations are from the NIV unless otherwise mentioned.

ISBN - 61-7916-011-6

Second Printing

Published and distributed by:
Biblical Counseling Worldwide
P. O. Box 547
Caledonia, MI. 49316

Printed in the USA by Dickinson Press Inc.

Dedication

This book is dedicated to
my and my wife's dear parents, Merle and Mina
Meengs and, Albert and Evelyn Derks. They did so
much to "Guard Our Hearts." How they prayed when
we needed protection and strength. We thank God for
placing us in our covenant families, who are precious to
us. May we as parents and grandparents live well,
finish well and be a testimony of the grace of God, as
our parents have been to us!

*"Above all else, guard your heart,
for it is the wellspring of life."
Proverbs 4:23*

Guard Your Heart

For It is the Wellspring of Life

366 Daily Devotionals

Thank You

There have been many efforts to get this devotional book out. I just wanted to acknowledge those who have helped. First of all, thanks to my dear wife Mary, who has been such a blessing for 46 years. She has been patient in reading and rereading as she edits these devotions for this publication and for others. She has corrected mistakes and has given good advice when something was not said as well as it could have been. There are so many helpful comments that are hers. Thanks also to our daughter, Becky, and my wife's sister, Donna, who spent so much time looking at these devotionals, checking references and helping to find mistakes before you do.

Above all, we want to thank our God who has written our names on His hand before the creation of the world. He is the one who calls us and equips us to serve Him and His church. He has blessed us, protected us and encouraged us every step of the way! May our God, His Son, His Word and Spirit, "Guard Your Heart"!

The Author,
David Meengs

January

February

Day	Text	Title of the Devotional

March

April

May

June

July

August

September

October

November

December

JANUARY

"Search me, O God, and know my heart;
test me and know my anxious thoughts.
See if there is any offensive way in me,
and lead me in the way everlasting."
Psalm 139:23-24

January 1

"This is what the LORD says: 'Stand at the crossroads and look; ask for the ancient paths, ask where the good way is, and walk in it, and you will find rest for your souls.'" Jeremiah 6:16

Walk the *"ancient paths"*

As we begin a new year, we are at a "crossroads" much like the people of Israel were. They had forsaken their relationship with God. As a result, they had personal and political turmoil. The hearts of the people and leaders had changed. By their actions, it was evident they thought the world had more to offer than God did. The people had clearly traded off the love of the Creator for the love of created things and pleasures of all kinds. God asked them, *"What injustice have your fathers found in Me, that they have gone far from Me?"* Jeremiah 2:5b NKJV. God was asking them, why did you break <u>covenant</u> with Me? This was not only Israel's problem. It's our problem too!

The Bible is a testimony of two covenants. God promised His people in a covenant, a binding agreement, that He would protect and care for His people if they would love Him in return. Well, the love for God had grown cold over the years, and God is warning them that He is not going to take much more of this! We wonder, "What was it that caused Israel, and us also, to leave God?"

We have had God's covenant blessings in abundance for many years! God kept His covenant promises! But over time, we begin to expect these blessings and even think that we deserve more of them! Like wandering Israel, we are more in love with the created things God gives, than a deepening relationship with Him the Creator and Giver of everything!

God sends Jeremiah to warn us, *"Stand at the crossroads and look; ask for the ancient paths, ask where the good way is, and walk in it, and you will find rest for your souls.'"* Jeremiah 6:16. Those *"ancient paths"* are outlined in the Bible for us to see God's will for our lives. Will we take this warning seriously? Israel didn't! And God allowed wicked countries to plunder them!

Prayer: Lord, we are guilty personally and nationally of forsaking You. Forgive us Lord. We want to walk Your *"ancient paths"* and love You more! Help us Lord, as we study Your *"ancient paths"*! In Jesus' name we pray. Amen.

January 2

*"In six days the LORD made the Heavens and the earth,
the sea, and all that is in them."* Exodus 20:11a

How long did it take God to create?

The Bible says *"six days."* Some argue these days could have been a million years each. Yes, but they weren't! I wonder why they never argue about the length of time a night is? God clearly said there was an evening and then a morning, just the way we see it today. One reason God created everything in *"six days"* was to set our standard workweek of working six days and resting one. Another proof is, *"God said, 'Let there be lights in the expanse of the sky to separate the day from the night, and let them serve as signs to mark seasons, and days and years,'"* Genesis 1:14. If the days of creation were not six literal days, how could they *"mark seasons, and days and years"*?

The book of Genesis is literal, historical and foundational to the Bible and Christian doctrine. The word Genesis itself means beginning or origin. Genesis details the beginning of the created world, the sun, the moon, and the stars. We have details about the beginning of plants, animals and man. We have the first marriage. We have the first sin. We have the first news of God's plan of salvation. The book of Genesis is God's introduction to what He wants to reveal about Himself!

Genesis shows us clearly that there is intelligence, meaning and purpose behind all that exists. Many important doctrines in the Bible are in Genesis or linked to it! If you eliminate the book of Genesis, particularly the first eleven chapters, you will have undermined Christianity. If God did not create man and all creation, good and perfect; if man did not sin and become separated from God, why would we need a Savior to restore us to God? Why would we need a new Heavens and earth some day. Fact is, Satan wants us unprepared for eternity! So Satan introduces his own theologies, like evolution, to cast doubt on the fact that God created and continues to sustain the world we now have.

Prayer: Dear Lord, we thank You for telling us that in the beginning You created the heavens and the earth. Help us to see how evolution is another religion. Lord, Your truth alone sets us free. In Jesus' name we pray. Amen.

January 3

"And God said, 'Let there be light,' and there was light. God saw that the light was good, and He separated the light from the darkness."
Genesis 1:3-4

Why did God separate?

Did you notice, God *"separated"* something on the first four days of creation? God is teaching us something! The first time we see this word in the Bible is in our text. There was only darkness in the newly created world. Somehow God *"separated"* it and made light on the first day. On day two, God *"separated"* *"water from water."* Without separation there was only water! With separation we now have sky also! There is now <u>distance</u> between the two!

On day three we have another water *"separation."* Now we have land also! Dry land is about 29% of the earth's surface. Water is 71%. With this *"separation,"* the land can *"produce vegetation: seed-bearing plants and trees,"* Genesis 1:11b. Again on the 4th day, God did another *"separation."* God made a daytime light (the sun), and nighttime lights (the moon and stars). What would we have without all these *"separations"*? We would still have darkness, no productive earth to sustain life! <u>Separation bore much fruit in our physical world!</u>

Think of how important *"separation"* is concerning our spiritual life! *"Your iniquities have separated you from your God; your sins have hidden His face from you, so that He will not hear,"* Isaiah 59:2. God created us to bear fruit also. We cannot do this until we are separate from the world, born again! The change chapter in the Bible ends with a major separation. *"Get rid of all bitterness, rage and anger,"* Ephesians 4:31a. If we are not bearing fruit for God, it is because we are not willing to separate self from sin! *"Get rid of all moral filth and the evil that is so prevalent and humbly accept the Word planted in you, which can save you,"* James 1:21.

Prayer: Lord, what a beautiful job You did *"separating"* things, to bring us a fruitful world. Lord, create in us clean hearts so we too can separate ourselves from sin! For Lord, You are coming again; this time to separate the sheep from the goats! May we be found ready and faithful. In Jesus' name we pray. Amen.

"Then God said, 'Let Us make man in Our image, in Our likeness, and let them rule over the fish of the sea and the birds of the air, over the livestock, over all the earth, and over all the creatures that move along the ground.' So God created man in His own image, in the image of God He created him." Genesis 1:26-27a

Created in the image of God!

These two verses are the Gospel message. Three times in two verses God says He *"created man in His own image."* The *"Us"* in *"Let Us make man"* refers to God the Father, the Son and the Spirit. One God, in Trinity, together made man, dwelt in man, and uniquely commissioned man for a higher purpose than the rest of His creation.

First, the context helps us define *"in His image."* In the first 25 verses, God is very personal in relating to His creation. God made man His representative to *"rule over"* His creation. Note that God did not make man to worship His creation!

Secondly, *"in His image,"* is a spiritual likeness. *"God is Spirit,"* John 4:24. God is only a Spirit. Man's *"likeness"* to God in creation was God's Spirit placed in man. Man is made of two parts, body and spirit. Yet man is even more spiritual than physical. For the physical body dies after a few years, but our spirit lives forever as Ecclesiastes 12:7 teaches. Like God, we not only have an eternal spirit, we <u>are</u> an eternal spirit!

Third, *"in His image,"* means man is different than an animal. If animals have a spirit, it goes into the ground at death, Ecclesiastes 3:21. Our text totally rules out evolution! How can man evolve from an animal when he has a *"spirit"* unlike an animal?

Fourth, *"in His image,"* is before sin. Man was created *"good,"* sinless, just like God. Man had complete, perfect unity and purpose with God. Their spirits were one! Sin changed all that. The Gospel message is: Man was created in the image of God, lost it in the fall, and can regain it in Christ. Our first parents were holy and happy, *"in the image of God"*! And so are we in Christ, restored to the image of God!

Prayer: Lord, we thank you for creating us in Your image, giving us a relationship with You. We thank you for recreating us through Jesus, Your Son. In His name we pray. Amen.

January 5

"The heavens declare the glory of God; the skies proclaim the work of His hands. Day after day they pour forth speech; night after night they display knowledge." Psalm 19:1-2

The creation points to the Creator

For thousands of years people have worshiped creation. Especially the sun, moon and stars, since they are literally "highlights" of God's creation. The trees and even the earth itself is worshiped. The creation itself is not God, but points to God! So when we look at God's beautiful creation, we need to see the more beautiful Creator. That is why our text begins, *"The heavens declare the glory of God."* The skies <u>shout</u>, "Your Creator gave you all this!" *"Day after day"* and *"night after night"* the Heavens <u>speak</u> about how great God is! Creation itself is rightly called God's "general revelation." It is a revelation about Him, for all to see!

We must see that God not only created a good world for us to live in, but that He also upholds it and keeps it running! The book of Hebrews tells us about the relationship of Jesus Christ to the created world. God *"appointed"* Him, that is Jesus, *"heir of all things, and through whom He made the universe."* Then it goes on to say that Jesus Christ as Lord sustains, *"all things by His powerful word,"* Hebrews 1:3b.

As Christians, we want opportunities to tell others the Gospel message. Let us then use our text to point to God! May we point discussions about the beauty of "nature," to the One who created everything. One thing we must learn from creation: It gives meaning and it is not selfish. The trees give fruit, nuts and shade to cool down man and beast! The trees wave in praise to God. Psalm 96 says, *"the trees of the forest will sing for joy."* And this is just the trees. All creation points to the Creator. May we learn great spiritual lessons from created things and worship God who thoughtfully and lovingly gave us such a beautiful creation to bless and sustain us!

Prayer: Lord, forgive us for ignoring You, the Maker of all things! *"For since the creation of the world, Your invisible qualities — Your eternal power and divine nature — have been clearly seen."* Romans 1:20a. Lord, we worship You. In Jesus' name we pray. Amen.

January 6

"And the LORD God commanded the man, 'You are free to eat from any tree in the garden; but you must not eat from the tree of the knowledge of good and evil, for when you eat of it you will surely die.'"
Genesis 2:16-17

Why was Adam's one sin so serious?

The first thing we see in our text is the absolute authority of God. He has just made Adam the crowning glory of all that He created. Since God made man, He now has the right to rule over him. God gives a single command to Adam; *"You must not eat from the tree of the knowledge of good and evil, for when you eat of it you will surely die."* It is significant that Eve is not yet made.

God specifically commanded Adam, because he alone is the representative father of every person who would ever live. If Adam obeyed God in this one simple command, he would live forever, along with all of his children through all the generations. Adam and later Eve were the only two people who truly had a free will! Eve is included because they were one flesh in everything. If Adam and Eve obeyed God, they would never die physically or spiritually.

God promises life forever if Adam obeyed, death if he did not! Adam and Eve were truly immortal until they sinned! After sin, as God promised, they and all their offspring lost their immortal status!

Herein lies much of the problem! It was a very small thing for Adam to keep this one simple command! But having a free will, Satan convinced the two of them that they could have more than they presently had if they would eat of the tree. Their sin had great consequences. For now, the whole created world is under the curse also. Even the animals will now die, even eating each other after the flood.

Prayer: Lord, we see the history of our failure to obey You. It is so amazing that soon after Adam and Eve sinned, the first death of any kind in the whole world was You killing an animal in Genesis 3:21. You covered man's sin! You shed innocent blood to pay for Adam's guilty life. By doing so, You pointed to Jesus who would some day come and shed His innocent blood for our sins. How beautiful is Your grace. We praise You for it. In Jesus' name we pray. Amen.

January 7

"'And I will put enmity between you and the woman, and between your seed and her Seed; He shall bruise your head, and you shall bruise His heel.'" Genesis 3:15 NKJV

Satan gets into a war!

God, the righteous and holy Judge, speaks here directly to a guilty Satan, sentencing him to death. God does not question Satan or ask him why he did what he did! God put Satan on death row! This verse is fully a preview of what is to come as the Bible and the history of the world unfolds. God here is clear about Satan's doom.

1. Satan gets into a war. Satan just declared war with God. Now God is telling him and us that Satan will lose. This battle is an 6000-year war to date, still going on today with even more intensity, as the world comes to an end! It is the battle between Satan and the Church! It is the battle for our eternal souls!

2. The war is a God-ordained hostility. It is between the forces of evil led by Satan, and the Church led by Christ. It is called the antithesis, meaning against God. And yes, it is God-ordained! That is helpful to remember as we study the Bible and interpret the battles going on in the world yet today. *"I will put,"* means God is behind the antithesis for His own glory and praise! The antithesis is the ongoing fight between good and evil. It is a dividing line clearly drawn, clearly fought, forever vicious. The two sides of this war are becoming clearer as the world nears the end. This war will not cease until the last elect soul is saved. Then Christ will stop it!

3. Christ wins the war. As soon as the snakebite was given, the antidote was administered. The grace of God quickly covered Adam's sin. Eve's "Seed" in our text is singular, not plural! It is Christ. He has already defeated Satan at the Cross! The book of Revelation completes the Bible with the final victory! But already in Genesis, God's grace to man is shown and promised in the future. God is now building His Church!

Prayer: Lord, how beautiful! Jesus Christ, born of a woman, perfect Man, yet fully God, has already defeated Satan! How much we need You Lord, so we too can defeat Satan! We praise You for Your grace and power! In Jesus' name we pray. Amen.

January 8

"Watch and pray so you will not fall into temptation." Matthew 26:41a

Satan calls a meeting

His opening address was, "My dear demon helpers, we need to plan! We need to keep Christians from going to church, from reading their Bibles, and from prayer. If they gain a connection with Jesus, our power is broken. Steal their time, so they don't develop a relationship with God and with other people either."

"How shall we do this?" asked his demons. "Keep them busy in the non-essentials of life. Invent schemes to occupy their minds. Tempt them to spend and borrow until they are broken. Persuade the wives to go to work for long hours. Get the husbands to work 6-7 days each week, 10-12 hours a day. All so they can afford their empty lifestyles. Keep them busy with sports, cinema and T.V. programs. Keep them from spending time together. Break their families so their homes will offer no escape from the pressures of work!"

"Go my demons go! Make sure you over-stimulate their minds so that they can't hear the voice of God. Fill their life with noise! Keep the TV, CDs, PCs, radios and cell phones playing and ringing. Jam their minds with junk and break their union with Christ."

"My demon friends, fill their homes with worthless newspapers and magazines. Pound their minds with news 24 hours a day. Invade their driving time with billboards of barely dressed men and women. Flood their mailboxes with junk mail, porn mail, mail order catalogs, etc... In their recreation, let them be so excessive that they return from play, exhausted. Keep them too busy to smell the flowers and reflect on God's creation. Keep them super busy!"

"And my dear demons, when they meet for spiritual fellowship, make them gossip so they leave with troubled consciences. Crowd their lives with so many good causes that they have no time to seek power from Jesus. Soon they will be working in their own strength, sacrificing their health and family for 'good causes.'" And the demons went out!

Prayer: Lord, we have many temptations! Satan wants us! Forgive us for giving in to his schemes. Fill us with Your Spirit so that we *"watch and pray"*! May we redeem the time! In Jesus' name we pray. Amen.

January 9

"Fight the good fight, holding on to faith and a good conscience. Some have rejected these and so have shipwrecked their faith. Among them are Hymenaeus and Alexander, whom I handed over to Satan to be taught not to blaspheme." 1 Timothy 1:18b-20

"Handed over to Satan"

What revealing words about how God works! Today in many churches, there is a preoccupation with casting out Satan! But here, two church members are *"handed over to Satan"* instead! Paul gives the reason, *"That they be taught not to blaspheme."* To blaspheme is to speak profanely or evil of God, or about the sacred things of God. It is to curse God and hold Him in contempt. This sin was punishable by death in Leviticus 24:16. But here in 1 Timothy, two blasphemers were *"handed over to Satan."* Why?

A similar situation happened in 1 Corinthians 5:1. A man *"had his father's wife."* He was a church member, and the church was proud or laughing about the matter. God wasn't! He commanded the church to *"hand this man over to Satan, so that his sinful nature may be destroyed and his spirit saved on the day of the Lord,"* 1 Corinthians 5:5. God was saying that this man should be put out of the church because he was currently not one of His children. Furthermore, *"you must not associate with anyone who calls himself <u>a brother</u> but is sexually immoral or greedy, an idolater or a slanderer, a drunkard or a swindler. With such a man do not even eat,"* 1 Corinthians 5:11b.

By handing these men over to Satan, God used Satan to afflict them! With much pain and misery from Satan, the former blasphemer turned to God for mercy! And that's the point. Yet another reason was God's church remained holy. One rotten apple makes the whole box rotten is also true spiritually speaking!

Prayer: Lord, You teach us much concerning Your holiness and the importance of us being holy. How gracious You were to the man who was put out of the church in 1 Corinthians 5. Later You saved this man. So great is Your grace! We need that same grace in great measure! Please Lord be merciful to us. In Jesus' holy name we pray. Amen!

January 10

"Wisdom calls aloud in the street, she raises her voice in the public squares; at the head of the noisy streets she cries out, in the gateways of the city she makes her speech." Proverbs 1:20-21

Student, wisdom is calling out to you!

Student, imagine this scene in your city or school. At the main gate or door, God is making a speech to all who enter! He knows terrorists and evil people are inside. He knows they want to lead you into a life of hatred, violence and corruption. So, enter with caution. But before you enter, God wants to further warn you!

"Fools hate knowledge," Proverbs 1:22b. You have an opportunity that everyone does not have! You can go inside and learn. But beware, in your school there are those who will tell you not to study, just have fun. Don't be foolish! Now is the time for you to learn and get knowledge! God said to the foolish person that He would have poured out His heart and made His thoughts known to him. *"But, since you rejected Me when I called and no one gave heed when I stretched out My hand, since you ignored all my advice and would not accept My rebuke, I will turn and laugh at your disaster; I will mock when calamity overtakes you like a storm, when disaster sweeps over you like whirlwind, when distress and trouble overwhelm you,"* Proverbs 1:24-27.

Dear student, problems will come to you! They come to everyone. You need God's mercy when they do come! God is clear. You can't ignore Him and then expect Him to protect and guide you! In fact, worse than not guiding you, God will *"laugh at your disaster."* If you mock God, He will mock you! You will call out for Him and He will not answer. *"They will look for Me but will not find Me. Since they hated knowledge and did not choose to fear the LORD,"* Proverbs 1:28b-29.

Basically then, if we love God and choose His wisdom, He will help us, bless us, and protect us! But scorn God's wisdom and He will scorn us. This is a most serious warning, especially for all who head to school or to work! No one can say, "God didn't warn me!"

Prayer: Lord, we thank You for warning us. We need it! How loving of You to show us wisdom's path, and to help us walk in it. In Jesus' name we pray. Amen.

January 11

"When tempted, no one should say, 'God is tempting me.' For God cannot be tempted by evil, nor does He tempt anyone; but each one is tempted when, by his own evil desire, he is dragged away and enticed. Then, after desire has conceived, it gives birth to sin; and sin, when it is full-grown, gives birth to death." James 1:13-15

Satan says, "gratify your selfish desires"

There are two spirits, an evil one and a Good One. The evil one is Satan and his fallen angels. The other Spirit is God. Both want us to do their will. Satan's nature is to "tempt" us to do what is evil and against God. Satan appeals to our *"evil desire." "Each one is tempted when, <u>by his own evil desire</u>, he is dragged away and enticed."* Satan is a problem. But, the main problem is the *"evil desire"* in our heart! What is needed is a new heart. If Jesus is in, Satan is out!

Satan is called the *"ruler"* of this world in John 12:31 NKJV. In his second book John wrote, *"Do not love the world or the things in the world. If anyone loves the world, the love of the Father is not in him. For all that is in the world — the lust of the flesh, the lust of the eyes, and the pride of life — is not of the Father (God) but is of the world,"* 1 John 2:15-16 NKJV. Satan tempts our *"evil desire"* in three ways.

A. *"The lust of the flesh."* Satan appeals to the cravings of sinful man, to live by our desires and feelings. "If it feels good, do it," is Satan's motto. He does not want us to think about if it is right or wrong. Eve, *"saw that the fruit of the tree was good for food,"* Genesis 3:6a.

B. *"The lust of the eyes."* Satan appeals to our desire for more; coveting, greed, and jealousy. The fruit was, *"pleasing to the eye,"* Genesis 3:6b.

C. *"The pride of life."* Satan appeals to our pride. He wants us to boast about what we have, and what we do. He wants us to build self up. Satan says, if you have much self-esteem, then you will be happy. Eve saw that the tree was, *"desirable for gaining wisdom,"* Genesis 3:6c.

Prayer: Lord, forgive us for following Satan's pleadings to please self. Forgive us also for blaming Satan when it is our own hearts that need to change. We praise You Jesus, that even though we and Eve failed, You did not fail when You were tempted the same three ways by Satan. Help us to see that the victory is in You! In Jesus' name we pray. Amen.

January 12

"Then Jesus said to His disciples, 'If anyone would come after Me, <u>he must deny himself</u>, and take up his cross, and follow Me.'"
Matthew 16:24

Jesus says to deny yourself

Deny self, yes, but what does this mean in our practical day-to-day living? It means to deny selfish importance of all kinds!

1. *"Deny"* self-love – Nowhere in the Bible are we told to love self. The summary of the whole Bible is love God first and others second, Matthew 22:37-40. Our problem is we love self too much! *"But mark this: There will be terrible times in the last days. People will be lovers of themselves, lovers of money..."* 2 Timothy 3:1-2a.

2. *"Deny"* self-assertiveness – Society says, "assert yourself, take charge." The Bible never teaches this. The earth is the Lord's and everything in it. As His servants, we are called to lift up His name and to edify others!

3. *"Deny"* self-confidence – *"Trust in the LORD with all your heart and lean not on your own understanding; in all your ways acknowledge Him and He will direct your paths,"* Proverbs 3:5-6 NKJV.

4. *"Deny"* self-esteem – We are sinners! The wages of sin is death, what we deserve. Apart from Jesus Christ, we have no value! Our value is in Him, knowing Him, and living for Him! Christ-esteem is what we need.

5. *"Deny"* self-righteousness – *"There is no one righteous, not even one; there is no one who understands, no one who seeks God. All have turned away, <u>they have together become worthless</u>; there is no one who does good, not even one,"* Romans 3:10-12.

6. *"Deny"* self-exaltation – Exalting self is characteristic of a person who is a rebel! *"Whoever exalts himself will be humbled, and whoever humbles himself will be exalted,"* Matthew 23:12. *"Deny"* boasting!

Prayer: Lord, we praise You for telling us what we are like! But with a relationship with You, Your Son and Your Spirit we can change from being self-centered to God-centered and other-centered! We praise You for this miracle! In Jesus' name we pray. Amen.

January 13

"Choose for yourselves this day whom you will serve."
Joshua 24:15b

To whom will you listen?

Joshua was wise. He knew evil was always present to entice the people to go astray. On his deathbed he gave some excellent advice, *"Choose for yourselves this day whom you will serve."* But why the word, *"Choose"*? And why the words, *"this day"*? There are two reasons, and this is your battle too! Satan will tempt you many times *"this day."* God will test you many times *"this day."* That is the reason for the question: "Whom will you listen to?" This is why Joshua said, *"Choose for yourselves this day whom you will serve."* Every single decision you face *"this day,"* both great and small, demands that you *"choose"* whom you will serve, God or Satan! For example:

- A spouse spends too much money. Will you get angry at them, or calmly discuss the matter?
- Your boss praises Mary, saying nothing to you! Will you be jealous? Or will you do the task at hand with a good attitude?
- You walk by a store window and see a beautiful dress you can't afford. Will you burn with envy? Or will you thank God for what you already have?
- A beautiful girl walks by and she is, wow! Will you lust for her, or thank God for what you have?
- Your fellow student offers you an answer to a test question. Will you take it or reject it?
- Your friend offers you drugs. What will you do?
- You lose your job. Will you worry and fear? Or will you trust God and begin to look for something different?

Prayer: Lord, You have tested us many times *"this day."* We do not always follow Your way of living. At times we decide to follow Satan. Forgive us Lord. Strengthen us to *"choose"* You every time. We want to be Your wise children that bring glory to Your most holy name. In Christ's name we pray. Amen.

January 14

"Search me, O God, and know my heart; test me and know my anxious thoughts. See if there is any offensive way in me, and lead me in the way everlasting." Psalm 139:23-24

"Search me"

This is one of the most beautiful prayers in the entire Bible. It begins with the personal request, *"search me."* It says, "Look at my life God. Am I living as I should? Are there adjustments I need to make in my relationship with You and with others?" The words, *"search me,"* plead with my Creator and Redeemer to examine my life today. Therein is the beauty of this prayer. My spiritual life is ultimately between God and *"me."* Today I am calling on God to draw closer to *"me"*, and *"me"* to God. I dare not wait until tomorrow, for that is the devil's day. If Satan can get me to put off doing something about my relationships today, he has won a small battle. Tomorrow he will do his best to get me to wait another day to get serious. *"Seek the LORD while He may be found; call on Him while He is near,"* Isaiah 55:6.

"Know my heart; test me and know my anxious thoughts," is a wise request to God! Why? We are told, *"the heart is deceitful above all things and beyond cure. Who can understand it? I the LORD search the heart and examine the mind, to reward a man according to his conduct, according to what his deeds deserve,"* Jeremiah 17:9-10. The verse asks the One who truly understands my heart, to examine it closely, according to His righteous standards.

There is a judgment coming. What I do today will be judged some day soon. When I own this verse, I pause in life's journey to ask God, "How am I doing? Am I living in the light of eternity? Does my heart care about what is near and dear to You, Lord?" *"Lead me in the way everlasting."* Lead me to those things that really matter!

Prayer: Lord, apart from Your holy Word and Will, I do not know what is "everlasting." Search me and test my heart today. Lord, lead me to You. Prepare my heart and use my life for that which is eternal! Prepare me for an eternity with You. Make me to love what You love. In Jesus' name I pray. Amen.

January 15

"To this you were called." 1 Peter 2:21a

"Called" to suffer

The *"this"* in our text is suffering. Peter writes to us plainly because most of us have a problem. We do not expect to suffer! Then someone treats us badly when we are doing good. We respond by becoming angry and bitter. We fly into a panic. Filled with tension, we can't sleep. We fall further into self-pity. Our mind races in circles. Some resort to drugs, alcohol, sex problems. Or, we bury ourselves in work. Some fall into a deep depression and are suicidal. What can we do? We must take to heart the words, *"to this you were called."*

Peter once thought that he should not suffer either. He denied Jesus three times. But then, <u>Christ strengthened him</u>. Christ changed <u>him</u>. Peter saw first-hand the sufferings of a perfect Christ and learned something! If Christ, who was perfect suffered, then a sinner should expect it also. Peter learned that suffering put his mind on eternal things. Suffering put Peter's eyes on God the Father, the Son, and the Holy Spirit. Peter began to look at life differently. Peter matured spiritually when he learned his response to suffering had to change!

Like Peter, we rejoice in our money and reputation, before our faith. Peter corrects us. *"<u>In this you greatly rejoice</u>, though now for a little while you may have had to suffer grief in all kinds of trials."* Why Peter? *"These have come so that your faith – of greater worth than gold, which perishes even though refined by fire - may be proved genuine and may result in praise, glory and honor when Jesus Christ is revealed,"* 1 Peter 1:6-7.

Peter learned, *"submit yourselves to your masters with all respect, not only to those who are good and considerate, <u>but also to those who are harsh</u>,"* 1 Peter 2:18. Why Peter? *"This is commendable before God. <u>To this you were called</u>, because Christ suffered for you, leaving you an example, that you should follow in His steps,"* 1 Peter 20b-21. We endure trials God's way by having a right attitude, the mind of Christ!

Prayer: Dear Lord, how radically different Your wisdom is than ours! Lord, change our hearts to have a right attitude towards all suffering. Help us to fully understand that we were *"called"* to suffer! In Christ's name we pray. Amen.

"But you, when you pray, go into your room, and when you have shut your door, pray to your Father who is in the secret place; and your Father who sees in secret will reward you openly." Matthew 6:6 NKJV

Fast and pray, but for whose will?

A Christian young lady called today. She said she had fasted and prayed 21 days for a marriage that she wanted to happen to an unbeliever. She prayed the man would step forward and finish the marriage arrangement. But he has still not called for the past two months. Now she is very upset!

I told her, "It is good that you fasted and prayed! But in this time, did you plead with God for your will to be done, or for His will to be done? You prayed for what you wanted, didn't you?" She said, "Yes, I prayed for God to agree with my choice for marriage!" She saw her mistake by understanding it was God's will that was important, and for Him to open her eyes to His will. I told her, "I believe God answered your prayer. He has greatly protected you from a marriage that was outside of His will!" Yet this lady's problem is often our problem!

In Luke 18:12, the Pharisees fasted, *"twice a week."* But it did them no good! Why? Jesus said they were selfish in their demands. They were also proud that they were fasting! Jesus told them about a cheating man who was a great sinner. He prayed, (it does not say he fasted) simply and humbly, *"God, be merciful to me a sinner!"* Luke 18:13b NKJV. Jesus said, *"I tell you, this man went down to his house justified rather than the other; for everyone who exalts himself will be humbled, and he who humbles himself will be exalted,"* Luke 18:14 NKJV.

When we fast and pray, or just pray, may we privately and humbly ask God for His will to be done! Jesus told us to pray like that in the Lord's Prayer. It is not that we don't take our will into prayer, but that we submit our will to His will!

Prayer: Lord, we thank You for openly telling us how to pray. We want to be like this humble sinner who acknowledged his sin and came looking for forgiveness and direction. Lord, direct us for Your own name's sake! In Jesus' name we pray. Amen.

January 17

"Arise, shine, for your light has come, and the glory of the LORD rises upon you." Isaiah 60:1

Don't cry about what you can't do!

She was in a terrible accident, now in bed with two broken legs. The doctor said she will never walk again. She is just 35 years of age. What often happens, happened. She gave in to despair and that was quickly followed by a long list of "I can'ts."

A man suddenly broke his back in a serious fall and is now paralyzed at the age of 25. His business was going great. He had lots of work. But suddenly he is not able to physically continue. He gave in to despair. Feeling more sorry for himself with each "I can't," he soon became quite depressed. He had so many dreams that would not happen now!

These are difficult, life changing tests when they happen. "Tests" from God Himself! The same test/trial is also a temptation from Satan to sink into despair, fear and worry! Our response, which is fully our responsibility, is so critical right here! Will we trust in God to get us through this trial? We will need hope from God to do it! There are many verses that direct us to hope in God, in His Spirit, in His Son and in His Word. Verses like 1 Corinthians 10:13 and Matthew 6:25-34 are very helpful. But in the end, we still need to respond!

"Arise, shine," our text says! Get up! Get going! That's not God's responsibility, it's ours. And in our getting up, in our *"arising,"* God will make us *"shine."* He will make our way plain! He has a purpose for our life. Saying "I can't" runs away from His purposes. We must not cry about what we can't do, but instead, do what we can. Then trust the Creator for the rest! He will never fail us! His desire is for us to be faithful in all circumstances. We are responsible to be faithful. After that, the results are totally His. Don't try do God's job! Let Him take care of the results while we remain faithful! We will quickly learn that the will of God never takes us where His grace will not guide and protect!

Prayer: O Lord, what a comfort You are! Your divine character is our hope! May we be able to say about our trials, "I consider them pure joy," just like James did. For You are busy building our faith, working all things for our good and Your glory. In Jesus' name we pray. Amen.

January 18

"Well done, good and faithful servant!" Matthew 25:21b

Jesus' words we want to hear!

I heard of a young woman who had this verse framed, and hung it on the wall of her home. What a great idea for a reminder of what is really important! We surely all know that this life is a testing ground to see if we are faithful in developing a close relationship with God and with others. But what are we doing about it? Are we letting the hours speed by while we pursue many selfish pleasures? That is by far the easiest thing to do!

Matthew 25 begins with the Parable of the Ten Virgins. Some of these ladies were wise and took advantage of the time they had to get ready for when the bridegroom came. Some were foolish and not prepared. They missed the marriage feast. The foolish virgins claimed to be saved. They even claimed to know God. But God did not know them! They never exercised true faith in Christ!

The second parable is about three servants. Two were faithful. One was not. The faithful ones heard the beautiful words: *"Well done, good and faithful servant,"* Matthew 25:21a. The unfaithful servant, the one with a big fear problem was told by the Master, *"You wicked and lazy servant,"* Matthew 25:26a.

Those who truly believe will be separated from those who pretend to believe. Work that is wise and faithful will flow from those who have true faith. Even though salvation is by grace alone, not by works, a saved person will exercise good works because their heart has been changed by God to do that. The Parable of the Talents teaches that it matters how our time on earth is spent! We must be prepared for the Kingdom of Heaven; busy working for it. Right faith leads to right works, which leads to God's kingdom coming. *"The time has come... the kingdom of God is near. Repent and believe the good news!"* Mark 1:15.

Prayer: Lord, help us to be more heavenly minded! May we believe so that we might repent. And may we repent that we might believe. Help us to live in You and for You! For You are the Way, the Truth and the Life. May we hear the words, *"Well done, good and faithful servant."* In Jesus' name we pray. Amen.

January 19

"I have been young, and now am old; yet I have not seen the righteous forsaken, nor his descendants begging bread." Psalm 37:25 NKJV

God's faithfulness to His children

God's faithfulness is praised much in the Bible. The truth about His faithfulness must not only comfort us, but direct us also!

1. God's faithfulness is to His children. That is what our text is teaching. But more than that, God's faithfulness is also to His children's children! Our God is a covenant keeping God. He blesses Christian families, even up *"to a thousand generations"* as He promised He would in Deuteronomy 5:10.

2. God's faithfulness is part of His character. You can count on God to do what He says He will do! His promises are "Yes, and Amen." God is gracious to those who serve Him. He is full of compassion to those who need Him. He is slow to anger when we offend Him. He is most merciful when we seek Him. He is just as ready to give, as He is to forgive. Faithfulness is part of God's character!

3. God's faithfulness is given to the obedient. Elijah was a faithful servant of God! When there was a huge drought in the land that came by the will of God, God did not forget obedient Elijah or a Christian widow and her son! *"For this is what the LORD, the God of Israel, says: 'The jar of flour will not be used up and the jug of oil will not run dry until the day the LORD gives rain on the land,'"* 1 Kings 17:14.

4. God's faithfulness must be worshiped. We are called to praise God for His covenant faithfulness, which is to <u>all generations</u>. The Bible wants us to be sure that we understand! *"It was not with our fathers that the LORD God made this covenant, <u>but with us</u>, with all of us who are alive here today,"* Deuteronomy 5:3.

Prayer: Lord, we do not deserve to be Your children, let alone receive Your blessings that come with our privileged covenant relationship. Lord, accept our worship and praise for Your eternal faithfulness! In Jesus' name we pray. Amen.

January 20

"For we know, brothers loved by God, that He has chosen you."
1 Thessalonians 1:4

God loves you and has chosen you

We have just seen Paul point out in the prior verse that the faithful Christian has <u>work</u> *"produced by faith,"* <u>labor</u> *"prompted by love,"* and *"<u>endurance</u> inspired by hope in our Lord Jesus Christ."* Paul now takes his encouragement a step further.

Christian, *"<u>we know</u>"* you are specifically *"loved by God"* and *"that He has chosen you."* The implication is, if God has *"chosen you"* for all eternity, He will take care of you in your present and future trials! In the many trials of life we need to remember this reassuring truth from God Himself! *"And, <u>we know</u> that in all things God works for the good of those who love Him, who have been called according to His purpose,"* Romans 8:28. Do we really trust God to work everything for our good? If we do, then why do we have unbelieving doubt, fear, and even worry in many of our trials?

Meditate on how much time and planning God has already invested in our life up to this point! Before the world was even made, our name, yes every Christian that would ever come, was written on the palm of His hand. Our name on His hand has always been visible to Him for an eternity past! Our present issues and our entire future is likewise in His hand. Do we trust Him to continue to care for us? Then for God's sake and for His worship, let us put our eyes on Him and get them off from our present trial.

Jesus died on that Cross for us! That is how much God loved us! What other proof is necessary? Why, O why, do we doubt God's ability to care for us?

Prayer: Dear Lord, our faith is indeed weak! You are the only author and perfecter of our faith, and we doubt it so often! Lord, forgive our ugly unbelief! You are worthy of our worship! Absolutely nothing can happen to us apart from Your perfect, holy and powerful will. And we know that it was and is Your will to love us for all eternity. In Jesus' name we pray. Amen.

January 21

"He will sit as a refiner and purifier of silver." Malachi 3:3a

God's refining grace

A group of women wondered what this verse meant. One lady offered to find out about this process of refining silver. So she made an appointment to watch a silversmith at work. She didn't mention anything about the reason for her interest beyond her curiosity about the process of refining silver.

As she watched the silversmith, he held a piece of silver over the fire and let it heat up. He explained that in refining silver, one needed to hold the silver in the middle of the fire where the flames were hottest, to burn away all the impurities. The woman thought about God holding us in such a hot spot; then she thought again about the verse that says, *"He will sit as a refiner and purifier of silver."* She asked the silversmith if he had to sit there in front of the fire the whole time.

The man answered, "Yes." He not only had to sit there holding the silver, but he had to keep his eyes on the silver the entire time it was in the fire. If the silver was left a moment too long in the flames, it would be destroyed. The woman was silent for a moment. Then she asked, "How do you know when the silver is fully refined?" He smiled and said, "When I see my image in it."

If today you are feeling the heat, remember God has His eye on you and will watch you until He sees His image in you. Be comforted! God is at work in you! He will never give you more than you can bear as 1 Corinthians 10:13 teaches. Daniel's three friends were not in the furnace alone either! Jesus was there with them so that they were preserved!

"In this you greatly rejoice, though now for a little while you may have had to suffer grief in all kinds of trials. These have come so that your faith - of greater worth than gold, which perishes even though refined by fire - may be proved genuine and may result in praise, glory and honor when Jesus Christ is revealed," 1 Peter 1:6-7.

Prayer: Lord, You tell us that You place us in the fire of affliction for our good! Lord, give us the spiritual maturity to accept that! More than that, give us the grace to, *"greatly rejoice."* In Christ's name we pray. Amen.

January 22

"Here is a trustworthy saying that deserves full acceptance: Christ Jesus came in to the world to save sinners – of whom I am the worst."
1 Timothy 1:15

Are you a perfectionist?

A perfectionist is one who is a master at seeing what is wrong with others, yet blind to their own mistakes! A perfectionist demands that everything around him is perfect, thinking, "I would never do that." What a miserable person to live with! At one time Paul was like that. He persecuted Christians, thinking he was right in doing so! That is part of the reason Paul says he was the "worst." But a real question for us is this: If we don't do what other sinners do, can that save us?

"No" is the answer! Yet this kind of thinking is present today! Some take their baptism and creeds and lay them at Jesus' feet saying, 'Here is what I believe." The implication is, "I did not do what others did, so let me into Heaven!" Nothing can damn a man quicker than claiming his own righteousness! Nothing but the righteousness of Christ saves!

It is possible to be lost by having too much "religion"! Christ's religion alone saves! If Christ does not intervene as He did in the case of the Apostle Paul, the self-righteous perfectionist is lost for all eternity. *"Unless your righteousness surpasses that of the Pharisees and the teachers of the law, you will certainly not enter the kingdom of heaven,"* Matthew 5:20.

A perfectionist makes a horrible parent, pastor, businessman, teacher, or friend! Seeing the mistakes of others, but unwilling to see their good points is a big mistake. The result of such a negative life is people flee from us, not to us. How can we do evangelism with our children and others this way? Even crops do not grow in sour ground! We need to honestly check the spiritual condition of our hearts. The Pharisees' outward zeal in following every part of the Jewish law, covered up their inner spiritual poverty. Let us not do the same thing.

Prayer: Lord, too often we are all law and no grace! It is killing our relationships with You and with others! Forgive us Lord. Give us the heart and strength to be gracious! May we be gentle and loving like Jesus our Lord! In His name we pray. Amen.

January 23

"Now the people complained about their hardships in the hearing of the LORD, and when He heard them His anger was aroused."
Numbers 11:1a

Why God hates complaining

We complain too much and God does not like it! Think of what God did for Israel and for us as Christians. He delivered us from Egypt, (our slavery to sin) and from Pharaoh's (Satan's) hold. God then gave Israel (us) His perfect law, His way of living. Why? Now that He delivered us from sin, we have the power to keep His loving laws. We now can live like a child that is on our way to Heaven, God's real Canaan!

After all God did for Israel and for us, we complain! Our complaining is *"in the hearing of the LORD"*! It shouts, "Lord, You have not given me enough! I want more now!" They *"began to crave other food, and again the Israelites started wailing and said, 'If only we had meat to eat! Remember the fish we ate in Egypt at no cost — also the cucumbers, melons, leeks, onions and garlic. But now we have lost our appetite; we never see anything but this manna!"* Numbers 11:4b-6. What was this *"manna"* in the New Testament?

Three times Jesus compared Himself to the *"manna"* of the Old Testament saying, *"I am the living Bread that came down from Heaven. If anyone eats of this Bread, he will live forever,"* John 6:51a. In the New Testament, Jesus fed 5000 with only a little bread. Suddenly Jesus was a hero! Yet by the end of John 6, all 5000 left Him because they only got a little *"Bread."* They only got Jesus! They wanted other blessings that Jesus could give, but not Jesus Himself. This is exactly why the people "complained" in the desert. They didn't crave a deep relationship with God! They craved more blessings. What about us? Do we forget what God has done for us in Christ? We do, every time we complain! The next time we complain may we remember Numbers 11:1.

Prayer: Gracious Lord, how ungrateful we are! We so quickly lose sight of the "Big Picture," that is Jesus! We forget that You have the words of eternal life. Lord, forgive us for complaining. Make us more and more thankful, because godliness with contentment is great gain. In Christ's name we pray. Amen.

January 24

"To keep me from becoming conceited because of these surpassing great revelations, there was given me a thorn in my flesh, a messenger of Satan, to torment me. Three times I pleaded with the Lord to take it away from me. But He said to me, 'My grace is sufficient for you, for My power is made perfect in weakness.'" 2 Corinthians 12:7-9a

Our thorn in the flesh

Perhaps, like Paul, we now have a severe trial. Paul said this about his trial: *"Three times I pleaded with the Lord to take it away from me."* God recognized Paul as a true servant of Christ, yet He chose not to heal him! So if we think it was a lack of faith on Paul's part, we are wrong. God saw Paul's suffering, heard his prayer, yet, God's answer was no. "No" is an answer to prayer! In not healing him, God had something better in mind to serve His righteous cause, and for Paul's good too! That something was the very special presence of God! He gave Paul the *"grace"* to bear this suffering!

Our suffering too is really a test from God to see how real our faith is! Yet, at the same time, our suffering is a temptation arrow from Satan to blame God, curse God, and even to hate God! If our <u>response</u> is faithful dependence on God, He will strengthen us. Our faith will grow, and He will see us through! This may not be what we want to hear, but it was true for Paul and it is true for us! God is building His eternal kingdom. In His own perfect way, God will use our weaknesses and imperfections to the glory of His name!

We also know that Paul was given a clear vision of exactly what Heaven was like. Paul was quite sure that a main reason for his thorn (no one knows what it is) was to keep him *"from becoming conceited"* or proud. I wonder, "How much pain does God need to put us through to teach us humility and to depend on His mercy?"

Prayer: Lord, You chose not to heal Paul. You chose to let Your perfect Son suffer! May we humbly accept that suffering is part of life! Like Paul, may we *"boast all the more gladly about my weakness, so that Christ's power may rest on me."* Lord, we have much to learn. Help us Lord to trust You more! In Christ's name we pray. Amen.

January 25

"Though He was rich, yet for your sakes He became poor, so that you through His poverty might become rich." 2 Corinthians 8:9b

Christ became poor to make you rich!

A well to do couple got caught one winter night in a severe snow storm. They nearly froze to death, but were able to find shelter in a poor man's house. The house was very cold. Few of the poor people had comfortable heat in their house. The couple vowed to help the poor. But then, they returned to their own beautiful home. Immediately, they had their tea and a nice dinner in front of the fireplace. They continued this privileged pattern of living and soon forgot about those left out in the cold. They did not end up helping the poor.

The point is, those who suffer think of others who are suffering! In the history of the world, Jesus suffered more than any other human being. Since Jesus knows what suffering is all about, He is able to have more sympathy for those who are poor and hurting! Because Jesus was poor there are at least three benefits for us.

Christ's poorness unites us to God. Christ became poor to make us wealthy, spiritually speaking! Jesus came to earth to wear our rags, to be able to clothe us in His righteous robes. We couldn't get His robes of righteousness on our own. Properly dressed, now God accepts us as His sons and daughters, even joint heirs for all eternity! Now that is riches beyond comprehension!

Christ's poorness identifies with our poorness. Had Christ remained in Heaven He could not have helped us! He had to identify with our poorness. So too, the rich saint communes with the poor when he helps them. Jesus became nothing, because we are nothing!

If Christ's poorness made us rich, think of what His glorification does for us! Now, Christ is ascended, sitting at the right hand of God, glorified, in full power. No one can ever snatch our soul away from Him! Our eternal riches are that guaranteed!

Prayer: Lord, we could not benefit from Your perfect holiness anymore than Satan could! So You did something about it. You became like us, so we could be like You. What amazing love You have for us! May we in turn be dedicated to You. In Jesus' name we pray. Amen.

January 26

"I will be a Father to you and you will be my sons and daughters, says the Lord Almighty." 2 Corinthians 6:18

"I will be a Father to you"

What an encouraging truth! *"Since we have these promises, dear friends, let us purify ourselves from everything that contaminates body and spirit, perfecting holiness out of reverence for God,"* 2 Corinthians 7:1. What are *"these promises"* spoken of here? We need to look back at what was said before, because originally there were no chapter breaks.

The content just before this is the words of our text. *"I will be a Father to you."* What a comfort this is today! Persecution is growing. Our economy is not good. The political landscape is frightening. Family members are suffering. We have pressures and problems each and every day. Foolishly, we so quickly focus on the size of our problems. How much wiser we would be to meditate on the truth of our text. Our God says, *"I will be a Father to you."*

God is aware of our problems! As *"a Father,"* He has promised to work all things for the good of His children. God is all-powerful. His wisdom is way beyond our understanding. He sees everything going on in the world. His storehouse of blessings is unlimited. His heart is gracious and kind. God is fully able and willing to move events and people in our daily life!

When we dwell anxiously on what may or may not happen in the future, we forget to look to our *"Father."* We refuse to be *"confident of this, that He who began a good work in you will carry it on to completion until the day of Christ Jesus,"* Philippians 1:6. The *"Father"* who feeds the birds of the air; clothes the lily of the valley; and gives strength to the deer in the woods when it is time to give birth, is our Heavenly Father.

Prayer: Dear *"Father"* in Heaven, we say we believe in You. Then some trial comes and we doubt Your ability to care for us. We doubt You who is our all in all. We doubt You our *"Father."* We doubt Jesus, our Brother. We doubt the Holy Spirit our Comforter. Forgive us for our small amount of faith. Lord, we praise You for the relationship You give us. In Jesus' name we pray. Amen.

January 27

"*Man is born to trouble.*" Job 5:7a

The sinking sands of life

Did you ever suddenly lose a pile of money? Did someone ever try to hurt your reputation? Have you ever had a painful sickness? Did you ever lose a dear loved one? Job had all of these things happen in just one day. His friend said to him, "*Man is born to trouble as surely as sparks fly upward. But if it were I, (if it happened to me) I would appeal to God; I would lay my cause before Him. He performs wonders that cannot be fathomed, miracles that cannot be counted,*" Job 5:7-9. We must learn to expect trouble! One of our problems is that we do not expect difficult days. Then when troubles come, we fall apart.

Trust is the right response to trouble. Fear is the wrong one. God said to Abraham and us, "*Do not be afraid, Abram. I am your shield, your very great reward,*" Genesis 15:1b. We look for the things of this world to be our "*great reward*"! We expect a life without trouble! But trouble will come. When it does, where is our hope? If it's mostly in money, reputation, health, friends or family we have a great problem! Our number one hope must be in God who will never fail us. I am ashamed at my panic-filled response to some trials. May we look to God who alone is our help and strength!

1. "My hope is built on nothing less than Jesus' blood and righteousness; I dare not trust the sweetest frame, but wholly lean on Jesus' name."

2. "When darkness veils His lovely face, I rest on His unchanging grace; in every high and stormy gale, my anchor holds within the veil."

3. "His oath, His covenant, His blood, support me in the whelming flood; when all around my soul gives way, He then is all my hope and stay."

4. "When He shall come with trumpet sound, O may I then in Him be found, dressed in His righteousness alone, faultless to stand before the throne." The refrain is: "On Christ the solid Rock, I stand, all other ground is sinking sand. All other ground is sinking sand."

Prayer: Lord, You are not just our Savior, You are our Lord. Thankfully, our life is in Your capable hands! In Christ's name we pray. Amen.

January 28

"The Son is the radiance of God's glory and the exact representation of His being." Hebrews 1:3a

Am I a role model of God? Part 1

I believe this question hits on a big problem among Christians today. The answer to this question is: No. We are not in any way role models of God! Jesus is the only one who is *"the radiance of God's glory and the exact representation of His being,"* Hebrews 1:3a. However the question, "Am I a role model of God?" needs to be asked. It becomes apparent by how we live, what we think we are.

How often do we as parents confess our sins to our children, meaning the sins we have committed against them? Rarely! We demand that our son or daughter confess their sins when they fail to respect their mom or dad. We make them say "I'm sorry." But then as parents, we don't respect our spouse even in the hearing of our kids. We don't say sorry! Why don't we admit our mistakes? Do we think we are some kind of god that does not sin?

How often does the businessman get angry at an employee, or is rude to a customer? When the employees are angry at each other or a customer, they get scolded. Is this boss somehow a little "god" who does not need to say, "Sorry I was wrong when I..."?

How often do teachers get upset when the students do not study or take the right things to class? Are teachers prepared? Does the teacher, ever say to the students, "Sorry, I did not prepare very well for this class?" If teachers are not accountable to the kids, how will the kids learn to be accountable?

Pastors tell the congregation they need to repent. They even give examples of how. Is the pastor repenting? Are they humble enough to say to the congregation, "Please pray for me, I am struggling with this sin that I am telling you not to do?" Is a pastor accountable to the congregation this way? If you say "No," then you believe the pastor is some kind of role model of God and does not have to do that.

Prayer: Lord, help us. We have not modeled our faith as we should. So often we say the right things but do not practice it. Forgive us. Teach us to lead by example. In Jesus' name we pray. Amen.

January 29

"The Son is the radiance of God's glory and the exact representation of His being." Hebrews 1:3a

Am I a role model of God? Part 2

We have a problem and it is our pride. We do not want to admit that we are a sinner! We want to pretend to others. We want them to think we are already mature Christians. The truth is that we are all babies in Christ, with a lot to learn. We are not role models of God. Jesus is *"the exact representation of His being"*! He is the only role model of God! <u>We are supposed to be examples of what it means to be a believer</u>! That is far different than being a role model of God.

We believers make mistakes. We actually sin! We need forgiveness. Therefore we believers need to confess our sins! As believers, we need to disciple others in what it means to live like Christ. What we say is important. What we do is even more important. What disciple of ours will believe what we say, if we ourselves do not live what we say?

Too often we are hypocrites. This hurts our discipleship efforts in the home, in the business, in the church and in the school. If we do not think these are all discipleship relationships, we don't even have a Biblical idea about why we are here. If we want to be God's servants and help others worship God and His holiness, then we need to act like a believer. May God convict us especially on three things believers do:

1. Confess sins. *"If we confess our sins, He is faithful and just and will forgive us our sins and purify us from all unrighteousness,"* 1 John 1:9.

2. Dump the garbage. *"Get rid of all bitterness, rage and anger, brawling and slander, along with every form of malice,"* Ephesians 4:31.

3. Forgive one another. *"Be kind compassionate to one another, forgiving each other, just as in Christ God forgave you,"* Ephesians 4:32.

Prayer: Dear Lord, Your Word sets before us what we must become. Lord, we plead, give us the will and the strength to follow Christ! We ask this because You are the author and perfecter of our faith. In Christ's name we pray. Amen.

January 30

"You shall have no other gods before Me." Deuteronomy 5:7

Has your job become your idol?

Our job, even ministry, becomes an idol when our zeal for our work is more important than our relationship with God. Truly, we are to be content in our work. That's important, yet not more important than our relationship with God. I am guilty also. It is one thing to meditate on God's Word to help others, but is this same Word changing me? And may we never forget, every Christian's daily work is ministry. If we do not think so, we don't understand the discipleship process.

The first commandment is, *"You shall have no other gods before Me,"* Deuteronomy 5:7. Nothing is more important than God Himself! If we are more thankful for the work God has given us, than with Him who gave it, then we are idolaters! Pagans are not the only idol worshipers!

Work becoming our idol, is a main cause of burn out! A church leader in China who was put in prison said, "The first time I went to prison I struggled wondering why God allowed it. Slowly I began to understand. He had a deeper purpose for me than just working for Him. He wanted to know me, and I to know Him."

Every pastor's job is to prepare people for the work of ministry. Yet how often don't pastors try to prevent gifted people from teaching, because they think, "that is my position." Jealousy is a real problem. If we have it, then our ministry is a big idol! God help us! We must do our work for God first. If we think "What am I going to gain by doing this?" we will not do our work for the right Person or for the right reasons. If only we would understand and remember, God is more interested in what we are <u>becoming</u> than what we are <u>doing</u>. Until we become more like Christ, we cannot do much for Christ. So if we are struggling in our daily work, we should examine our hearts to see if we might just have an idol problem that needs confessing and correcting.

Prayer: Lord, we see that You do not need some proud professional to do Your work, but common brokenhearted men and women who are willing to serve You and others! You want weak but willing vessels to display Your grace! Make us like that! In Jesus' name we pray. Amen.

January 31

"Faith by itself, if it is not accompanied by action, is dead."
James 2:17b

Saved to a living faith!

By reading the book of James, we should understand that there are two kinds of faith: a living faith and a dead faith. A living faith is dependant on God, busy working for God. The prostitute Rahab was not saved because she let the spies go free. She let the spies go free because she had faith in God to protect her. She had a living faith!

Our good works do not save us either! Doing good works to earn salvation says that the perfect Judge God, will accept a bribe from us to enter Heaven! The good work for our salvation, has been done by God! Jesus or James never taught that good works were ever the basis for our salvation. We are saved by God's grace <u>alone</u>, through faith <u>alone</u>, by Christ <u>alone</u>. Eternal life is completely a result of what God did in us. With salvation, God gave us new hearts that now beat for Him! With changed hearts, we now have new thoughts, new words and new actions, that we were created in Christ to do according to Ephesians 2:10.

Good works are a heartfelt response of thanksgiving for what God has done in us. God always saves a person to a living faith not a dead faith. The heart that is now alive, loves much and it shows. We help the hurting. We reach out in love. We share the Gospel. Just because we are saved by grace alone, through faith alone, by Christ alone, does not mean that our faith stands alone.

Spurgeon once said, "A man declared to his minister that God had done His part in his salvation, and he had done the rest. 'Well,' said the minister, 'What part did you do?' 'Why,' said the poor man, 'God did it all, and I stood in the way.'" Yes, even our best works are stained with sin, so how can they possibly save us?

Prayer: Dear gracious Lord, how amazing is Your salvation! Forgive us sinners for thinking we had something to do with our salvation. Lord, continue to convict us about what grace really means: All of You, none of us. In Christ's name we pray. Amen.

FEBRUARY

"You are worthy, our Lord and God,
to receive glory and honor and power,
for You created all things, and by Your will they
were created and have their being."
Revelation 4:11

February 1

"See to it that you complete the work you have received in the Lord."
Colossians 4:17b

The importance of finishing well!

Dad just passed away. He was 86. We learned much about him the last 5 years as God allowed the trial of Alzheimers to afflict him. He bore up in all of this with a ready smile, in true patience. We never saw him angry! We kids all learned something important. You can tell how big a person is, by what it takes to discourage him!

One day two nurses said (with a smile) "May we tell you what happened with your dad?" Then one said, "A couple of days ago I was working on your dad, I gave him a hug and a little kiss on the cheek and told him he was a good man. Another nurse was watching, so she asked your dad if she could also give him a little hug. He looked at her with a smile and said, 'Sorry, but I am not here for that reason.' We all had a good laugh!" But think about it, that is quite a statement for someone in his very last days with a disease that robs your mind! Dad knew where he was! And, what a testimony of faith! He still knew it was important to be faithful, and he lived it to the end. And by the way, she was a cute, young nurse. He could have taken advantage of the situation.

Dad lived a favorite verse of his. *"Therefore, my dear brothers, stand firm. Let nothing move you. Always give yourselves fully to the work of the Lord, because you know that your labor in the Lord is not in vain,"* 1 Corinthians 15:58.

Dad is in Heaven now, with his Lord. He is having a reunion with the saints who have gone on before him. They met him at Heaven's door. He has personally seen Christ on the throne. He has heard the angels singing. No disease is in sight. No one is crying. Not even one person is struggling with sin. He basks in a sun that never sets. He is picking the most perfect fruit from trees that are always in season. If he could, he would tell us, "Finish well!"

Prayer: Lord, we know we are personally responsible to keep the command, *"See to it that you complete the work you have received in the Lord."* We thank You for putting Your sovereign grace and power in us so we can finish well. In Jesus' name we pray. Amen.

February 2

"We continually remember before our God and Father your work produced by faith, your labor prompted by love, and your endurance inspired by hope in our Lord Jesus Christ." 1 Thessalonians 1:3

Good reasons to be remembered

Paul tells his Christian friends that he thanked God for them, even *"mentioning them in our prayers,"* 1 Thessalonians 1:2b. He tells them what was noteworthy in their life! Will you be remembered for these same three reasons? And notice how the order of these reasons produces a peace from God!

1. Is *"your work produced by faith"*? Your good work comes from *"faith."* Faith literally produces all good work. If you need more work out of someone, they need to have more faith first! What is the point of working, if someone thinks it doesn't matter? If we work little for the Lord, we have a faith problem! If we work little in business, in school, in the home and in our relationships, we have a faith problem! *"Your work"* is *"produced by faith."* God loves good workers!

2. Is *"your labor prompted by love"*? It is called *"labor"* here, because we need to work to the point of exhaustion! Remember, real Biblical love is a <u>sacrificial</u> concern for God and for others. God is not only pleased with our hard work, but even more pleased when it is done in love, with the right attitude! We have only one life to make a difference. Plus, "love labor" is solid worship! Is our *"labor prompted by love"*?

3. Is *"your endurance inspired by hope"*? *"Endurance"* does not happen simply because we want to be diligent! *"Endurance"* in life is rooted in hope! So then, do we lack *"endurance"*? Do we give up easily? Do we have a motivation problem? When we do, we need a *"hope"* adjustment! May God give us the spiritual eyes to see beyond all of our immediate problems! May we see the big picture of what God is doing in our world. May we then put our hope in God! Based on His faithfulness, He will never fail us!

Prayer: Lord, we don't endure much because we don't hope much. We do not labor tirelessly for You because we do not love You much! Our work is little because our faith is little. Correct us Lord for Your glory and for our good! In Jesus' name we pray. Amen.

February 3

"Thou art worthy , O Lord, to receive glory and honour and power: for Thou hast created all things, and for Thy pleasure they are and were created." Revelation 4:11 KJV

Whose pleasure am I here for?

A friend recently said, "You must really enjoy traveling all over India teaching." I was a little surprised by the comment because deep inside I must admit, I do not always enjoy it. It's not easy to be away from home, from your loved ones, and from that which is far more comfortable. But then we are not on this earth for "our pleasure." We are here for His good pleasure! Our text says God created *"all things"* for His pleasure. The *"all,"* includes you and me!

The Westminster Catechism correctly begins with a good question! 'What is the chief end of man?' The answer is: "Man's chief end is to glorify God, and to enjoy Him forever." You would not know this is a foremost Christian concern by seeing how many of us live. If our main concern in life is, "to glorify God," then it is not to bring glory to self. Yet that is what our sinful, human nature still wants to do!

One main way we seek our own glory and pleasure is by not honoring God in keeping the Sabbath Day holy! God warned us! *"'If you keep your feet from breaking the Sabbath <u>and from doing as you please on My holy day</u>, if you call the Sabbath a delight and the LORD's day honorable, and if you honor it by not going your own way and not doing as you please or speaking idle words, then you will find your joy in the LORD, and I will cause you to ride on the heights of the land and to feast on the inheritance of your father Jacob.' The mouth of the LORD has spoken,"* Isaiah 58:13-14.

We must humble ourselves before Almighty God! We must confess the ways we have lived in excess for our own pleasure. For each of us the specifics are different! If we confess our selfish pleasures to God, He will forgive us and redirect us for His glory!

Prayer: Lord, forgive us for looking for pleasure in created things before a deeper relationship with You! For You are the only way, the only truth, and the only life! In Jesus' name we pray. Amen.

February 4

"Not that I have already obtained all this, or have already been made perfect, but I press on to take hold of that for which Christ Jesus took hold of me." Philippians 3:12

Paul's hunger for the Gospel

The words, *"not that I have already obtained all this,"* shows the humility of Paul. He admits he has a lot to learn! Are we so open to learning? Are we still hungry for the Word of God? Paul is talking about his sanctification, his lifelong process of growing up in Christ. He never thought that he had sufficiently arrived in his knowledge of, and his obedience to His Lord, Jesus Christ.

Many years ago my pastor asked me, "Are you satisfied with your spiritual progress?" I proudly said, "Yes." How wrong and self-righteous I was! The one person Jesus could not teach was a self-righteous Pharisee! He could teach sinners of all kinds! But a self-righteous person thought he had already arrived! If this is us, we must ask God to open our heart as He did Paul's and many others.

Matthew Henry said, "Those who think they have grace enough, give proof that they have little enough, or rather that they have none at all; because, wherever there is true grace, there is a desire for more grace, and a pressing towards the perfection of grace."

The grace of God selects every believer specifically. Every believer only reaches for God, because God put that desire in their heart. John the Baptist said, *"A man can receive only what is given him from Heaven,"* John 3:27. Salvation is 100% a gift from God! *"All who were appointed for eternal life believed,"* Acts 13:48b. Those who are justified will grow up in Christ, because God never leaves or forsakes them! God's promises are a reality!

Paul hungered to walk with God and to walk with others in living for God. How we must do this is in the next three devotions.

Prayer: Lord, we so often desire other things more than You! Lord forgive us. Kindle a flame in our hearts to love You! You created us for that purpose. We know that it is eternally important! May we live for Your glory and praise. In Jesus' name we pray. Amen.

February 5

"One thing I do: <u>forgetting what is behind</u> and straining toward what is ahead. <u>I press on</u> toward the goal to <u>win the prize</u> for which God has called me heavenward in Christ Jesus." Philippians 3:13b-14

"Forgetting what is behind," Part 1

Paul presents the proof of saving grace with his statement of faith. There are three points. First, *"Forgetting what is behind."* Second, *"press on."* Third, *"win the prize."* Learn these. Practice these. And we will be like an eagle, soaring above earth's problems.

This *"forgetting what is behind,"* is the first half of the life long <u>process</u> of repentance, summarized in Ephesians 4:22-24. It is the putting off of the old nature. It is how we change Biblically. It is part of the ongoing <u>process</u> of sanctification, our growing up in Christ. So how are we <u>not</u> *"forgetting what is behind"*? That is what must be corrected before we can move onto point two, which is *"press on."* To *"forget what is behind"* we must confess our sin, thus remove it, then replace it!

If we do not forget *"what is behind,"* we are a slave to the "victim mentality." Not forgetting is refusing to let go of how someone hurt us! Dwelling on how others wronged us is 100% bitterness, called *"demonic"* in James 3:14-16. It is the opposite of forgiveness! Think of those who have a problem with anxiety, fear, worry, depression, drugs, alcohol, and even sex problems! They are not <u>willing</u> to *"forget what is behind"*! Think of a two-year old crying hysterically for a long time, beating their head on the floor! They do not want to forget what lies behind! But then, we practice these same habits until they are part of our character, and then we wonder why we have such a problem!

Many people are in mental institutions because they refuse the part of *"forgetting what is behind."* By focusing intently on the wrongs of others, they are like hypnotized, in another world, in an altered-state of consciousness! Then they are often given drugs to put them in yet another world. Granted, they are then *"forgetting what lies behind,"* but they are not really "better" because it is not the change our text is teaching!

Prayer: Lord, forgive us for not *"forgetting what is behind."* We want to live like Your child. Help us to dump our sin garbage at the foot of the Cross! In Christ's name we pray. Amen.

February 6

"One thing I do: forgetting what is behind and straining toward what is ahead. I press on toward the goal to win the prize for which God has called me heavenward in Christ Jesus." Philippians 3:13b-14

"I press on," Part 2

This is something we must all <u>learn</u>, and the quicker the better! When we finally learn to *"press on"* we begin to live like a child of God! The old is gone. Let it be gone! Make sure it is gone. We can't *"press on"* when we want to hang on to how others have hurt us. Focusing intently on what needs to be "put off," prevents Biblical change. I know we discussed this yesterday but it needs to sink into our heads because this is killing us spiritually, mentally, physically, even financially. Let's give an example.

Ruth was hurt by her ex-husband in horrible ways. But when discussing forgiveness (a major part of pressing on), Ruth said, "I can't ever forgive this creep for what he did to me." I told her, "don't lie." The truth is, you <u>won't</u> forgive him, not that you <u>can't</u> forgive him! Ruth, if your ex-husband died, after ten years, he would still control you! You are letting him do that by the insane bitterness in your heart. If you only knew that it is your hard heart that is mostly killing you, not what your ex-husband did to you many years ago! But you don't know that, because you do not know what it means to *'press on'*!"

I continued, "True, your ex-husband does not deserve to be forgiven! But did you deserve to be forgiven by God? Yet, God forgave you even when you were dead, <u>still in your trespasses and sins</u>, (Ephesians 2:5). You were still God's enemy, (Romans 5:10) when He forgave you. Grace means that God gave you what you did not deserve, His forgiveness! Now God is demanding that you do the same thing. *'If you hold <u>anything</u> against anybody, forgive him,'* Mark 11:25b. This wipes out any excuse you have! You must forgive *'just as in Christ God forgave you,'* Ephesians 4:32. And Christ forgives all sin."

Prayer: Lord, how great is Your grace! You never bring up our sin to our face again! You never tell others! You never sit in Heaven and dwell on it either! Yet we do all of these. Lord, forgive us! Help us to dump our bitterness and *"press on"* for Your Glory, for others good, and for our own good too. In Jesus' name we pray. Amen.

February 7

"One thing I do: forgetting what is behind and straining toward what is ahead. I press on toward the goal to win the prize for which God has called me heavenward in Christ Jesus." Philippians 3:13b-14

"Win the prize," Part 3

An Olympic participant has their eyes on a gold medal. Heaven is the prize of the Christian. So the point here on earth is to live in the light of eternity, with Heaven in mind. Focus on what God has called you to.

Important to our discussion is to see how our text fits perfectly into the process by which we all change to live God's way instead of man's way! In fact, our text is a summary of what we must do to change! In the next chapter Paul teaches us how to press on heavenward!

In Philippians 4:2-3, put off your hard feelings and fighting. In 4:4 *"Rejoice in the Lord."* Find your joy in Him and His will! More joy will come when you, in 4:5, *"let your gentleness be evident to all."* And then, in 4:6, *"do not be anxious about anything,"* instead pray, and with thanksgiving also.... This is exactly how you can *"forget what is behind."* You do it when you *"press on toward the goal to win the prize."* When we concentrate on living the Christian life God's way, with all of our heart, we will change!

Think of it this way. Can we shoot a gun and hit a target if we are looking back? No, our aim will be off. Can we plow the first furrow through a open field by looking back? No, if we do, the whole field will be crooked! Many people live crooked lives because they are always looking back. They are not willing to *"forget what is behind."* They are not willing to *"press on"* and live the Christian life. And because of this they are not able to *"win the prize."* Paul here is laying out God's way of living! He is presenting a life that will result in not only eternal peace, but a peace that passes all understanding today!

Prayer: Lord, how gracious You are in giving us a beautiful road map to win the prize of Heaven and for us to be with You for all eternity. Lord, change our hearts to live with Heaven in mind. Convict us by Your Spirit to change. Forgive our sins. Take our guilt away. Give us Jesus. You are our everything! In Christ's beautiful name we pray. Amen.

February 8

*"Even when I am old and gray, do not forsake me, O God, till I declare
Your power to the next generation, Your might to all who are to come."*
Psalm 71:18

The prayer of an elderly Christian

Psalm 71 is a beautiful prayer. The elderly Christian fully realizes that
God is *"my rock of refuge, to which I can always go,"* Psalm 71:3. David
feels the effects of aging. His mind is not as sharp as it once was. Aches
and pains are his constant companion. But one thing he knows from
experience, God is and will always be his strength. That's why David
calls out to God, *"Do not cast me away when I am old; do not forsake me
when my strength is gone,"* Psalm 71:9.

David is aware of his sins and shortcomings as a parent and leader.
But he doesn't dwell on these, thinking, "If only I had done it differently!"
Long ago God forgave him of all these sins and David is profoundly
grateful! He knows he did not deserve God's abundant mercy. God has
taught David that his Lord and Savior can be fully trusted. So David
cries out to God, *"I will always have hope; I will praise You more and
more,"* Psalm 71:14.

David has greatly grown in humility. More and more he looks out
into the church and the world. He sees the multitudes and realizes they
do not have the hope he does. He knows they don't realize how strong
and mighty God really is! If they would just turn to God. So David has
one goal in life now, *"My mouth will tell of Your righteousness, of Your
salvation all day long,"* Psalm 71:15a. Do you see the humility and how
he longs for the people to have God's righteousness?

David pleads with God, *"Do not forsake me, O God, till I declare
Your power to the next generation, Your might to all who are to come,"*
Psalm 71:18. And that is our prayer today and every day.

Prayer: Lord use us as Your mouthpiece to communicate the beauty of
who You are. Lord give us the strength to do that! Lord, the song rightly
says, "Years I spent in vanity and pride, caring not my Lord was crucified."
That is our song too. By Your grace we know You are our everything,
our all. Strengthen us in every way to communicate that Jesus saves! In
His name we pray. Amen.

February 9

"He was driven away from the people and given the mind of an animal; he lived with the wild donkeys and ate grass like cattle; and his body was drenched with the dew of Heaven, until he acknowledged that the Most High God is sovereign over the kingdoms of men and sets over them anyone He wishes." Daniel 5:21

The importance of God's sovereignty

We have here an amazing historical event that demonstrates the absolute and amazing sovereignty of God in the affairs of all people. The subject is the great King Nebuchadnezzar. He was one of the greatest earthly kings ever! In the height of his extreme wealth and comfort we hear the king's own testimony: *"I, Nebuchadnezzar, was at home in my palace, contented and prosperous,"* Daniel 4:4. He had a dream of a large, strong tree! Daniel interpreted the dream and told the king that the tree was him, the king! And that God had made the king, very strong. But God was warning the king. He was going to take the kingdom away from the king for 7 years. Then, when King Nebuchadnezzar finally *"acknowledge that Heaven rules,"* Daniel 4:26b, God will restore his kingship once again.

God gave the king a year to repent. Then, exactly *"Twelve months later, as the king was walking on the roof of the royal place of Babylon, he said, 'Is this not the great Babylon I have built as the royal residence, by my mighty power and for the glory of my majesty?'"* Daniel 4:29-30. While the words were still on his lips, God made the king go crazy so then the people put him out in the field *"like cattle."* Why? It was to teach the king and us a lesson! *"Everything that was written in the past was written to teach us, so that through endurance and the encouragement of the Scriptures we might have hope,"* Romans 15:4.

So how are we doing? Do we recognize the sovereignty of God? Are we thankful for it? Be assured! God is far bigger than any circumstance! He wants us to look to Him in faith to be our all in all.

Prayer: Almighty God, we too are proud of our accomplishments. Forgive us! May we keep our eyes on You in humility, for we know this is right and what You want. Help us Lord. In Jesus' name we pray. Amen.

February 10

"Be always on the watch, and pray that you may be able to escape all that is about to happen, and that you may be able to stand before the Son of Man." Luke 21:36

Be prepared!

The chapter begins with the disciples commenting on how beautiful the stones and other things in the temple are. Jesus responds, *"As for what you see here, the time will come when not one stone will be left on another; every one of them will be thrown down,"* Luke 21:6. Jesus was speaking of the coming overthrow of the Jewish empire by the Roman army, that happened by Nero, about 70 AD. But then, after Jesus' life and death, the whole Jewish system was finished anyway. <u>Jesus became the Temple. Jesus became the place of worship. Jesus became the sacrifice itself</u>! Therefore, let us not put our faith in a world that is failing, but in Christ who is our everything and our all.

There is another application to the text. As our own world passes away, we will be hated by some, betrayed by others. We will be persecuted for bearing the name of Christ. Through it all, we must be faithful to what God has called us to. Let us not be sidetracked by the things of this world that will someday burn up. Not only is the end of the world coming, our personal end is coming. May we be prepared for that Day of Judgment.

We are totally unworthy and unable to stand in The Judgment in our own righteousness. It is when we realize our unworthiness, and cry to Christ, that He makes us worthy and able to stand before Him! We need to pray, asking God to give us His righteous in exchange for ours and give us His clothes of righteousness for our unrighteous ones.

"Be always on the watch." Understand the times that we live in. Compare it to the times in the Bible. Know that no country and no person that is becoming increasingly wicked will continue that way very long. Jesus is coming again. Watch and pray.

Prayer: Lord, if we come to You with any righteousness of our own in our hand, make us drop it and plead for Your mercy. For we can *"stand before the Son of Man"* with Your righteousness alone! In Christ's name we pray. Amen.

February 11

"Surely I was sinful at birth, sinful from the time my mother conceived me." Psalm 51:5

Why do the innocent suffer? Part 1

Psalm 51 teaches us about "original sin" and is a psalm of confession. Convicted of his sin, David pours his heart out to God. By doing so, he is worshiping the holiness of God! It is good for us to see how our text fits into the question in our title. Telling you a true story will help.

Fifty year old James told me his life's story! Bitterly, he told how his younger brother was born with cerebral palsy. This brother suffered for 45 years. He had to be carried everywhere. In time, even the mother could not care for him. Many times James mentioned the innocence of his brother and how he did not deserve this. According to James, his family suffered wrongly. He implied that God made a mistake in allowing this to happen. But we know this is not true, because God cannot sin.

What can we tell this man to comfort him? He is asking, "Why do the innocent suffer?" That is not the right question. Asking it assumes there are innocent people. The truth is, *"there is no one righteous, not even one,"* Romans 3:10b. David said it still stronger in our text! *"Surely I was sinful at birth, sinful from the time my mother conceived me,"* Psalm 51:5. David did not claim innocence, neither can we, not even a baby!

The reason a baby is not innocent is the Gospel message itself. Adam was created sinless, innocent and perfect. But when he chose to sin, everything changed! As our earthly representative, his one willful sin changed the course of human history. Now all are born sinners. Asking the question, "Why do the innocent suffer?" is a very misleading question! The heart of man is now, *"only evil, all the time,"* Genesis 6:5b. It is the truth. We guilty people need the grace of God, every one of us! Tomorrow we will see the rest of the story.

Prayer: Gracious Lord, forgive us for asking wrong questions that show our unbelief. You have lovingly showed us that we are not innocent, but are born with Adam's sin, and then sinning some more on top of that! Lord, You in love show us how lost we are, so that we will seek Your mercy and grace! In Jesus' name we pray. Amen.

February 12

"For the wages of sin is death, but the gift of God is eternal life in Christ Jesus our Lord." Romans 6:23

Why do the innocent suffer? Part 2

A man in class told me he believed in the doctrine of "total depravity." Yet, he still believed innocent people suffer. He correctly believed that man's problem is, he is *"a slave to sin,"* Romans 6:16b. But still he thought many people suffer innocently. His doctrines simply do not agree with each other. That's why we continue looking at how the question, "Why do the innocent suffer?" is a wrong question.

If we believe all people deserve eternal life, we will logically come to the conclusion that innocent people suffer. Therein lies a big part of the problem. Not one of us deserves salvation! Our text teaches that all deserve death, meaning our sin earns that for us! Our wages are death. It is just payment for what we did! For *"all"* have sinned and fallen short of the glory of God. Adam was warned about this before he sinned. With this in mind, how can anyone be innocent?

Another part of the problem is, some are saying God loves everybody. The truth is, only in Christ does God love us. We are born separated from God, under the wrath of God. The message of the Cross is that everyone needs to be rescued from God's wrath. Innocent Jesus satisfied the wrath of God on the Cross.

Man is presently under the wrath of God, if he is not saved! See what comes after John 3:16. The chapter ends, *"Whoever believes in the Son has eternal life, but whoever rejects the Son will not see life, for God's wrath remains on him,"* John 3:36. The word *"remains,"* is a present tense word that means God's wrath is presently, or is now on those who do not believe.

Prayer: Dear merciful Lord, there is so much we don't know. But You have revealed that we are not innocent. You tell us we all need Your grace and mercy to make it to Heaven. We know that You can give Your salvation at any age. We also know from Acts 13:48 that *"all who were appointed for eternal life believed."* Lord, move us to this saved position, because as dead sinners we cannot move ourselves to You! In Christ Jesus' name we pray. Amen.

February 13

"The LORD God commanded the man, 'You are free to eat from any tree in the garden; but you must not eat from the tree of the knowledge of good and evil, for when you eat of it you will surely die.'" Genesis 2:16-17

The Bible and two covenants, Part 1

A covenant is a contract that God makes with man, to bless man. The first covenant is the one God gave to Adam called the covenant of works. God promised to give man life forever (salvation), if man was completely obedient to God. Both parties had obligations or conditions. God the originator of the agreement needed to test man's loyalty. Man failed the test! He broke covenant with God when he ate from the tree. It was called a covenant of works because it was based on Adam's performance. If he was 100% obedient, he could earn salvation and live forever. He and his children would die forever if he broke it.

The second covenant, the covenant of grace comes to Abraham later on. It points to God's redemption. Yet God gives a preview of the covenant of grace, already in Genesis 3:15. Again in Genesis 3:21, a picture of the covenant of grace is an animal's blood being shed to cover man's sin. Grace, because man did nothing!

Throughout the Old Testament, the covenant of works remains unfulfilled. Jesus comes, fully man, the second Adam. His perfect life of obedience finally keeps the covenant of works! That is exactly why Paul wrote, *"When the fullness of time had come, God sent forth His Son, born of a woman, born under the law, to redeem those who were under the law,"* Galatians 4:4-5a NKJV. Jesus fulfilled the covenant of works for the Old Testament believer, and for us. Christ said, *"This is My blood of the covenant, which is poured out for many for the forgiveness of sins,"* Matthew 26:28. Understanding the covenant of works is important to understand the Old Testament. Understanding the covenant of grace is important to understand the whole Bible.

Prayer: Lord, we are doubly sinners! We have Adam's sin. We have our own. We thank You for Jesus who fulfilled the covenant of works by His obedience, and by shedding His blood to provide a covenant of grace. In Jesus' name we pray. Amen.

February 14

"O Sovereign LORD, what can you give me since I remain childless?"
Genesis 15:2b

Can God keep covenant? Part 2

Genesis 15 begins with God promising Abram to be his *"very great reward,"* Genesis 15:1b. The sovereignty of God initiated this contract with Abram! God <u>called</u> Abram by name, telling him not to fear! Be encouraged, this great man of faith had some fears too! God noticed Abram's fear, and was still patient and willing to help! But then, God mercifully does these same things for every Christian son and daughter! So, God in grace moved to Abram and now Abram obeys. Do not miss the fact that Abram here also delights in the sovereignty of God!

Abram responds to God, *"What can you give me since I remain childless?"* Genesis 15:2. Abram questions God's ability to keep His part of this covenant contract! After all, he has no son or heir at this point! We too question God at times. We should learn from Abram!

Abram does not complain to <u>others</u> about his difficult situation. He does not complain <u>about</u> God either. Instead, Abram brings his concern <u>to</u> God. See the big difference between these two responses. God respects and delights for us to <u>come to Him</u> with our petitions and concerns. It is really idolatry for us to bring our complaints and needs to the notice of others, who cannot do anything about it. Instead bring them to God who is able to help us. After all, it is God who is *"sovereign,"* all wise, all powerful and all seeing. He has the world's largest storehouse of blessing, is gracious and loves to give it to us. May we respond in obedience and trust in God's ability to keep His contract in the covenant of grace through Jesus Christ!

Prayer: Dear gracious Lord, by Your sovereign will, You promised Abram that his descendants would be like the stars in the sky. Lord, Abram fully believed in the truth of that promise. Abram was <u>certain</u> that You would do exactly as You said. This so fits the definition of faith. Lord, how blessed we are. Just as father Abraham was justified by his faith in You, so too we are justified by our faith through Christ Jesus, the Mediator of the new covenant. Lord strengthen our relationship with You! In Christ's name we pray. Amen.

February 15

"So the LORD said to him, 'Bring Me a heifer, a goat and a ram, each three years old, along with a dove and a young pigeon.' Abram brought all these to Him, cut them in two and arranged the halves opposite each other." Genesis 15:9-10a

The covenant of grace, Part 3

There are two ways to have salvation. 1. Keep the covenant of works perfectly. 2. Rely on the covenant of grace. Since Jesus was the only one who kept the covenant of works perfectly, there is only one option left for us, the covenant of grace! Adam foolishly tried to cover his own sin with fig leaves, to still keep the covenant of works, but he couldn't! God graciously provided a sacrifice for Adam's sin in Genesis 3:21. That's the first picture of the covenant of grace! The innocent blood of the animal was shed in exchange for Adam and Eve's sin. The covenant of grace is further defined in our text, again pointing to what Christ will do on the Cross!

Genesis 15 shows how God is the originator of the covenant, our salvation! He promises Abram a miracle son, pointing to Jesus the real "miracle Son." God says to Abram, "Look up... count the stars if you can." "So shall your offspring be." This points to God's many children in the history of the world. We see a picture of the promises that God will fulfill in the new covenant (New Testament) of God's grace! "Abram believed the LORD, and He credited it to him as righteousness," Genesis 15:6. Faith is man's requirement in the new covenant!

All covenants need to be clearly written down and then sealed with blood. "So the LORD said to him (Abram), 'Bring Me a heifer, a goat and a ram, each three years old, along with a dove and a young pigeon.' Abram brought all these to Him, cut them in two and arranged the halves opposite each other," Genesis 15:9-10a. The halves of the bloody sacrifice are lined up, with a gap between the matching pieces! Abram sleeps. This is how much we contribute to our salvation, nothing!

Prayer: Lord, we thank You for the covenant of grace, our salvation. We see the bloody sacrifices laid out: Christ for our sin. The penalty which is ours to pay, is paid for by You, our God! Lord, thanks for Your amazing grace! In Jesus' name we pray. Amen.

February 16

"See to it, brothers, that none of you has a sinful, unbelieving heart that turns away from the living God. But encourage one another daily, as long as it is called today, so that none of you may be hardened by sin's deceitfulness." Hebrews 3:12-13

Love respects the Law of God, Part 1

God's truth is presented. The Bible tells us how we need to live before a just and holy God. The Scriptures demand <u>a response</u> to who God is! We will either become <u>hardened</u> and hide from the Law of God. Or, we become <u>softened</u> and sensitive to the Word. We will look at the two different responses in the Bible itself.

1. The Law of God softened the heart of a king. *"On the first day of the seventh month Ezra the priest brought the Law before the assembly, which was made up of men and women and all who were able to understand. He read it aloud from daybreak till noon as he faced the square before the Water Gate... and all the people <u>listened attentively</u> to the Book of the Law,"* Nehemiah 8:2-3. Israel had forgotten the Law of God. So now, for seven days, the Levites read and explained the Law to them again. The Israelites were convicted. They confessed their sins. True love respects the Law of God! The people even stood up! *"Ezra praised the LORD, the great God; and all the people lifted their hands and responded, 'Amen! Amen!' Then they bowed down and worshiped the LORD with their faces to the ground,"* Nehemiah 8:6.

Then there was King Josiah. He heard the Law read. After he heard it, *"he tore his robes,"* 2 Kings 22:11. Josiah then sent the prophet to inquire of God. What should they do? The prophet returned with a message from God, *"'Because your heart was responsive and you humbled yourself before the LORD when you heard what I have spoken against this place and its people, that they would become accursed and laid waste, and because you tore your robes and wept in My presence, I have heard you,' declares the LORD,"* 2 Kings 22:19. True love respects the Law of God, and then God in love responds to them again!

Prayer: Lord, we see a king was softened by Your Word, then restored. We have also ignored Your law and did what is right in our own eyes. Lord, forgive us and restore us also. In Christ's name we pray. Amen.

February 17

"The king was sitting in the winter apartment, with a fire burning in the firepot in front of him. Whenever Jehudi had read three or four columns of the scroll, the king cut them off with a scribe's knife and threw them into the firepot, until the entire scroll was burned in the fire."
Jeremiah 36: 22b-23

Hate rejects the Law of God, Part 2

We have seen that the Law of God always gets a response. In the last devotion, King Josiah's heart was softened by the Word of God. Now we are going to see the opposite response.

2. The Law of God hardened the heart of the king. What makes this response in our text so alarming is, King Jehoiakim was Josiah's son! In one generation, the law of God was burned! God's rules for holy living were ignored. What do you think God did to the people and nation that burned His righteous law? God removed that king. More than that, God said, *"I will punish him and his children and his attendants for their wickedness,"* Jeremiah 36:31a. And God did just that. Another son of Josiah, a God-fearing man, was put into power. God can not and will not be mocked.

How do we respond to law burners who are unconcerned about the holiness of God? Well first of all, we need to care about the lost and dying souls of the lawbreakers. We need to care that they face an eternity that will not be pleasant. We need to pray earnestly for them. We need to ask the Holy Spirit to break their hearts of stone. We need to plead with them and tell them of the One who can give them new hearts and a new reason for living. We need to plead with God to spare their souls.

Jeremiah was surrounded by those who hated God's law, yet he humbly prayed, "LORD change me!" Why? Jeremiah knew he could not change others. Neither can we change anyone! That's God's job! We must change ourselves, witness and pray. See how Jeremiah prayed in Chapter 10:23-24.

Prayer: *"I know, O LORD, that a man's life is not his own; it is not for man to direct his steps. Correct me, LORD, but only with justice - not in Your anger, lest You reduce me to nothing."* In Jesus' name we pray. Amen.

February 18

"And when you pray, do not be like the hypocrites." Matthew 6:5a

How not to pray

Jesus told His disciples how not to pray in Matthew 6:5-8. Then Jesus taught them how to pray the Lord's Prayer. Jesus did this because the other rabbis introduced prayer practices that were not pleasing to God. Jesus said, *"When you pray, do not be like the hypocrites, for they love to pray standing in the synagogues and on the street corners to be seen by men. I tell you the truth, they have received their reward in full,"* Matthew 6:5. Those who pray so others will think they are great prayer warriors, will get the praise of men, but never the praise of God! Prayer is designed to give thanks to God for who He is, for what He has done. Prayer is meant to strengthen our relationship with Him, and to plead for His mercy. How foolish it is then to pray for our own praise. If we want the praise of men, pray like the Pharisee. It we want the mercy of God, *"go into your room, close the door and pray to your Father, who is unseen. Then your Father, who sees what is done in secret, will reward you,"* Matthew 6:6b.

The Pharisees prayed at certain hours of the day as a ritual. They prayed at 9am, 12 noon, and again at 3pm. The rabbis wrote specific wordy prayers for every occasion. This may sound good, but the people could pray these prayers without thinking of the content. Prayer had become a formal duty, not heartfelt, nor humble devotion to God.

The people believed that if they just said lots of words at the right times God would automatically bless them. That is why Jesus said, *"When you pray, do not keep babbling like pagans, for they think they will be heard because of their many words,"* Matthew 6:7. The people's lips were moving but their brains were not engaged. Their hearts were not seeking the heart of God. So, Jesus gives them an example of how they need to get serious about prayer.

Prayer: Dear Lord, forgive us for praying the same way the Pharisees did. We are so quick to pray the same prayers over and over again. Lord, move our hearts to seek You. We need a deeper relationship with You! Lord grant us Your mercy, peace and grace. In Christ's name we pray. Amen.

February 19

"This, then, is how you should pray:" Matthew 6:9a

Introduction to the Lord's Prayer

The Lord's Prayer given here, is a type of prayer Jesus wants His disciples to pray. This same prayer was given to the Gentiles by Luke to teach them how to pray in Luke 11:2-4. This prayer is perfect for every disciple, perfect in its order, perfect in its construction, and perfect in its wording! Jesus knows the real needs of every disciple! He also knows the heart of God, like no one else. Jesus mercifully teaches us how to communicate effectively with God. *"This, then, is how you should pray:"* Matthew 6:9a. Jesus never prayed this prayer Himself, because verse twelve asks God to forgive our sins. Jesus never sinned. This really is a disciple's prayer.

Every part of this prayer has its origin in the Old Testament Scriptures, primarily from the Psalms. Our prayers must have the wisdom of the Scriptures in them to be acceptable to God! *"This is the confidence we have in approaching God: that if we ask anything according to His will, He hears us,"* 1 John 5:14. We can't know the will of God if we are ignorant of the Scriptures. That is why it is much easier to pray after meditating on God's Word.

Some say we should not pray this prayer often because it will lose its meaning. Yes, that is possible. But then, every good and perfect thing in the Bible, can be and is, misused by us sinful creatures! We break the Law of God daily. Should we then not use it as a pattern for living? The Law drives us to Christ. So too, this prayer is the Gospel abbreviated. It drives us to God and a relationship with Him. We were created to know God and to enjoy Him forever. This prayer was given to us to strengthen our relationship to God, and to man also!

Prayer: Lord, You are so gracious in giving us this prayer. The disciples said, *"teach us how to pray."* You have beautifully done that for the glory of the Father and for our good. Forgive us for praying so little. Lord, we thank You for not only encouraging us to pray, but for teaching us how to do it! Your prayer here is so personal, so fresh, so timeless and so suitable for any occasion. May Your kingdom come! In Jesus' name we pray. Amen.

February 20

"Our Father in Heaven." Matthew 6:9b

Praying to God, our Father

Our prayer is addressed to God, our Father. The words, *"Our Father,"* show the paternal relationship every believer has with God. Since we are children of God, we should call Him, *"Father."* The words, *"Our Father,"* are not some doctrine of Christianity. It is Christianity itself, because Christianity is a relationship. The words, *"Our Father,"* teach us that the God of the universe who is all powerful, all seeing, all wisdom, and has the biggest storehouse, is our very own, <u>loving</u>, Abba Father. Contrast that to the millions of people who pray to gods that can't hear!

Think about the huge change coming in the world when Jesus gave this prayer. A believer will no longer be bound to the Law. Bondage to sin and the Law will soon be broken. All the shadows, the vague pointing to what will some day be when Christ comes, are almost over with. The ascended Christ will soon come to live in our hearts. As our very personal great High Priest, He introduces us to our Father in Heaven. We are privileged! Jesus, the Son of God who gave us this prayer, is also our personal and only Mediator to God!

Concentrate then. Focus on *"Our Father."* Don't think like those who meditate much on how they are a "victim" of someone's hate. We believers must grab these words, *"Our Father,"* and not let go. The words, *"Our Father,"* are provided to not only get our eyes on God, but to keep them there. We have what the world does not have. God adopted us. He loves us. He is our Father! Jesus prayed, *"Righteous Father, though the world does not know You, I know You, and they (the disciples) know that You have sent Me. I have made You known to them, and will continue to make You known in order that the love You have for Me may be in them and that I Myself may be in them,"* John 17:25-26. We have a *"Father in Heaven."*

Prayer: Lord Jesus, we thank You that as our Divine Mediator and High Priest, You reveal the Father to us! We thank You for showing us the Father because we were separated from Him, lost, because of Adam's sin and from our own sin. What a privilege and blessing that our very own *"Father"* is Lord of all. In Christ's name we pray. Amen.

February 21

"Hallowed be Your name." Matthew 6:9c

Praying, God's name be honored

This is the first petition of the Lord's Prayer. Praying *"hallowed be Your name,"* is to hold up and to be in awe of the holy character of God. We sinners are taught here by Jesus to embrace a holy God through prayer! We who were born with Adam's sin, we who have our own sin and continue to sin, are brought into the presence of God. Jesus knows we do not think highly enough of God or esteem Him for who He really is. Jesus knows we do not strive enough for personal holiness in order to bring Him honor!

Praying *"hallowed be Your name,"* humbly lowers us and elevates God. Way too often we sinners are proud of our own name, of our own accomplishments, of our own goals. He who sits in the Heavens will not be mocked! He who created us to glorify the Creator, Sustainer, and Redeemer will receive the glory that is due His name! For even God's continually creation testifies to His existence. The leaves are uplifted to God. Fruits hang in the Heavens before Him. The sea sparkles for God. How much more then, should we, the crown of God's creation, bring praises and glory to Him!

To swear or take the name of God lightly is the opposite of hallowing His name. Shouting our prayers or making loud demands of God is not respecting God! Neglecting to read God's Word is not hallowing His name. We fall so greatly here. There is so much we should know but don't because we do not hunger for God's Word and esteem it as we should! God took great care to give us His holy, infallible and unchanging Word. God reveres His Word even more than His creation, while we sinners are far quicker to worship the creation and ignore His Word! God will not be mocked when we respect Him so little. As people, we need respect. What lengths we go through to try to get it. But how much more must God be respected and His name hallowed!

Prayer: Father, forgive us for trying to bring honor to our own name instead of Yours! *"Hallowed be Your name."* May You be God and may we be Your willing subjects. Lord, make us honor You! In Christ's name we pray. Amen.

February 22

"*Your kingdom come.*" Matthew 6:10a

Praying, God's kingdom come

This second petition covers the kingdom of God. Every king has a kingdom. God's sovereignty rules His! We have the following:

1. The kingdom of God over His creation. Every living thing, plant, animal, and the whole solar system belongs to God. All were made by God for the glory of God first, for the benefit of man second. Because of sin, the earth is wearing out. Some day God will reconcile all things to Himself! When we pray, "*Your kingdom come,*" we are also praying for the earth to be liberated from its present bondage to decay.

2. The kingdom of God in us. As a Christian, "*You yourselves are God's temple and that God's Spirit lives in you,*" 1 Corinthians 3:16b. "*For those God foreknew He also predestined to be conformed to the likeness of His Son,*" Romans 8:29a. Praying "*Your kingdom come,*" is praying for God to complete the work of sanctification in all believers.

3. The kingdom of God in the world. When we pray, "*Your kingdom come,*" we are asking God to extend the rule of Christ and bring it to completion. We are praying for Christ's kingdom to stand victorious over the kingdom of Satan. So when we pray "*Your kingdom come,*" think of God working out His plan of salvation and redemption. Think of God bringing many souls to Heaven just as He brought the animals to the ark. Jesus said, "*And this Gospel of the kingdom will be preached in the whole world as a testimony to all nations, and then the end will come,*" Matthew 24:14.

Every Christian is a steward of the mysteries of God. A steward is required to be faithful! Jesus gave different talents to three men in Matthew 25. When the first two men were faithful in their work, Jesus said, "*Well done, good and faithful servant.*" Our Lord is looking for us to be faithful, as we live and work for His kingdom!

Prayer: Lord may Your kingdom come in all of creation. May it come in us. May it come in all the world. Use us to promote Your kingdom for that will give You great glory and give us our greatest joy! In Jesus' name we pray. Amen.

February 23

"Your will be done on earth as it is in Heaven." Matthew 6:10b

Praying, God's will be done

This is the 3rd petition of the prayer. God's *"will"* spoke the world into existence. Every event here *"on earth"* and *"in Heaven,"* is on God's eternal timetable. God's *"will"* is revealed in the Biblical genealogies showing that the *"earth"* is just over 6000 years old. This is just one example of God's revealed *"will"* which many do not believe, to their ignorance! But God also has His secret *"will"* that is not published for all to see. In praying this prayer we are invited to access God, to align ourselves to think, act, and promote His overall *"will."* Praying *"Your will be done on earth,"* is pleading with God to make us live according to His agenda for us. The glaring truth is that we are too often on a different page than God!

Praying, *"Your will be done,"* is praying with a submissive and obedient spirit! Jesus, our perfect human example was always submissive to the *"will"* of God! Jesus *"learned obedience."* And since Jesus never sinned, this can only mean that Jesus lived completely in the center of God's will! *"Jesus <u>increased</u> in wisdom and stature and in favor with God and man."* This verse explains Jesus' childhood and life. How much more then, must we and our children pray in a submissive spirit, *"Your will be done on earth"*! This is also why we and our children need to learn obedience. A parent who fails to teach "No" to a child that is wrong, is not teaching the child to be submissive to God's will. The child who is not submissive, quickly grows up only to become an adult who is not submissive to God or man!

God's *"will"* is going to *"come."* Will we be in the center of it? Satan continues to plot his evil. The heathen still rage against God and against His Anointed. And yes, even against us, the children of God. What eternal comfort there is in the center of God's will! *"Blessed are all who take refuge in Him,"* Psalm 2:12b.

Prayer: Lord, may Your will be done! Train our eyes to see as You see. And Lord, even when we can't see Your hand, may we learn to trust Your heart! Mold our hearts after Your heart. May every step we take have its purpose in Your will! In Jesus' name we pray. Amen.

February 24

"Give us today our daily bread." Matthew 6:11

Praying, God supply our needs

This is the fourth petition of the Lord's Prayer. There were three petitions to pray for the kingdom of God. Now here in the 4th petition, we turn to the needs of man. It is a Biblical prayer that keeps in mind this God-ordained pattern: God first, others second. The Ten Commandments do the same.

We are asking our Father to supply all that we need, yet all the Trinity is involved. The Father provides our *"daily bread"* in this petition. The Son forgives our sins in the next petition. We are delivered from evil, by the working of the Holy Spirit after that. We are that dependent on God the Father, the Son and the Holy Spirit! And that is exactly why we are praying these prayer points.

The petition, *"give us today our daily bread,"* is more than asking God for sufficient food. It asks God for the appetite to eat and for the nourishment of the body after we eat. *"Daily bread,"* to the Hebrew people included all the <u>necessities</u> of life. "Lord please supply us with all our daily <u>needs</u>, not wants." *"Give me neither poverty or riches, but give me only my daily bread. Otherwise, I may have too much and disown You and say, 'Who is the LORD?' Or I may become poor and steal, and so dishonor the name of my God,"* Proverbs 30:8b-9. If God provides more than this, we are blessed. We see <u>God's providing grace</u>.

We are asking God for our daily needs because we don't deserve them. Ever since father Adam fell for all of us, *"the wages of sin is death,"* Romans 6:23a. That is what we deserve. Since, *"the earth is the LORD's and everything in it,"* Psalm 24:1a, we need to ask for it. We may think, "My labor purchased my food." Yes, but who gave us the work, and the strength to do it?

Prayer: Lord, we are a proud and independent people. In this prayer, and especially this point, You teach us to depend *"daily"* on You! We need that reminder! Lord, our hope is in You, in Your ability to supply our every spiritual, physical, and financial need, right on time. May Your name be praised. In Christ's name we pray. Amen.

February 25

"Forgive us our debts." Matthew 6:12a

Praying, God forgive us, Part 1

Our text here is the 1ˢᵗ half of the fifth petition. The other half is, *"as we forgive our debtors."* Praying, *"forgive us our debts,"* acknowledges our debt of sin we owe to God. We are asking Him to forgive that debt. This petition follows asking God to *"give us our daily bread,"* because without forgiveness, what use are the good things of life? Matthew Henry said, "Our daily bread does but feed us as lambs for the slaughter, if our sins are not pardoned!"

I have always wondered, "Can a non-Christian really pray this prayer?" It starts out with *"Our Father."* A non-Christian does not have God as his or her father! Yet still this prayer is prayed in families and in churches where all are not Christian. I think part of the answer concerns this part of the prayer. *"Forgive us our debts,"* covers both the justification debt of becoming a Christian and the sanctification debt of our ongoing sins. We all still need daily forgiveness because our ongoing sin hurts our relationship with God, and with others too. This is also the reason Jesus washed the disciple's feet in John 13. So here in this 5ᵗʰ petition we pray for <u>Jesus' pardoning grace</u>.

We are guilty before the righteous, Most Holy Judge. His forgiveness is totally an act of mercy! That is exactly why we are asking for it! Also notice the closeness of the words *"give us"* and *"forgive us"*! Without the *"forgive"* of God, we do not get much of the *"give"* of God!

Being sorry for our sin must come before we confess it, and before God forgives us. The Christian life is so much all of God, that He even has to make us sorry for our sin. God the Holy Spirit *"will convict the world of guilt in regard to sin and righteousness and judgment,"* John 16:8b. So dependent are we on God's pardoning grace!

Prayer: Dear Father in Heaven, we are so thankful that You love to hear the cries of Your children. And when we can't pray, Your Spirit groans for us! What privilege is ours, that Your love just keeps on giving. May You, our holy God in Trinity be praised now and forever. In Christ's name we pray. Amen.

February 26

"As we also have forgiven our debtors." Matthew 6:12b

Praying, God forgive us, Part 2

This is the second half of the fifth petition. As we begin the second part of this petition, notice that as in all the petitions, we have plural words like *"we" "our"* and *"us."* This means that this prayer is for the entire body of Christ. This is a family prayer, for God's family!

Praying, *"as we also have forgiven,"* is a polite argument to God: "Since we have been faithful in forgiving others by grace alone, not looking for them to do anything to earn our forgiveness; so too Lord, forgive our every sin, even though we do not deserve it!" That is the plea Jesus wants us to pray.

Have we really forgiven others? If we are not forgiving others, this part of the prayer will curse us, not heal us! Are we serious about the command, *"Get rid of all bitterness, rage and anger, brawling and slander, along with every form of malice,"* Ephesians 4:31? We must put off that first, before we can forgive anyone. The replacement behavior is now given: *"Be kind and compassionate to one another, <u>forgiving each other, just as in Christ God forgave you</u>."*

Since Christ in grace forgives us of <u>every</u> single sin we have committed against Him, God demands that we have the same heart of grace to others! So *"all"* of our *"bitterness"* and *"anger"* must go so we can grow, spiritually speaking! This prayer commits us to live a life of grace! We should know what we are saying when we pray it!

Jesus counsels us, *"And when you stand praying, if you hold <u>anything against anyone</u>, forgive him, so that your Father in Heaven may forgive you your sins,"* Mark 11:25. Jesus rules out <u>any</u> excuse we might come up with for not forgiving someone. Grace can't say, "When you prove to me that you deserve forgiveness, then I'll do it." Forgiveness can only be given to those who do not deserve it! We pray for that kind of forgiveness from God, and then we must give it to others.

Prayer: Dear Lord, we need to do much soul-searching here. So often we pray this prayer without thinking much about what it means. Lord soften our hard hearts. Move us from being forgiven, to forgiving. In Christ's name we pray. Amen.

February 27

"And lead us not into temptation." Matthew 6:13a

Praying, God keep us from sin

This sixth petition of the Lord's Prayer follows the cry for forgiveness. Now that I have been forgiven, now that my guilt is removed, my prayer is: "Lord, do not let me plunge back into this or that sin again! Build a protective wall around me, Lord." This prayer point really highlights **the Holy Spirit's preventing grace!**

"Lord protect me from that *'other spirit,'* the one who is not holy. Protect me from Satan and his demons, from the one who tempts us!" Keep in mind here that Satan is a created angel. As such, God has complete control of him! Think about the history of Satan. Know what he is up to, and why we must pray, *"Lead us not into temptation."*

God said about Satan: *"You were anointed as a guardian cherub, for so I ordained you. You were on the holy mount of God; you walked among the fiery stones. You were blameless in your ways from the day you were created till wickedness was found in you. Through your widespread trade you were filled with violence, and you sinned. So I drove you in disgrace from the mount of God, and I expelled you, O guardian cherub, from among the fiery stones. Your heart became proud on account of your beauty, and you corrupted your wisdom because of your splendor. So I threw you to the earth,"* Ezekiel 28:14-17a.

Satan fell. He who once guarded the Holy of Holies as the chief *"guardian angel"* wants you to fall with him! He is mad at God, mad at the other holy angels, mad because God has His loving hand on you!

Remember that, every temptation from Satan, is also a test from God! Our cry must be: "Lord, *'Lead us not into temptation.'* Lead us with Your strength to resist temptation. Lead us to pass Your tests by standing firm. Do not let Satan or his workers have any piece of us!"

Prayer: Lord, we are no match for Satan. We are in the same position as Daniel's three friends. This world is a fiery furnace, getting hotter all the time. Satan can walk on coals. We can't. Without Your divine protection Lord, we get burned. Lord, we don't want to even smell like smoke. Protect us so completely! *"Lead us not into temptation."* In Jesus' name we pray. Amen.

February 28

"Deliver us from the evil one." Matthew 6:13b

Praying, God deliver us from evil

This is the seventh and the last petition of the Lord's Prayer. Notice what this petition does not do. We are not pleading with God to free us from the power of sin or evil. Christ has already done that at the Cross. In Christ, God <u>has already</u> set every single Christian free from <u>the guilt</u> of sin and from <u>the power</u> of sin. Paul argued, *"You used to be slaves to sin,"* Romans 6:17b. But now set free, we *"have become slaves to righteousness,"* Romans 6:18b. The petition here is for the Lord to <u>keep</u> delivering us from Satan's power. We see the Holy Spirit's <u>preserving grace</u> in the words, *"Deliver us from the evil one."* The Holy Spirit <u>keeps</u> us holy. Yet there is more to *"evil"* than just Satan. Some versions say *"deliver us from evil,"* meaning *"all that is evil."*

<u>Lord, deliver us from the evil world</u>. One of the reasons for Christ's death, was our death to the world. We read, *"He gave Himself for our sins, that He might deliver us from this present evil world."* When God delivered His people from Egypt, it was from the evil gods and the evil people. But God also delivered them to something! Christ and His abundant grace *"delivers"* us to live a righteous life. We are praying for the Lord to continue leading us to righteousness.

<u>Lord, deliver us from evil men</u>. Free us from those who profess to know much of religion but practice evil. Paul prayed, *"Brothers pray for us that we might be delivered from unreasonable and wicked men: for not all men have faith."* And, deliver us from doing evil to all men.

<u>Lord, deliver us from the evil in our own hearts</u>. *"Each one is tempted when, by his own evil desire, he is dragged away and enticed,"* James 1:14. Satan, as a roaring lion, appeals to evil desires that still remain in our hearts. Satan can't possess us because Christ lives in our hearts. But Satan is permitted to harass us, trouble us, and take some of our peace. In the end, it only draws us closer to God as He answers this prayer!

Prayer: Dear Lord, deliver us from every temptation of the evil one. For You are the Author and Perfecter of our faith. You are the Way, the Truth, and the Life. Our life is in You, our Deliverer! In Jesus' name we pray. Amen.

February 29

"For Yours is the kingdom and the power and the glory forever. Amen."
Matthew 6:13c NKJV

The Doxology to the Lord's Prayer

"Doxa" is "glory" in Greek. The word doxology means glory to God. So the end of the Lord's Prayer is praising God. The words, *"For Yours is the kingdom and the power and the glory forever"* repeats and reinforces the first three petitions.

"For" is a conjunction, a connecting word. It pleads with Christ to plead with God the Father <u>for</u> us to be heard. Together we have just placed seven petitions before our Heavenly Father. Seven, God's perfect number, to a perfect and complete God. *"For"* God is <u>willing</u> to hear this kind of prayer. *"For"* God is <u>able</u> to answer this prayer.

"<u>Yours is the kingdom</u>" is saying, "Lord, You reign supreme over all Heaven and Earth. Both are fully under Your sovereign control. As King, defend us, Your subjects. We are vulnerable. We belong to You in covenant. We depend on You."

"<u>And the power</u>" says, "Lord You have the right to exercise Your will in Heaven and Earth. Nothing is too hard for You! No one can resist You! So Lord, use Your power on behalf of Your servants who are powerless without You."

"<u>And the glory</u>" appeals to God to answer this prayer for His Own glory. "Lord, help us to mean this fully, because You deserve all the glory and all the praise!"

"<u>Forever</u>," a word that contrasts God's eternal attributes to the weakness of any temporary earthly ruler. *"From everlasting to everlasting You are God,"* Psalm 90:2b. *"Forever,"* is a worship word that sets our minds to live in the light of eternity!

"<u>Amen</u>," a word of faith. *"Amen,"* a humble reminder of submission to God will for us. *"Amen,"* a word of expectation, of looking forward to God's timely answer. *"Amen,"* so let it be. Amen.

Prayer: Lord, what a beautiful gift this prayer is! How fitting that we end this prayer in doxology, praising You and Your most Holy name. What a privilege for us to bless You with our lips and lives because You have so blessed us. In Jesus' name we pray. Amen.

MARCH

"The Lord is my Shepherd, I shall not want.
He makes me lie down in green pastures,
He restores my soul."
Psalm 23:1-3a

March 1

"The LORD is my Shepherd." Psalm 23:1a

Introduction to Psalm 23

I recently read a book by Philip Keller, who was a shepherd for many years. He wrote, "A Shepherd Looks at Psalm 23." It is a very good book! David wrote this particular Psalm for our comfort and for the worship of our Shepherd. Psalm 23 is perhaps the most favorite of all the Psalms, rich in its pictures of how God by His grace leads us. Our hope and faith as Christians, are in our God, our "Good Shepherd." May we learn more of Him, so we can follow Him in true faith and duty!

God, the maker of Heaven and earth is "my" personal owner. He is concerned about "my" welfare. That is exactly what a good shepherd does. In this Psalm, David speaks as a sheep, proud to belong to its divine owner! He is amazed that as a child of God, he is the object of God's deepest affections.

Sheep are not able to take care of themselves! They are about the dumbest and most stubborn of all animals. And we are all like sheep! It's no wonder then, that we need "the author and perfecter of our faith." How terrible it is that so many do not know the love and attention "The Good Shepherd" gives to His sheep! How tragic that so many follow the false shepherd, Satan, who will never care for their soul, but instead, will work to destroy it.

Think carefully on the individual words as this Psalm begins. Don't read this Psalm too fast! "The Lord," the Maker of all Heaven and earth, the King of the universe, is "my" God, and "my Shepherd." He watches over me and cares for me! The One who has the best eyes in the world, the most power, unbelievable wisdom and the biggest storehouse of blessings in the universe, "is" my Lord. This God "is," meaning present tense, meaning today and always, "is" mine, He owns me, and I own Him.

Prayer: Loving Lord, forgive us for not meditating enough on the fact that You are presently and forever our personal and loving God. Absolutely nothing about us ever escapes Your divine attention! Your power is able to reach the weakest lamb. Your grace is sufficient for the most unworthy soul. We are so thankful that we belong to You, body and soul. In Christ's name we pray. Amen.

March 2

"I shall not be in want." Psalm 23:1b

God provides all our needs

We are all like sheep. When a sheep thinks *"I shall not be in want,"* it has everything it needs in abundance. More than that, the sheep is confident the abundance will be there tomorrow. This sheep is content with its owner and supplier of his daily needs. A content animal is a healthy animal. A content person is a healthy person. This is true physically as well as spiritually. One thing lacking among Christians today is contentment. A main reason is: we still have too many other gods. When we look to other gods, we are not content with our "Shepherd" God! That is a huge problem! "The Good Shepherd," is proud of His reputation of being the very best. If we will own Him as such, He will own us. Paul said, *"My God will meet all your needs according to His glorious riches in Christ Jesus,"* Philippians 4:19.

"I shall not be in want," is primarily a spiritual fullness that God gives to us, His sheep. Jesus said, *"I have come that they may have life, and that they may have it more abundantly,"* John 10:10b NKJV. It is also true that as our Shepherd, God will also give us sufficient food and clothes. Jesus gives us the example of how God clothes and feeds the birds in Matthew 6. The problem is: we so easily put our hope in the money god, instead of putting our hope in God! Our money, our material blessings we have in this world are good, if they are a slave to us. But if we make them our master we have a god that is a false shepherd. No one ever took any money out of this world but we will all take our spiritual blessings with us as our spirit never dies! We might know this truth, but too often we live like we do not. We need to remember this principle here: God is the Shepherd and we are the sheep.

Now that God is clearly identified as the "Shepherd," the rest of the Psalm explains how God gives His life to His sheep – true Christians.

Prayer: Dear Shepherd of our soul, help us to be content. We know that we need to trust the things of this world less and trust You more. The problem is that we are like dumb and rebellious sheep. Without You, the Good Shepherd, rescuing us, we are lost! Help us, we pray in Jesus' name. Amen.

March 3

"He makes me lie down in green pastures." Psalm 23:2a

God protects us, Part 1

See the grace and goodness of our *"Shepherd"* in the word *"makes"*! It is not what the Christian does to lie down in a peaceful sleep, content in life; it is what God does! This word *"makes"* should cause us to fix our eyes on our God in awe! It must drive our prayer life too. There are four main ways our Shepherd *"makes"* His sheep *"lie down,"* because sheep have four problems that will not let them *"lie down."*

1. Sheep will not lie down if they are afraid.

The slightest sound, a glimpse of a snake, dog, wolf, or any other animal causes sheep to run in fear. The Shepherd spots the danger, beats the snake, chases the dog, shoots the varmint, and then draws near to His precious sheep. The shepherd's very presence calms the sheep. This is exactly what God does for us! Before Jesus left this world He said, *"In this world you will have trouble. But take heart! I have overcome the world."* Remember, our Shepherd is *"The Prince of Peace."* The way He calms our fears is nothing short of a miracle, and we love Him dearly for it! Israel saw the size of the 9 foot Goliath and trembled! David saw the size of His God! Like Israel, we often think our Goliath (trials) are bigger than our God, and we sinfully fear. Then our tender Shepherd comes along and shows us again and again that He can be trusted. He *"makes"* us *"to lie down"* when we have a fear problem!

2. Sheep will not *"lie down"* if they are fighting one another.

Animals and birds fight for "pecking order." All want to be number one. Sheep butt heads to get the best. When they are fighting, neither are lying down. So the shepherd disciplines the bossy sheep, so much so, that the sheep who tried to be first is now last in the affections of the shepherd. Surely, this is what Jesus meant when He said, *"the last will be first, and the first will be last,"* Matthew 20:16. Jesus' disciples were fighting for position, and so do we, to our own hurt! Praise God, our Shepherd makes us stop fighting and then, we *"lie down."*

Prayer: Lord, we have wasted so much time in our worthless fighting. We are like sheep! Forgive us Lord and make us useful, building others up for Your kingdom. In Jesus' name we pray. Amen.

March 4

"He makes me lie down in green pastures." Psalm 23:2a

God cares for us, Part 2

3. Sheep cannot *"lie down"* if something is bugging them.

No animal can *"lie down"* or rest if flies and bugs are after them! In the hot summer the flies get bad, so the sheep move to a place of shade or where there is a breeze, to escape the bugs. An alert shepherd will protect his sheep by treating them for insects and providing some shade from the hot sun. God, "The Good Shepherd," does these same things for us! When people "bug" us too much, we pray to God and He changes us, and often God changes the person who is hurting us too. Even if the "bugging" does not stop, God through His Holy Spirit, gives us grace and mercy to accept our situation with joy, knowing that He could remove it if it is His will. In the end, God *"makes"* us to *"lie down"* and rest as nothing is "bugging" us any longer.

4. Sheep will not *"lie down"* until they are free from hunger.

A hungry sheep is a restless sheep. Sheep need lots of good food. If they have it in abundance, they will quickly *"lie down"* and chew their cud. They will quickly gain weight, the goal of the shepherd. However, the *"green pastures"* the sheep need, do not just grow up on their own. Farmers spend much time cultivating the ground, planting the right seed, and even watering the ground if possible. This is hard work on the shepherd's part! It is a picture of how tirelessly and diligently our Shepherd cares for us. "We *know that in all things* God _works_ *for the good of those who love Him, who have been called according to His purpose,"* Romans 8:28. What love God has for His sheep! Our Shepherd here mainly satisfies our spiritual hungering. His Word is just the right spiritual food. Good grass is exactly the right food for the sheep. When we stay grazing in the Word of God, He satisfies us, making us *"to lie down in green pastures."* Are we grazing in the Word?

Prayer: Lord, what a beautiful Shepherd You are. Your Word is always fresh and filling. We will never, in a thousand lifetimes, be able to eat of all the abundance. Lord, how good You are to us by *"making"* us lie down and rest in You! May we learn to fully trust You, our Shepherd, keeping our eyes on You. In Jesus' name we pray. Amen.

March 5

"He leads me beside quiet waters." Psalm 23:2b

God leads us to Christ

All creatures need good, clean water. One of the quickest ways for sheep to get sick is to drink polluted water. They will quickly do that, if the shepherd does not lead them to good water. Even on the way to good water, some sheep will drink water that has parasites and other crud in it. Then they quickly get sick and stop eating. What a clear picture of how we also drink from polluted streams! We stop on our Christian journey to get a drink of lust, useless TV, or even water that has alcohol in it. And then we get sick from it all. Why don't we just follow our Shepherd, who leads us to the pure mountain stream? St. Augustine said, "O God! Thou made us for Thyself and our souls are restless, searching, until they find their rest in Thee." Why don't we follow our beautiful Shepherd more earnestly? The reason is that we are dumb and disobedient sheep. It is God who leads us to the quiet waters, as we could never find it on our own!

In our own wisdom we would go to the "rushing waters" and drown. We would go to the absolutely calm waters that are stagnant. God, our Good Shepherd leads us to the stream that tumbles quietly along and is safe, clean and refreshing. In fact, only the Spirit of God can satisfy our souls. *"He leads me beside quiet waters."*

Proud sheep need to be led! Jesus said, *"Blessed are those who hunger and thirst for righteousness, for they will be filled,"* Matthew 5:6. God makes us hungry and thirsty as *"He leads me beside quiet waters."* The Holy Spirit leads us to Christ. It is Christ who unites us to God the Father. Christ sends us back to the Holy Spirit to dwell in us. Our God in Trinity quiets our souls. We can only cry out to our Shepherd, "make us hungry and thirsty." And even such a cry is God leading us to Himself.

Prayer: Dear Lord, Your amazing grace gets more amazing every day. You indeed are the author and perfecter of our faith. You are our all in all. Lord, accept our worship and praise for leading us to the quiet waters. Keep us by that beautiful refreshing pool. In Christ's name we pray. Amen!

March 6

"He restores my soul." Psalm 23:3a

God restores us, Part 1

Sheep get lost and wander mindlessly. Then they cannot figure how to get back to the shepherd and to the flock. This pathetic picture is also real in the Christian "sheep" camp. We often try to ignore the fact that we wander because it is embarrassing. It is not just a non-Christian that needs to be restored! The point in this Psalm is that sheep, or believers, need restoration! Sooner or later, usually sooner, every Christian will fall because we gave into some temptation. After falling, we need the tender love of God to get up again. David speaks often about how he had fallen, and how God lifted him up, restoring him. A good example of David's need of restoration is when he chides himself three times for being *"cast down"* in Psalm 42. *"Why are you downcast, O my soul? Why so disturbed within me? Put your hope in God, for I will yet praise Him, my Savior and my God,"* Psalm 42:5. What is true of David is true of us! We become *"cast down"* or depressed.

Philip Keller, a shepherd, explains how a sheep becomes *"cast down."* It is upside down, feet up, beating the air. A *"cast"* sheep is <u>unable</u> to "restore" itself to a standing position, <u>unable</u> to protect itself! The shepherd is the only one who can right the sheep, and get it up! Knowing a sheep is easily cast down, a shepherd carefully watches to see if any of the sheep are missing. A shepherd will even count his sheep to see if all are present. If missing, the shepherd will quickly go searching just as Jesus did in leaving the 99 in Matthew 18:12. <u>This wandering, cast down sheep is us, not an unbeliever!</u> This is not a story to emphasize evangelism, but one to encourage loving discipleship with believers that need restoration! The next 8 verses of Matthew 18 prove just that! This *"lost sheep"* could not find the Shepherd, so the Shepherd found the sheep.

Prayer: Dear Lord, we see the love and dedication You have for us poor, wandering sheep! May this reality, cause us to love You more. You not only put us back on our feet, You make us walk again, and again, and yet again if necessary. We praise You and pray in the name of Jesus, the Shepherd of our souls! Amen.

March 7

"He restores my soul." Psalm 23:3a

God restores us, Part 2

"Cast down" sheep have three problems that need restoration.

First, sheep that look for the softest spot to lie down are more easily *"cast down."* If there is a slight dip in the ground, they can easily go from lying on their side, to flipping onto their back, and then are not able to get up. How many of us are so busy trying to "get comfortable," that we become cast down? Perhaps the biggest god in the Christian camp today is "the god of comfort." This god does more to keep us soft spiritually than any other god! It may be the worst god of all, because it is the one god we do not fear.

Second, sheep that have too much wool are easily *"cast down."* Long wool gathers mud and manure. This extra weight on the bottom of a sheep does much to keep it from getting up. Wool in the Bible was often a sign of sin. A priest could not wear wool. Too much sin and we get weighed down. Do you know what the shepherd does to the sheep that becomes cast down because of heavy wool? The shepherd shears that sheep! It is very uncomfortable for the sheep as they will get a few cuts from the shearing. God shears us for our good! He cuts the sin out. He restores us to righteous living!

Third, sheep that are too fat are easily *"cast down."* A fat sheep is often a lazy and a weak sheep. A shepherd puts sheep that are too fat on poorer grass. Some of us need poorer grass! Our Lord wants us in shape, sharp and active for Him. God has called us to be warriors, not couch potatoes! The Great Commission says, "Go;" a lazy person says, "No." Besides our love for food, we love clothes and many other pleasures. A Christian's body is the temple of the living God. Our bodies contain our souls and God lives there. God wants our individual temples to be clean and orderly. We need to live as soldiers of the Cross!

Prayer: Shepherd of our souls, what a comfort to see how You look out for us cast down sheep! You run to us. You gently put us back on our feet again. You forgive our sins and restore us. You are a beautiful Shepherd. In Jesus' name we pray. Amen.

March 8

"He guides me in paths of righteousness for His name's sake."
Psalm 23:3b

God guides us

Part of God's restoration process is His guiding us, *"in paths of righteousness."* Cattle of all kinds will use the same *"paths"* when going in and out of the pasture. They will wear a track into the grass that soon becomes a washout. By nature, sheep do not go down the "right" paths either. They spread their manure along these same paths, eat the grass by them, and then get sick from the parasites. A new pasture not only has better grass, it is free from bugs also. A good farmer makes sure the old pasture gets a rest and the animals get fresh grass. Otherwise, both the sheep and the ground suffer from poor health.

When sheep and cattle are put into a new pasture they will jump for joy. When Christians follow God's way of living in new ways, they too jump for joy! It is actually God's Spirit that gives the Christian this new joy. But more than that, God in Trinity <u>makes</u> the Christian focus on the new way of living, and by that process is changed. The Biblical process of change is laid out for us in Ephesians 4:22-24. We first must put off the old habits or *"paths."* We then replace them, and walk in the new *"paths of righteousness."* Through the help of the Spirit, we complete the change process when we focus intently on the new *"paths of righteousness."* We never "get healthy" by going down the old path. We won't get healthy even looking at it! Concentrating on the old corrupt way of living prevents change! So like sheep we need a new pattern, a new path! Praise God, He *"makes"* us go down the right, new path. *"He guides me in paths of righteousness."*

"For His name's sake," God guides us! He guides us for His own glory, *"for His name's sake."* God wants us to be trophies of His grace! He wants our lives to reflect our divine owner. Are we living holy lives to respect, honor and worship God?

Prayer: Lord, thank You for Your abundant grace to us, Your precious sheep! We are so unworthy. You are so worthy. May we stay close to You, loving You with all our hearts! In Jesus' name we pray. Amen.

March 9

"Even though I walk through the valley of the shadow of death."
Psalm 23:4a

God carries us

When the summer heat comes, the low lands are no longer tender and good for the sheep. So the shepherd leads the sheep to higher ground, to the green *"table"* spoken of in the next verse. On the way, the shepherd has to take the green valleys up the mountain. In these valleys there is good grazing, but there are also many snakes, hazards and places for the sheep to fall. This is the only way up the mountain. You can see the imagery for us on our way to Heaven.

"Though I walk," shows the believer, hand in hand with God, enjoying His presence, calmly and purposely finishing life's journey. *"Through the valley,"* are great words of hope! Our *"Shepherd,"* will never leave us in that *"valley"* which is filled with despair and dangers! He will lead us *"through"* it! We must not look so intently at all the cliffs and snakes! God will get us all *"through the valley."* Keep our eyes on the Shepherd! *"Do not let your hearts be troubled. Trust in God; trust also in Me. In My Father's house are many rooms; if it were not so, I would have told you. I am going there to prepare a place for you,"* John 14:1-2. Jesus is leading us *"through the valley,"* to that *"place."*

"The valley of the shadow of death," shows that for a Christian, dying is merely a *"shadow."* Can a shadow harm us? Can the shadow of a knife or gun hurt us? No! Neither can death hurt us if Christ is our Shepherd! He has conquered death. The grave could not hold Him because He had no personal sin. We are one of His precious sheep, He bought us with His own blood. He paid a big price for us! He is in the process of taking one of His prized possessions to Heaven. Our body will sleep for some time, but our soul will never die! We will pass from life on this earth, to life everlasting with the *"Shepherd"* of our soul!

Prayer: Dear Shepherd of our soul. What a comfort that You know exactly the way to Heaven. You are the Way, the Truth, and the Life. When our life is hid in You, we are safe, loved, and so privileged. Lord, train our eyes to gaze upon You in awe! You are our forever Shepherd. In Your name we pray. Amen.

March 10

"I will fear no evil, for You are with me." Psalm 23:4b

God is with us

Sheep have a fear problem! When the wind blows a tumbleweed or a plastic bag across the pasture, the sheep run in panic. Can this rolling weed hurt the sheep? No! So what caused the sheep to fear? The sheep thought it might hurt them. This is the very heart of the matter! The weed did not cause the fear! The fearful heart of the sheep was the problem. And this is so true of us! We have many <u>temptations</u> to fear, like a loss of money, job, health, or spouse. Yet the <u>cause</u> of the fear is in us. It is in our hearts! What is it that finally quiets us?

Our "Shepherd," Jesus, comes and calms our trembling hearts! *"I will fear no evil, for You are with me."* We know from 1 John 4:18 that *"perfect love drives out fear."* Jesus Himself is perfect love! God's law tells us to love Him first and others secondly, is perfect! Fear comes when we put self and our selfish interest first!

Our problem is not that we don't trust God. Even as a Christian, we don't trust Him <u>fully</u>! Our spirit of self-sufficiency is still very proud. Our selfish nature still loves idolatry. We still want other "things" more than God. Our spiritual love life again becomes, me first.

God in His infinite wisdom sends yet another difficult trial our way. He builds our faith in Him a little more! We learn once again how weak we really are. We learn for the hundredth time that we need God more than anything else. It is good that the Shepherd knows how to build our faith! If our selfish hearts had to do it, it just wouldn't happen! *"For it is God who works in you both to will and to do for His good pleasure,"* Philippians 2:13 NKJV. What a beautiful experience our Shepherd God is! *"I will fear no evil, for You are with me."* God pours His perfect love into us! His perfect love casts out our many fears.

Prayer: Lord, You not only killed David's lions and bears, You kill ours. You who eliminated David's Goliath, eliminate ours. You who are perfect in love, perfect in power and perfect in wisdom, belong to us! Because You are with us, we *"will fear no evil."* In Jesus' beautiful name we pray! Amen.

March 11

"Your rod and Your staff, they comfort me." Psalm 23:4c

God disciples and disciplines us

The wooden *"rod"* and *"staff"* were the main tools that a shepherd used to care for the sheep. The Psalmist David was very familiar with these tools, as are shepherds yet today.

1. The rod was a symbol of power and authority. The shepherd was very good at throwing the rod or using it as a club to protect the sheep from snakes, dogs, lions, bears, etc. The rod of Moses was used as a symbol of God's authority over Pharaoh and the gods of Egypt. Sheep are greatly comforted by the rod, as were the children of Israel. Moses' rod was even put in the Ark of the Covenant!

2. The rod was used to examine the sheep. The shepherd used the rod to move the wool to see if the sheep skin was healthy. David knew this when writing, *"Search me, O God, and know my heart; test me and know my anxious thoughts. See if there is any offensive way in me, and lead me in the way everlasting,"* Psalm 139:23-24. No one can pull the wool over God's eyes. His omniscient eye sees everything!

3. The rod was used to discipline the sheep. It is amazing how a shepherd can throw the rod at a sheep that wanders away from him. I remember a new dog we once had. I was picking vegetables and he was wandering by the road. I called, but he wouldn't come. So, I threw a stone at him and hit him. Thereafter, he came when called! The dog got the rod, and with it got the message. In much the same way, *"God disciplines us for our good, that we may share in His holiness. No discipline seems pleasant at the time, but painful. Later on, however, it produces a harvest of righteousness and peace for those who have been trained by it,"* Hebrews 12:10b-11. God says, *"He who spares the rod hates his son, but he who loves him is careful to discipline him,"* Proverbs 13:24. Like sheep, we and our children are foolish! We need the rod then, and love must always deliver it!

Prayer: Lord, You tell us, *"Folly is bound up in the heart of a child, but the rod of discipline will drive it far from him,"* Proverbs 22:15. Truly, *"Your rod and Your staff, they comfort me."* How privileged we are to have a "Shepherd" of our souls. In Jesus' name we pray. Amen.

March 12

"Your rod and Your staff, they comfort me." Psalm 23:4c

God comforts us

The *"staff"* is designed by the shepherd to help the sheep. A staff is a long and strong stick with a hook on one end. The *"staff,"* more than anything, identifies a shepherd as a shepherd. The *"staff"* is a picture of the deep concern the shepherd has for the welfare of the sheep. The *"staff"* is a tool of love in the hands of the shepherd. God's staff is His Spirit with us, helping us in life's journey as a Christian.

1. The shepherd uses the *"staff"* to reach up and pull tree limbs and bushes down so the sheep can eat. God gives us our daily bread!

2. The shepherd uses the *"staff"* to bring a newborn lamb close to the mother. If he touches the lamb the mother could reject it because of the smell of his hand. God covenantly works in us and our children to bring us together with one heart and purpose!

3. The shepherd uses the *"staff"* to bring a shy sheep closer to Him, or lift a fallen sheep. So too, *"The Lord will rescue me from every evil attack and will bring me safely to His Heavenly kingdom,"* 2 Timothy 4:18.

4. The shepherd uses the staff to search for danger. There are snakes hiding under brush and logs that can hurt the sheep. There are small caves. The shepherd uses his long staff to search for various problems. God's Word is often called the Shepherd's staff. It searches out dangers in our lives and it brings us *"comfort"*!

5. The shepherd uses the end of the *"staff"* to guide the sheep down the right path, or to make them change direction. The *"staff"* gives the shepherd a nine foot arm to direct the sheep. The staff quickly makes personal contact with the sheep, giving encouragement and love. In the same way, our Lord leads us in the paths of righteousness, making us holy. When Jesus left this world He told His disciples, *"when He, the Spirit of truth, has come, He will guide you into all truth,"* John 16:13a NKJV.

Prayer: Lord, what a loving concern You have for our spiritual condition! You feed us, care for us, comfort us and protect us perfectly! No one else could ever lead us to an eternity with You! We worship You for being our wonderful Shepherd. In Jesus' name we pray. Amen.

March 13

"You prepare a table before me." Psalm 23:5a

God prepares a table for us

In the spring the shepherd goes ahead of the sheep to the flat, high areas called a *"table,"* or mesa. There the grass grows well in the hot summer. We must fall in love with this gracious word, *"prepare."* Shepherds *"prepare"* waterholes, put up salt blocks, and remove poisonous weeds. See a picture here of how a pastor must work for the congregation! Farmers *"prepare"* a pasture and put up a fence to keep the animals from wandering! The animals do not realize how much this fence protects them from outside dangers. God puts up many fences to *"prepare a table before me."*

1. God prepares the *"table"* of marriage for us. The grass on the other side of the fence is tempting. It may look greener, but poisonous weeds and the deadly HIV snake is there. We are worse than sheep! Animals don't understand the danger when they try to get out. As a boy, I helped the neighbor get the cows from the pasture for the evening milking. One day four cows were missing. We found them dead, hit by a train that ran on the other side of the fence. If only the cows knew that they were free and safe, <u>within the pasture that was prepared for them</u>! They rejected the "green pastures" for an early death. A cow can smell the electric fence to see if the current is on. If there is no immediate shock in the fence wire, they will put their heads through and start eating. Soon they stretch the wire and end up on the other side! We do the very same thing! We smell the fence by playing with lust and watching rotten T.V. Praise God for His Holy Spirit that shocks us when we stick our neck through the fence!

2. God prepares two *"tables"* of the Law for us. The first table is to love God, the second is to love others. When we feed in these pastures we will be filled with peace and be most blessed.

3. God prepares a *"table"* of communion for us. What a huge blessing it is to see and experience this picture of the Gospel and commune with God and fellow Christians as we remember Christ's sacrifice!

Prayer: Lord, You put us in many green pastures. Help us to appreciate them and praise You for them. In Christ's name we pray. Amen.

March 14

"In the presence of my enemies." Psalm 23:5b

God delivers us

The fact that God prepares a table of everything that a Christian needs is a miracle in itself. But the fact that God does so right *"in the presence of my (our) enemies"* takes our breath away! David is shouting to us that conditions do not need to be perfect for God to give us what we need. Even when conditions seem impossible, God can do anything!

Think of David's situation. Saul, king of the most powerful country in the world, could not find David, even with the best of his soldiers! And Saul knew about where David was. However, hundreds of men who were in desperate need were able to find David! So too, we find Christ when our "enemies" can't see to locate Him! God supplied all of David's needs, and his small army too. Our Good Shepherd supplies our every need! God can even feed us from the tables of our enemies if He so chooses. That is how much our God cares for us!

It is a huge test of our faith to see if we will trust God when we are surrounded by those who want to hurt us. We are then forced to make a "faith decision." Will we foolishly in fear, look at the size of our enemies and tremble? Or, will we wisely in faith, look at the size of our God and rejoice? It is my experience that at first, we see the size of our enemies and tremble! Then we pray to God and He opens our eyes to the fact that He is in complete control! He matures our faith, right *"in the presence of my enemies."*

There's another way God *"prepares a table before me in the presence of my enemies."* In Christ, God has already defeated our enemies at the Cross! The penalty and the power that sin has over us is broken and destroyed. Our number one enemy, Satan, still has some power! But compared to God's power, Satan's power is nothing but weakness.

It is our God in Trinity that gives us a table of blessings in the presence of our enemies. He has in covenant promised us that He will never leave us or forsake us, especially when our enemies are in our presence!

Prayer: Lord, we praise and thank You for giving us a table right in the presence of our enemies. So great is Your power! We worship You. In Jesus' name we pray. Amen.

March 15

"You anoint my head with oil; my cup overflows." Psalm 23:5c

God anoints us

In the summertime, flies and bugs that sheep hate, come in abundance. When "bugged," the sheep will not gain weight or lie down in contentment. Today a shepherd will commonly run the sheep through tanks or pools of chemicals that will protect the sheep's skin from various ailments, including the bugs. But of course, the sheep does not put his head into the brew! He would drown! So, many shepherds still put a special oil mixed with other medicines on the sheep's head to protect the sheep's head from bugs, scabs, and other skin problems.

Just as a shepherd anoints the sheep, God anoints our *"head with oil."* The Holy Spirit, *"anoints"* us at the time of salvation. *"The fruit of the Spirit is love, joy, peace, patience, kindness, goodness, faithfulness, gentleness, and self-control,"* Galatians 5:22-23a. If our Christianity is real, this fruit of His presence will become more and more noticeable! Some say they are going to "get the anointing," or they are going to "get more of the Holy Spirit." Friends, no one ever "gets" the anointing on their own! It is <u>given</u>! It is a gift! God *"anoints my head with oil."* <u>Getting</u> is works righteousness. <u>Given</u> is the grace of God! Read Ephesians 1:1-14 and see how the grace of the Father, the Son, and the Spirit is freely given. This idea of "getting" is really another gospel!

Has any sheep ever walked up to a shepherd and said, "I am coming to you to get anointed." No way! The loving Shepherd sees the difficulty the sheep are going through and mercifully anoints them! In fact, the sheep does not like it when this concoction is put on its head. They simply like it after the flies and skin diseases are history. Not only that, what sheep ever went to the market and purchased oil for its head? Our Good Shepherd, sees our need and then supplies it. Glory to God!

Prayer: Dear Lord Jesus Christ, our Shepherd, You have so graciously anointed us with oil. You have freed us from sin and every defect. You have filled us with Your Spirit and changed us from being fearful to peaceful, from lost to found, from hopeless to hopeful. Thank You for Your loving attention. In Christ's name we pray. Amen.

March 16

"Surely goodness and mercy shall follow me all the days of my life."
Psalm 23:6a

God's mercy and goodness follow us

This verse begins with an absolute truth and a promise that flows from the faithfulness of our "good" God. Since God is self-existent, His *"goodness"* had no beginning. Since God is eternal, His *"goodness"* has no end. Since our God is infinite, His *"goodness"* has no limit. Because our God is all wise, His *"goodness"* will always be perfect. Since our God is all powerful, He can give His *"goodness"* anytime and anyplace! Since our God is omniscient, His *"goodness"* is never blind to our need. Since God is holy, His *"goodness"* is always pure. Because our God will never leave us or forsake us, His *"goodness"* will never leave us either. God's *"goodness"* is everything we need in life's journey.

In times of great trials, Satan will tempt us to doubt the *"goodness"* of God, just as he did to Eve. But we have a promise built on the faithfulness of God: *"Goodness... will follow me all the days of my life."*

God's *"mercy"* also follows us! *"Mercy"* is God's forgiveness of our sins, *"all the days of my life"*! It will never leave us! May we meditate on how God takes care of His sheep forever!

There is another part to this *"goodness"* and *"mercy"* that *"shall follow"* us. God expects us to give *"goodness and mercy,"* to others. For example, *"Religion that God our Father accepts as pure and faultless is this: to look after orphans and widows in their distress and to keep oneself from being polluted by the world,"* James 1:27. The *"world"* selfishly thinks of getting good, not giving it! They want others to be good to them but do not want to do this to others! We must selflessly leave a trail of *"goodness"* behind us! We must <u>show</u> the love of Christ. Preach to all people, and if necessary use words. The *"goodness and mercy"* that must *"<u>follow me</u>"* is a fruit of God's love in me. Praise be to God!

Prayer: Dear gracious and merciful Lord, often we are like the wandering children of Israel. We demand the comforts of Egypt instead of meditating on how Your *"goodness and mercy"* both leads and follows us. We appreciate and need Your mercy that follows us, all the days of our lives. In Christ's name we pray. Amen.

March 17

"I will dwell in the house of the LORD forever." Psalm 23:6b

God forever claims us

We have seen the dedication of the Shepherd to the sheep. But here we see the contentment of the sheep to have such a great Shepherd. We see the sheep content to belong to the flock. A question that begs us is: "Are we content to love and be loved by our fellow church members?" Even dumb sheep know when they are part of a caring flock. They will lie down together, content. If we are not content in the flock, is there something wrong with us, or is our church the problem?

In Psalm 37, a lack of contentment came about by being *"envious"* of wicked people. The same concept is true for believers! Do not be filled with a longing for what the wicked have! *"Trust in the LORD and do good; dwell in the land and enjoy safe pasture. Delight yourself in the LORD and He will give you the desires of your heart. Commit your way to the Lord; trust in Him and He will do this. He will make your righteousness shine like the dawn, the justice of your cause like the noonday sun. Be still before the LORD and wait patiently for Him,"* Psalm 37:3-7a.

God here encourages us to delight in Him by moving to the center of His will for our lives. Then we will find that life will become satisfying and worthwhile. Why does it take us so long to learn these lessons? Probably because by nature we do not have the hearts to trust in God, or commit our ways to Him. But thanks be to God, our Shepherd poured out His life for us. Our Shepherd had pity on us and loved us so much that we can not help but trust Him more! This is the condition of the sheep in Psalm 23. The Shepherd is in love with the sheep. The sheep respond by loving the Shepherd.

Prayer: Dear Shepherd of our souls. Our only comfort in life and in death is that we are not our own, but belong in our bodies and souls to You, our faithful Savior and Shepherd. May Your name be lifted up forever. You are so worthy of praise. The fact that You care so completely for us dumb and rebellious sheep takes our breath away. We know that we love You only because You first loved us. We not only love You today, but will love You for all eternity. In Your name we pray. Amen.

March 18

"If you suffer for doing good and you endure it, this is commendable before God. To this you were called, because Christ suffered for you, leaving you an example, that you should follow in His steps."
1 Peter 2:20b-21

Is your bottle half full or half empty?

If I am counseling a person who has a very negative attitude I often hold up a bottle that is at the half-way mark. Then I ask him or her, "Is this bottle half full or half empty?" It is a good question to get them to think. A negative person will say the bottle is half empty. A positive person will see it as half full. Every day we must choose whether we will be either negative or positive. If we live a negative life, we will be no fun to be around. People will avoid us like the plague. But how do we change from being so negative?

We need God's wisdom in our text. If we are *"doing good,"* when people trouble us, and we patiently endure their harsh words, God says, *"this is commendable."* More than that, *"to this you were <u>called</u>."* This is how Christ lived! Spiritual maturity is keeping our eyes on God in difficult circumstances. God will surely use this difficult time to build our faith and may use it to teach others some important lessons also.

Peter was a very negative man, that is until Christ changed his heart. He did not see the need to suffer or go through trials. But when Christ came out of the grave, his whole attitude changed! He finally understood his own suffering <u>in light of the Cross</u>. Suddenly his bottle was half full! This must shout to our attitudes! <u>We must see our personal trials as appointments instead of disappointments</u>! God knows what is best for us and for the advancement of His kingdom. His timetable is different than ours. We need to trust His divine appointments! Then our attitude will be *"commendable."* C. S. Lewis said about trials: "If they are unnecessary, then there is no God, or a bad one. If there is a good God, then these tortures are necessary, for not even a moderately good Being could possibly inflict or permit them if they weren't."

Prayer: Lord, C.S. Lewis was also right when he said that pain is Your megaphone to a deaf world. Lord, help us to follow in Your steps, with the right attitude! In Jesus' name we pray. Amen.

March 19

"Flee from sexual immorality. All other sins a man commits are outside his body, but he who sins sexually sins against his own body."
1 Corinthians 6:18

Immorality has its price now! Part 1

The problems caused by immoral wanderings are many! The Bible warns us! The medical community warns us! Yet we often ignore the subject because it's so personal. Then our youth learn from other youth and they experiment. Then they get hurt for the rest of their lives, and are very sorry for it. The truth is that when anyone gives into the temptation to have sex outside of marriage, they are making a mistake physically, mentally, socially, financially, and spiritually! We need to tell our children why purity is so priceless!

1. The physical problem – Sex with any person is also sex with any person they have been active with! A young woman had a relationship with only one young man and became infected with multiple STD's (sexually transmitted diseases)! The man she was with, was with just one other woman! But, this woman was intimate with 5 men. These men were active with prostitutes. As a result, this young woman came into contact with diseases of about 100 different people! It is a big physical mistake to go for immoral sex! Truly, *"He who sins sexually sins against his own body."*

2. The mental mistake – Sexual activity is addictive. Some say it's worse than drugs. When we mentally crave something, we cannot focus on what we should be doing. Plus, when we do sin, we will experience guilt. This is even more true when we know better! The heavy load of guilt will also spoil our mind, making us unstable.

3. The social seclusion – A person who gets involved sexually is making themselves socially acceptable to some! But, the crowd they are playing with doesn't play fair socially! They want your body, not you! That's major rejection! When your body is no longer appealing, you are finished! Plus, sex just for fun, desensitizes you from being able to have a real intimate relationship.

Prayer: Lord, You appeal to us for our good. You show us that a few minutes of immoral pleasure is not worth a lifetime of misery. Lord, protect us and fill us with Your Spirit! In Jesus' name we pray. Amen.

March 20

"Flee from sexual immorality. All other sins a man commits are outside his body, but he who sins sexually sins against his own body."
1 Corinthians 6:18

Immorality has its price later! Part 2

4. The financial foolishness - We have seen that immorality exacts a heavy tax on the body physically, mentally and socially. But it also taxes us financially! If you think it's not true, then look at all the medical bills from STDs and HIV. Consider how much the time off from work will cost! What will be the expense of divorce over the years? Those who are loose sexually, lose financially! If we play, we will pay! We may sin in secret, but we will pay in public!

5. The spiritual sin – Sin separates us from both God and man. The spiritual implications of an immoral lifestyle are bad in the present, worse yet in eternity. God asks us a simple question, *"Do you not know that the wicked will not inherit the kingdom of God? Do not be deceived: Neither the sexually immoral...will inherit the kingdom of God,"* 1 Corinthians 6:9-10. Why not? Because, *"The body is not meant for sexual immorality, but for the Lord, and the Lord for the body,"* 1 Corinthians 6:13b. In fact, *"Your bodies are members of Christ Himself,"* 1 Corinthians 6:15a. God never condemns people for using their sexual desire within marriage! He condemns them for misusing it outside of marriage!

I have heard young people say they were interested in missions, yet they had serious sexual "issues." How can anyone lust after other people's bodies, and at the same time care for their souls! Purity is precious! May we desire it for us and for others. May God block every opportunity that we face to be involved in an immoral way!

Prayer: Dear Lord, we all stand guilty of sexual sins either in thought, in word, or in deed. We can see the harm it does to You, to others, and also to ourselves. Forgive us and change us because we belong to You, were bought by You, and are indeed a temple of the living God. May we not defile Your temple! Help us to fix our eyes on Jesus, the Author and Perfecter of our faith. In His name we pray. Amen.

March 21

"In Me you may have peace. In this world you will have trouble. But take heart! I have overcome the world." John 16:33b

"Peace" in a difficult world

Satan will throw everything at us to take our eyes off from our God! Peace is keeping our eyes on God the Father, the Son and the Holy Spirit! Jesus' our perfect example was hated by the religious leaders, persecuted by them, and finally killed. So when Jesus speaks here in our text about *"peace"* in difficult circumstances, He knew from His own experience what He was talking about!

Our text is also a final summary of chapters 15 and 16. Jesus began by saying, *"I am the true vine, and My Father is the gardener,"* John 15:1. God the Father was His secret to *"peace."* We are a branch, connected to Jesus, *"the true vine."* We wither up when we become detached and distant to Jesus, our only source of spiritual food. In fact, Jesus said, *"Apart from Me you can do nothing,"* John 15:5b. It is also true that apart from Christ, we <u>are nothing</u>!

So what can we do to know peace? Remain in Jesus' love! Jesus said that in verse 9, *"If you obey My commandments, you will remain in My love, just as I have obeyed My Father's commandments and remain in His love,"* John 15:10. The first four commandments are all about loving God more than anything else! Jesus did this. Satan tries to get us to love something more than God! Commands 5-10 teach us to love others. That order, will give us contentment in a difficult world!

Paul wrote much of the New Testament while he was in jail. He was content! King David was chased all over the country by King Saul and the Psalms speak of his contentment! David, Paul, and Jesus all lived in a wicked and cruel world, just like we do! May we respond to evil and cruelty as they did, not with bitterness, but in finding ways to love God, through our kindness to others.

Prayer: Lord, how amazingly simple. *"In Me you may have peace."* We look for peace in so many other "things" and then wonder why we don't have Your peace in us! Lord make us believe in You and remain in You. Hold us tight Lord. In Jesus' name we pray. Amen.

March 22

"And He took bread, gave thanks and broke it, and gave it to them saying, 'This is My body given for you; do this in remembrance of Me.' In the same way, after the supper He took the cup, saying, 'This cup is the new covenant in My blood, which is poured out for you.'"
Luke 22:19-20

Views on the Lord's Supper

1. Catholic view of the Lord's Supper. About 500 AD the Catholic Church began teaching that the Lord's Supper is a sacrifice, and a priest is required to offer it. They believe that when a priest pronounces the sacramental words, the bread and wine are miraculously changed into the actual body and blood of Christ. This is called the doctrine of <u>transubstantiation</u>, because it is a <u>change in substance</u>! Only the priests take of the wine, because the laity could spill it and Christ's blood would flow again. The laity receives the bread in the form of a wafer called, the host, which is placed on the tongue by the priest.

2. Protestant views of the Lord's Supper.

    A. Martin Luther - changed the Catholic practice of the Lord's Supper. He pointed out that the mass wrongly offered up Christ again and again as a sacrifice. Hebrews 9:25-28 tells us not to do this. The church members began to take of the bread and wine themselves. Yet still Luther believed that Christ's body was present in the Lord's Supper because Christ is everywhere present. Luther's view is called <u>consubstantiation</u>.

    B. John Calvin - denied there was any bodily presence of Christ in either the bread or the wine. He believed the supper was a memorial in which Christ was present, spiritually speaking. And just as we can see the bread and wine and take it in, so too we must take in Christ spiritually! Calvin believed that the Lord's Supper was a picture form of the Gospel. Calvin's view is called <u>Biblical.</u>

Prayer: Lord, we are so grateful that You gave us the Lord's Supper to remind us to "remember and believe" what You did on the Cross. May we take You in spiritually, never forgetting Your sacrifice for us personally! In Jesus' name we pray. Amen.

March 23

"So we say with confidence, 'The Lord is my helper; I will not be afraid. What can man do to me?'" Hebrews 13:6

Who do we live for?

Where do some of our greatest fears come from? Is it not a big concern over how other people perceive us? We know we should not be so selfish like this! How can we change?

1. We need to see that the problem is in us! In my youth I wanted to be the center of attention, so I was naughty in school. Now I know why, I was very selfish. I wanted people to like me! So, I would do things to get their attention hoping they would notice me. Later in the work world as a young man I wanted everyone to know I could do more than anyone else. I still wanted TO BE NOTICED! And if I wasn't noticed for what I did, then I was upset. I finally burned out! And that was a good thing! You see, the problem was not <u>in others</u> liking me! It was <u>in me</u> liking me too much! I was living my life to please myself and to impress others. I was not living for the approval of God at all. And that was my problem!

2. We need to see that the solution is in God! Only when we are emptied of self, do we have room for God! That only comes from God working in us, giving us a relationship we never had. God shows us that what He thinks of us is infinitely more important than what others think! United to Christ, God thinks a lot of us! In Christ, we have a full and permanent acceptance that will never falter or fail. We have complete acceptance because of what Christ has done. We do not need to do anything! We don't have to earn anything. Christ earned our standing before God! He prays for us constantly and the Spirit seals us in His eternal love. What a relief! All we have to do is live for the glory of God, not earn a thing! Now we hope and pray God will use our lives so others will have a relationship with Him! It never was all about me!

Prayer: Lord, You are correct in telling us that man's life is not his own. You also tell us that You direct our steps! So we can only pray, *"Correct me, LORD, but only with justice – not in Your anger, lest You reduce me to nothing,"* Jeremiah 10:24. In Jesus' name we pray. Amen.

March 24

"On the outside you appear to people as righteous but on the inside you are full of hypocrisy and wickedness." Matthew 23:28b

What is a hypocrite?

Our text shows us a hypocrite is a person who says one thing and does another! Jesus often called the Pharisees "hypocrites." He also called them "whitewashed tombs," another good description of a hypocrite. White on the outside, dead inside. It is one thing to preach the Gospel. It's another thing to live it. The hypocrite who preaches it, but does not live it, will have his words fall on deaf ears! Why? The blind cannot lead the blind! But what about us? Are we a hypocrite?

A hypocrite in the church is far worse than one in the world! Filled with self-righteousness, a hypocrite sees no need for the righteousness of Christ! Jesus said to all of us, *"You hypocrite, first take the plank out of your own eye, and then you will see clearly to remove the speck from your brother's eye,"* Matthew 7:5. If we want to be a witness for Christ, then we need to clean up our act! If we can't see the sin in our own lives and overcome it, how will we be able to see sin in others, and help them change? Besides, it is the Holy Spirit who changes all of us and a hypocrite is missing out on the power and presence of God!

Hypocrites are not limited to the church! Some give lame excuses for not going to church! They say, "I'm not going to any church because they are filled with hypocrites." No doubt. Churches are! But is this not all the more reason for us to go and be a good example of a believer? Churches need sincere and honest members! God will not accept any excuse for not developing a sincere relationship with Him and with others. We will all stand before God soon in The Judgment. We will be tested!

It's not hypocritical to do things we don't feel like doing. We may not feel like doing some work, but we do it anyway, because we know it is our responsibility. We are a hypocrite when we do things that we don't feel like doing, and then say we really enjoy it!

Prayer: Lord, too often we have been hypocrites. You speak to our hearts and we fail to listen, but then want others to listen! We have failed to take the sin out of our own life. Lord, don't give up on us! Work in us! In Christ's name we pray. Amen.

March 25

"Grace and peace to you from God our Father and the Lord Jesus Christ, who gave Himself for our sins to rescue us from the present evil age, according to the will of our God and Father, to whom be glory for ever and ever. Amen." Galatians 1:3-5

The passion of Jesus

As we enter into discussions on Passion Week, think of our text! The passion of Christ is more about life than it is about death. The way to life is through death. A seed must die before it can give life. Jesus died to give us a victorious and eternal life, now and forever!

Trace the events in the last week of Jesus' life. Mary Magdalene anointed Jesus. He rode into town on a donkey. Priests rode donkeys. Jesus was soon to become our High Priest to God.

People were oppressive. The government was oppressive as they used and abused the people. They sold food that was meant for the poor, and kept the money for their own personal profit. The rulers were tyrants. They lorded it over the people, insteading of serving them! The priests and church were oppressive! The leaders took the widows property. The poor had to borrow money just to marry a son or a daughter. They could not pay the money back and were in debt to the temple and to the priests, the church leaders. It was so wicked!

Jesus lived with a passion to stop the injustice of sin. This passion for good, was in stark contrast with what the church and government was doing. Jesus cursed the fig tree, damned the temple, and called the leaders whitewashed tombs. And the leaders tried furiously to stop Him!

The passion of Jesus must affect us! We need a right attitude to pain and trials! There is no cross without pain. It's still hard to fight injustice in the church and government. Try it and you will see! Jesus carried a heavy burden to Calvary! We shouldn't expect ours to be light when the world is still so wicked. The gap between rich and poor is growing. Jesus was not against the rich, but against the rich that didn't care about injustice. Easter was personal to Jesus! How personal is Easter to us?

Prayer: Lord, we can see that Easter involved a lot of passion for You! May we hate injustice and sin of all kinds. Help us to have a passion for You and Your kingdom! In Jesus' name we pray. Amen.

March 26

"The LORD said to Moses, 'Make a snake and put it on a pole; anyone who is bitten can look at it and live.' So Moses made a bronze snake and put it up on a pole. Then when anyone was bitten by a snake and looked at the bronze snake, he lived." Numbers 21:8-9

Why a snake on a pole?

The people had sinned much, so God sent fiery serpents to bite them. They were called fiery, because the people who were bitten had their body temperatures get so high that some died. They cried out to God to remove the poisonous, fiery serpents. God heard their prayers! But instead of taking away the snakes, He provided a cure!

See the Gospel in the lessons of the bronze serpent! 1. <u>People were bitten and many died.</u> 2. <u>The bronze snake was the only remedy God provided for the snake bite!</u> 3. <u>The cure was personal as each person had to look for himself or herself!</u> 4. <u>The people had to actually look to live.</u> Just believing that a cure existed was not enough. 5. <u>The healing was so immediate that the looking and the healing went together.</u>

Forgiveness or salvation is ours instantly, if we will just look to Christ! God does not completely remove Satan from us either, instead He provides the cure - Christ! Why are some churches trying to remove Satan and sin without looking to Christ? Do you see the Gospel, the grace of God through Christ alone in these five points above? The whole event of the bronze serpent points to Christ on the Cross!

The fiery serpent, Satan, still causes death! God still has the only cure! God set the Cross above the earth so sinners could clearly see the Christ. Christ's broken body and shed blood is for our personal sin, if we will look up at that Cross! Do we now see why it had to be a snake on a pole? <u>That which was cursed by God, Jesus, became the very means of the cure!</u> Our sin must be put to death. Our sin must be paid for. We cannot do it! God in His mercy provided the cure. Will we look to the Cross and be cured?

Prayer: Lord, how beautiful! Even Jesus said, *"Just as Moses lifted up the snake in the desert, so the Son of Man must be lifted up, that everyone who believes in Him may have eternal life,"* John 3:14-15. Thank You Lord for taking our fiery curse from us! In Jesus' name we pray. Amen.

March 27

*"Say to the Daughter of Zion, 'See, your King comes to you, gentle
and riding on a donkey, on a colt, the foal of a donkey.'"*
Matthew 21:5

Why did Jesus come on a donkey now?

Jesus came into Jerusalem on Palm Sunday as the Messiah. Peaceful,
humble, a common man, yet He was God. Jesus quietly continues to
move His earthly agenda for the busy upcoming week. Because of the
crowds, the Pharisees wanted to wait until after Passover to do away
with Jesus. But that would not happen because Jesus is the Passover
Lamb. With the crowd all stirred up in favor of Jesus, the Pharisees act
now. All the world events are fully on Jesus' schedule, not on man's!

A king or warlord would surely have come into town on a horse. So
will Jesus when it is time for His Second Coming, when He comes in
Judgment. But here He comes in peace, *"on a donkey."* This Palm Sunday
event was foretold in Zechariah 9:9. The Jews rightly shouted *"Hosanna,"*
meaning "save us now Lord!" They were right on the Messiah part but
they were wrong in thinking Jesus was about to set up David's political
kingdom here on earth again.

Jesus also is here on "Palm Sunday" to be the Savior of the Greeks.
In John 12:20-22, the Greeks wanted to see Jesus. They were hungry to
be filled spiritually. Jesus' answer to them is: *"The hour has come for the
Son of Man to be glorified. I tell you the truth, unless a <u>kernel</u> of wheat
falls to the ground and dies, it remains only a <u>single seed</u>. But if it dies, it
produces <u>many seeds</u>,"* John 12:23-24. What a beautiful answer Jesus
gives! Palm Sunday is for all of us now! And, Palm Sunday makes the
Great Commission possible!

Prayer: Sovereign Lord, our amazing God! You, who hung the stars in
place, hung by nails in our place! What a gentle and loving Savior You
are today. But Lord may we realize when You come again that You will
not be on a humble donkey. You will not be bringing peace and salvation!
Instead, You will come again as a King on a horse, in judgment, condemning
all who did not follow You. Today is the day of salvation! Someday soon
it will be too late! Hosanna Lord, move us to Yourself today. In Jesus'
name we pray. Amen.

March 28

"Then Jesus went with His disciples to a place called Gethsemane, and He said to them, 'Sit here while I go over there and pray.' 'My soul is overwhelmed with sorrow to the point of death. Stay here and keep watch with Me.'" Matthew 26:36 & 38b

In the Garden of Gethsemane

One of Satan's last attacks against Jesus as the Son of Man is in the Garden of Gethsemane. Satan would have loved it if Jesus had died in the Garden, without going to the Cross. Then Jesus would have gone to Heaven alone. He would not have been able to pay the price required for the sins of every believer. So the spiritual agony of Jesus in the Garden is beyond horrible. He was *"overwhelmed."* We can't really understand what Jesus went through, for no one in the history of the world went through anything like this.

Notice what Jesus said to His disciples and to us: *"Sit," "stay," "watch."* Jesus talks to us like we do to the family dog. He keeps it simple, but to the point! *"Sit, stay, watch."* A dog could understand, but the disciples went to sleep! This is our problem too! *"Sit"* and think. Stop running! *"Stay"* for some time. Don't hurry. *"Watch"* what is happening! *"Watch,"* our personal salvation is almost accomplished! *"Watch"* and see how the Son of Man is the perfect Lamb of God to take away all our sin. *"Watch"* so we can learn from Him. See His commitment. See how Jesus did what Adam did not do! *"Watch"* Him pray. See the importance of prayer for our coming trials. Don't forget His commitment to the Father and to us. Wake up son. Now isn't the time for sleeping!

"Watch," Him? We'd rather think about how He watches us! No, *"watch"* Him! *"Sit," "stay,"* meditate on His living and dying example! He *"is overwhelmed with sorrow"* for lost souls, NOT feeling sorry for His physical and spiritual pain. He is in a spiritual war with the evil forces and He is praying intensely! *"Watch,"* see how He does it!

Prayer: O dear Lord, we can't imagine what You went through! We can only see that You were so dedicated to the will of Father. You were so selfless in Your love for us. Wake up our spiritual souls. Lord, help us to do as You say, *"Sit," "stay,"* and *"watch."* In Jesus' name we pray. Amen.

March 29

"Jesus turned and said to them, 'Daughters of Jerusalem, do not weep for Me; weep for yourselves and for your children.'"
Luke 23:28

"Weep for yourselves," Good Friday

It is "Good Friday." Jesus is going to die! Pilate granted the demand of the people to crucify Jesus. The news circulates quickly around Jerusalem. Jesus' disciples are beginning to understand. They are in shock. They are thinking about losing their dear friend. And now, their beloved Jesus is going to give them some "deathbed" advice. Others around the world do this also! The jokes are finished. Food is not an issue. Bank accounts are meaningless! Now the important stuff is discussed! Since we are disciples of Jesus, this deathbed scene is for us personally!

Jesus lovingly says, *"Do not weep for Me; weep for yourselves and for your children,"* Luke 23:28. Jesus is saying it is better that we shed our tears for the sin that is in our life, and in our family who does not know Jesus! He is trying to get His disciples to keep their eyes on the big picture of His life and His dying! He came to this world because we have a sin problem. It separates us from God. Jesus does not want us to gaze so intently on the pain of the crucifixion, that we do not see the reason for it! It is our sins that put Jesus on that Cross, therefore, weep over our sins. Our sins caused the Father to beat His perfect Son and shed His blood! May we then weep over our transgressions that nailed the Redeemer to that cursed tree.

Weeping over the dying Savior is to cry about the remedy for our sin! Jesus knew better than to wail over the disease we gave to Him who was perfectly healthy! To weep over the dying Savior is like crying about the doctor's knife that must cut out a spreading deadly tumor. That knife is a blessing in the hands of the surgeon. The Cross is a blessing to us! May we then cry about our sin that made the Cross necessary.

Prayer: Lord forgive us for getting so sentimental about Your dying while we ignore the sin in our lives. Lord, our sin did this to You! "My sin, not in part, but the whole is nailed to the Cross and I bear it no more." We praise You for healing us for all eternity. May we live like Your holy children! In Jesus' name we pray. Amen.

March 30

"As the Father knows Me, even so I know the Father; and I lay down My life for the sheep." John 10:15 NKJV

For whom did Christ die?

Many Christians believe that God from all eternity elected only some souls to eternal life and that the work of missions in general, proceeds to the saving of these. Others deny the doctrine of the election of believers. They say Christ died for every single person in the world. Who did Jesus come to redeem? Our answer is in our text.

Jesus' coming is clearly rooted in a covenant of redemption that exist between the Father and the Son. The Father clearly gave the Son a particular work to do in sending Him to this earth! In John 17:4 Jesus said to His Father, *"I have brought You glory on earth by completing the work You gave Me to do."* Jesus clearly came at a specific time, for a specific reason. Now the question is: Did Jesus come for a specific people?

We must agree, Christ Jesus is the Redeemer. He redeemed Abraham, Isaac and Jacob. Why? Was there something good in them that was not in the other people? A man called Boaz redeemed a woman named Ruth. Why? What is God showing us? Boaz is a type of Jesus, he is even in Jesus' ancestry line. Boaz' life points to a greater Redeemer who would buy and care for the ones He redeemed.

Christ's shed blood as the Redeemer was <u>sufficient</u> for all! But that is not the question! Did Jesus come only for the sheep, those who would believe? Or did He come for the goats also, those who never believe? Our text says He came for the sheep. His blood's <u>effect</u> was <u>specific</u>.

Jesus did not come to make salvation "possible" for all and then leave the rest up to man! No, like Moses, He delivered the people from Egypt, that is, from sin. In Ephesians 5:25, Jesus gave Himself for His Church. Grace means, we are saved by God's decision, not by ours, per John 15:16. Praise Him for His amazing selecting grace!

Prayer: Lord, we are humbled. Our salvation is all You from start to finish. Your grace just keeps on getting bigger as we learn more. Thank You for adopting us! In Jesus' name we pray. Amen.

March 31

"They stripped Him and put a scarlet robe on Him." Matthew 27:28

The King of the universe stripped naked!

Matthew tells us the authorities had the soldiers take Jesus' clothes off. He was naked before them! After stripping Jesus' clothes, they put a *"scarlet robe"* on Him, a crown of thorns on His head, a staff in His hands, and then they spit on Him. As they mocked Jesus, they hit Him over the head with the staff, surely pounding the thorns into His sinless head. After all this, the authorities stripped Jesus again. They took off the robe and *"put His own clothes back on Him. Then they led Him away to crucify Him,"* Matthew 27:31b. Later by the Cross, verse 35 tells us, the soldiers again took His clothes off and gambled for them.

Can there be any greater shame than innocent Jesus, both God and man, was stripped naked before a sinful world? He calmly endured a very public execution, so we could be privately healed. God allowed Himself to be so humiliated, to bear the shame of our sin. The guiltless One became guilty so we who are guilty could be guiltless!

Think about what Jesus had in Heaven before coming to earth! He had all honor, power, comfort and wealth. He was worshiped and praised. Jesus had everything in Heaven! Yet still, He came to earth to be obedient to the will of His Father. He gave up His honor to love us more!

We in turn, are obsessed with having more honor, highly concerned about our reputation! What does Jesus' humility teach us? Does it not show us that the world will mock us and hate us just like they hated Him? Yet, we sinners deserve to be hated. We are not sinless like Jesus! We would have a much better attitude if we expected to be mocked and hated just for loving Jesus.

Prayer: Lord, as we meditate on the fact of how Jesus was stripped completely naked for the world to view, we are moved that You, our God, endured such horrible shame for us! Lord, it is we who deserved this shame. We are the ones who are the sinners. Lord, help us to calmly "endure it" when we are shamed for the sake of Your name. Take our pride away from us, Lord, and give us Your humble Spirit. In Jesus' name we pray. Amen.

APRIL

*"For He has rescued us
from the dominion of darkness
and brought us into the kingdom
of the Son He loves."*
Colossians 1:13

April 1

"From the sixth hour until the ninth hour darkness came over all the land. About the ninth hour Jesus cried out in a loud voice, 'Eloi, Eloi, lama sabachthani?' which means, 'My God, My God, why have You forsaken Me?'" Matthew 27:45-46

Why did Jesus hang on a tree?

Matthew 27 begins with Judas hanging himself. The chapter continues with the Father hanging the Son. Both were under the wrath of God. Judas died because of his own sin. Jesus died because of our sin! Judas died because of his selfishness. Jesus, because of our selfishness! Jesus had to be perfect to do what the first Adam didn't do and we can't do! The world didn't want a perfect man who was also perfectly God! So they/we put Him to death. <u>Jesus hung on a tree between Heaven and earth because no one wanted Him. He was cursed by God, and rejected by man!</u> He became our sacrifice to God, our sin payment!

Our feet have sinned. Our hands have sinned! So Jesus' innocent feet and hands were pierced for our guilty ones! The proof of God's judgment was that it was dark out, right in the middle of the day! From noon till three o'clock it was fully dark! At the end of this time of experiencing Hell for us, Jesus cries out, *"My God, My God, why have You forsaken Me."* Matthew 25:46b. This was literally the scream of the damned for every single Christian who will ever live! The perfect lamb of God took our sin and reunited us to God.

When Jesus died, the thick curtain in the temple was ripped from top to bottom. This shows that now God opened the way for us to go through Jesus who is our Mediator, to God the Father. Suddenly three things happened: 1. The old temple was rendered useless. 2. The old sacrifices were replaced. 3. The priests were no longer needed. Jesus suddenly became all three! He is our High Priest. He is our sacrifice. And He lives in our hearts which are temples of the living God!

Prayer: Lord, help us to see what You did for us on the Cross. Make it personal for us. May we not say only that You are a Savior, but that You are my personal Savior. How great Thou art! In Jesus' name we pray. Amen.

April 2

"Contend for the faith that was once for all entrusted to the saints."
Jude 3b

How contentious should we be?

We have a faith that is worth contending for. We have a faith worth standing up for. We are talking about using the Word of God to clear any doubts or accusations that a person may have about what is written in the Bible. *"Contend,"* because Jesus commanded us to in the Great Commission. *"Contend"* for His honor!

"Contend for the faith that was once for all entrusted to the saints."

Teach what is in the Bible! The older versions say *"earnestly contend."* It does not say *"furiously"* contend as some have the habit of doing! The point here is teach the Holy Word that God has given to the saints by His own hand. Contend because God's Word changes hearts by the working of His Spirit. Preach Christ crucified to fellow sinners all over the world. If God did not spare His only Son, the One on whom He had placed the sin of us all, will God somehow spare sinners whose sins are their own? No! Every single person's eternity will depend on their response to *"the faith that was once for all entrusted to the saints."*

Never *"Contend for a faith that was <u>not</u> entrusted to the saints"*!

Some are contentious when they shouldn't be. For example, it's the parents' responsibility to bring up their children in the fear of the Lord. However, where and how the parents "educate" should not be argued! Some argue for religious freedom but then restrict where a child should go to school. Also when some people meet a Christian they do not know, they start asking them questions about what they believe. As soon as they find a point in which they do not agree with, they want nothing to do with them. That is being too contentious!

Prayer: Lord, forgive us for being contentious in things that do not matter. Forgive us also for not being contentious for things that do matter! Lord give us the hearts to *"contend for the faith that was once for all entrusted to the saints"*! In Christ's name we pray! Amen.

April 3

"For He has rescued us from the dominion of darkness and brought us into the kingdom of the Son He loves." Colossians 1:13

Can a believer be demon-possessed?

Jesus and the apostles cast out demons! Demon-possession is still a problem. But a big question is: in the Bible, were demons ever cast out of a believer? Is it even possible for a demon to enter a believer? These questions are really important. We need to be absolutely sure of the answer, because we need to know whether to do Biblical evangelism with a non-believer or biblical discipleship with a believer!

After Jesus converted Paul on the Damascus road, He said, *"I will rescue you from your own people and from the Gentiles. I am sending you to them to open their eyes and turn them from darkness to light, and from the power of Satan to God, so that they may receive forgiveness of sins and a place among those who are sanctified by faith in Me,"* Acts 26:17-18. At the time of salvation, Paul was delivered from the *"power of Satan."* Does any believer ever need to be redelivered?

In Luke 10:17, when the 72 returned saying the demons were subject to them, Jesus said, *"Do not rejoice that the spirits submit to you, but rejoice that your names are written in Heaven,"* Luke 10:20. Pastors may brag about casting out demons, but Jesus living in any heart is a far greater truth! If Jesus is in, Satan must be out, and stay out! Both cannot live in the same heart, as 2 Corinthians 6:14-18 shows. Christians *"are the temple of the living God,"* 2 Corinthians 6:16b.

I have seen Christians who had a sinful week, enter church guilty and sad. In church, they kneel before the pastor who puts his hand on their head shouting "Satan get out!" Who made this Christian guilty? Was it Satan or the Holy Spirit? Who is the pastor telling to get out? Discipleship by casting out demons is saying the sin is the fault of demons! What happened to confession and repentance? No wonder so little is happening in the area of discipleship in some churches!

Prayer: Lord, what protection we have as believers when You in Trinity indwell us! What John said is true, *"The One who is in you is greater than the one who is in the world,"* 1 John 4:4b. We praise You for Your loving protection! In Jesus' name we pray. Amen.

April 4

"Put on the full armor of God so that you can take your stand against the devil's schemes. For our struggle is not against flesh and blood, but against the rulers, against the authorities, against the powers of this dark world and against the spiritual forces of evil in the heavenly realms." Ephesians 6:11-12

Why is magic so dangerous?

Magic is not innocent fun! Both the Old and New Testaments warn against it because there is a war going on in the supernatural, between both good and evil spirits. The enemies of God and His people are not limited to this present physical world. The forces of God (for good) are *"against the spiritual forces of evil in the heavenly realms."* Magic gains access to the powerful, evil spirit world to interact with it, to cooperate with it!

The power in the spirit world that is good, is God and His network of angels! God hates it when people seek out "other" evil powers. God put us on this earth to worship Him, alone! God spoke very strongly about this! *"When you enter the land the LORD your God is giving you, do not learn to imitate the detestable ways of the nations there. Let no one be found among you... who practices divination or <u>sorcery</u>, interprets omens, engages in witchcraft, or <u>casts spells</u> or who is a medium or spiritist or who consults the dead. Anyone who does these things is detestable to the LORD,"* Deuteronomy 18:9-12a.

The staff of Moses became a snake. The magicians of Pharaoh did the same thing! But their power was demonic! Now the people were going to a new land where magic was widely practiced so God warns them. Sorcery is much like magic. Sorcery gets into the evil spirit world and into the drug culture. Interestingly, the word *"sorcery"* in the New Testament is *pharmakeia*, from which we get the word pharmacy. The drug scene holds hands with demons! If we play with evil, we will be pulled away from God!

Prayer: Lord, You said, *"I will set My face against the person who turns to mediums and spiritists to prostitute himself by following them, and I will cut him off from his people. Consecrate yourselves and be holy, because I am the LORD your God,"* Leviticus 20:6-7. Lord, we cling to You to make us holy! In Jesus' name we pray. Amen.

April 5

"You shall not make any cuttings in your flesh for the dead, nor tattoo any marks on you; I am the LORD." Leviticus 19:28 NKJV

What is wrong with tattoos?

God wants His people to reflect His holy character. When leading them to Canaan (to Heaven itself), He warned them sternly! God said, *"You shall"* many times. He also said, *"You shall not"* many times. Putting a tattoo on your body was on the *"You shall not"* list. God didn't want His children to imitate the evil practices of the pagans.

When a heathen died, their friends would cut their bodies, as a sacrifice, to appease their gods. Do you know why? They didn't want the demons to torment the deceased further, or to come after them next! So they gave some of their blood as a sacrifice. God on the other hand, gave His Son's blood as a sacrifice for us!

The pagans also marked their bodies with tattoos. This showed their loyalty to their god and was literally, an act of worship! Can you see why it made God angry? He was the One that made them, protected them, and cared for them! <u>Cuttings and tattoos were a pagan statement on a body that God created</u>!

Fifty years ago people got a tattoo when they were drunk, when they were out of their right mind. A tattoo was laughingly called a permanent sign of temporary insanity. But it's no laughing matter! Tattoos are currently the rage with many sports heroes. They think it makes them look tough and on the wild side. Now many in society get tattoos to show that they are part of the "in crowd." But we need to carefully consider, "Is it worth it to be with the 'in crowd' if it displeases God?" Besides this verse in Leviticus that says no tattoos, we also have instruction in the New Testament. *"Offer your bodies as living sacrifices, holy and pleasing to God, this is your spiritual act of worship,"* Romans 12:1b. Tattoos are not pleasing to God!

Prayer: Lord forgive us for wanting what the world wants when it is against Your holy will. May we never try to be wiser than You in any area in life, but to depend on You. For You made us to worship and to love You! In Jesus' name we pray. Amen.

April 6

"The sacrifices of pagans are offered to demons, not to God, and I do not want you to be participants with demons." 1 Corinthians 10:20b

The sacrifices of pagans are to demons

Last week was a Hindu festival. My wife and I went into the city where I needed to teach. On the way, there were many people purchasing their 18 inch tall elephant god. They were carrying their god. They were bringing their god into their home. Within a week they will put their god into the water by the sea, or in their own drinking well. This is all part of their sacrifice. What is wrong with that Biblically?

Compare such sacrifices to what our God does for us. He purchased us! Not with just a few coins, but with His Son's own blood. After purchasing us, He carries us! He will take us into His home forever, not just for a week. He put us under the water in baptism, a sure sign of how clean we really are from Jesus' blood. May we have a burden for the lost, and thank God for what we have by His grace!

In the verses surrounding our text, the new believers of Corinth wanted to know how they should behave with their pagan neighbors concerning their old festivals or holidays. Paul's explanation is both interesting and instructive. Paul contrasted the Christians taking of the Lord's Supper to pagans participating with demons in their festivals! That brings a lot of clarity concerning the different pagan holidays all around the world! Let us dwell on what God offers us!

By God's grace, we never have to go to a temple and ring a bell to wake up our God. He never slumbers or sleeps! Far more than that, God makes us His Temple! He lives in us! He tells us that He will always live in us. We will always live with Him. God's Son is our elder Brother. God adopted us into His family. We are joint heirs to all the blessings His beloved Son receives. And there is far more we are currently unaware of! *"No eye has seen, no ear has heard, no mind has conceived what God has prepared for those who love Him,"* 1 Corinthians 2:9b.

Prayer: Gracious Lord, we don't deserve Your abundant grace. We pray that many will see the hope that they can have in You as their Father, Jesus as their Savior, and the Holy Spirit as their Friend. In Jesus' name we pray. Amen.

April 7

"Keep watch over yourselves and all the flock of which the Holy Spirit has made you overseers. Be shepherds of the church of God, which He bought with His own blood." Acts 20:28

Why the office of Elder?

There are many reasons that "the flock" is weak today. One big reason is a failure to keep the clear command in our text, that elders (plural), must lead God's church. We know this is plural because Paul is writing to a single church! The command is part of Paul's farewell address to the Ephesian elders. Many had different ideas for leadership. Paul points out God's way in church government!

1. The authority for elders is from God. The command in our text originates in the *"Holy Spirit."* The command reasons that because Jesus owns the church, *"bought with His own blood,"* He has the right to determine who should lead it.

2. The elders' purpose is; *"Be shepherds of the church of God."* These are not board members, not advisors, but *"shepherds."* These elders are to care for the health of the flock, to feed the flock with real spiritual food. Jesus said to Peter, *"feed My sheep."* Today many sheep are starved and leaving for other churches because they are hungry spiritually. The elders are to protect the flock! After our text, Paul warned the Ephesian elders, *"I know that after I leave, savage wolves will come in among you and will not spare the flock,"* Acts 20:29. Already the early church did not protect the flock. The book of Ephesians is an elder's handbook. It is addressed to them with lessons on leadership for today!

3. The pastor is one of the elders! *"To the elders among you. I appeal as a fellow elder, a witness of Christ's sufferings and one who also will share in the glory to be revealed: Be shepherds of God's flock that is under your care, serving as overseers, not because you must, but because you are willing, as God wants you to be; not greedy for money, but eager to serve; not lording it over those entrusted to you, but being examples to the flock,"* 1 Peter 5:1-3. How much this advice is needed today!

Prayer: Lord, we pray for the elders of Your church. May they be true shepherds. In Jesus' name we pray. Amen.

April 8

"Deacons, likewise, are to be men worthy of respect, sincere, not indulging in much wine, and not pursuing dishonest gain. They must keep hold of the deep truths of the faith with a clear conscience. They must first be tested; and then if there is nothing against them, let them serve as deacons." 1 Timothy 3:8-10

Why the office of Deacon?

Paul also wrote Timothy some instructions for the office of deacon. He gave his reason for doing so. *"Although I hope to come to you soon, I am writing you these instructions so that, if I am delayed, you will know how people ought to conduct themselves in God's household, which is the church of the living God, the pillar and foundation of the truth,"* 1 Timothy 3:14-15.

The term "deacon" simply means servant. The deacons are to assist the elders in their ministry of spiritual oversight. They are to especially take care of the physical and practical affairs of the Church. In Acts 6, the apostles ministered to the needy, but they were so overburdened with this service that some were neglected. The office of deacon flows from the love that Christ has for His Church. This interest is so great that Jesus says that what is done unto one of the least of His brethren is done unto Him personally! Jesus places the "needy" in churches to test the members, to see if they will love them and reach out to them!

Jesus said to church members about The Judgment; *"For I was hungry and you gave Me something to eat, I was thirsty and you gave Me something to drink, I was a stranger and you invited Me in, I needed clothes and you clothed Me, I was sick and you looked after Me, I was in prison and you came to visit Me,"* Matthew 25:35-36.

A healthy church needs both elders and deacons to function well. The number one qualification for these offices is to *"conduct yourselves in a manner worthy of the gospel of Christ,"* Philippians 1:27a. It is the mission of an elder or deacon to live right, to be a Christian example. Woe be it to us if we neglect these important things!

Prayer: Dear Lord, we see deacons are important to You. You even test us to see if we are acting graciously in reaching out to the needy. Forgive us where we have failed. In Jesus' name we pray. Amen.

April 9

"Now the overseer must be above reproach, the husband of but one wife, temperate, self-controlled, respectable, hospitable, able to teach, not given to drunkenness, not violent but gentle, not quarrelsome, not a lover of money. He must manage his own family well and see that his children obey him with proper respect." "He must not be a recent convert." 1 Timothy 3:2-4 & 6a

God's qualifications for a Pastor

Paul is writing concerning the Ephesian church which he started as a missionary a few years before. He shows them a model for the New Testament Church. The term *"overseer"* includes the office of pastor or teaching elder. God carefully explains the practical qualifications for this office:

- *"**Above reproach"*** – One should not be able to accuse him of anything. He must have a good standing in the community!
- *"**Husband of but one wife"*** – A man, and not a polygamist.
- *"**Able to teach"*** – Must have the gift of teaching. This is far more than knowing what to teach. It is also being able to communicate it!
- *"**Not given to drunkenness"*** – Does not have a drinking problem.
- *"**Not violent but gentle"*** – Must be a loving and gentle man.
- *"**Not quarrelsome"*** - Gentle persuasion was Jesus' approach!
- *"**Not a lover of money"*** – Not money-minded!
- *"**Must manage his own family well"*** – A family man who manages with love and not by fear or threats. And it must show!
- *"**His children obey him"*** – The proof he manages well is, *"his children obey him."* "If anyone does not know how to manage his own family, how can he take care of God's church?"* 1 Timothy 3:5.
- *"**Not be a recent convert,"*** – He needs to learn about Christ before he teaches about Christ to others.

Prayer: Lord, we have not followed Your listed qualifications! We have looked more at how much schooling someone has instead of how much Christ and Your Spirit is visible in them. Forgive us! May we who say we believe in grace, live graciously! May Your church be built Your way. In Christ's name we pray. Amen.

April 10

"The Spirit clearly says that in later times some will abandon the faith and follow deceiving spirits and things taught by demons. Such teachings come <u>through hypocritical liars</u>, whose consciences have been seared as with a hot iron." 1 Timothy 4:1-2

False teachers are "hypocritical liars"

After Paul started the Ephesian church, false teachers started to move in. Paul saw it coming! In his farewell speech to the elders, Paul said, *"Keep watch over <u>yourselves</u> and all the flock of which the Holy Spirit has made you overseers. Be shepherds of the church of God, which He bought with His own blood. I know that after I leave, savage wolves will come in among you and will not spare the flock. Even <u>from your own number</u> men will arise and distort the truth in order to draw away disciples after them,"* Acts 20:28-30. This still happens!

Apostate pastors lead people astray. That reality will increase as we near the end. Why? The antichrist needs demonic deceivers to work with, to further his wicked agenda. Paul has warned us in 2 Thessalonians 2:9-10 about "false teachers." Paul very pointedly was saying, <u>expose them now</u>, by examining how they are <u>living</u>. This is what they will look like. They will be *"hypocritical liars."* They will say one thing and do another! They will be a law unto themselves! Don't be fooled by an educational degree. Without a good conscience, they do not work for God! That's why Paul told Timothy, *"set an example for the believers in speech, in life, in love, in faith and in purity,"* 1 Timothy 4:12b. The context of 1 Timothy 3 is for good leaders. In Chapter 4, false teachers were not doing what good leaders were supposed to do. So Timothy and all leaders, guard yourselves! May it be evident whose side we are on!

What can church members do? Plenty! Look at the leaders in our churches. Are they in office based on how they live and treat people? If not, why not? Be aware, false teachers are in churches to tempt members to *"abandon the faith and follow deceiving spirits."*

Prayer: Lord, many of our churches are in serious trouble. We have not followed Your guidelines for leaders! You have warned us repeatedly about false teachers and we have not listened. Forgive us and help us to see what You see! In Jesus' name we pray. Amen.

April 11

"A time is coming and has now come when the true worshipers will worship the Father in spirit and in truth, for they are the kind of worshipers the Father seeks." John 4:23

What is Biblical worship?

This is a serious subject. We were put on earth to worship God. Therefore worship is not optional. God requires it, defines it and regulates it. We do not get to *"worship"* as we please, but as God commands us. In His mercy, God tells us what our worship must look like!

1. The person of worship is critical. Our text is part of the answer Jesus gave to the Samaritan woman. She asked Jesus in verse 20, "What *"place"* should we worship, Jerusalem or Samaria?" Jesus is telling her plainly, *"a time is coming and has now come."* What has *"now come"*? It is Jesus Himself in the flesh! The point is worship God through Jesus! It's the <u>person</u>, not the place that is important.

2. *"Worship God acceptably with reverence and awe."* Hebrews 12:28b. Do not worship God casually, in speech or in manners and this includes dress. Too many speak lightly, jokingly, without real respect. God told Moses, take off your shoes you are standing on holy ground. Pulpits that used to be elevated to preach the Word, have been replaced with a stage and drama. The results are more in line with Hollywood. We used to dress up to go to church. Now we dress down! Why? Whose approval do we seek?

3. We must worship God in *"truth."* The truth is an equal balance of God's love and justice. One attribute of God must not be emphasized more than the other! Mistakes are made on both sides of this issue. Too much teaching on God's love does not show the holiness of God and the depth of man's sin. Too much teaching on God's holy justice keeps people from knowing God in a loving, fatherly relationship. Our God is gracious in loving us, yet He hates our sin. We need God's balance!

Prayer: Dear Holy Lord, when we search the Scriptures, *"true worshipers"* are the only ones that You ever seek! Lord, forgive us when we have not been true worshipers of You. Teach us to worship as You desire. In Christ's name we pray. Amen.

April 12

"Come, let us bow down in worship, let us kneel before the LORD our Maker; for He is our God and we are the people of His pasture, the flock under His care. Today if you hear His voice, do not harden your hearts." Psalm 95:6-8a

Corporate worship is commanded

Our text is a good example of a call to worship that the pastor gives at the beginning of the Sunday service. For God is actually calling us into His presence! We must do as the verses command! *"Come," "bow down,"* and *"kneel."* This is our position in corporate and private worship as we are transported into the throne room of Heaven. It is here we offer our praises to God! We do not go to worship to be an audience, but as an adoring assembly! There are 3 main parts to corporate worship.

1. Singing - The Psalms were written to be sung back to God. When our hearts are full of Christ, we must sing. God has put a song in our hearts and He wants to hear it! Think of how beautifully the birds sing to God! What do they have to sing about compared to us? We must sing in worship, with all our hearts!

2. Praying - God taught us to pray, encourages us to do so, and greatly delights in it. Prayer belongs in corporate worship for three good reasons. 1. God the Holy Spirit is the author of our prayers. 2. God the Son presents our prayers to the Father. 3. God the Father accepts our prayers. Corporate prayer worships God in Trinity. Prayers that come from the hearts of God's people go to the heart of God! We must pray with all of our hearts!

3. Hearing of the Word of God - *"Everyone who calls on the name of the Lord will be saved. How, then, can they call on the One they have not believed in? And how can they believe in the One of whom they have not <u>heard</u>? And how can they <u>hear</u> without someone preaching to them?"* Romans 10:13-14. In worship, the Gospel enters our hearts by way of the ear! We must hear then, with all our hearts!

Prayer: Lord, You alone are worthy of praise. Hebrews 10:25 is right. *"Let us not give up meeting together, as some are in the habit of doing, but let us encourage one another - and all the more as you see the Day approaching."* In Jesus' name we pray. Amen.

April 13

*"Praise the LORD, O my soul; all my inmost being, praise His holy name.
Praise the LORD, O my soul, and forget not all His benefits."*
Psalm 103:1-2

What are *"His benefits"*?

The young orphan children would recite Psalm 103:1-2 at the end of their prayers. The children learned these excellent verses from adult caregivers! But the children, could not think of even one *"benefit"* that God gives to them! How about us as adults? What kind of list of *"His benefits"* would we put together? Would we list material blessings first? God has His own list of *"His benefits"* that He gives to us in verses 3-19. It is an impressive list. Instead of complaining, it would do our souls much good to meditate on these important *"benefits"*!

Notice how the *"benefits"* section begins. The Lord *"forgives all your sins,"* in verse 3. What a profound truth! Look at all the people carrying rice bags on their heads all the way to North India, just to dump them in the Ganges River. They think their sins are forgiven by doing this! Think of all the other ways people try to have their sins forgiven! But there is only one way! *"All your sins"* are forgiven by *"the LORD"* alone. May we think about that often and praise God for His complete forgiveness!

Another benefit, the Lord *"redeems your life from the pit."* So Jesus doesn't just forgive our sins, He first had to pay the price for our sins. That is what *"redeemed"* means. Therefore, death can not hold us in the *"pit"* or grave, anymore than death could hold the sinless Jesus there! When we do come out of that grave in the resurrection, He *"crowns us."* Another undeserved benefit!

The Lord also *"satisfies your desires with good things"* in verse 5. God's love satisfies you in this world as well as in the next. No other love in this world truly satisfies like God's! What benefits we have from our Lord, and we have only looked at a few of them!

Prayer: Dear father in Heaven, what amazing benefits You bestow on us when we are Your redeemed children! When we really do think of Your *"benefits"* we can only say, *"Praise the LORD, O my soul."* In Jesus' most holy and precious name we pray. Amen.

April 14

"Finally, all of you, live in harmony with one another; be sympathetic, love as brothers, be compassionate and humble." 1 Peter 3:8

"Live in harmony with one another"

Life can be stressful! But there's a way out, if we live God's way. The command here to *"live in harmony with one another,"* is a practical call to live out the Christian life. If we believe Christ is Lord, then we must expect to live as He wants us to. Peter's overall context here is a call to submissive Christian service. That's the secret to *"live in harmony with one another."* Peter outlines a Christian pattern of practical living in chapters 1-3. It is also a call to daily worship, since the words serve and worship come from the same word. See the consistent pattern.

"Servants, be submissive to your masters with all fear, not only to the good and gentle, but also to the harsh. For this is commendable," 1 Peter 2:18-19a NKJV. In verses 21-24, Christ was submissive. Wives are taught to be *"submissive"* in 1 Peter 3:1-6. Finally, husbands are taught to be *"considerate"* to their wives in 1 Peter 3:7. And then our text, *"Finally, all of you, live in harmony with one another."*

In our morning devotions we may commit ourselves to worship and serve God. We say we want to be servants. But then, after prayer, someone treats us like a servant and we get upset. We are mad. We selfishly think, "Do you think I'm your servant?" Our desire to be proud is displayed! We want to serve the god of self, not the Almighty God, and surely not others!

I met with a lady who gets very angry on a daily basis with those she works with. She lashes out at them and often stays mad for days. She considers herself a Christian, and might be. But one thing is evident: she doesn't have a heart to serve anyone else! She is not *"in harmony,"* with others. Not *"sympathetic;"* not loving others; not *"compassionate and humble."* She is not very happy either! What about us? How is our daily worship going out in the world?

Prayer: Lord, we can see that the call to live as a servant, gives a living testimony of our love for You and others. Lord expose our proud hearts. Teach us how to really serve one another as our Savior did. May we be like Him. In Christ's name we pray. Amen.

April 15

"All of you, clothe yourselves with humility toward one another, because, 'God opposes the proud but gives grace to the humble.'"
1 Peter 5:5b

For Christ's sake, dress right!

The words *"clothe yourselves with humility,"* means to wear our *"humility"* like clothing! If we take our "humble" clothes off, our naked pride will be exposed for all to see! Spiritually speaking, *"humility"* must go with us throughout our day just like our clothes do! Imagine the laughing, mocking and even crying that would go on if we were not clothed! Well, God notices it when our humility comes off. He's telling us, for Christ's sake, keep our humble clothes on! For the good of others, stay dressed! For our own peace, keep our own spiritual clothes on!

Is there even one single place in our daily living for pride? Think about the good things that we do every day! Do we do any of them in our own strength? How about our righteousness? Do we ever do anything in our own righteousness? The Bible is very clear about this! *"For it is God who works in you to will and to act according to His good purpose,"* Philippians 2:13. So much so that, *"We are God's workmanship, created in Christ Jesus to do good works, which God prepared in advance for us to do,"* Ephesians 2:10. With this in mind, what place does pride have in our wardrobe of spiritual clothes?

"God opposes the proud." Notice, there is no neutral ground here! If we do not wear the humility set of clothes, we will be wearing the pride set! It's the only two sets of clothes we have until we enter Heaven! There God gives us white robes to wear!

Prayer: O Righteous Lord, in Revelation You tell us that Christians were *"arrayed in white robes."* The question was asked, *"Where did they come from?"* And You tell us, *"These are they who came out of the great tribulation, they have washed their robes and made them white in the blood of the Lamb. Therefore, 'they are before the throne of God and serve Him day and night in His temple; and He who sits on the throne will spread His tent over them,'"* Revelation 7:14b-15. Lord, You do dress us for all eternity! May we wear Your clothes today to bring honor to the One who bought us with His blood. In His name we pray. Amen.

April 16

"The LORD inflicted serious diseases on Pharaoh and his household because of Abram's wife Sarai." Genesis 12:17

"Playing around" will plague you

In Genesis 12:10-20, there is a brief account of Abram going to Egypt. Why did Abram go to Egypt? You might say because there was a severe famine in the countries around Egypt. True, but that information is covered in verse 10 alone. The next nine verses deal with a larger truth God is trying to teach us.

Abram's wife was a very beautiful woman. So beautiful that Abram feared that those who were in power in Egypt would kill him, just so that they could take his wife. So Abram told the Egyptians that Sarai was his sister. Sure enough, *"when Pharaoh's officials saw her, they praised her to Pharaoh, and she was taken into his palace,"* Genesis 12:15. Pharaoh did not know that Sarai was married! Yet still, we read that *"The LORD inflicted serious diseases on Pharaoh and his household because of Abram's wife Sarai,"* Genesis 12:17. If God severely plagued Pharaoh for taking a woman into his house, not knowing she was married, and not even touching her, how much quicker will God plague those who knowingly do these things?

God asks some hard questions for our good! *"Can a man scoop fire into his lap without his clothes being burned? Can a man walk on hot coals without his feet being scorched? So is he who sleeps with another man's wife; no one who touches her will go unpunished,"* Proverbs 6:27-29. The punishment of God will be both quick and sure! *"A man who commits adultery lacks judgment; whoever does so destroys himself,"* Proverbs 6:32. No one should blame God for the difficulties He will rain on the guilty. Those who *"commit adultery,"* are challenging God, "I dare You to bring on the punishment."

Prayer: Lord how blind we sinners are. We are willing to exchange a moment of pleasure for an eternity of suffering. Lord, we thank You for the many warnings that You give us to help us to see the truth about willfully sinning against You. Lord, we pray for those who have fallen. May they, like King David, go to You for forgiveness. Lord forgive us from all of our sins. In Jesus' name we pray. Amen.

April 17

"Don't let anyone look down on you because you are young, but set an example for the believers in speech, in life, in love, in faith and in purity." 1 Timothy 4:12

Youth, "set an example"!

Christian young person, do you think that you are only the future church? That is not just your mistake! It is also ours who are older. <u>Like Timothy, the youth are today's church!</u> It's also important that you start acting like today's church. *"Set an example"* now. That is Paul's advice. Many believing children are being used by God to call unbelievers of all ages to repentance. You are called by God to, *"Set an example for the believers in speech, in life, in love, in faith and in purity."*

Those who think, "I am young now but I will get serious tomorrow," are presently in the devil's camp. His favorite trick is to get you to wait until tomorrow to get serious about a relationship with God! When tomorrow comes, he will again move us to wait one more day. While all the tomorrows come and go, we get further into the camp of the wicked! Or worse yet, we die. Hell is filled with people who had intentions of getting serious with God, "some day."

I once spoke at an opening ceremony for a Bible college in India. I asked the students how many of them were planning to be in ministry while they were in college. Only a few hands came up. I asked the rest to pack their bags and go back home. What better time is there to serve the Lord and be a witness for Him than in Bible school among the students? It is a God-ordained privilige to pray together, study and together reach out to those in and around the school. School isn't just a time to learn about ministry, it's a time to do it! If we can't find time to "do ministry" in school, how will we find time when we get out? This is true for every Christian youth today. Preach by *"setting an example."*

Prayer: Lord, we thank You for instructing young Timothy and us. We need to hear *and see the words,* "set an example" in how we live! How sad it is that some youth live like hell, yet expect to go to Heaven. Lord, correct us all. Turn us around. We want to act like Your holy children. In Christ Jesus' name we pray. Amen.

April 18

"I urge, then, first of all, that requests, prayers, intercession and thanksgiving be made for everyone — for kings and all those in authority, that we may live peaceful and quiet lives in all godliness and holiness. This is good, and pleases God our Savior." 1 Timothy 2:1-3

When we grumble, we stumble!

How often we grumble about those *"in authority."* Is any of this grumbling changing the wrong they do? See how our text fits into the rest of 1 Timothy 2. The chapter is about worship. Praying for, *"all those in authority,"* is part of our worship. Grumbling is the opposite of worship. When we grumble we stumble in our worship.

1. Grumbling does not submit to our *"governing authorities."* *"Everyone must submit himself to the governing authorities, for there is no authority except that which God has established. The authorities that exist have been established by God,"* Romans 13:1. Our grumbling does not *"submit"* to God's authority.

2. Grumbling will *"bring judgment"* on us. Those who rebel *"will bring judgment on themselves,"* Romans 13:2b. Even an evil leader can be, *"God's servant to do you good,"* Romans 13:4a. God often uses evil leaders to discipline His people, to turn them back to Himself! We are called by God to be witnesses, not lawyers or judges. God Himself does not judge a man until he dies. Why should we?

3. Praying changes hearts! If we want the heart of any leader to change, pray. If a parent, teacher, government, boss or co-worker is difficult, pray. If we want a better pastor, pray for him. At least our own bitter heart will then change. Grumbling fuels demonic bitterness in us. Our text commands; *"Live peaceful and quiet lives in all godliness and holiness. This is good and it pleases God our Savior."*

Prayer: Lord, we grumble about so much! If we would quit grumbling we would have better relationships with everyone, including You. The Bible says, *"Do everything without complaining or arguing, so that you may become blameless and pure, children of God without fault in a crooked and depraved generation, in which you shine like stars in the universe,"* Philippians 2:14-15. Lord, help us to live like this. In Jesus' name we pray. Amen.

April 19

"For which of you, intending to build a tower, does not sit down first and count the cost, whether he has enough to finish it."
Luke 14:28 NKJV

Jesus has counted our cost!

If we are a missionary or a kingdom worker for any length of time, we have counted <u>our</u> cost. We know the loneliness, the separation from family, the hardships that are too numerous to count. And if we continue to count <u>our</u> cost and meditate on that, it will be our ruin. We can't follow Christ by counting our cost. We need the strength of Almighty God. We need the encouragement, prayers and help from others in the body of Christ. We must look to Christ who has counted our cost!

Consider how much it cost Him to redeem us! It cost Him everything, even His life. <u>He knows exactly what it will cost us and takes great pleasure in meeting our need.</u> Look to God and see how our cost is already "covered." The following Acronym will help:

J - Justified by His blood. We are God's adopted child, His relative. He will never leave us or forsake us; He promised.

E - Energized by God's power. We can say, *"I can do everything through Him who gives me strength,"* Philippians 4:13.

S - Sufficient by His Spirit. *"Not that we are sufficient of ourselves to think of anything as being from ourselves, but our sufficiency is from God, who also made us sufficient as ministers of the new covenant... the Spirit gives life,"* 2 Corinthians 3:5-6 NKJV.

U - Unlimited is His grace to keep us going. *"It is God who works in you to will and to act according to His good purpose,"* Philippians 2:13.

S - Safety is in His arms. *"In this world you will have trouble. But take heart! I have overcome the world,"* John 16:33b.

Prayer: Lord, we thank You for paying the cost for our salvation, for our sanctification, and even for our glorification. You left Heaven to live on this earth in horrible conditions! How fully You know the cost of discipleship! You are our everything, our all! We praise You for not only counting our cost but for paying for it and giving us what we need to serve You. In Jesus' name we pray. Amen.

April 20

"You who fear Him, trust in the LORD – He is their help and shield."
Psalm 115:11

He is our help and shield!

What a beautiful statement concerning the loving care of our Lord! Three times the psalmist repeats these words so that we will dwell on them and absorb its truth. The psalmist begins by questioning the people on why so many of them have turned to idols that cannot do anything for them. He reminds them that their idols can't see, hear, smell, or even move a finger to come to their aid. In fact, we will be just like them if we cling to them. Everyone is like what his or her god/God is like!

What does our text mean for us as Christians? Our God sees us! He never slumbers or sleeps. He hears us, even if we lose our voice. Our God has all wisdom, all power and the biggest storehouse, all to bless and protect us as He builds His kingdom. The Psalm doesn't say that, He will be our help and shield! It says, *"He is their help and shield."* This is fully as much a present reality as it is a future promise! Why then do we fear our enemies? Why do we fall to pieces when we read of economic disaster? Why do we wonder what will happen to our loved ones? Why do we give in to senseless self-pity that kills us physically, mentally and spiritually?

This Psalm is for today! God is our *"help and shield."* God is on the offensive for us and at the same time He defends us. Meditate on what this means! God will give us what we need exactly when we need it as Hebrews 4:16 teaches. It does not say that God will give us what we want, when we want it. It says, what we need, when we need it! Our comfort is in the fact that God knows what we need! He knows whether the medicine of pain or the medicine of pleasure is best for us.

Defensively, who can do what God does? The prophet Elijah was correct! *"Don't be afraid,... those who are with us are more than those who are with them,"* 2 Kings 6:16. God has twice as many good angels to defend us, than Satan has demonic angels to hurt us.

Prayer: Sovereign Lord, Elijah's powerful prayer is ours. Open our eyes that we may see. What a blessing You are to us, Your adopted children. We thank You! In Jesus' name we pray. Amen.

April 21

"Do not be yoked together with unbelievers. For what do righteousness and wickedness have in common?" 2 Corinthians 6:14a

You want to marry an unbeliever?

"But, he is such a nice person." "He is very caring." "He loves me a lot!" "I know he's not perfect, but better than any boy in our church!" Secretly she thinks that the bad points will surely change and that she will change him. What can we say to this girl who wants to marry an unbeliever?

The boy says, "I am in love with this girl." "She is very beautiful!" "Her parents are educated and good." "There is no other girl like this!" Secretly he hopes, she will come to church. In the meantime, he thinks he will be so happy because she is so beautiful and that she will always be so beautiful. She will never change. What can we say to this boy?

It is always outside of God's will for a Christian to marry an unbeliever. There is a common "false hope" of both the girl and the boy. She thinks she will change his wild spirit. He thinks her outward beauty will never change. This is not logical thinking. We could say love is blind but the truth is: lust is that blind. Love through the eyes of God is never blind.

To the girl we must say, only God can change a heart to believe! In Ezekiel 36:26-27a, God says, *"I will give you a new heart and put a new spirit in you; I will remove from you your heart of stone and I will give you a heart of flesh. And I will put My Spirit in you and move you to follow My decrees."* Once Jesus lives in the heart of this young man, he will grow in grace. This means as he loves God more, he will increasingly treat you gently and with more respect.

To the boy we must say that God calls him to love far more than just this girl's body. What about her soul? Do you love what she is on the inside? Her soul, who she really is, will continue to grow more beautiful as she ages, if she really is a child of God! This girls' outward appearance will surely change when age and gravity attack her body. Then what will you love?

Prayer: Lord, we can be so blind because too often we have wrong ideas about what true love is! Lord, it is Your truth that sets us free. We are so thankful that You give it to us! May Your name be lifted up in our relationships. In Jesus' name we pray. Amen.

April 22

"Then the LORD God made a woman from the rib He had taken out of the man, and He brought her to the man. The man said, 'This is now bone of my bones and flesh of my flesh; she shall be called 'woman,' for she was taken out of the man.'" Genesis 2:22-23

My very own flesh

All the animals, birds and fish had a partner. Adam, the crown of God's creative genius, did not. God in mercy to man, took a bone out of Adam's side. He made Eve, while Adam slept! Then God presented her to Adam. What a beautiful surprise! Surely Adam's eyes about came out of his head. Here stood the most beautiful woman in the world, even if she was the only one. She was of the same flesh as he was. The meaning here is important physically and spiritually.

God gave man exactly the kind of partner he needed in marriage and in life. God gave the woman exactly what she needed. God demands that the two of them cling to each other physically and spiritually because they are made of the same flesh and bone. But our text has even a greater meaning for every Christian.

As Christians we are remade of the same Spirit as Christ. God in grace also gave us what we needed, just like He did to Adam. Our spiritual life was non-existent just like when Eve was not yet made. We were dead because of our sin! Then God pierced the side of Christ to give us life. He pierced the side of Adam to give Eve life! He broke Christ's body and shed His blood so that we could partake of it! When we take the Lord's Supper we celebrate this. As Christians we do this because we are bone of His bones, flesh of His flesh! Because of the second Adam, we have life everlasting! Now Christ's sufferings, His death, resurrection and ascension are all ours. We are even given His name, "Christian," just like Eve was given the name "woman."

Prayer: Lord, like Adam before us, we admire Your creative genius in marrying us to Christ! You made us one flesh with Him. What a privilege and benefit it is for us. What a blessing to be declared righteous and have all our sins forgiven. We worship and praise You. In Jesus' blessed name we pray. Amen.

April 23

"'Haven't you read,' He replied, 'that at the beginning the Creator 'made them male and female,' and said, 'For this reason a man will leave his father and mother and be united to his wife, and the two will become one flesh?' So they are no longer two, but one. Therefore, what God has joined together, let man not separate.'" Matthew 19:4-6

Separation instead of divorce?

Can <u>two believers</u> in a marriage just separate instead of divorcing? Note we are not talking about an unbeliever and a believer. Neither are we talking about two unbelievers. Jesus is saying "no" to separating two believers because they are literally one flesh. Paul also wrote about divorce and separation. He said "no" concerning two believers separating. Two believers have the Spirit of God in them. They have the grace and power to work things out. How can they learn how to work together if they want to live separately?

Isn't the real problem selfishness for both spouses? Isn't it true that those who want to separate think, "I want to do what I want to do, and this marriage is getting in my way"? What if Christ, the head of the church was not committed to us, His body? Where would we be for all eternity? Husband, in God's eyes you are the head of your wife. If the head leaves the body, the body dies! Is this what you want? If you say "Yes," you have a big problem with God. And wife, "Can a body leave the head?" "How will you function without eyes and ears?" "How will you eat?" You can't live if your body separates from your head.

If you are a believer, you can and must work it out. In fact, God is testing your faith right here, to see if you are really committed to Him and to your spouse. Make sure you pass this big test for the glory of God, for the good of your family, and for your own good.

Prayer: Lord, if we have wanted to separate from our spouse because we have been unable to change them, make us see that we are only responsible to change self (Matthew 7:1-5), not others. For You will hold us personally accountable for how we lived! May we see that as we love others, You change them, because that is Your responsibility. In Jesus' name we pray. Amen.

April 24

"Now the Spirit of the LORD had departed from Saul, and an evil spirit from the LORD tormented him." 1 Samuel 16:14

God sends an *"evil spirit"*

This text really grabs my attention! We know Satan sends out his evil spirits to raise havoc in the world! But can and does God Himself really send an *"evil spirit"* into a person? And if this is true, what does this truth have to say to those who try to cast out evil spirits when God may have put them there? There is not a translating error in our text. The next verse shows that even Saul's servants recognized something serious and life-changing had happened in Saul's life. *"Saul's attendants said to him, 'See, an evil spirit <u>from God</u> is tormenting you,'"* 1 Samuel 16:15. What can we learn from this? Scripture does interpret Scripture.

Satan reports to God! We know this from the life of Job. *"One day the angels came to present themselves before the LORD, and Satan also came with them. The LORD said to Satan, 'Where have you come from?'"* Job 1:6-7a. This question concerning the Spirit/spirit world shows that God is in total control of it! If this were not true, how could Jesus teach us to pray, *"deliver us from the evil one"*? But, there is a big difference between the righteous covenant-keeping Job, and unbelieving covenant-breaking King Saul. With Job, God allowed Satan to afflict him according to limits God set. He did this to show His power and protection of His believer! With Saul, God used an evil spirit to show what happens when He removes His protecting hand to a covenant member!

How about us? Were we brought up in the church? Were our parents and grandparents believers? If so, then we were brought up in the covenant, meaning we agreed to serve God and love Him. Are we doing that? We must, if we desire not only God's salvation, but His continued covenant protection also!

Prayer: Father in Heaven, we thank You for giving us warnings through the lives of real people who had huge problems when they rejected You. May we see these truths and confess our sins, seeking Your forgiveness. May we live for Your eternal kingdom! In Jesus' name we pray. Amen.

April 25

"Saul has slain his thousands, and David his tens of thousands."
1 Samuel 18:7b

Jealousy tries to stop God's mission

God promoted David rapidly. 1. He killed the giant. 2. David became friends with Jonathan, Saul's son and heir to the throne. 3. David successfully performed his job well, quickly rising in the ranks of the army and in the esteem of the people. 4. The ladies in the towns of Israel danced and sang the song in our text; *"Saul has slain his thousands, and David his tens of thousands."* And guess what! *"Saul was very angry; this refrain galled him,"* 1 Samuel 18:8a. David was credited with more success then Saul who was the king! *"And from that time on Saul kept a jealous eye on David,"* 1 Samuel 18:9. And get this, immediately, *"The next day,"* 18:10, Saul throws a spear at David.

Here we see the real heart of jealousy. It is soon filled with much anger and bitterness. The evil thoughts of the heart quickly moves the mouth, hands and feet into action! Saul works quickly to remove the one who is perceived to be a threat to his desire for greatness! That's why Saul hurled a spear at David. And since God put David where he was, this evil attitude is really directed at God.

Because of jealously, we too have relationship problems in our families, schools, businesses, and yes, our churches also. Our jealousy quickly tries to remove others so that our prideful self can be lifted up. We do it. Others do it to us. Many ask me, "Do you face persecution?" The answer is, "Yes!" But it is not coming from where they think it is. They think it's the radicals from other religions that are trying to stop you. They are! But what comes from within the church is far more harmful to the kingdom of God than what comes from the outside. Sad to say, it's often those in authority in the church who in jealously throw spears to pin you to the wall. We must be aware of these things so we can examine our own hearts and see if we are throwing any spears.

Prayer: Lord, we throw spears! Change our hearts for Your glory, and for our good! You tell us to love others, *"especially those who belong to the family of believers."* May Your kingdom come in our hearts today. In Jesus' name we pray. Amen.

April 26

"And David behaved wisely in all of his ways, and the LORD was with him." 1 Samuel 18:14 NKJV

Respond wisely to spears thrown at you!

As David becomes more widely known as a child of God, the spears start coming. Now David will need the grace of God to <u>respond </u>well to those who try to hurt him. David's faith and his ability will be tested by how he responds to the spears that are thrown at him. This is huge! Because David's response must be our response!

David is quickly invited to Saul's house, where he became friends with Saul's son Jonathan. Such a relationship is not common at all. Jonathan had more of a reason to be jealous of David than his father did! After all, David was going to be the next king instead of Jonathan. David was friendly and moved freely with those in the palace.

"David went out wherever Saul sent him, and behaved wisely," 1 Samuel 18:5a NKJV. This too is important. We see that the Spirit of the Lord remains in David, keeping him humble and productive for God. But then the women sang about David killing his ten thousands. Saul could not handle the competition for popularity. Saul throws his first spear at David. He even sends David into battle hoping he would be killed. What does David do? *"<u>David behaved wisely in all of his ways</u>, and the LORD was with him,"* 1 Samuel 18:14 NKJV. <u>He knew that he was in the Lord's will</u>. Another lesson for us.

Saul continues to try eliminate David. He even tries to trap him by using someone from his own family. Jealousy is so evil that even our family can be sacrificed for it! Saul demands David to kill 100 of the enemy, hoping he will die! And what does David do? He kills 200 men. *"And so it was, whenever they went out, that David behaved more wisely than all the servants of Saul, so that his name became highly esteemed,"* 1 Samuel 18:30b NKJV. Let us pray to God for this kind of response to those who do evil things, trying to hurt us.

Prayer: Lord, what a testimony of Your Almighty hand in the life of David, and in every believer. When others in jealousy try to stop our service to You, You protect us. If You are for us, who can be against us? You are such a wonderful God! In Jesus' name we pray. Amen.

April 27

"Wives, submit to your own husbands, as is fitting in the Lord."
Colossians 3:18 NKJV

Wives *"submit,"* Part 1

Paul is setting down rules for a Christian home. That is the context of this command. Paul's concern is that the Gospel is taught by what we do, not just by what we say. What a great idea! Paul lists many sinful practices that we all need to personally put off. He tells us what to put on to complete the change process! *"Therefore, as God's chosen people, holy and dearly loved, clothe yourselves with compassion, kindness, humility, gentleness and patience,"* Colossians 3:12. "Now that would be an easy spouse to live with!" "I want a spouse like that." Yes but, we must all become a spouse like that. If we all lived for our spouse *"with compassion,"* we would all have awesome marriages.

Paul then describes a most important rule for every good relationship. *"Bear with each other and forgive whatever grievances you may have against one another,"* Colossians 3:13. In case we do not know what *"forgive"* means, he ends the verse with, *"Forgive as the Lord forgave you."* Jesus forgave us when we were still sinning, when we were still His enemy, and when we were dead. Which is what saved by grace is all about! We neither deserve forgiveness nor do <u>anything</u> to earn it. Because God put His forgiving grace into us, He now wants to see it openly displayed for all the world to see!

With this instruction as background information, Paul says, *"Wives, submit to your <u>own</u> husbands, as is fitting in the Lord."* I used NKJV because it includes the word, "own." A wife is not to submit to other men, but to <u>her own husband</u>! This subject of submission is important. If we sum up the duties of a wife, her overall attitude must be to *"respect"* her husband! The Colossian women may have had a *"submit"* problem, because the same "information" to the Ephesians in chapter 5 was summed up, *"the wife must respect her husband."*

Prayer: Lord, what needed instruction for us to have Christian marriages. May we have a right respect for Your rules, to live holy lives. In Jesus' name we pray. Amen.

April 28

"Husbands, love your wives and do not be harsh with them."
Colossians 3:19

Husbands *"love,"* Part 2

The chapter in the Bible that teaches a lot about how we need to live as Christians, ends with the summary, *"Husbands, love your wives."* How practical! If a husband does not live the Christian life in his marriage, what's left? Why specifically this command to love? Most likely, Paul looked around and saw a lot of husbands who were not very loving! Sad to say, there are still unloving husbands, even in the church! A husband may look good in church, but what is going on behind the closed doors of his house? Since God sees everything, His Spirit knew what to put on the pages of the Bible.

Jesus and Paul both kept coming back to this theme that marriage is a one flesh relationship. Every person in this world is committed to, and in love with his or her own body. Because of this truth, *"Husbands ought to love their wives as their own bodies. He who loves his wife loves himself,"* Ephesians 5:28. No husband can get out of this God-given responsibility by claiming that he somehow hates himself! So Paul strengthens the argument by saying, *"After all, <u>no one ever hated his own body</u>, but he feeds and cares for it, just as Christ does the church — for we are members of His body,"* Ephesians 5:29-30.

Biblical love is a sacrificial <u>action</u> for another, that needs to be noticeable. We live in a culture that does not want to openly show our love for each other. Colossians 3 is all about how we need to demonstrate our commitment to each other. And husbands and wives need to lead the way. How a wife has to *"submit,"* is also true for how a husband must *"love."* Since God poured His great love into us, He demands that it comes out of us! In Proverbs, a husband must praise his wife. *"Her children arise and call her blessed; her husband also, and he praises her,"* Proverbs 31:28. Christian husbands display their *"love"* to their wives.

Prayer: Lord, You love us when we are not very lovable! Help us to do the same in our marriages. May any harshness be replaced with patience and kindness. In Jesus' name we pray. Amen.

April 29

"Children, obey your parents in everything, for this pleases the Lord."
Colossians 3:20

Children *"obey,"* Part 3

What a beautiful order of verses here in Colossians for having a good family life! Hopefully we can see how the last three verses fit together. If mother is *"submissive"* to the father, and if father *"loves"* the mother, then both <u>obedience</u> and <u>love</u> will be openly displayed in the home. The children's problem is just like mom and dad's, they are fully selfish. There is no desire in a child to be *"submissive"* or *"loving"*! In fact their greatest desire is to be independent and get their own way in all things. *"Folly is bound up in the heart of a child,"* Proverbs 22:15a. If allowed, children will gladly run the home their way. Children need to be lovingly disciplined so that they will obey. This is a major point. If we disagree, we will find out when it is way too late, that we were wrong! Listen to God who is all wise. He says, to discipline the child, and by doing so we will *"deliver his soul from hell,"* Proverbs 23:14b NKJV. Obedience works to drive hell out of a child's eternity. How is this possible?

When a child <u>learns</u> obedience to the parents, they <u>learn</u> obedience to God. In fact, a child must start learning obedience before the age of one. It is not important for a very young child to understand why! They just need to learn a <u>pattern of consistent obedience</u>! Specifically, they must submit to the parents when told "No." Early obedience prepares a child for life on this earth and points them to Heaven.

<u>If a wife will not *"submit"* to her husband and even says bad words about him to others, why should the child *"submit"*? If a husband is *"harsh"* with the child's mother, instead of *"loving"* her, why should the child be *"loving"*? The whole point of Colossians 3 is that sinful behaviors must be put off by everyone in the family and loving habits must replace them. God adds His blessing to these families!</u>

Prayer: Dear Heavenly father, we love Your wisdom! You want us parents to be loving and serving examples in the home, so the children can see clearly with their own eyes how it is done. Help us all in that. In Jesus' name we pray. Amen.

April 30

"'Are you still so dull?' Jesus asked them. 'Don't you see that whatever enters the mouth goes into the stomach and then out of the body? But the things that come out of the mouth come from the heart, and these make a man 'unclean.' For out of the heart come evil thoughts, murder, adultery, sexual immorality, theft, false testimony, slander. These are what make a man 'unclean.'" Matthew 15:16-20a

"I can't eat chicken today!"

That's what the orphanage cook said when I asked her why she didn't eat some of the chicken soup she made for all of us. She is a Hindu, but some Christians and other religions have this same fasting idea. Why do some people think that eating certain foods on certain days will defile their body and soul? What can we say in this situation to help them see the truth? What Jesus said in our verse would be a good place to start. We do need to be concerned about this!

We live in the slum area. It is common for a man to have up to 4 wives. He may even live with number 4 and have another "friend" he is working on. These "marriages" were not performed in a church or a temple but they consider themselves married, with no real commitment! But guess what? They fast and pray regularly!

Cheating to try get more money is another passion. Pagans manage their relationships with extreme fighting, physically and verbally. Some say that 90% of the women in the slums are regularly beaten! The women are not innocent either. They are not submissive. But they too, fast and pray regularly!

The favorite drink in the slums is not water or milk, tea or coffee, It is something with alcohol in it. Drinking problems are the norm. The kids roam the streets because it's safer in the street than in the house, The children study their parents more than books in school! Then they imitate their parents. And the practice continues. But they do fast and pray regularly. The point is: they all need Jesus and a new heart.

Prayer: Lord, convict us of our sins also! Create in us new clean hearts. We pray for those who are so lost. Find them Lord. Do this for Your own glory. In Jesus' name we pray. Amen.

MAY

*"May the words of my mouth and the
meditation of my heart be pleasing in Your
sight, O Lord, my Rock and my Redeemer."*
Psalm 19:14

May 1

"I anointed you king over Israel, and I delivered you from the hand of Saul. I gave your master's house to you... And if all of this had been too little, I would have given you even more." 2 Samuel 12:7b-8

Sexual sin has private consequences! Part 1

When our sins are forgiven, the <u>guilt</u> is removed completely! That's good news. But here is the bad news. There are serious consequences that remain! If we sin sexually thinking that some day God will forgive that guilt, we are on dangerous ground. Besides that, our sin displeases God and our sin is harmful for others. But first we need to see more clearly that our sin has private consequences!

When God confronted David's sexual sin, he confronted David's pattern of sin in this area. David had many wives and concubines. His problem was he was not close to any of them. They were basically sexual objects. Lust does that! He wanted Uriah's wife to be his next lover. But it will not end there if his pattern of sin does not change. God strongly confronts David and us about sin patterns.

God's principles in the Bible have not changed, only the names have. Now we are on the world's stage. Do we see the Biblical principle for our life in our text verses? In salvation God delivers us from sin just as he delivered David *"from the hand of Saul."* God makes us joint heirs with Jesus Christ, just as David was given his *"master's house."* Then God says to David, *"I would have given you even more."* God will give us more also if we will love and serve Him! A consequence of our sin is that we give up many of God's blessings! Then we bitterly complain that God does not bless us! Why don't we stop sinning so He can? *"Do not be deceived: God cannot be mocked. A man reaps what he sows,"* Galatians 6:7. The point then is this: God will give us serious consequences for our sin, so we will stop sinning. Will we stop? Sexual sin has everything to do with lust and nothing to do with love. If we really are looking for love, then we must turn to God, not mock Him!

Prayer: Lord, we deserve Your wrath and displeasure, but we need Your forgiveness and mercy instead. Lord, send your Spirit to convict us and turn us to You. In Jesus' name we pray. Amen.

May 2

"The LORD has taken away your sin. You are not going to die. But because by doing this you have made the enemies of the LORD show utter contempt, the son born to you will die." 2 Samuel 12:13b-14

Sexual sin isn't just private! Part 2

We know our sin hurts us, but so often we sin anyway. We must also consider how much our sin hurts God and others too! We know from 2 Samuel 11 and 12 that David sinned sexually and killed an innocent man to try cover his adultery. After David failed to confess these, God sent Nathan the prophet to convict him. We also know David confessed his sin and the guilt was removed! BUT, his sin still hurt God!

David's sin hurt the honor of his holy God. Chapter 11 ends with the words, *"But the thing David had done displeased the LORD,"* 2 Samuel 11:27b. God poured His grace into David starting at a young age. Then David failed to act in grace when he sinned with Bathsheba. David thought very little of his relationship with God when he did this! We do the same! When David sinned, people talked! When we sin, people will talk. God's holy name is quickly blasphemed all over!

David was <u>unavailiable</u> for God's service when he held on to his sin. Surely he didn't write many Psalms and his harp was out of tune when he did not confess his sin! This is true for us also. When our communion with God is interrupted by sin, we are not useful for God. Our willful sin treats Jesus' suffering and shed blood as if it were common blood. Our sin breaks covenant with God. How incredibly ungrateful, arrogant and unholy it is for us to covet what God forbids. May God help us to see how He is *"displeased"* with our sin.

Despite the fact that David's sin *"displeased"* God, in love God still sent Nathan the prophet to instruct and counsel him. God brought David back to his spiritual senses. When we sin, God is *"displeased,"* yet still He sends His Word and Spirit to wake us up.

Prayer: Merciful Lord, we don't think enough about how good we have it that You are our God! Lord may it register in the depths of our souls, how *"displeased"* You are with our sin. Forgive our wanderings, even if it is in only in thought. Strengthen us to live for You. We want to be a blessing to Your holy and precious name. In Jesus' name we pray. Amen.

May 3

"This is what the LORD says: 'Out of your own household I am going to bring calamity upon you. Before your very eyes I will take your wives and give them to one who is close to you, and he will lie with your wives in broad daylight. You did it in secret, but I will do this thing in broad daylight before all Israel.'" 2 Samuel 12:11-12

Sexual sin isn't just private! Part 3

That truth that our sin hurts others is a general principle in our text. God's strong rebuke here to David is a rebuke for us too. God's principles in Scripture are for all generations. When God gave the terms of His covenant to Israel and to us, He said this about all idols, *"You shall not bow down to them or worship them; for I, the LORD your God, am a jealous God, punishing the children for the sin of the fathers to the third and fourth generation,"* Deuteronomy 5:9a. This underlined reference to *"punishing the children"* is about consequences. In Ezekiel 18:1-20, it is clear that the guilt of the fathers does not pass on to the next generation. We must take this instruction personally, because that was God's intention when He wrote it down for us in the Bible.

The consequences of sexual sin is: It will affect *"your own household"*! Father or mother if you are sinning sexually, it will affect *"your own household."* Unmarried young men and women, if you sin sexually and do not turn from it, *"your own household"* will be affected. Are we prepared for the fact that if we play, the rest of our household will pay. Down the road we will see many of the ways our *"own household"* was indeed affected!

"Thus says the LORD: 'Behold, I will raise up adversity against you from your own house,'" 2 Samuel 12:11a NKJV. What an ugly consequence for selfishly sinning, doing what God hates. We have visions of a happy family life where love for each other is openly shared. That picture will be tarnished by all sexual sin. We need to know this.

Prayer: O Lord, what a sobering truth to see how our sexual sin is especially harmful to others. Lord, what consequences we bring on others when we love sin and don't turn from it. Lord, convict and change us. In Jesus' name we pray. Amen.

May 4

"Elijah went before the people and said, 'How long will you waver between two opinions? If the LORD is God, follow Him; but if Baal is God, follow him.' But the people said nothing." 1 Kings 18:21

"If the LORD is God, follow Him" Part 4

We have talked about some serious sexual issues in the past devotions. It is not easy to talk about this topic because it's such a personal subject! To some degree, we all sin in this area. There is an alarming trend that needs further discussion. The reason is: lust is just as strong of an addiction as drugs and alcohol are.

The T.V. shows way too much skin and immorality. Internet porn is a problem. Many kids from our churches are getting involved in recreational sex, which is sex for fun, no relationship expected. We have seen that there is a private and public concern.

Sexual problems start when we don't have a strong relationship with God or our parents! Granted, parents are part of the problem, but in the end, a small part. No one will be able to stand before God on Judgment Day and blame their parents for anything! We are personally responsible to be one with God. When Israel wandered the most from God they were confronted. *"How long will you waver between two opinions? If the LORD is God, follow Him; but if Baal is God, follow him!"*

We quoted this verse about Baal, because he was more than anything else, a sex god. The people were more in love with him than the covenant God of their family. When Elijah confronted the people, *"The people said nothing."* What about us? God showed us what happened to the priests of Baal. All of Satan's disciples will have a horrible end. If any of us continue to serve Baal, our fate will be the same. Perhaps the best question to ask is: "Where do we want to spend eternity?" It is the height of foolishness to think we can live like Hell and still go to Heaven.

Prayer: O Lord have mercy! Some covenant youth are being very foolish. Lord move their hearts to love You. Move our hearts to love You! We know we will never be sorry! In Jesus' name we pray. Amen.

May 5

"My son, do not forget My teaching, but keep My commands in your heart, for they will prolong your life many years and bring you prosperity." Proverbs 3:1-2

Five blessings for making wise choices!

As we study Proverbs 3:1-10, we quickly see five commands of God. If we are faithful, God promises us five blessings.

Command - *"Keep My commands in your heart,"* Proverbs 3:1a.

Blessing - *"They will prolong your life many years and bring you prosperity,"* Proverbs 3:2.

Command - *"Let love and faithfulness never leave you,"* Proverbs 3:3a.

Blessing - *"Then you will win favor and a good name in the sight of God and man,"* Proverbs 3:4.

Command - *"Trust in the LORD with all your heart,"* Proverbs 3:5a.
"In all your ways acknowledge Him," Proverbs 3:6a.

Blessing - *"He will make your paths straight,"* Proverbs 3:6b.

Command - *"Fear the LORD and shun evil,"* Proverbs 3:7b.

Blessing - *"This will bring health to your body and nourishment to your bones,"* Proverbs 3:8.

Command - *"Honor the LORD with your wealth,"* Proverbs 3:9a.

Blessing - *"Then your barns will be filled to overflowing,"* Proverbs 3:10a.

If we think God's commandments are burdensome, our hearts are hard! God gave these commands in love, to guide us down a path to eternal happiness, that begins when we keep them!

Prayer: Dear Lord, Your commandments are good and right! They are how You created us to live! Lord help us to obey and trust in You! For You tell us, *"Trust in the LORD with all your heart and lean not on your own understanding. In all your ways acknowledge Him, and He will make your paths straight,"* Proverbs 3:5-6. Lord, how amazing You are! You not only give us the will and the power to be obedient, but then You bless us also. We worship You Lord! In Christ's name we pray. Amen.

May 6

"He was taken up before their very eyes, and a cloud hid Him from their sight. They were looking intently up into the sky as He was going, when suddenly two men dressed in white stood beside them. 'Men of Galilee,' they said, 'why do you stand here looking into the sky? This same Jesus, who has been taken from you into Heaven, will come back in the same way you have seen Him go into Heaven.'" Acts 1:9b-11

Why did Jesus ascend up to Heaven?

Mission accomplished! Jesus has now lived a perfect life. He is the perfect Son of man, our representative. He is also the perfect Son of God, His representative. With a body and soul just like us, He went to God. The ascended Jesus brings us together again in full union and communion with God. Jesus lived to give us life! He died to give us eternal rest. He arose from the grave to give us full freedom. Now He ascends to give us honor, dignity and glory. How wonderfully amazing. The once despised and rejected Jesus now rules in Heaven as our Prophet, Priest and King. The honors that our Mediator Jesus now enjoys are ours as His redeemed saints.

Jesus ascended because He had to go back home to Heaven. The perfect and exalted Jesus couldn't live on this corrupt earth again until it is purified and remade in the new Heavens and Earth.

Jesus had to go back to God to be our High Priest. There He fulfills His office until the resurrection and Judgment Day.

Jesus had to ascend so that the Holy Spirit could come to earth to convict us of our sin and make us righteous, John 16:7-8.

Jesus had to ascend to Heaven *"to prepare a place for you,"* John 14:2b. *"And if I go and prepare a place for you, I will come back and take you to be with Me that you may also be where I am,"* John 14:3. Jesus is now completing His work in Heaven for you.

Prayer: Loving Father, what hope we have! The ascended Jesus is our representative, our glory. What a benefit we have even now. Jesus hears our prayers and takes them to You the Father. Jesus sends us the Holy Spirit. Jesus prepares a place for us. Your grace is beyond amazing to us who deserved death. Accept our praise. We look forward to being with You in glory. In Jesus' name we pray. Amen.

"Let the words of my mouth and the meditation of my heart be acceptable in Your sight, O LORD, my strength and my Redeemer."
Psalm 19:14 NKJV

True worship asks God to accept us!

As we begin Sunday corporate worship, the minister rightly calls us into the presence of the Lord using verses like our text. In worship we go right into the throne room of Heaven. Our text is a beautiful call to worship our God. Here we humbly ask the Lord, *"Let the words of my mouth and the meditations of my heart to be acceptable in Your sight."* That is Biblical worship!

In the Old Testament, it was always God, the covenant giver, who needed to accept the sacrifices and offerings of the people. When the people hardened their hearts towards God, He warned them. *"They have loved to wander; they have not restrained their feet. Therefore the LORD does not accept them; He will remember their iniquity now, and punish their sins."* Jeremiah 14:10 NKJV.

In the New Testament, salvation was still God's purpose and plan. In Ephesians 1:5, He *"predestined us to be adopted."* That is God accepting us because He did the adopting. Peter knew clearly who had to accept whom. He said to the Christians, *"You also, as living stones, are being built up a spiritual house, a holy priesthood, to offer up spiritual sacrifices acceptable to God through Jesus Christ,"* 1 Peter 2:5 NKJV. Praise God, He accepts our worship of Him through Jesus Christ who is *"my strength and my Redeemer"*!

Why then, do we so often hear the question, "Did you accept Christ as your Savior and Lord?" Is such a question really Biblical? Is it accurate theologically? Perhaps in a secondary sense it is true. But we cannot find even one verse that clearly says we must accept God or Jesus! It is possible to accept God as a savior and still go to Hell. But if God knows and accepts us, then we are bound for Heaven!

Prayer: Dear Redeemer of our souls. Strengthen us to serve You as Paul encourages Timothy to do. *"That we may lead a quiet and peaceable life in all godliness and reverence. For this is good and acceptable in the sight of God our Savior."* In Jesus' name we pray. Amen.

May 8

"Let them alone. They are blind leaders of the blind. And if the blind leads the blind, both will fall into a ditch." Matthew 15:14 NKJV

No faith vs. *"great faith,"* Part 1

First, we'll look at no faith. Jesus said the religious leaders were blind, with no faith at all, but they thought they had great faith. We have a home for the blind next door. When they go out, they form a line of 3 people or so. The front person plots the course. The rest follow, basically just talking. Jesus warned the people, don't be so relaxed in following blind leaders. What did the people do that was so wrong?

1. They broke God's commands for the sake of tradition! The Bible goes against all "special rules" that the church has. If any "church rule" disagrees with the Bible, it is wrong. For example, the 5th command says don't dishonor or curse your parents. The Pharisees instead said to the adult children, don't give money or gifts to your needy parents, give it to us, the priests. Jesus taught that denying service to a parent was to curse them, which the Pharisees were advocating. This is just one example in Matthew 15:3-9 of tradition vs. the Bible.

2. They honored God with their lips but not their hearts! God is never impressed if our lips say one thing and our actions do another. If we think our sin is so small, why don't we just confess it, turn from it and then replace it? Matthew 15:18-19 shows us that what comes out of our hearts defile us. Not something outside of us.

3. They worshiped in vain because they followed the will of man! Jesus said of the Pharisees, *"In vain they worship Me,"* Matthew 15:9a NKJV. If we don't know the Son, we can't worship God.

4. The people didn't do evangelism because they were waiting for the "blind leaders" to do it! Those in the pew who wait for the "professionals" to do their "thing," need to wake up. But, it can also be just as much the fault of the clergy when they think the people in the pew are not qualified. It's the clergy's job to make them qualified.

Prayer: Lord, if we are blind to Your grace, open our eyes. Help us not to follow *"blind leaders."* Give us the eyes to see who is truly Your kind of leader. Also, may we learn to follow You and Your plan for our lives. In Jesus' name we pray. Amen.

May 9

"O woman, great is your faith." Matthew 15:28b NKJV

Jesus gives a "great faith," Part 2

In Matthew 15:21-28, Jesus teaches us how He brings a Canaanite woman (and us) into a *"great faith."* There are three points.

First, Jesus gives the woman no answer. *"And behold a woman of Canaan came from that region and cried out to Him, saying, 'Have mercy on me, O Lord, Son of David! My daughter is severely demon-possessed,'"* Matthew 15:22 NKJV. The woman recognizes Jesus as Lord and begs for mercy! *"But He answers her not a word,"* Matthew 15:23a NKJV. Why? Jesus is testing her to see what she will do. She knows Jesus is Lord and is the promised Messiah. She called him *"Son of David."* She knows Jesus can heal!

When God is silent, a true Christian seeks Him all the more! After all, no one can satisfy but God. His silence only intensifies our faith! Isn't it strange then, that so many people say, "If God doesn't answer you, it's because your faith is weak." This event in Matthew shouts to us that the health and wealth gospel is not about true faith. What is going on in many "churches" resembles the prophets of Baal dancing around the altar, cutting themselves and shouting. Elijah and this Canaanite woman both plead respectfully. Yet Jesus answers this woman, *"not a word."*

In Psalm 28:1 NKJV, David pleads, *"To You I will cry, O LORD my Rock: do not be silent to me, lest, if You are silent to me, I become like those who go down to the pit."* Even though David cries, he learns that through God's silence, God moves us closer to Himself. Through it all, God drains away our selfishness, to pour in His fullness. God is always working all things for the good of every true believer, Romans 8:28. The next time God is silent may we not panic but in faith wait to see how God is going to be glorified in His silence!

Prayer: O Sovereign Lord, Your ways are higher than our ways! You were silent for two days when Lazarus was dying, and how You loved him. Then when You did go to Lazarus, You did more than anyone thought possible! Lord may we not forget that You know what You are doing, all the time. We praise You for the silent times that teach us to walk by faith and not by sight. In Jesus' name we pray. Amen.

May 10

"Send her away, for she cries out after us." Matthew 15:23b NKJV

Jesus gives a *"great faith,"* Part 3

Second, the Canaanite woman is sent away, rejected. Here again, Jesus is showing His disciples and us what happens when a person like the Canaanite woman has true faith. It appears like Jesus is rejecting her. Even His disciples came and urged Him, *"Send her away, for she cries out after us,"* Matthew 15:23b NKJV. Now we get to see the persistent faith the woman has in Jesus. We also get to see how deep the woman's love is for her daughter.

Jesus answers His disciples' request. In the hearing of the woman He says, *"I was not sent except to the lost sheep of the house of Israel,"* Matthew 15:24 NKJV. Some say that Jesus said this because it was not yet the time of the Gentiles. At this point in time, it was basically Jews only. Yet remember that true faith is always *"a gift of God,"* Ephesians 2:8b. God gave the gift of faith to other Gentiles, many in the lineage of Jesus. This woman's response to Jesus was one of worship. She knew who He was. Remember earlier in the chapter the Jewish religious leaders did not know who Jesus was. She did! This shouts to us. Not all who appear to have true faith, have it.

Amazingly, even as she was pushed away, she came back. True faith never leaves the Savior. *"Then she came and worshiped Him, saying, 'Lord help me!'"* Matthew 15:25 NKJV. What a fantastic, short and sweet, personal prayer. When did the Pharisees ever say *"Lord"* to Jesus? In fact they *"lorded"* it over Jesus and all others. When did the Pharisees ever say, *"help me,"* asking Jesus to mediate for them? Yet this Gentile woman desires God with all of her heart. This completes the second of three tests Jesus gave the woman. She keeps coming back to Him with the eyes of faith.

Prayer: Lord help us! Like the Canaanite woman, we worship the fact that You are Lord. Like the Canaanite woman, we need Your divine help. Be merciful to us because we are weak and we too need Your divine healing. Protect us from the evil one, just as this godly woman prayed. We are so grateful that You hear our prayers. May Your kingdom come in our hearts and in our lives. In Jesus' name we pray. Amen.

May 11

"But He answered and said, 'It is not good to take the children's bread and throw it to the little dogs.'" Matthew 15:26 NKJV

Jesus gives a "great faith," Part 4

Third, Jesus now insults the woman. What will she do? Jews commonly called Gentiles "dogs." By calling her a *"little dog"* Jesus is trying to teach the woman and us something. This woman has no right to the kingdom of God. No right by birth. No right by nationality. No right by education. No earthly right to a relationship with Him. In fact, the words of Jesus point to the fact that she is a good for nothing sinner. And this is what we all are too!

Still the Canaanite woman does not leave Christ. She begs Him for just a little bit of mercy. *"She said, 'Yes, Lord, yet even the little dogs eat the crumbs which fall from their masters' table,'"* Matthew 15:27 NKJV. Street dogs rely on handouts. This woman is saying, "Even little dogs survive on crumbs, so can I. Lord, give me just a few crumbs of blessing." She knows Jesus is the way, the truth, and the life. *"Crumbs"* from Jesus are better than the riches of the world. Have we experienced this? We must have much in common with this woman. We need a faith that has eyes for Jesus and His lifesaving mercy!

Through our emptiness, we are able to desire and request the riches of God. One of the greatest problems we have is: we do not see that we are the blind spoken of in the Bible. We do not see that we are the lepers! We don't see that we are like this poor widow. These events are in the Bible to teach us to rely on the grace of God for our fullness.

By these three tests, can you see how God uses trials to test our spiritual maturity? You can see how God teaches us to think His thoughts after Him. By His grace, by His providence, by His leading, He matures our faith just like He did the Canaanite woman. After all this testing, Jesus responds to the Canaanite woman, *"O woman, great is your faith,"* Matthew 15:28b NKJV. May our faith be great in the eyes of God!

Prayer: Lord God, Father in Heaven, may we personally pass Your tests for Your glory and for our good. Forgive us for loving the things of this world more than You! Help us to be like this Canaanite woman, hungry for You. In Jesus' name we pray. Amen.

May 12

"You will be My witnesses in Jerusalem, and in all Judea and Samaria, and to the ends of the earth." Acts 1:8b

Why missions? Part 1

Christ Himself came to this earth on a mission. What kind of mission did the Father have in mind by sending Jesus? Why would God send His perfect and only Son into our filthy and sinful world? Why did Christ when leaving this world, hand off the responsibility for missions to His disciples? Why did these disciples of His, again hand off the responsibility to still other disciples until finally "the call" has reached you and me? Why must we be His *"witnesses"*? What is the purpose of missions? Missions have two main goals.

1. For the <u>glory of God</u> demands we are His *"witnesses."*

Jesus clearly said, *"You <u>will be</u> My witnesses."* This means we are to be a witness concerning who Jesus is. Not so much about what He has done, but about who He is. Missions flow from the heart of God. If we want to be near the heart of God, then we need to love what He loves. God loves His Son dearly. His work of redemption is at the heart of missions. Through Jesus, God is calling those whom He will redeem to have a restored relationship with Father, Son and Spirit. God commands we go into all the world. We do not know whom He will save! That part is God's business alone! Ours is to go. <u>The command of His "to go," is even more important than the needs of the lost</u>! We obediently go and He changes hearts, one at a time, and He is glorified.

2. For the <u>benefit of man</u> demands we are His *"witnesses."*

God did not call us to Himself just to be saved and sanctified, but to be of service to Him! We do the work of missions because we are His, and He is accomplishing His work and purposes through us, to others! With His power and authority we speak and live before others and that makes all the difference. Broken lives are healed; many are restored.

Prayer: Lord Jesus, You were broken for us, that we might be broken of our pride and work to restore others to You. We are called to that. We praise You for giving us Your name and Your Spirit and for sending us to tell others about You! In Jesus' name we pray. Amen.

May 13

"Now the word of the LORD came to Jonah the son of Amittai, saying, 'Arise, go to Nineveh, that great city, and cry out against it; for their wickedness has come up before Me.' But Jonah arose to flee to Tarshish from the presence of the LORD." Jonah 1:1-3a NKJV

Is God calling us to missions? Part 2

Jonah thought he had a choice on whether or not he should follow God's call into missions. God said, "Go." Jonah said, "No." I think you know who won! God wins out every time! The life of Jonah teaches us that in the end, he didn't really even have a choice.

If God is calling us to missions, we may think we have a choice. We may, temporarily resist the call. As with Jonah, God will convince us. God will compel us, if He is calling us. If we refuse, God in His love will convince us. In the end, we will go. If we go the wrong way at first, like many of us do, we will end up very convinced when God turns us around. Jonah was! I know that I was.

1. Jonah knew why there was a great tempest in his life! Jonah said to the others on the ship, *"I know that it is my fault that this great storm has come upon you,"* Jonah 1:12b. Is God calling you today through great storms? Do we recognize that many of our troubles are from a refusal to do what God called us to do? God will make us willing to listen if He has called us to serve Him! How much more must God squeeze us before we will listen? When we finally do, and the storm passes, we will know that God was in the storm!

2. When times got tough later on, Jonah did not doubt that God was calling him to missions! This will also happen to us. There will be great difficulties in mission life. We will often be lonely, uncomfortable, miserable, and discouraged. But, in the midst of it all, we will fully know that we are in the center of God's will. Knowing that we are called by God to *"cry against the wickedness that has come up before God,"* we will do it. In the end, we will listen to God, because just like Jonah, God has made us willing to be on a mission for Him.

Prayer: Lord, give us the attitude of Jesus. May we pray like Jesus did. Lord, not my will but Yours be done. Give us the words of Isaiah, *"Here am I. Send me!"* In Christ's name we pray. Amen.

May 14

"Jonah ran away from the LORD." Jonah 1:3a

Jonah, saved by grace alone! Part 3

We are continuing our discussion from yesterday. The story of Jonah is a picture of how God saves every child of His by grace alone, through Christ alone. But this picture also pinpoints a particular grace of God. Jonah was saved by God's irresistible grace! Jonah ran the other way, but God <u>made</u> Jonah come to Him. Jonah could not refuse or resist!

The book of Jonah begins with God calling Jonah. Like many today, Jonah wasn't serious about listening to God! Yet when God calls a specific sinner, they come, every single time. Jonah is living proof that man cannot resist the call of God when He marks them for salvation and service! Thinking he had a choice, Jonah went the other way! Well, God planned from all eternity that Jonah would come. Romans 8:28-29 explains that. God sends *"a violent storm,"* as part of His grace in making Jonah come! Do we see our storms and trials as the grace of God turning us? Or, are we bitter at God for them?

This *"running away"* is not unique to Jonah! *"<u>When we were God's enemies</u>, we were reconciled to Him through the death of His Son,"* Romans 5:10a. Considering that the wages of sin is death, Jonah deserved to drown in his misery. And so do we! Then in our deepest misery, when we are without strength, as spiritual beggars, like Jonah in the belly of the big fish we cry to God for mercy! Do we now see that God set this all up? Dear friend, do not think you had anything to do with God's salvation for you. *"God, who is rich in mercy, <u>made us</u> alive with Christ even <u>when we were dead</u> in transgressions – it is by grace you have been saved,"* Ephesians 2:4b-5. A dead person can't choose Christ!

Prayer: Gracious Lord how much like Jonah we really are! We run from our relationships. We run from our responsibilities. In all of our running, we are running from You. Lord how great is Your patience to put up with us running sinners. If it were not for Your pursuing grace, we would drown in our sin and misery. Lord may Your kingdom go on and on. May Your kingdom come! In Jesus' name we pray. Amen.

May 15

"But the LORD provided a great fish to swallow Jonah, and Jonah was inside the fish three days and three nights." Jonah 1:17

Jonah, chased by God's grace, Part 4

"But the Lord provided." Is this not the testimony of all true faith? Even the smallest amount of faith *"provided"* by God, is a gift. Every fiber of our spiritual life is God-ordained and God-given. This thought must structure our prayers. For God is fully able to use any method He chooses to bring us to faith and obedience. He can even use a big fish!

Jonah did not deserve a big fish! That is a main point of the forgiveness God gives! He gives us what we <u>need</u>, not what we <u>deserve</u>! That is exactly what grace is. Even though Jonah ran from grace, grace found him, right at the appointed time! And, this is true for every Christian. *"You see, at just the right time, when we were still powerless, Christ died for the ungodly,"* Romans 5:6. If we think we had something to do with our salvation, then we think Jonah had something to do with the fish picking him up. Let us not rob God of His glory and cheapen His grace!

Jonah's life points to Jesus. The whole Old Testament points to Jesus. Jesus spent three days and nights in the depths of a tomb that could not hold Him. Jonah came out of that fish after three days because his life was pointing to Jesus. The tomb that could not hold Jesus, cannot hold us either! *"Do not be amazed at this, for a time is coming when <u>all who are in their graves will hear His voice and come out</u> - those who have done good will rise to live, and those who have done evil will rise to be condemned,"* John 5:28-29. Death cannot hold anyone in the grave. Where will we go when we do come out? There are only two places: Heaven or Hell. That was Jonah's message, and it is ours also.

Like Jonah, we have a commission from God. We too are called to go to Nineveh, to the lost! We have this big fish story to help us understand the importance of Jesus' command to *"<u>go</u>."* This is our necessary response to God's grace, as we shall see next.

Prayer: Loving Lord, how great is Your grace. The song says it is amazing. But more than that, it is a miracle. You took our sin and gave us Jesus' righteousness. Now we have eternal fellowship with You. May we now live and teach about a life of grace! In Jesus' name we pray. Amen.

May 16

"Those who cling to worthless idols forfeit the grace that could be theirs." Jonah 2:8

Jonah replaces his idols for grace, Part 5

On the ship Jonah saw many idol worshipers who faced certain death. The ship was about to go down. Each pagan man prayed to his favorite idol god. <u>Nothing happened</u>! Jonah had his idols too! Do we have idols? Do we have something that is more important to us than a good relationship with God. That's what an idol is. What do we worship the most? How much time do we spend before a mirror, as compared to the amount of time we spend in the Word of God and in prayer? The sailors asked Jonah a good question! "Who is your God?" He said, *"I worship the LORD, the God of Heaven, who made the sea and the land,"* Jonah 1:9b. He did, yet he was running from God.

What about you young person? You are already outwardly beautiful! But did you know that outward beauty, without inner grace, isn't really beautiful for long? Real beauty always starts in the heart! If you do not have it, you will be as blind to grace as Jonah and his travelers were! Worse yet, you will be blind to true love for eternity.

It took a big fish for Jonah to realize his idols. Jonah was in love with who he was and what he wanted to do. He ran from God and His grace. God got lip service from Jonah, but not much more. Jonah's heart was set on his own pleasures. When Jonah's eyes were opened, he said, *"Those who cling to worthless idols forfeit the grace that could be theirs,"* Jonah 2:8. Jonah found out the hard way, selfishness literally stinks! It smelled rotten in the belly of that fish.

Young person, don't age before your time. Grace preserves! Experience God's grace and true love now, and for all eternity. Then you will be all that God wants you to be. And you will find your purpose in life too.

Prayer: Lord, Your grace makes us beautiful. With it You exchange our idols for Your forgiveness. With it, we have a heart that becomes more loving and kind. Lord, increase Your grace in us so we can be *"pure, children of God without fault in a crooked and depraved generation."* In Christ's name we pray. Amen.

May 17

"Be kind and compassionate to one another, forgiving each other, just as in Christ God forgave you." Ephesians 4:32

Jonah, saved to live graciously! Part 6

The story of Jonah is not finished when he lands on the beach! Saved by grace, he now needs to teach about the grace of God and the need for repentance. Chapters 1-3 of Ephesians teach us about our running from God's gracious and miraculous rescue. Ephesians 4 demands a response to the grace God puts in us! *"I urge you to live a life worthy of the calling you have received,"* Ephesians 4:1b. Chapter 4 explains what our response to His grace must be. This is what our repentance must look like. *"Get rid of all bitterness, rage and anger, brawling and slander, along with every form of malice. Be kind and compassionate to one another, forgiving each other, just as in Christ God forgave you,"* Ephesians 4:31-32. How did God forgive us?

God's forgiveness was 100% by grace, meaning that, He forgave every sin of ours at salvation. Now we must forgive every single sin others do to us. Why? To model God's grace to us in Christ. Yes, we must forgive as God did, Ephesians 4:32. Grace means we cannot ask anyone to prove their repentance before we will forgive them. Did Jonah prove his repentance to God? How could he? Jonah was in a fish. We are just as dead spiritually. For us to forgive as God did, means we must forgive other dead sinners. We must give them what they need, not what they deserve, just like God did to Jonah! We must not think of using the argument that our enemy doesn't deserve forgiveness. Neither did we.

Jonah didn't want to go to Nineveh. He refused to go. God had to teach him what His grace was all about by using a big fish. Jonah got the point of why he had to go to dead sinners in Nineveh. Just as Jonah had to go to God's enemies and work for reconciliation, so must we! His going was only modeling what God had done for him. As Christians, we have Jonah's grace and Jonah's responsibility to go.

Prayer: Lord, forgive us for not understanding that we must have a response to the grace You put in us. It was hard for You to forgive us rotten sinners! You beat and abused Your perfect Son to do it. May we not expect it to be easy either. In Jesus' name we pray. Amen.

May 18

"In fact, everyone who wants to live a godly life in Christ Jesus will be persecuted." 2 Timothy 3:12

Does our Gospel include suffering?

Paul is concerned! He knows he will soon leave this world for an eternity with God. In fact, the apostles are all dying. Paul is concerned about passing the torch to the next generation. Even Timothy was unsure of what to do without Paul around to teach him. Are we sure about what we must do to pass the faith on? Paul told Timothy, *"Do not be ashamed of the testimony of our Lord, nor of me His prisoner, but share with me in the sufferings for the Gospel according to the power of God,"* 2 Timothy 1:8 NKJV. Timothy needed to see that Paul's being in prison could advance the Gospel! We also read, *"Demas has forsaken me, having loved this present world,"* 2 Timothy 4:10a NKJV. The advice is: Timothy, don't let your love for "worldly things" outgrow your labor for the Great Commission!

When we love things in the world more than Jesus, we are unfaithful and unfruitful! Paul warns, "Don't go that way Timothy." "Don't let your fire for the Gospel go out!" Paul knew it could happen because he said, *"Only Luke is with me,"* 4:11a. The others all deserted Paul. So he is writing to Timothy, pleading with him to stand firm because Timothy needed to answer an important question: <u>Does his view of the Gospel have room for suffering?</u> That's our question too! If we believe in a "prosperity gospel" we have already failed the question.

Have we considered how Jesus was deserted, even more than Paul? Luke was still with Paul and perhaps Timothy. Jesus did not even have Peter. Many will desert us if we are serious about the Gospel! It will happen and it will be painful and difficult. Expect it! May we stand firm to the end. It will be worth it all when we see Jesus!

Prayer: Lord, the repentant Peter wrote, *"Beloved, do not think it strange concerning the fiery trial which is to try you, as though some strange thing happened to you; but rejoice to the extent that you partake of Christ's sufferings, that when His glory is revealed, you may also be glad with exceeding joy,"* 1 Peter 4:12-13 NKJV. Lord help us to fully believe this! In Christ's name we pray. Amen.

May 19

"Then the contention became so sharp that they parted from one another. And so Barnabas took Mark and sailed to Cyprus; but Paul chose Silas and departed." Acts 15:39-40a NKJV

Contentions in the ministry

Fighting in the family of God started with Adam and Eve, progressed to Cain and Abel, and it has not stopped. It is both embarrassing and wrong. You may think that "ministry workers" are so proper that this would not happen, but it does. In fact, it is the main reason ministry workers leave the mission field.

In seminaries and in Bible schools, cross-cultural missions are studied to get us used to the different ways other people think and act. We look forward to working alongside others to bring the love of Christ to other cultural groups. But then, shock of all shocks! We get on the job and quickly realize that it is the co-workers that we are not getting along with, and we are in the middle of it!

The Apostle Paul also had his disagreements. After working together with Barnabas for a long time, they suddenly had a big fight. *"Now Barnabas was determined to take with them John called Mark. But Paul insisted that they should not take with them the one who had departed from them in Pamphylia, and had not gone with them to the work,"* Acts 15:37-38 NKJV. Paul felt so strongly about this that he found a new partner and Barnabas left with Mark.

Stubborn individualism causes trouble. There is no "I" in the word "team." We may know that ministry is about being a servant, but we're more comfortable acting like kings. That is why the main qualification for all "ministry" is to first demonstrate that we are serving our own families well.

Satan is alive and still working hard in believers. Being precious to God, we are important to Satan! He tempts us in many ways to get us off course in completing the Great Commission. May the Holy Spirit work in us a spirit of cooperation with co-workers which is so essential.

Prayer: Lord, our egos are way too big. May we truly serve You by serving each other. We know the glory belongs to You. Help us live like servants! In Jesus' precious name we pray. Amen.

May 20

"The Spirit helps us in our weakness. We do not know what we ought to pray for, but the Spirit Himself intercedes for us with groans that words cannot express." Romans 8:26

Dad's birthday

I just returned from India and went to see Dad. Would he still recognize me? He is in a home for two years now, well cared for. He is 85 years old today. At times we wonder, "Why is dad going through this time of losing the mind, almost completely unaware of what is going on in the day to day world?" We know that God does not make mistakes! We know that *"from one man, He (God) made every nation of men, that they should inhabit the whole earth; and He determined <u>the times set for them and the exact places they should live</u>,"* Acts 17:26.

Based on our text and others, Dad is spiritually growing, even though mentally and physically he is shrinking. Yesterday Mom said something to Dad and he thought she asked him to pray. Dad said, "I can do that." I was surprised by this simple sentence. But then he started to pray, *"Our Father which art in Heaven."* All the words did not make complete sense, but Dad was sincerely praying! Then he ended the prayer; *"In Jesus' name we pray. Amen."* It was one of the most beautiful prayers I ever heard! Dad knew exactly what he was saying, because, *"the Spirit Himself intercedes for us with groans that words cannot express."* How great is our God!

I wondered, will Dad know me and my wife? His face lit up when he saw us. He even told my wife she was looking good! He didn't say that about me. Dad knew us. But more importantly than that, he knows God! More important still, God knows Dad. God promised him, *"Never will I leave you; never will I forsake you. So we say with confidence, 'The Lord is my helper,... what can man do to me?'"* Hebrews 13:5b-6. What can Alzheimers do to Dad in the light of eternity? Absolutely nothing!

Prayer: Precious Lord, what a treasure we have. We have Jesus, our High Priest in Heaven, interceding for us. We have the Holy Spirit praying for us. We have You, the Father watching over us. You are such a great God. Accept our worship and praise. In Jesus' name we pray. Amen.

May 21

"The LORD, the LORD, the compassionate and gracious God, slow to anger, abounding in love and faithfulness, maintaining love to thousands, and forgiving wickedness, rebellion and sin."
Exodus 34:6b-7a

Who is God?

What an important question for witnessing! We will never witness productively to lost sinners until we figure out this age old question: "Who is God?" Our text is God's description of who He is. He gave it to Moses on Mount Sinai. The verse is also for us.

With our text in mind as a definition of God's character, think of how we commonly respond to someone who has caused us much trouble! Think of how we respond to numerous other horrible acts of hate. Should we fight fire with fire? Hopefully we all know that we have just two options. We can hate back OR we can love and forgive. Which one of these two options is God's kind of response? What did Jesus do? Look at our text and then decide.

The question is not, "What do we feel like doing?" But, "What should we do?" The truth is: We will never witness to our enemies until we first show some love to them! If we think this is not right, then consider, "<u>When we were God's enemies</u>, we were reconciled to Him through the death of His Son," Romans 5:10a.

A common question comes up. "Are there consequences for the wrong actions of others?" Yes, if a person gets caught stealing, they go to jail. If a person gets HIV as a consequence of sharing a dirty needle, they will likely die. The point is: Do we love the one who is in jail or is sick? Or do we turn our back on them saying, "This is what you deserve?" What did our own ugly sins deserve? Are not the wages of our sin, death? Yet, Jesus loved us and gave us life instead! We must learn some important life lessons from what Jesus did. May our responses reflect our view of God. May we respond graciously to those who oppress us.

Prayer: Gracious Lord, give us the mind of Christ Jesus. May we follow that perfect Man, who is our God. Lord mold us and make us after Your own character. Make us compassionate, gracious and slow to anger. In Jesus' name we pray. Amen.

May 22

"God made Him who had no sin to be sin for us, so that in Him we might become the righteousness of God." 2 Corinthians 5:21

How righteous are we?

Are we a super saint yet? Are we as righteous as the apostle Paul who wrote our text? Or better yet, are we as righteous as the Lord Jesus Christ is? If we are a true Christian, we are! That is not overstating the issue. Nor is it being overconfident as a Christian. Yes, we all still sin much! But the issue here is what does it mean to be justified by the blood of the Lord Jesus Christ? It does us much good to examine this doctrine of justification.

1. ***"God made Him who had no sin to be sin for us."***

Adam sinned not only for himself, but for all of us. Jesus came as the first and only one to live a perfect life. As perfect man, He is perfectly righteous, for all of us. Jesus did what Adam failed to do and what we cannot do. God in grace, seeing our inability to earn our own righteousness, provided a way for us to be made righteous. He did that in and through His Son. Jesus takes away the guilt of our sin. God as the perfect Judge accepts this blood payment for our sin. Most Christians understand this part, that Jesus gets our sin, but this is only half of the Gospel message.

2. ***"So that in Him we might become the righteousness of God."***

We receive Jesus' righteousness. It is God's own righteousness. This is the other half of the salvation transaction! In Christ we are just as righteous as Christ is, just as righteous as God the Father is, just as holy as the Holy Spirit is. God accepts Christ's righteousness as our own and imputes (gives) it to us. This is what it means to be justified. It is to be made fully righteous, just as if we never sinned.

Prayer: Father, how wonderful it is that You do not see our sinful rags anymore! In Christ, You see us dressed in the same white robes Your righteous Son wears. We are today just as fully righteous as we will ever be, fully fit for Heaven. You have fully adopted us as Your sons and daughters and fully made us joint heirs with Jesus Christ. You give us the name of Christian. We belong to You forever! In Jesus' beautiful name we pray. Amen.

May 23

"Now may the Lord of peace Himself give you peace at all times and in every way. The Lord be with all of you." 2 Thessalonians 3:16

Peace is not what's in our hand!

We notice that Paul's letters begin with a salutation of *"peace"* from God. In our text, the letter ends with a benediction calling again for the *"peace"* of God to us His hearers. This subject of peace is that important! What is the *"peace"* of God? Our sinful nature thinks peace is what we have in our hand. The difficult times we have economically, help to teach us lessons we should have learned long ago. Theologically, we may know peace is not what we have in our hands, but that is not how we have been living!

We commonly think, "If I make good money I will have peace." Or, "If this person would give me some respect I would have peace." Or, "If I could get married I will certainly be at peace." Another person thinks, "If I was not married I would really have peace!" Or we may think, "If only we could have children truly we would have peace." And yes, others are thinking, "When the kids leave the house I will finally have peace." "If I could just get a better car, I would really have some peace in my life." We look for better clothes, food, and housing then cry if we lose any of it. Perhaps the biggest mistake of all is thinking, "When I finally retire, then surely I will really have a peaceful life." The last peace people look for is their physical health coming back. And that too eventually dies! The world's peace is like that, always flying away! Real peace is simply not what we have in our hands. It is Jesus in the heart. He is the Prince of Peace!

It's so sad, we can live a whole lifetime looking for "peace" in all the wrong places! See the words of our text clearly. *"Now may the Lord of peace Himself give you peace at all times and in every way. The Lord be with all of you,"* 2 Thessalonians 3:16. It is the Lord "with us" that puts peace in our hearts!

Prayer: O Lord, help us weak sinners to look to You. Jesus said, *"In Me you may have peace. In this world you will have trouble. But take heart! I have overcome the world,"* John 16:33b. Lord, our hope is in You! In Jesus' name we pray. Amen.

May 24

"Daniel replied, 'No wise man, enchanter, magician or diviner can explain to the king the mystery he has asked about, but there is a God in Heaven who reveals mysteries.'" Daniel 2:27-28a

The God who reveals mysteries

Be assured, all Scripture is written for the glory of God, and for our personal good! The book of Daniel begins with the children of Israel going into captivity because of their unfaithfulness in keeping covenant with God. This is a serious warning for us. We are then presented with the evil King Nebuchadnezzar. He is the ruler of the most powerful nation on earth at this time.

In chapter 2:1 of Daniel, we see that King *"Nebuchadnezzar had dreams; his mind was troubled and he could not sleep."* So he calls for his advisers who are *"magicians, enchanters, sorcerers, and astrologers,"* Daniel 2:2b. All four of these are 100% connected to demonic powers and are the religious leaders of the land. The king asks these pagan advisers to not only interpret his dreams, but even to tell him exactly what the dreams were! Of course, no one can possibly do that.

See what God is doing? He not only gave the king these troubling dreams, but is in the process of arranging a major confrontation to show everyone that He alone, is the Lord God Almighty! Remember that Israel should have been proclaiming the greatness of God, since they were placed at the crossroads of the then known world. But they were not willing to serve God and be His witnesses.

So Daniel prayerfully asks God to reveal to him the mystery of both what the dreams were, and the meaning of them. God answers Daniel's prayer. The king is grateful and places Daniel in a high government position. God is still in the process of revealing Himself and His powerful attributes.

Prayer: Lord, how great and powerful You are. How You want Your name to be known, and made known. You gave us a commission from Jesus Christ in Matthew 28:19-20. Forgive us for not being more concerned about Your holy name. Strengthen us to be like Daniel, faithful, bold and true. In Jesus' name we pray. Amen.

May 25

"Make it your ambition to lead a quiet life, to mind your own business and to work with your hands, just as we told you, so that your daily life may win the respect of outsiders." 1 Thessalonians 4:11-12a

"Win the respect of outsiders"

Paul knew respect was important. He ended Ephesians 5, by telling wives to respect their husbands. A husband is to encourage that respect by loving his wife, which is also respecting her. Even a child needs respect. Did you ever notice how even a baby is easily offended? We all crave respect. Many will go to great lengths to try get respect from others. They will dress differently, paint their faces, pierce their bodies, get tattoos, have sex, get drunk, and the list is actually endless. God knows we all need respect. But how do we get it is the big question!

Paul simply says, *"win the respect."* Respect is earned. The problem is that many of us would rather demand respect than *"win"* it. A bully demands respect using rough tactics but that only gets a temporary obedience based on fear. Real respect is based on love. Paul gives us three points on how to win respect.

1. *"Lead a quiet life."* Don't be loud and bossy! We may get some attention if we are loud but that is not respect. We do not need to take over the "show" but need to serve others. Jesus Christ is our perfect example. We need to imitate Him!

2. *"Mind your own business."* Each of us has enough to do without minding what others are doing. It is our own business that we are held accountable for, both now, and in The Judgment. The problem is many would rather meddle in the affairs of others than care for their own!

3. *"Work with your hands."* Honest work is priceless. It will please God. It will bless others. Even we will be greatly blessed with a clear conscience, a peaceful sleep and wealth that will not just fly away. In fact, God made man to work. Work is honorable. *"One who is slack in his work is brother to one who destroys,"* Proverbs 18:9. Doing quality work is a moral commitment to serve faithfully. Work is worship!

Prayer: Lord, we have much to learn about respect. Help us to lead a quiet life, to mind our own business and to work faithfully. Accept our work as worship. In Jesus' name we pray. Amen.

May 26

"Dishonest money dwindles away, but he who gathers money little by little makes it grow." Proverbs 13:11

Accumulating wealth God's way

"Dishonest money dwindles away" is an amazing truth. Many cheat and steal to try get ahead. They think they are so smart, and that *"dishonest money"* is good business. God has a way of turning their easy gain into a quick loss. Paul warned, *"Do not be deceived: God cannot be mocked. A man reaps what he sows,"* Galatians 6:7. The omniscient, all-powerful, all-wise God can and will make some kind of loss come to those who go for the *"dishonest money."* Those who cheat others will have someone cheat them! Two points to increase our wealth God's way:

1. God owns everything in this world. *"The earth is the LORD's, and everything in it, the world, and all who live in it,"* Psalm 24:1. There isn't anything in this world that God doesn't own! God expects us to manage everything we have, because it is His! God placed us in this world as a steward - one who is hired to supervise a large estate. The one thing that we own that is 100% ours, is our sin! God owns everything else and the more He gives us, the more we are in debt to Him!

2. Spend less than we make to become financially secure. Person after person says: "If I had just a little more money each month I could make it financially." It does not matter if that person makes $2,000 a month or $8,000. The story is the same. We are by nature, undisciplined, spending more than we should. Then we borrow to make ends meet. Millions of people owe more than they own! The proverb is so true, *"The borrower is servant to the lender,"* Proverbs 22:7b. It is by spending less than we make, that we build wealth. It is not quick. It is not easy! It takes discipline to spend less than we make. But God rewards the disciplined!

Prayer: Loving Lord, we have sinned against You by going so far into debt. We truly have become a servant to the one we have borrowed from. We have not been content with what You have given us. You call us to serve You first and foremost. Lord, help us to be more disciplined. In Christ's name we pray. Amen.

May 27

"I hate the work of those who fall away, it shall not cling to me."
Psalm 101:3b NKJV

Help Wanted! Part 1

Companies need to hire and promote good people. But what are the main qualities that a business needs to succeed in today's competitive environment? It is commonly believed that companies simply go for the brightest people. But that simply is not true. What if that bright person uses his "smarts" to cheat you? Then that person would be a problem, not a solution! Being bright may get an interview, but the ones who get the best jobs will have to pass a few tests.

1. Do you have integrity? What is your moral make-up or character? You know it is wrong to lie, cheat, or steal. But do you do it? Would you lie, cheat or steal to advance your new company? If you said, "Yes," I wouldn't hire you! What you are in your heart, leads to what you do on a professional level. A person with integrity has an inner conviction, a moral compass. They will always act according to their tender conscience. So integrity is more than knowing what is right. It does right! *"The integrity of the upright guides them,"* Proverbs 11:3a.

2. Are you faithful? Will you be loyal to the new company? In today's world, workers jump ship and run to a competitor so quickly. No business wants to train you to be the competition! One of the questions a company is going to assess is: What kind of a flight risk are you? The company needs to be convinced you will be faithful. *"He guards the lives of His faithful ones,"* Psalm 97:10b. Companies do also!

3. What is your attitude? A person with a good attitude is teachable. You will be required to learn new things from many people! You must be able to be corrected without getting angry or bitter. A good attitude keeps a person productive, a team player, easy to work with. A person with a bad attitude is destructive! *"An angry man stirs up dissension,"* Proverbs 29:22a.

Prayer: Lord, You know we live in a corrupt and violent world that loves to cheat. May we be found faithful! May Your name and those we work for be lifted up by how we work. In Jesus' name we pray. Amen.

May 28

"The people worked with all their heart." Nehemiah 4:6b

Help wanted! Part 2

4. Will you work? God made man to work. Work is good! When a man or woman hires into a company they are agreeing to work hard to help make the company successful. Godly workers have a moral obligation in their heart! The company has the same commitment, promising to pay for valuable services. Both the employer and employee have a contract to keep!

I have seen bright people in business, who were eager to pretend that they worked hard! They had a smooth mouth, lazy bones, and a lying heart! What a waste of a life! They were selfish with a huge ego. No one can produce real customer service without having a heart that is willing to work at serving others! If you won't serve the customer, you won't serve the company. The company that hires you must be convinced that you will work, especially when no one is watching.

5. Are you reliable? You may work when you are at your place of employment, but will you always show up? It takes moral commitment to come to work also. What Paul said about ministry workers is also a need in the workplace, *"Reliable men who will also be qualified to teach others,"* 2 Timothy 2:2b.

6. Are you flexible? Are you willing to adjust your services to meet the changing needs of the business. A company's reputation is at stake. Without flexible people, a company cannot remain competitive. So "Are you flexible?" is a major question. Those who are not flexible when asked to do something different from what they normally do, have a bad "attitude"! Companies are forced to hire extra people while customers wait, all because workers are not very flexible.

Prayer: Lord, we see that You are much like an employer and demand more than our brains. You also want our heart in our work everyday for Your glory. Lord, help us to see that our work matters, and that it is here that we need to excel as Christians! Help us to refine our character so that we are worth more to the "business" You placed us in! May Your name be lifted up by our faithful work. May all employers see that Christians are the best workers. In Jesus' name we pray. Amen.

May 29

"We always thank God for all of you, mentioning you in our prayers. We continually remember before our God and Father your work produced by faith, your labor prompted by love, and your endurance inspired by hope in our Lord Jesus Christ."
1 Thessalonians 1:2-3

"It's the way that you're right that I hate!"

My boss said to me years ago, "I want to commend you in the fact that when it comes to business concerns, you are usually right. But too often, it is the way that you're right I hate." What he said was true. I was proud that I knew the best way to do things. Humility was greatly lacking. Who wants to be remembered for being proud and arrogant? How can we be truly successful in God's or man's eyes if we think so highly of ourselves? We do need to be on the right side of truth, but with humility, to serve both God and man!

How is it going for you? Are you too proud of your accomplishments? Do you think you are great because you are at the head of the class? Do you think that you are quite special because your children are all successful? Your church is growing, do you think it is so because you are such a great preacher and leader? Is your business a big success? Do you think it was your ability and drive that has made you a success? Where is God in all of this?

God is the giver of ability, strength, stamina and even looks. We are all nothing apart from God who is the giver of all good gifts. May we acknowledge God's hand in our lives. May we live for Him, and to be a blessing to His kingdom. May we be remembered as children of God whose work was *"produced by faith, our labor prompted by love, and our endurance inspired by hope in our Lord Jesus Christ."* This will keep us humble. Then no one will think about us, "I hate the way you are right!"

Prayer: Gracious Lord it is good that You are working in us, to change us. You tell us clearly in Philippians 2:13 that *"it is God who works in you to will and to act according to His good purpose."* Lord, the glory and honor belongs to You. Forgive us for trying to steal it from You. In Jesus' name we pray. Amen.

May 30

"Then Peter came to Jesus and asked, 'Lord, how many times shall I forgive my brother when he sins against me? Up to seven times?'"
Matthew 18:21

The Parable of the Unmerciful Servant

Jewish tradition taught we must forgive three times. In Matthew 18:15, the offended one must go to his brother alone and tell him his fault. If the sinning brother does not repent, (verse 16) he should ask one or two others to go with him to repeat the message. If the sinning brother still does not repent, tell it to the church. Peter knew this! Trying to show humility, Peter asked Jesus if he should forgive seven times. Jesus said no, seventy times seven, meaning an unlimited number. Peter was shocked!

Jesus said this because He forgives sinners an endless amount of times. We are called to *"forgive each other, just as in Christ God forgave you,"* Ephesians 4:32b. The parable shows how Jesus forgave each of us Christians, and what He will do if we don't forgive others.

"Therefore, the kingdom of Heaven is like a king who wanted to settle accounts with his servants," Matthew 18:23. A servant owed the king ten million dollars. The man couldn't pay it, so the king cancelled the debt, a picture of Jesus forgiving us. A fellow servant owes the forgiven man a day's wage, a small debt. He chokes the guy because he could not pay a small debt! The king hears about it and is enraged! The king now tortures the man who he had forgiven the huge debt. Jesus promises to do this to us if we don't stop our anger and bitterness, which is a lack of forgiveness! Why is this so serious?

Hebrews 12:15 teaches that an unforgiving person, *"misses the grace of God."* In salvation, God gave us what we <u>needed,</u> not what we <u>deserved</u>! Now, God requires us to give others what they need, not what they deserve! An unforgiving bitter person *"causes trouble and defiles many."* Forgiveness heals relationships. Bitterness *"causes trouble."* It is the *"duty"* of every Christian to forgive in Luke 17:3-10.

Prayer: O Lord, we are that unmerciful servant! You gave us the power to forgive at salvation. Our rebellion makes excuses not to forgive. Lord, thank You for the pain You give us, so that we will obey You. In Jesus' name we pray. Amen.

May 31

"Blessed are you when people insult you, persecute you and falsely say all kinds of evil against you because of Me. Rejoice and be glad because great is your reward in Heaven." Matthew 5:11-12a

Are we rejoicing?

"Are we rejoicing?" The question is a major one on our Christian exam. Jesus makes the important point in our text because too often we have the wrong attitude about difficult trials! Our normal response is to be angry and bitter when someone troubles us. So Jesus gives us a necessary reminder of what a God-honoring response must be! Then a chapter later (yet the same discussion), Jesus teaches us that the secret to rejoicing is to forgive those who trouble us. This is important for three reasons!

Forgiving brings glory to God. Forgiving blesses others. Forgiving blesses us with rejoicing. Plus *"great is your reward in Heaven."* If we are a Christian, God has put His grace in our heart. Anger and bitterness are not a grace response; forgiveness is! We may think our anger points a finger at others who need to change. The opposite is true. Our anger is a sign that we need to change. It is also evidence that we are lacking in grace. James wasn't lying when he said, *"Man's anger does not bring about the righteous life that God desires,"* James 1:20.

We insist, a person has hurt us really bad and not only that, they have done it again and again. Must we keep forgiving them? What about the person who keeps saying things that are not true? Peter's question to Jesus is important. He asked, "Must I forgive seven times?" Jesus said, you must forgive *"7 times 7,"* or *"70 times 7"* in another place, an unlimited amount! But don't start counting! Dietrich Bonhoeffer a martyr who stood up to Hitler, wisely said, "As long as you are counting, you haven't forgiven even once." Most of our hurts come through relationships, and so will our healing!

Prayer: Lord, You forgive us again and again. You forgave us while we were still Your enemies. On the cross Jesus said, *"Father forgive them."* Lord, we have been poor witnesses of Your forgiving grace by holding on to our anger and bitterness. May we forgive even if we don't feel like it! And Lord, thanks for giving us rejoicing in the midst of difficult trials. In Jesus' name we pray. Amen.

JUNE

*"Create in me a pure heart, O God,
and renew a steadfast spirit within me.
Do not cast me from Your presence
or take Your Holy Spirit from me."*
Psalm 51:10-11

June 1

"No one has ever seen God, but God the One and Only, who is at the Father's side, has made Him known." John 1:18

The seven "I AM" sayings of Jesus

Our text introduces the seven "I AM" sayings of Jesus, because through these, God *"has made Him known."* Seven is a heavenly number, one of perfection. It is God's number. Jesus spoke seven "I AM" sayings to fully proclaim that God Himself had arrived. Moses was the only person to put these same two "I AM" words together. Since then, no one was permitted to use these words together. So sacred was the name of God. So when Christ said, *"I Am the Bread of life,"* the people really took notice. The One greater than Moses had finally arrived, 1400 years later! The Old Testament is fulfilled. The long-awaited Lamb of God is here. The seven "I AM" statements are very clear in showing the purpose, the life, the death, and the resurrection of Jesus.

In the early church, God's name, "I AM," gave way to Yahweh when referring to God. Later on, Jehovah was preferred. About the year 1900 the name for God was changed to Lord. Yet all of these names are really the same "I AM" name of God. The meaning of the words, "I AM," shows God is complete in Himself, is ever-present, has all knowledge, is everywhere at once, and is all-powerful.

Focus on the one small word that appears right after every "I AM" statement about who God is. It is the word *"the,"* as in *"the Bread," "the Light,"* and *"the Door."* In Greek, this is called a definite article, first person, singular, meaning the one and only *"Bread."* Jesus is not *"a Bread"* of life, as if there are others. He is the one and only *"Bread of life."* This means that Jesus is not a god. He is the God. This very important distinction is also clear in John 1:1.

Before we move into the devotions on the seven "I AM" sayings of Jesus, we will look at how and why God first introduced Himself as "I AM" to Moses. Then we will move into the seven descriptions of who God is and what He is doing in the world.

Prayer: Dear Lord, help us to see more clearly who You are, so we can worship You more fully. May Jesus, as both God and Man, be praised. In His name we pray. Amen.

June 2

"Moses said to God, 'Suppose I go to the Israelites and say to them,
"'The God of your fathers has sent me to you,'" and they ask me,
"'What is His name?'" Then what shall I tell them?' God said to Moses,
'I AM WHO I AM. This is what you are to say to the Israelites: I AM
has sent me to you.'" Exodus 3:13-14

The "I AM" delivers through Moses

Moses was called by God to free His people from 400 years of slavery. He was afraid! If he showed up in the court of Pharaoh he would likely be put to death. Who would dare to ask the most powerful ruler on earth to set all his slaves free? And if Moses lived, the first question from Pharaoh would be, "Why should I let go of these people who built Egypt into the greatest country in the world?"

Moses arrived on the scene as God's ambassador. Moses is a type of Christ. He points ahead to the kind of person Jesus will be. Moses also had a miraculous birth. All the other boy babies under two years were killed. Moses delivered the people from slavery, symbolizing our deliverance from the bondage to sin. There was nothing those in bondage could do to remove themselves from slavery! They were born into it. They died in it. Both Moses and Jesus rescued people from bondage.

Abraham, Isaac, and Jacob are long gone. Joseph and all he did is now forgotten. But did God forget His people? No, not at all! The 400 years since Joseph's death were used by God to build up a great number of people. Why? A deliverer needs people to deliver. And now the people were ready for that deliverance.

Do you see the reality of our sin problem that the Israelite people personally understood! They were 100% in bondage, complete bondage. It would take the grace and power of God to rescue them! By using many miracles, the "I AM," God Himself, convinced them that Moses was their deliverer. Years later, with even more miracles, God again convinced His people that He had sent His "I AM" called Jesus.

Prayer: Dear Lord, it is good that You give us a very clear picture along with a detailed account of how much we too need a deliverer. We praise You for sending a perfect, powerful and complete deliverer in Jesus Christ. In His name we pray. Amen.

June 3

"I Am the Bread of life." John 6:35a

The first *"I AM,"* Part 1

We read about how Jesus is the Bread of life from John 6:35 to John 8:11. Yet, the discussion really begins in John 6:4 when Jesus fed the 5000 with only a little bread in His hand. Jesus did this miracle as, *"the Jewish Passover was near."* The real Bread, the Passover Lamb has arrived! At the end of this meal, 12 baskets of bread were picked up. Jesus is popular! He can give physical food and blessings! At the beginning of chapter 6, He is a hero. By the end of chapter 6, Jesus is a zero. All will leave Him. The people wanted physical food, but not spiritual food!

After this *"Bread"* miracle, even Jesus' 12 disciples are seen sailing through life without Him. But they could not make much headway in the storms of life. Then suddenly Jesus appears, walking on the water. Amazingly, as soon as the disciples take the *"Bread"* of life into their boat, they *"reached the shore."* When we take Jesus into our hearts, we too are immediately on the shores of the Promised Land – even Heaven itself!

Jesus uses *"bread"* to describe Himself because that was the main food that kept man alive. Without bread many people would starve. But bread keeps us alive for just another day. Jesus wanted them to know that He is not just bread for a day, but *"the Bread of life."*

Think back to the 40 years in the desert. God miraculously gave daily manna (bread) from Heaven to keep His people alive. This manna pointed to Jesus who would be the Manna from God to keep them alive spiritually! Three times Jesus compared Himself to the manna in the Old Testament. Then Jesus said, *"I am the living Bread that came down from Heaven. If anyone eats of this Bread, he will live forever,"* John 6:51a. Again, this is why the 5000 people who ate the bread and fish left Him. At this point, Jesus asked the twelve a big question. *"You do not want to leave too, do you?"* John 6:67. Peter then said a most amazing truth! *"Lord, to whom shall we go? You have the words of eternal life,"* John 6:68b.

Prayer: Lord, our deliverer, You still have the words of eternal life. We worship and praise You for rescuing us! In Jesus' name we pray. Amen.

June 4

"I Am the Bread of life." John 6:35a

The first *"I AM,"* Part 2

Why *"Bread"*? Bread is made to be eaten. If we were literally starving to death and someone placed a beautiful loaf of bread in front of us, what would we do? Would we merely take the bread and touch our lips with it? No way! We would rip into that bread! We would be quick to get it into our stomach. We have the same spiritual problem. We are starving and dying spiritually. Jesus invites us to take of Him, to be filled with Him spiritually. But what do we do?

We may have Jesus on our lips on Sunday but do we digest Him? Does *"the Bread of life"* ever get past our lips! May we not forget! Five thousand people saw a huge miracle and then all left Jesus when He told them they needed to take Him into their hearts! They were not prepared to get that serious about a relationship with Jesus. They wanted the blessings of God in the basket, but they did not want anything to do with the One who was holding the basket!

After teaching the 5000 and His 12 disciples, *"the Bread of life"* secretly goes to the Feast of Tabernacles, in Leviticus 23:33-34. This was the third of the three major feasts that all males were required to go to Jerusalem for. This celebration looked back on how God provided in the wilderness for 40 years. This feast also looked forward to how God would continue to provide for His people in the future. In this week, the priest sacrificed 70 bulls, representing the 70 nations that came from Noah. The hope and prayer was that these 70 Gentile nations would someday accept the God of Abraham, Isaac and Jacob.

"On the last and greatest day of the Feast, Jesus stood and said in a loud voice, 'If anyone is thirsty, let him come to Me and drink. Whoever believes in Me, as the Scripture has said, streams of living water will flow from within him,'" John 7:37-38. *"The Bread of life,"* is also the *"living water,"* complete nourishment for our souls! Amazingly, the word "tabernacle" means God dwelling with us.

Prayer: Dear Lord, forgive us for being so cold to You, the real *"Bread of life"*! Make us hungry for You! Make us thirsty for You! Draw us to Yourself we pray. In Jesus' name we pray. Amen.

June 5

"I Am the Light of the world." John 8:12b

The second "I AM," Part 1

Jesus is not a light in the world. He is not one of the gods. Jesus is *"the Light,"* the only Light. Real light eliminates darkness. The Pharisees tried to tell Jesus that His testimony of being *"the Light"* was not valid. Jesus corrects them saying; *"I know where I came from and where I am going,"* John 8:14b. If they only knew that Jesus existed before light, and even created it! Jesus also said, *"I am not alone. I stand with the Father, who sent Me,"* John 8:16b. Jesus rebuked the Pharisees by saying, *"In your own Law it is written that the testimony of two men is valid. I am one who testifies for Myself; My other witness is the Father, who sent Me,"* John 8:17-18.

The Pharisees were blind to the fact that Jesus was the Son of God, fully God in the flesh. The amazing part is that the Pharisees were the leaders in the church, yet they were totally in the dark. Chapter 8 ends with the people throwing stones at Jesus. The ones who still throw the most stones at Christians are the self-righteous in the church who want a form of religion, but not Jesus Christ!

The Light of the world, *"saw a man blind from birth,"* John 9:1. Spiritually blind is the main point here. David wrote, *"Surely I was sinful at birth, sinful from the time my mother conceived me,"* Psalm 51:5. This story of the blind man teaches that we blind sinners need *"The Light of the world."* Notice an important "grace point" here. Jesus *"saw"* a man. This blind man could not see Jesus, nor can we. Grace means Jesus sees us when we can't see Him! He opens our eyes, our sinful natures are that blind. Ephesians 2:4b-5 says, *"God, who is rich in mercy, made us alive with Christ even when we were dead in transgressions - it is by grace you have been saved."* Since dead people can't see Christ, Jesus *"spit on the ground, made some mud with the saliva, and put it on the man's eyes,"* John 9:6b. Open our eyes too, O Lord!

Prayer: Dear Lord, You show us in so many ways that we are poor, wretched, blind, and unable to find You. But then, You shine Your light into our hearts and wake us up. So Lord, open our eyes to see *"the Light of the world."* In Jesus' name we pray. Amen.

June 6

"The man they call Jesus made some mud and put it on my eyes. He told me to go to Siloam and wash. So I went and washed, and then I could see." John 9:11

The second "I AM," Part 2

The people questioned the blind man about who healed him. His testimony is beautiful and simple. This man was surely not very educated, but he had, *"the Light of the world"* in him! Listen to his simple but absolutely brilliant three-point sermon. It is his response to the grace of God, now in him. His three points are, "I went, I washed, I see." God in Trinity selected this person and moved his heart to obey the call of salvation! But still, this is what the man did and saw by faith in Jesus.

Do these simple words move us? Has this been our experience? Can we say, "I went, I washed, I see"? Or, do we say, "I think I'm saved?" If we do not yet know, then we must get on our knees and plead for God to move our hearts to the assurance of our relationship with Him. This formerly blind man did not doubt his sight! Faith that can say, "I went, I washed, I see" is real faith! Jesus gives clear sight.

Now the blind Pharisees question salvation by grace alone through Christ alone. These educated teachers did not understand the healing of this blind man, because it was not their experience! To them, religion was one of heritage, one of gaining more and more knowledge. It was about keeping every law perfectly! They were proud of who they were. They thought the people should follow them, to learn from them. Jesus pointed out they didn't even have a relationship with Him. They were the ones that were really blind.

Do not think that this has changed today. A man recently came to me who had asked four pastors what it means to be a "new creation." All four had no idea! What does this tell you? Are we a new creation? Has Jesus opened our eyes? Who do we say that He is?

Prayer: Lord Jesus, open our eyes today! We want to know You. And Lord, if there is any self-righteousness in us, please remove it! Because Your grace cannot fully work where self-righteousness still rules! How much we all need Your righteousness! In Jesus' name we pray. Amen.

June 7

"I Am the Door. If anyone enters by Me, he will be saved."
John 10:9a NKJV

The third "I AM"

The NIV reads, *"I am the Gate for the sheep."* Christ is the only way by which we enter into the kingdom of God by faith. Jesus Christ is the only substitutionary atonement for our personal sins. This means there are false shepherds who do not know about the real Door, about the only way. The sheep pen is a picture of safety in the body of Christ! It should be obvious that many people try get to God by wrong doorways and are thus without safety, without Jesus Christ, the Good Shepherd!

Anyone who wants to get into the sheep pen other than through *"the Door"* comes in to steal, kill, and destroy the sheep. Jesus points out that the real agenda of the Pharisees and all false shepherds, is like that of a robber. *Jesus said "The thief comes only to steal and kill and destroy; I have come that they may have life, and have it to the full,"* John 10:10. Two things must be obvious to us!

First, false shepherds come over the wall to get at the sheep. They pretend to love the sheep. Their real agenda is stealing the sheep, or stealing from the sheep. With this in mind, how many TV programs pretend to teach the Bible while their real scheme is to get money out of people? And it's not just T.V. programs.

Secondly, *"They (sheep) will never follow a stranger; in fact, they will run away from him because they do not recognize a stranger's voice,"* John 10:5. We wonder, why don't some people recognize these false shepherds for who they really are? This verse in John opens our eyes to an important truth! Only sheep (real believers) recognize false shepherds. The Holy Spirit opens their eyes to what is false.

Prayer: Lord, it is only by Your grace that we go to the right Door. Just like there was only one door to get into the ark, there is one Door to get into Heaven! You alone are that Door. You alone open the Door. You alone close the Door. Without Jesus, *"the Door,"* we are eternally shut out of Heaven! We praise You, Father, Son, and Spirit for pushing us to that one Door, and into Your holy presence. In Christ's precious name we pray. Amen.

June 8

"I Am the Good Shepherd." John 10:11a

The fourth *"I AM"*

If Jesus is the *"Good Shepherd,"* what does the word *"Good"* mean?

A. <u>A Good Shepherd protects the sheep</u>. Without God, we sheep are dinner for wolves and bears, those who are false teachers!

B. <u>A Good Shepherd feeds the sheep</u>. Sheep can't feed themselves *"good"* food, in a *"good"* amount. So God feeds His sheep from His pure Word, not from other polluted sources.

C. <u>Evil shepherds exist, and God hates them</u>. God told Jeremiah, *"Son of man, prophesy against the shepherds of Israel; prophesy and say unto them: 'This is what the Sovereign LORD says: Woe unto the shepherds of Israel who only take care of themselves! Should not shepherds take care of the flock?'"* Ezekiel 34:2.

D. <u>Jesus is the Good and only Shepherd</u>. The *"Good Shepherd"* <u>leads</u> the sheep. You cannot drive sheep! A sheep that knows the shepherd will follow him everywhere, trusting him. But sheep will not follow a stranger! Sheep, that is true believers, recognize false shepherds and run from them because they know the danger.

E. <u>Jesus only rescues His sheep, all Christians</u>. Jesus tells this allegory to show the people and corrupt leaders that He came to rescue His <u>sheep</u>. He said, *"I am the good Shepherd; I know My <u>sheep</u> and My <u>sheep</u> know Me,"* John 10:14. Jesus further said, *"I lay down My life for the <u>sheep</u>,"* John 10:15b. This is exactly what the grace of God to believers is! Jesus came for the <u>sheep</u>, not for all of Israel. Later Jesus said, *"I have other sheep (Gentiles) who are not of this sheep pen (Israel). I must bring them also. They too will listen to My voice, and there will be one flock and one Shepherd,"* John 10:16.

Prayer: Lord, You indeed are a *"Good Shepherd."* Please open our eyes to that more and more. For what You did for us sheep, You did not do for all others. *"To all who received Him, to those who believed in His name, He gave the right to become children of God,"* John 1:12. In Christ's name we pray. Amen.

June 9

"I Am the Resurrection and the Life." John 11:25a

The fifth *"I AM,"* Part 1

The words *"I AM"* point to a present reality, not just a future promise. A Christian's *"resurrection"* and *"life"* are that guaranteed! But there is also a resurrection that ends in eternal death if a person is not covered by the blood of the *"I Am."*

Jesus is *"the Resurrection."* Jesus opens the door to a real eternal life with Him, through a real physical resurrection. To prove Jesus could do this, He brought Lazarus, the brother of Mary and Martha back to life. What happened to Lazarus will happen to every one of us!

Each of us is made of two parts, body and soul/spirit. At death our soul separates from our physical body. Our body is put into the ground to sleep until the day of our resurrection. Cemeteries are literally resurrection gardens. While the body is sleeping in the grave, the souls of Christians are alive in Heaven, Revelation 20:4. For those who are not Christians, their souls are alive in Hell after death. The story of the rich man and Lazarus the poor man, in Luke 16:19-23, shows an immediate going to either Heaven or Hell. On the Cross, Jesus said to the thief He saved, *"Today you will be with Me in Paradise,"* Luke 23:43b.

Paul said about the resurrection, *"We believe that Jesus died and rose again and so we believe that God will bring with Jesus those* (the souls) *who have fallen asleep in Him,"* 1 Thessalonians 4:14. John said, *"a time is coming when all who are in their graves will hear His voice and come out - those who have done good will rise to live, and those who have done evil will rise to be condemned,"* John 5:28b-29. There is a resurrection of the just and of the unjust on the very same day.

Some do not want to think about facing a resurrection! But the fact remains, *"all who are in their graves will hear His voice and come out."* What kind of resurrection will we have in our eternity? If we are forgiven by Christ's perfect blood, we are perfect already. If we are not covered, we are condemned already.

Prayer: Lord Jesus, You are the only One we can go to. You alone are *"the Resurrection and the Life."* We worship You and thank You for securing our future by Your blood. In Jesus' name we pray. Amen.

June 10

"I Am the Resurrection and the Life." John 11:25a

The fifth *"I AM,"* Part 2

Jesus is *"the Life."* Death could not hold Christ in the grave. He had a complete victory over sin and Satan's power. Jesus alone can say, *"I am the Resurrection and the Life. He who believes in Me will live, even though he dies,"* John 11:25. How is this *"life"* possible? Go back to Adam again. If man would not have sinned in the Garden of Eden, every person would have lived forever. God said to Adam, *"You must not eat from the tree of the knowledge of good and evil, for when you eat of it you will surely die,"* Genesis 2:17. Adam did not listen. *"Therefore, just as sin entered the world through one man, and death through sin, and in this way death came to all men, because all sinned,"* Romans 5:12.

Finally, after years of animal sacrifices to pay for man's sin, (Leviticus 17:11), Christ becomes the Lamb of God. He lived a perfect life. It was our sin that put Him to death! Once He paid the penalty for our sin, the grave could no longer hold Him. His resurrection proved He was sinless. His resurrection proved that God accepted His perfect life and then death for our sins. Jesus' life in Heaven without sin is our life. Because He lives forever, we will live forever, joint heirs to all the eternal blessings of God. This is the truth of the Gospel. Christ crucified for me! Christ's resurrection for me. Christ's eternal life for me.

Paul explains the resurrection of a believer to life everlasting: *"But Christ has indeed been raised from the dead, the firstfruits of those who have fallen asleep. For since death came through a man, the resurrection of the dead comes also through a Man. For as in Adam all die, so in Christ all will be made alive. But each in his own turn: Christ, the first fruits; then, when He comes, those who belong to Him,"* 1 Corinthians 15:20-23.

Prayer: Dear Lord, You give us real hope in Christ! We have Your promise! *"Just as we have borne the likeness of the earthly man, so we shall bear the likeness of the Man from Heaven,"* 1 Corinthians 15:49. What an amazing guarantee of a life that is above and beyond what we could ever imagine. What a beautiful day that will be! In Jesus' name, accept our praise and prayer! Amen.

June 11

"I Am the Way and the Truth and the Life." John 14:6a

The sixth *"I AM"*

"Do not let your hearts be troubled. Trust in God; trust also in Me," John 14:1. Comfort is the theme of chapter 14. The disciples are emotionally upset in the midst of the rapidly changing events leading up to Christ's trial and crucifixion. Judas has just left to betray Jesus. Then Jesus told Peter that he also would deny his Lord. Jesus tells the disciples He will leave them to go to Heaven. The disciples plead with Jesus to show them the way to where He is going. They want to be with Him. That's why He says, *"I am the Way and the Truth and the Life,"* John 14:6a.

1. *"I Am the Way."* In verse 5, Thomas said, *"Lord, we don't know where You are going, so how can we know the way?"* The disciples wanted directions to where Jesus was going, perhaps even the road Jesus was taking. Jesus instead told them that He Himself is the Way to God, the only Mediator by which they could get to God. We too are saved by this person Jesus, not by keeping the commandments, not by reciting a creed, and not by being baptized! Jesus is the one and only Way to be reunited with God!

2. *"I Am... the truth."* Remember that the Old Testament was in shadows and types. It was vague. Now the New Testament is here in a clearer truth. Jesus is the only source of redemptive revelation. Any other way that promises to get us to God is a lie. It is amazing, Pilate asked Jesus what is "truth," and he was looking at *"the Truth"* and did not know it! If we want to see God, we need to <u>know</u> *"the Truth."*

3. *"I Am... the Life."* Jesus has every perfect attribute of God according to Colossians 2:9. Jesus is the giver of eternal life according to John 3:16 and John 11:25. He guarantees it! *"I give them eternal life, and they shall never perish; no one can snatch them out of My hand,"* John 10:28. If Christ were not fully God and man, there would be no *"way"* to the Father, no redemptive *"truth,"* and no everlasting *"life."*

Prayer: Lord, You show us the Way. You open our eyes to the truth. You give us Life forever. Lord, Your gift of Jesus is good because we are blind and stubborn sinners. Make us accept Your beautiful gift, Your Son. In His name we pray. Amen.

June 12

"*I Am the true Vine.*" John 15:1a

The seventh "*I AM,*" Part 1

The context of this final "*I Am,*" is like the last one. Jesus is leaving them. Jesus comforts and encourages the eleven remaining disciples not to be like Judas. Jesus knows that after He leaves, the disciples will be greatly tempted to go back to Moses and all the Old Testament teachings. Jesus knows that false teachers will come to try lead them astray. So Jesus makes it clear that He is not just another vine, or "a vine," but "*the true Vine.*" There is a big difference! Jesus encourages His disciples to maintain their faith in Him and lovingly stick together. Jesus warns them that the world will hate them. But a key point is: stay attached to Jesus, "the true Vine," and bear fruit for Him! The chapter ends with Jesus promising to send the Holy Spirit to help them bear fruit. This seventh "*I Am,*" could be summed up with the 5th verse. "*I Am the Vine; you are the branches. If a man remains in Me and I in him, he will bear much fruit; apart from Me you can do nothing,*" John 15:5. There are six points in this verse that show the relationship between Jesus and His people.

1. "*I Am the Vine; you are the branches.*" Jesus here compares Himself to the main trunk of a grapevine. The Christian is the branch. We must remember our relationship to "*the Vine*"! The vine taps the ground for nutrients and is firmly rooted to the soil. Only branches that are solidly attached to the vine draw strength and have vitality. Grape branches spread far and wide. The Gospel spreads out over the earth by branches that are grafted into Christ. Is our sufficiency in Christ alone?

2. "*He cuts off every branch in Me that does not bear fruit,*" John 15:2a. A branch that doesn't bear fruit is called a sucker. It sucks the life out of a tree. It takes but does not give! Such a worthless branch is cut off flush with the vine. This way the sap can flow to the productive branches. "Pretending Christians" are these sap-sucking, unproductive branches that are cut off from the kingdom of God.

Prayer: Lord, so often we feel dead spiritually! We do not remain firmly attached and then wonder why we have so little "sap." It is because we leave You! Lord, don't cut us off. Strengthen our wilting hearts we pray. Have mercy on us. In Christ's name we pray. Amen.

June 13

"I Am the true Vine." John 15:1a

The seventh *"I AM,"* Part 2

3. *"Every branch that does bear fruit He prunes,"* John 15:2b. If a man undergoes severe trials, it is not necessarily because of a lack of faith! A branch that is good for something also gets trimmed. It is not cut off, but cut back a little to be more productive. Lord, give us the faith to see that this "pruning" is from You, to improve us!

4. *"Remain in Me."* The NKJV reads, *"Abide in Me."* This word is used 11 times in John 15. We are to *"remain"* or *"abide"* in Christ by faith. Let us consider the different ways we are to remain or abide in Christ. Jesus said, *"Remain in Me, and I will remain in you,"* John 15:4a. Christ promises communion with the believer if the believer will stay focused on Christ and all of His holy attributes.

5. *"Bear much fruit."* The words *"bear fruit"* is said 9 times in John 15. Grapevines make grapes! Christians make disciples! Are we? Years ago monks hid in caves and monasteries. Are we? We are called by God to be light and salt in a world that has lost its spiritual compass. *"What good is it, my brothers, if a man claims to have faith but has no deeds? Can such a faith save him?"* James 2:14. *"Was not our ancestor Abraham considered righteous for what <u>he did</u> when he offered his son Isaac on the altar?"* James 2:21. Abraham's *"faith and his actions were working together, and <u>his faith was made complete by what he did</u>,"* James 2:22b. God saves us, then uses us to tell others about Christ. Jesus said, *"show yourselves to be My disciples,"* John 15:8b.

6. *"Apart from Me you can do nothing."* We want to "do" something meaningful. The only way to do that is by staying attached to Christ. Our text gives us insight into what lasts for all eternity. True meaning in life is being connected to Jesus Christ alone! He says, *"apart from Me <u>you can do nothing</u>."* Just imagine! Everything we do that is not connected to Christ will burn up.

Prayer: Dear Lord, we can see that You are most pleased with us when we are most satisfied with You. We thank You for being our Vine and for making us productive. In Jesus' name we pray. Amen.

June 14

"'You are exacting usury from your own countrymen!' So I called together a large meeting to deal with them and said: 'As far as possible, we have bought back our Jewish brothers who were sold to the Gentiles. Now you are selling your brothers, only for them to be sold back to us!' They kept quiet, because they could find nothing to say... 'What you are doing is not right. Shouldn't you walk in the fear of our God to avoid the reproach of our Gentile enemies?'" Neh. 5:7b-9

The evil of "Usury," Part 1

The Israelites just came out of slavery to foreigners! Now they were trying to enslave each other through *"usury,"* which is charging excessive interest. Responsible governments pass laws to stop the practice of excessive interest. Let me give you an example of the problem.

Ruby's husband left her. She has a daughter to bring up alone. The money she gets as a cook did not cover her expenses last month. Her daughter's school fees are due. If Ruby does not pay the fees, her daughter will not be admitted next year. Ruby can't borrow from a bank. She has nothing of value to secure a loan. The only option she knows of is going to a neighbor to get 5000.00 rupees, about $100.00. But, the interest on this money is 1000.00 rupees a month, 250% interest. Ruby makes 1500 rupees a month and will not be able to repay it!

Ruby goes to a big church, but she never considered asking there. They never helped anyone in her situation before. The tithes and gifts all go into the pastor's pocket. Like many churches, there are no elders or deacons to help provide accountability for the money that comes in. Isn't it sad? Shame on a "church" that does not act like a church should!

When I see this I wonder, does her pastor know the following verses: *"Do not take advantage of a widow or an orphan. If you do and they cry out to me, I will certainly hear their cry. My anger will be aroused, and I will kill you with the sword; and your wives will become widows and your children fatherless,"* Exodus 22:22-24.

Prayer: Lord, You told us throughout the Bible about the use and the abuse of money. Lord, please convict those who need to learn more about the proper use of money. We pray for Your mercy and grace for those suffering. In Christ's name we pray. Amen.

June 15

"If you lend money to one of <u>my people</u> among you who is needy, <u>do not be like a moneylender</u>; charge him no interest." Exodus 22:25

The evil of *"Usury,"* Part 2

This charging of excessive interest or "usury" is wicked! The local Marwaris or moneylenders are brutal! They carry on their "business" in such a way that once a person falls into their hands, it usually means total ruin. And if you don't pay the money back, friends of the one who loaned you the money will beat on you! We all know stories about these things. Desperate parents sell a child for child labor or prostitution, just to try pay the moneylender. Others sell a kidney or other body parts, just to try to pay back the unrelenting crooks. Where is our outrage? Where is our sense of justice? Be sure of this: our Lord sees everything! The God who made everyone has some very definite ideas about how we as Christians should act. See our text and this next verse also.

"Do not charge your brother interest, whether on money or food or anything else that may earn interest. You may charge a foreigner interest, but not a brother Israelite, so that the Lord your God may bless you in everything that you put your hand to in the land you are entering to possess," Deuteronomy 23:19-20. God here wanted to bless His people. But, He would not do so until they acted like His children! How many are not receiving the blessings of God because they are not concerned about those who are being cheated? How many governments would prosper if they cared about the ones who suffer?

A woman I know goes to a fasting prayer meeting every week. At the same time, she also charges 36% interest, 3% a month to a poor neighbor! She does not understand God who says, *"Is not this the kind of fasting I have chosen: to loose the chains of injustice and untie the cords of the yoke, to set the oppressed free and break every yoke? Is it not to share your food with the hungry and provide the poor wanderer with shelter,"* Isaiah 58:6-7a. If we fast and pray and then cheat others, God doesn't hear our prayers!

Prayer: Lord, those who charge excessive interest are sucking the lifeblood out of the poor! Lord, help us to stop this evil! In Jesus' name we pray. Amen.

June 16

"There are six things the LORD hates, seven that are detestable to Him: haughty eyes, a lying tongue, hands that shed innocent blood, a heart that devises wicked schemes, feet that are quick to rush into evil, a false witness who pours out lies and a man who stirs up dissension among brothers." Proverbs 6:16-19

Seven things detestable to God, Part 1

The Bible speaks often about foolish living. God wants us not only to believe right, but to <u>live</u> right! God wants us to live a holy life, to worship Him, and to be a blessing to others. From these verses in Proverbs we can see the mind of our Holy God. We see exactly what He "hates." Notice specifically how the various <u>parts of our bodies</u> carry out the wicked practices that God hates:

1. "Haughty <u>eyes</u>," have a bad attitude! Our eyes are the headlights to our spiritual engines, the windows of our soul! "Haughty eyes," reveal what is in our hearts. "Haughty eyes" say to God, Your rules are not for me. "Haughty eyes" say to other people I am better than you. "Haughty eyes" walk about like a cocky rooster or a proud hen. We should know this from God, *"Pride goes before destruction, a haughty spirit before a fall,"* Proverbs 16:18. David said about God, *"You save the humble, but Your eyes are on the haughty to bring them low,"* 2 Samuel 22:28.

2. "A lying <u>tongue</u>," is out of tune with its Creator. David said of the Father, *"All Your Words are true,"* Psalm 119:160a. Jesus said, *"I am the way, the truth, and the life,"* John 14:6a. The Holy Spirit *"guides you into all truth"* in John 16:13b. Satan is the father of lies. We can see that God in Trinity hates lies! God is truth.

3. "<u>Hands</u> that shed innocent blood." People cheat so that they can rise up above others. Cheating hates others and seeks their destruction. God is a God of justice. He pays back hurt to those who hurt others! *"Blessed are the merciful, for they shall be shown mercy,"* Matthew 5:7.

Prayer: Lord, we say we want to worship You more faithfully. Here You show us how. We thank You for being so practical. We also thank You for giving us the power to live in a right way. You alone give us a spiritual life! In Jesus' name we pray. Amen.

June 17

"There are six things the LORD hates, seven that are detestable to Him: haughty eyes, a lying tongue, hands that shed innocent blood, a heart that devises wicked schemes, feet that are quick to rush into evil, a false witness who pours out lies and a man who stirs up dissension among brothers." Proverbs 6:16-19

Seven things detestable to God, Part 2

4. "A <u>heart</u> that devises wicked schemes." There is no shortage of wicked schemes in men's hearts! It may appear that they succeed for a while, but *"Do not be deceived: God cannot be mocked. A man reaps what he sows. The one who sows to please his sinful nature, from that nature will reap destruction; the one who sows to please the Spirit, from the Spirit will reap eternal life,"* Galatians 6:7-8.

5. "<u>Feet</u> that are quick to rush into evil." We read in Proverbs 1:17, *"How useless to spread a net in full view of all the birds!"* Even a bird with a brain the size of a pebble can see what we are doing. Do we somehow think that God, who sees absolutely everything in His creation does not know what we are doing? Evil men *"lie in wait for their own blood; they waylay only themselves! Such is the end of all who go after ill-gotten gain; it takes away the lives of those who get it,"* Proverbs 1:18-19.

6. "A false witness who pours out lies." Did you notice that number 2 was also about lying? God doubly hates lying. If we lie and think we are living in the Spirit, we are not. Jesus was clear, *"God is Spirit, and His worshipers must worship in spirit and in <u>truth</u>,"* John 4:24.

7. "A man who stirs up dissension among brothers." God is for peace. Jesus is called *"the Prince of peace."* God hates it if we try to harm any of His children. He loves His children and has said He will protect them. If we attack them, whose side are we on? We must remember that Satan wants relationships destroyed and is for demonic bitterness.

Prayer: Lord, when we see how the various parts of our bodies dishonor You, we are ashamed! Lord be merciful to us and forgive us. We want to hate what You hate, and love what You love. May we take Your words to heart, *"Therefore, I urge you, brothers, in view of God's mercy, to offer your bodies as living sacrifices, holy and pleasing to God,"* Romans 12:1a. In Jesus' name we pray. Amen.

June 18

"He made us accepted in the Beloved." Ephesians 1:6b NKJV

What does *"accepted"* mean? Part 1

There are a lot of Christians who are suffering because they do not see how God in Christ sees every true believer. Let us ask a few questions to check our understanding of some Biblical facts.

Does God love and accept us fully as much as He did Moses, Elijah, David, Matthew, Mark, Luke, John, Paul, etc...? Are we today as righteous as these Bible saints? Are we as righteous as God's own Son, Jesus Christ? Is God as pleased with us as He was with Jesus when He said, *"This is My beloved Son, in whom I am well pleased,"* Matthew 3:17b NKJV. The answers to these questions are all a big, "Yes!" In Christ, we are just as loved, accepted, and righteous! Why? Because we are justified, made righteous because of what Christ has done. We are restored! No Christian gets more justified as they grow up. We grow in sanctification but not in justification.

Meditate on the word *"made"* in our text. If God *"made us accepted,"* can we ever earn a better standing with God after salvation? No, Christ has already earned it for us! So then why do we so often have the mentality that if we do good things, God will finally like us? He already likes us. In fact, He loves us, just as He loves His own Son. May we start living like a thankful son or daughter of God!

Too often we live the Christian life believing half of the Gospel! We believe that Jesus forgave our sins at salvation/justification. That's good, but that is only half of the deal. Every Christian also receives the righteousness of Christ! Listen to Paul. *"For He (God) made Him (Jesus) who knew no sin to be sin for us, that we might become the righteousness of God in Him,"* 2 Corinthians 5:21 NKJV. So then, when God *"made us accepted in the Beloved,"* Christ takes our sin and we get His righteousness. He accepts us in the salvation process.

Prayer: Dear Lord, even though we see this truth on the pages of Scripture we cannot imagine how Christ takes all our sin! What a beautiful and gracious God You are in making us righteous. We know that we will sing praises for all eternity for what You have done. May we begin today! In Christ Jesus' name we pray. Amen.

June 19

"For it is by grace you have been saved, through faith — and this not from yourselves, it is the gift of God — not by works, so that no one can boast." Ephesians 2:8-9

Don't cheapen the grace of God! Part 2

We know from Ephesians 1-2 and from Romans 8 that God wrote the name of every Christian on His hand even before the world was created. Jesus came to claim those who were His own, His sheep. He did not come for those who would not believe, the goats. Our salvation is based solely on God's grace. Please hear two reasons why we must fully believe in the grace of God.

1. For the glory of God. The primary reason we worship God is for His amazing grace. God's grace is not very amazing if we had something to do with our salvation! Our text clearly says, *"not from yourselves,"* *"not by works."* At another time Jesus said, *"You did not choose Me, but I chose you and appointed you to go and bear fruit,"* John 15:16a. Think of Adam. He could not even cover one sin! God in grace had to shed the blood of the first sacrifice in Genesis 3:21. He clothed both Adam and Eve. They did not put the righteous clothes on! God put the *"skins"* on Adam and Eve. Jesus also said, *"I am the good Shepherd. The good shepherd lays down His life for the sheep,"* John 10:11.

God as Judge chooses to pardon some sinners! If Jesus came to pardon all sinners, they would come. Think of how God called the Apostle Paul when he was still God's enemy. God chose us when we were His *"enemy,"* Romans 5:10. Did any of the dry bones in Ezekiel 37 choose God? How could they? They were dead! God puts His Spirit into some dead bones. That is what makes grace, grace. This is why we will eternally sing, *"Worthy is the Lamb who was slain"*! He is worthy. We are 100% unworthy. He chose us who deserved death. He gave us life. All Christians were destined to become sheep simply because those names were written in His hand!

Prayer: Gracious Lord forgive us when we think we had something to do with our salvation, wanting a little glory for ourselves. Nothing in my hand I bring, simply to Thy cross I cling. In Jesus' name we pray. Amen.

June 20

"Get rid of all bitterness, rage and anger, brawling and slander, along with every form of malice. Be kind and compassionate to one another, forgiving each other, just as in Christ God forgave you."
Ephesians 4:31-32

Don't cheapen the forgiveness of God! Part 3

We have seen that we must believe in grace for the glory of God. We must also believe in grace for an important second reason.

2. For our own good. We must understand the grace of God to live a life of grace! John said, *"If anyone says, 'I love God,' yet hates his brother, he is a liar. For anyone who does not love his brother, whom he has seen, cannot love God, whom he has not seen. And He has given us this command: Whoever loves God must also love his brother,"* 1 John 4:20-21. We love others by being forgiving. Anger and bitterness in our text, is the opposite of the grace and forgiveness of God.

Here is where so many have a problem. If we think we chose God's forgiveness of us, then we will also think we may choose whether or not to forgive others. We are commanded to forgive *"each other, just as in Christ God forgave you."* That was by grace alone, by Him coming to us when we were unwilling and unable to come to Him. After the Lord's prayer, Jesus said, *"If you forgive men when they sin against you, your Heavenly Father will also forgive you. But if you do not forgive men their sins, your Father will not forgive your sins!"* Matthew 6:14-15.

God's forgiveness by grace alone means we did not prove in any way that we deserved it. Instead, we proved the opposite, and God saved us anyway. Now God demands we give grace to others who don't deserve it. If we cheapen God's grace with a different kind of forgiveness, God will not be pleased with us, just as God was not pleased with the *"unmerciful servant"* in Matthew 18:21-35. God handed the one who would not forgive over to be tortured until he was willing. Jesus said: *"This is how My Heavenly Father will treat each of you unless you forgive your brother from your heart,"* Matthew 18:35.

Prayer: Lord, You teach us the most important lessons about interpersonal relationships! May we forgive others as in Christ, You forgave us, by grace alone. In Jesus' name we pray. Amen.

June 21

"Jesus said to them, 'My food is to do the will of Him who sent Me, and to finish His work.'" John 4:34 NKJV

Are we "finishing" our work?

The *"will"* of His Father consumed Jesus. Satan tried everything he could to derail Jesus from doing the will of God. He worked up some people to attack Jesus' theology. He worked on Jesus' obedience in doing the will of the Father. Yet Jesus remained steadfast to the will of God.

How are we doing? Does the will of God drive us? Do we even know the will of God in the Bible? Are we easily distracted from learning and doing the will of God? Like Jesus, we are here in the world to do God's will. He put each of us here exactly when He wanted us to be here. We know that God has *"determined the times set for them and the exact places they should live,"* Acts 17:26b. We know from the following verse in Acts 17 that God put us here to seek Him and to find Him. So, if that is true, and it is, then it stands to reason that we are here to do His will! Are we doing it? Or are we slaves to created things instead of to the Creator of everything?

The word *"food"* in our text talks about desire. Our bodies long for food. That's how Jesus longed to do the will of His Father. On one occasion Jesus said, *"I have come down from Heaven, not to do My will, but to do the will of Him who sent Me,"* John 6:38. What is our *"food"* for living? Is it to do the will of God? To do God's will, we first need to know Him. Then we will be able to serve Him and love Him. If we do not have a close relationship with God, we will not have a strong desire to live for Him! At the end of Jesus' life, He said in prayer to His Father, *"I have glorified You on the earth. I have finished the work which You have given Me to do,"* John 17:4 NKJV. At the end of our lives, may we be able to say the same. May we start living out God's will today!

Prayer: Dear Father in Heaven, may the words of Jesus be our words, our passion for living! May our *"food"* be Your Holy will. We confess that we have been driven by things that are less important. Forgive us and place us directly in the center of Your will each day. In Christ Jesus' name we pray. Amen.

June 22

"He traveled through the area, speaking many words of encouragement to the people." Acts 20:2a

How balanced are we?

This passing comment about Paul's new lifestyle reveals a lot about his effectiveness as a Bible teacher and leader. There was a time when Paul did not give *"encouragement,"* but instead stole it from the people as he persecuted them! By the grace of God, Paul changed from a discourager to an encourager. It is important for us to see how this change became possible and how encouragement works!

First, Jesus met Paul on the road to Damascus and changed his heart! Jesus softened the heart of Paul to see the struggles of others. Paul suddenly had a burden to carry the burdens of others, just as Jesus carried his. Notice that *"encouragement"* is a sweet gift from God to help others understand and get through the struggles of life. <u>Jesus alone gives this heart of grace and the power to be gracious!</u> The source of *"encouragement"* is the grace of God.

Second, Paul had balance! Paul was able to lovingly rebuke others effectively. How did he get away with this? He spent more time giving *"encouragement"* to others. We too must give a loving rebuke when it is needed, when others need to change. We can do this effectively if we balance it with lots of encouragement! The question is: How balanced are we? If we want to ruin someone, just keep up the rebukes constantly! We will drive them away from us. Hear this plainly. We all need to work on *"encouragement."*

Our greatest failings as parents, teachers, employers or pastors are when we see the negative in others, but ignore the positive. Then we wonder why people run away from us. Paul knew this very well from his experience. He persecuted the church of Christ more than anyone. By the grace of God, Paul changed to become an amazing encourager. May we do the same!

Prayer: Lord, we read that Paul, *"traveled through the area, speaking many words of encouragement to the people."* May we speak, *"many words of encouragement."* Help us to be more like Jesus and Paul. In Christ's name we pray. Amen.

June 23

"Children, obey your parents in everything, for this pleases the Lord."
Colossians 3:20

"Children, obey your parents"

This command is necessary because children are born selfish! Paul is very brief in this command to children, *"obey your parents in everything."* It does not say in some things. It says, *"in everything."* No excuses allowed. Paul gives a good reason: *"For this pleases the Lord."* In the Ten Commandments God gave us two more good reasons to obey. *"Honor your father and your mother… so that you may live long and that it may go well with you,"* Deuteronomy 5:16a. Children have at least three good reasons to obey their parents.

These three reasons apply to all children. Those under three do not need to know the three reasons just yet. At that age, child must learn to obey simply because mommy and daddy said so. They do not need to know the why at first. The problem a child has is that by nature, they do not want to listen to a parent. If a little one doesn't listen to a parent's "No," and if the parent doesn't ever say "No," or enforce it, the child will have a difficult life. More than that, a child may not have a happy eternal life. A child that doesn't learn to respect his or her parents will not easily respect God or others.

This same *"obey"* principle is even true for training a dog! We let our family dog come into the house at times, but he had to stay on the rug by the door. He would try to sneak off the rug a little at a time. So we would say, "Buddy, are you on the rug?" And Buddy would quickly put his foot back and touch the rug. Or, he would just flop his tail on the rug. If we did not say anything, he would sneak further into the house! The point is that, every child and every one of us must learn to obey. God wants us to keep a foot on the rug, obedient to His will.

Prayer: Lord, You are so kind to us. You even tell us why we need to obey, because it *"pleases"* You and it blesses us also. Lord, Your ways are the best ways! We praise You for revealing them to us. In Jesus' name we pray. Amen.

June 24

"He who spares the rod hates his son, but he who loves him is careful to discipline him." Proverbs 13:24

Why should we discipline a child?

There is much confusion in the world today about the discipline of children. However, God is not confused about the issue! He uses strong language to show us that discipline is essential.

1. All children belong to God. Whoever owns the children has the right to say how to bring them up! God's ownership is clear. He says, *"every living soul belongs to Me,"* Ezekiel 18:4a. *"The earth is the Lord's, and everything in it, the world, and all who live in it,"* Psalm 24:1. God loans the children to parents to raise them His way.

2. God tells us to discipline children. *"Do not withhold discipline from a child,"* Proverbs 23:13a. This instruction is not up for debate. This is a command, not an option, not up to us to decide. God has very good reasons for saying this.

3. Discipline is a main way we show love to our children. *"He who spares the rod hates his son, but he who loves him is careful to discipline him,"* Proverbs 13:24. I hear people say, "I will not discipline my children because I love them." God says the opposite.

4. Discipline a child because they are foolish. *"Folly is bound up in the heart of a child, but the rod of discipline will drive it far from him,"* Proverbs 22:15. A child is born foolish, not innocent! King David said, *"Surely I was sinful at birth, sinful from the time my mother conceived me,"* Psalm 51:5.

5. Discipline a child to turn them away from Hell. *"You shall beat him with a rod, and deliver his soul from Hell,"* Proverbs 23:14 NKJV. The word "discipline" is part of the word disciple, part of the discipleship process. Ignore it and our discipleship in the home is incomplete!

Prayer: Dear Lord, we thank You for not just telling us to discipline, but clearly why we need to! Forgive us for not being faithful in this and continue to work change in us. In Jesus' name we pray. Amen.

June 25

"Discipline your son, for in that there is hope; do not be a willing party to his death." Proverbs 19:18

When should we discipline a child?

1. Discipline while there is still hope. Discipline changes a heart making it straight. A little tree that is crooked can be easily straightened. A big tree cannot be straightened with a big truck or tractor. A little child is like a little tree. A big person is like a big tree, not easily straightened! Not disciplining a child is to be a *"willing party to his death."*

2. Discipline is needed when the child acts like a fool. *"Folly is bound up in the heart of a child, but the rod of discipline will drive it far from him,"* Proverbs 22:15. Don't discipline a child when they spill milk or do some accident. That is clumsy, not acting like a fool.

3. A child is foolish when they question God's or a parent's commands. Know what the battle is. Your child wants to be in charge. Your child wants your chair, even God's throne. A child selfishly wants to do what they want, when they want. If we let them, they will. So then, the child is foolish when (not if) they rebel against God and the parent's authority. A fool willingly disobeys God's Ten Commandments listed in Deuteronomy 5 and Exodus 20.

Even before age one, a child needs to understand one word, "NO." They can't understand the why yet. They need to quickly learn when we say "No," we mean it. If we don't teach a child "No," and their immediate obedience to it, then we hate our child and do not care about how their life turns out! That is what God is teaching us in our text. Loving discipline works the foolishness out of a child's heart. Following God's way, there is hope for our child!

Prayer: Lord, we see Your amazing wisdom. We are so glad You know the heart of a child better than we do. For we are stubborn, even blind with our own foolish ideas! You tell us, *"There is a way that seems right to a man, but in the end it leads to death,"* Proverbs 14:12. How true this is especially concerning discipline. May Your ways be in the hearts of Your children! In Jesus' name we pray. Amen.

June 26

"Train a child in the way he should go, and when he is old he will not turn from it." Proverbs 22:6

How should we discipline a child?

1. Use some pain to discipline. *"A whip for the horse, a halter for the donkey, and a rod for the back of fools!"* Proverbs 26:3. If we control the head of a horse or donkey we can control their direction. What's true for donkeys and horses is true for children. A little pain on the backside of a child quickly turns their heart! One swat that hurts is enough. Some pain is necessary. No pain, no gain, is Biblical. Don't over discipline or under discipline. Both extremes are wrong. *"You shall beat him with a rod, and deliver his soul from Hell,"* Proverbs 23:14 NKJV. Better to feel pain for a few minutes than face an eternity of pain. The word *"beat"* means to hit, not to injure or almost kill them. One swat works.

2. Discipline without anger. This too is critical. Our anger will not build respect or obedience in a child. Fear, yes. Respect and love, no. God said, *"Get rid of all bitterness, rage and anger, brawling and slander, along with every form of malice,"* Ephesians 4:31. The reason is: *"Man's anger does not bring about the righteous life that God desires,"* James 1:20. Not in us! Not in a child! *"Bitterness,"* is a type of anger called *"demonic"* in James 3:15 NKJV. Demons don't disciple or bring encouragement. They torment to break people. Don't discipline in anger.

3. Forgive the one being disciplined. Don't confuse forgiveness with consequences. Discipline is a consequence of sin, a reminder not to do it again. The prior point on anger fits here. If we are angry or bitter when disciplining, it will be difficult to forgive the one we are correcting. When God disciplines us, and we confess our sin, He forgives us. He doesn't hold a grudge, and neither must we! Discipline, confession, and forgiveness together work for reconciliation and restoration. That is the goal of discipline. Sinners need to be restored to God and man. <u>When the act of discipline is over, it needs to be over on the part of the giver and the receiver of the discipline!</u>

Prayer: Lord, You tell us, *"those I love I rebuke and discipline,"* Revelation 3:19a. May we understand that, so we have the right attitude. In Christ's name we pray. Amen.

June 27

"But as for me, my feet had almost slipped; I had nearly lost my foothold." Psalm 73:2

I'm almost crazy!

I'm just about ready to lose it! The pressure is too much. I don't know how much more I can stand. I'm close to going crazy. These are exactly the psalmist's thoughts. We must admit they are ours at times too. The ones in the mental hospital are not the only ones who have mental stress. It's a good thing that God writes to us about our struggles, so that we can see the way out!

The Psalm starts by saying *"God is good."* Meaning, my poor mental outlook is not God's fault. God is not the problem. After saying he *"almost slipped,"* the psalmist admits his problem exists because of how he has been thinking. He envied those who he thought had it better than he did. The psalmist was thinking, "It's not fair what I am going through!" He was looking at *"the arrogant"* and *"the prosperity of the wicked."* He saw, *"their bodies are healthy and strong."* He saw others that were *"violent," "wicked,"* and *"carefree."* He openly says, *"Surely in vain have I kept my heart pure,"* Psalm 73:13a. He is saying, "I'm not so sure it is worth it!" The psalmist is feeling sorry for himself. That is a problem.

Then, he says, *"I entered the sanctuary of God; then I understood their final destiny,"* Psalm 73:17. Suddenly, he has a huge mind adjustment! The psalmist now realizes the great comfort and glory is in Heaven, not always here. Instead of focusing on the temporary blessings of God to the multitudes, he now sees the eternal blessings of God's grace to just a few, including himself! When the significance of this fact sunk into his soul, something happened! Now he says to God, *"You place them on slippery ground,"* Psalm 73:18a. He has finally moved from self-pity and the worship of self. He now worships God who is worthy of our adoration! May God help us to do the same.

Prayer: Lord, we are *"senseless and ignorant,"* when we lose sight of Your amazing grace! May we say with the psalmist in Psalm 73:26, *"My flesh and my heart may fail, but God is the strength of my heart and my portion forever."* In Jesus' name we pray. Amen.

June 28

"Each one should use whatever gift he has received to serve others, faithfully administering God's grace in its various forms." 1 Peter 4:10

What is our spiritual gift?

After becoming a Christian, God gives *"each one"* a special gift or ability to be used in the building up of His Church. The gifts come in *"various forms."* With our *"gift"* we are to *"serve others, faithfully administering God's grace."* *"Gifts"* are meant to be given! Peter lists two basic gifts: *"If anyone speaks, he should do it as one speaking the very words of God. If anyone serves, he should do it with the strength God provides,"* 1 Peter 4:11a. *"God's grace in its various forms,"* put in us by God, must flow out to others!

We say, "I don't know what my spiritual gift is?" Then we should pray and start serving others with our life. If we are a Christian, we will be given a gift to serve others. When we serve others in various ways, they will tell us how we are a blessing to them. Paul wrote three full chapters on spiritual gifts, 1 Corinthians 12-14. In the middle of his explanation on spiritual gifts we have the famous love chapter. This must shout to us that love is serving others, foundational for exercising our spiritual gift.

If we are not interested in finding out what our spiritual gift is, then we are interested in staying selfish! That needs to change because the words "a selfish Christian," do not belong together! In 1 Corinthians 12:1 Paul begins, *"Now about spiritual gifts, brothers, I do not want you to be ignorant."* Paul lists some of the gifts that make up a loving church and then adds, *"God works all of them in all men,"* 1 Corinthians 12:6b. Notice also that the Spirit, *"gives them to each one, just as He determines,"* 1 Corinthians 12:11b. This means, we do not choose our gift! God gives it! He gives speaking gifts, organizational gifts, financial gifts and to others the gift of encouragement. But the point is: *"serve others"* with our life, not self. Develop our gift of love and be a blessing to others.

Prayer: Lord, You alone build Your church. You put Your grace in us. You make it flow out of us to others. May the church get serious in identifying the gifts people have. Then, may the church encourage all believers to use their gifts for Your glory. In Christ's name we pray. Amen.

June 29

"Do not neglect your gift, which was given you." 1 Timothy 4:14a

"Do not neglect your gift"!

We just looked at the subject of spiritual gifts. Paul also wrote to Timothy on this subject. Timothy was given the gift of preaching and teaching. Paul here encourages Timothy to meditate on the fact that he had a gift from the Lord that he was to treasure and use carefully. And these same things are true for each of us! Paul knew that as we progress in the Christian life, Satan will always be right there to discourage us. Satan does not want us to exercise our spiritual gifts and be a blessing to others! Paul also knew that our gifts will wither away, if they are not used.

The words, *"do not neglect your gift"* come as a warning. Not to use our God-given gift is to abuse it. If we are not for God and what He has given to us, then we are against Him. *"Do not neglect your gift,"* because God Himself gave it to us. It is so easy to get so caught up in the cares and snares in life that we turn inward, selfish. It is then that we do not serve others. God did not give us Christ, His grace, and His blessings to become more selfish! Jesus did say, *"deny yourself."*

God gave us a specific gift to use in gathering in His children, and in discipling them! *"Be diligent in these matters; give yourself wholly to them, so that everyone may see your progress. Watch your life and doctrine closely. Persevere in them, because if you do, you will save both yourself and your hearers,"* 1 Timothy 4:15-16.

Do you see the urgency? Faithfulness matters! We must use our gift diligently to minister to others and not stop. We must not become lazy or weary. Use it or lose it. Pray about it. Look to God to bless it. If our gift is giving for the growth of God's church, do so prayerfully. If we are a pastor or a teacher in the church, prepare diligently. Encourage others with our spiritual gifts. For we are God's workmanship, created to be useful for His purposes!

Prayer: Lord, how amazing that You use redeemed, yet wicked sinners like us, to call other sinners to repentance. Lord, forgive our unfaithfulness. Make us faithful for Your glory and for the good of many lost souls. In Jesus' name we pray. Amen.

June 30

"Watch your life and doctrine closely. Persevere in them, because if you do, you will save both yourself and your hearers." 1 Timothy 4:16

"Watch your life and doctrine closely"

These are revealing words of warning and encouragement to Timothy, a young pastor. They show what is important to be "qualified" in ministry. Some emphasize life experiences, but pay no attention to doctrine. Others, emphasize doctrine, and count how we live as nothing. Both of positions are wrong! We need to watch our life and our doctrine.

What happens when leaders who are brilliant in understanding theological *"truth,"* are very proud of what they know, but not humble in how they live? They will demand that others have all their "doctrines" perfect, as if good doctrine is what Christainity is all about. Their Bible studies will be geared mostly to head knowledge! But practically, it does matter how much we pray. It does matter how much we are in the Word of God. It does matter how we relate to our family and to others. Practical, gracious living is a heart-felt response to the grace of God in us. Believing all the good doctrines of grace without living graciously makes for a pathetic believer and leader.

There are also leaders who are very kind and loving. They are great in how they deal with people. But when it comes to doctrine, anything goes! They wrongly think it does not matter what you believe as long as everybody is happy. Their Bible studies and messages are geared to keeping it light and fun. They are not willing to call sin what it really is. Rarely is anyone convicted of sin. In fact, the doctrine of Hell is never preached. Repentance is not important. What matters is that we just get along. There is no foundation for what they believe.

God's emphasis is, *"Watch your life and doctrine closely." "Persevere in them."* Keep doing both consistently! *"Because if you do, you will save both yourself and your hearers."* That is good reasoning on God's part, important for us to put into practice!

Prayer: Lord, we make mistakes in these areas. Convict us where we need a better balance between *"life and doctrine."* For we know that it will matter in The Judgment how how we lived and what we believed. Help us to focus on what matters. In Christ's name we pray. Amen.

JULY

"Trust in the Lord and do good;
dwell in the land and
enjoy safe pasture.
Delight yourself in the Lord and
He will give you the desires of your heart."
Psalm 37:3-4

July 1

"The acts of the sinful nature are obvious: sexual immorality, impurity and debauchery; idolatry and witchcraft; hatred, discord, jealousy, fits of rage, selfish ambition, dissensions, factions and envy; drunkenness, orgies, and the like. I warn you, as I did before, that those who live like this will not inherit the kingdom of God." Galatians 5:19-21

The deeds of the flesh

Our text calls these behaviors, *"the acts of the sinful nature."* All of us are born with the roots of these sinful habits in us. We have all inherited Adam's sinful nature, as Romans 5:12 teaches. These words describe the depths of our depravity! We need to know this, because apart from the truth of God, we may think we are innocent.

We have a heart problem! *"The heart is deceitful above all things and beyond cure. Who can understand it? 'I the LORD search the heart and examine the mind, to reward a man according to his conduct, according to what his <u>deeds</u> deserve,'"* Jeremiah 17:9-10. God shows us the condition of our hearts, and it's a slavery to sin problem. A slave must be set free, and God is the only one who can free us from sin and give us His righteousness through Christ.

Since we cannot see the heart like God does, we can only observe what comes out of the heart, which are the sinful <u>deeds</u>. That's why Paul says, *"I warn you… those who live like this will not inherit the kingdom of God."* If the deeds of the flesh describe our normal living pattern, then we have a conversion problem. If we are still known as *"angry," "bitter," "envious" "and the like"* we are lovingly warned, we *"will not inherit the kingdom of God."* These are God's words to move us to change!

Because the deeds of the flesh defile us, we need to study them. Because they are the opposite of living a life of grace, we need to get rid of them. Because these deeds keep us out of Heaven, we need to get serious concerning them. For this reason we will examine some of these sinful actions.

Prayer: Lord, we thank You for showing us what our sinful natures are like and how a real relationship with Christ changes our pattern of living. In Jesus' name we pray. Amen.

July 2

"For man's anger does not bring about the righteous life that God desires. Therefore, get rid of all moral filth and the evil that is so prevalent and humbly accept the Word planted in you, which can save you." James 1:20-21

Our *"anger"* is not righteous!

We make all kinds of excuses for our anger. We claim we get over it quickly. We say that God made us that way. We even say that our anger is righteous. God says it is not. Our text is clear. There are many other verses that teach the same thing. In yesterday's devotional we saw Galatians 5:19-21, where eight different kinds of anger are listed. These are all the opposite of the grace God expects to come out of us.

Ephesians 4 is one of the "change" chapters in the Bible. The first three chapters of Ephesians show us how the grace of God is put into us. Then chapters 4-6 demand that we now walk by grace! Chapter four ends in saying, *"Get rid of all bitterness, rage and anger, brawling and slander, along with every form of malice,"* Ephesians 4:31.

Putting off the deeds of the flesh doesn't save us. Christ alone does that! However, the ability to remove the deeds of the flesh is evidence that we are saved. This is why Paul ends the description of the deeds of the flesh by saying, *"I warn you, as I did before, that those who live like this will not inherit the kingdom of God."* When counseling people with serious anger problems, it is necessary to show them these verses for them to see that their anger is wrong. Until anyone is convicted by the Word and Spirit of God, they will not cry out to God in confession, or be interested in repentance.

Matthew 21:12-15 is helpful to see that Jesus was not angry in the temple. Many people say He was, and then use this as an excuse for their anger. It was the Pharisees who *"were indignant"* in that scene. We are like Pharisees when we exhibit graceless, loveless anger! May God help us to live out a life of grace!

Prayer: Lord, forgive our ugly sins of anger. We want to be examples of Your grace, testifying by our actions that You change hearts. In Jesus' name we pray. Amen.

July 3

"For I see that you are poisoned by bitterness and bound by iniquity."
Acts 8:23 NKJV

Our *"bitterness"* poisons us!

Bitterness is a very common evil. It afflicts young and old, rich and poor, male and female. It steals our beauty and beats our body and soul. Why? The devil is the father of bitterness, James 3:14-16. His demonic helpers are parasites that will eat at us until nothing is left. We will become a walking shell, without feelings. Our friends will leave us. Our life will move from empty to emptier. And while this demonic bitterness is busy devouring us, we are busy defending it! We believe we have a right to be bitter because the people that should have loved us, have hurt us! We feel alone, deserted by God and man. We want to escape a life that we say is unfair! We think we deserve so much more than what we are getting! The grudges of a bitter person are the heaviest thing we can possibly carry. A story will help us see the truth of it.

"A woman was in town shopping. She left town with her horse and wagon. It was an hour to her house and it was getting dark. She should have started earlier. Suddenly, she saw a man following her. She urged her horse to go faster to get away. She raced home in a panic, desperate to put some distance between the one chasing her. As she jumped from her wagon to run into the house, the man following her, ran to her wagon and lifted the tarp over her purchases from town. He exposed a robber with a knife."

This running woman represents us who are bitter. The man on the horse is the Holy Spirit. The robber with the knife is Satan trying to take all we have. God wants to help us, but we run from Him. We must stop our panic-filled running and turn to God, the Prince of Peace! He forgives every sin! He wants us to *"get rid of all bitterness,"* Ephesians 4:31a, and start forgiving, Ephesians 4:32.

Prayer: Lord Jesus, You were hurt more than we will ever be! When they were killing You, Your response was the opposite of our bitterness. You said, *"Father forgive them for they know not what they do."* Help us to be like You. In Christ's name we pray. Amen.

July 4

"Do not worry about tomorrow, for tomorrow will worry about itself. Each day has enough trouble of its own." Matthew 6:34

Our *"worry"* is a killjoy!

"Worry" is one of those sins that we easily get hardened to. We think it is not so bad because when we look around, so many people are worried! We even say, "I worry about my children," as if it is a virtue. In various parts of the Bible God shows us that worry is very wrong, even a sign of a weak faith. In fact, Jesus questions us on the subject by saying, *"Why do you worry,"* in Matthew 6:28a. Then to get our attention some more, Jesus calls the one who worries, one who has *"little faith."* I know that got my attention!

God is our Heavenly Father and He will take care of us! That is the message He promises to us, if we will just come to Him in true faith. The truth is, the world is not on our shoulders! It is on God's! He puts those in power who He wants in power! Nothing can happen apart from His sovereign control. The question is, "Do we trust God to be able to care for us today and tomorrow?" <u>If we cannot trust God to care for us in the present, how can we trust Him to care for our souls for all eternity?</u> This is exactly why Jesus calls worry, *"little faith."*

Can you imagine if our name was Mr. or Mrs. Killjoy Worry? That is what *"worry"* will do to us! "Worry" never solves tomorrow's problems! It only kills today's joy! A worrier demands to carry his or her own burdens, but they can't. Jesus came to carry them. The big question is, "Will we give them up?" Let us go humbly in prayer to Him who is so strong!

Prayer: Lord, You tell us openly, *"Come to Me, all you who are weary and burdened, and I will give you rest." "For My yoke is easy and My burden is light,"* Matthew 11:28 & 30. Lord, You give us a beautiful invitation! May we bring our concerns to You the King of kings and the Lord of lords! May we do as Peter advised us to do, *"Cast all your anxiety on Him because He cares for you,"* 1 Peter 5:7. We praise You Lord for being able and willing to handle *"all"* our anxieties. What a wonderful God You are! In Jesus' name we pray. Amen.

July 5

"And I saw that all labor and all achievement spring from man's envy of his neighbor. This too is meaningless, a chasing after the wind."
Ecclesiastes 4:4

Our "envy" is "meaningless"!

"Envy" harms God's kingdom. It harms others, and it even hurts ourselves. *"Envy"* is a sin! *"Envy"* breaks the tenth commandment, *"Do not covet."* *"Envy"* desires what others have, their looks, their money, their houses, their grades in school, their loving families, or possibly the gifts that God has given them. But even more than hurting others, this sin is most displeasing to God. Our envy actually breaks all the commandments of God! Plus, "envy" may well reward us with ulcers, for which we will probably take more medication. Yet still we refuse to confess it as sin! Now that is *"meaningless"*!

"Envy" is against God because it points an accusing finger at God, telling Him that He is not being fair to us. If we think that way, we claim to know more than God does about what is needed! Such pride places us above God, as if He needs to explain some mistake to us. How can God sin or ever make a mistake? God is perfect and holy! We must repent of our *"envy."*

Why "envy" is so meaningless? When we "envy," we are out of tune with the rest of God's creation! Trees live to give fruit, lumber and firewood. Plants give us vegetables! Chickens give us eggs. Their lives has meaning! When we "envy," we want to take, not give! God shows us even from nature that "envy" is meaningless! Not only that, "We brought nothing into the world, and we can take nothing out of it," 1 Timothy 6:7.

What is meaningful? *"Godliness with contentment is great gain,"* 1 Timothy 6:6. Spurgeon said, "A man's contentment is a matter of the heart, not in the extent of his possessions. God has given us gifts and talents. What we do with the gifts God has given us is what God will judge us on." That is what is important!

Prayer: Lord, we have a passion for things You have not ordained for us to have. Yet how rarely we confess our sin of "envy." Forgive us for loving created things more than You. Help us to say, "You are my portion and delight!" In Jesus' name we pray. Amen.

July 6

"For of this you can be sure: No immoral, impure or greedy person — such a man is an idolater — has any inheritance in the kingdom of Christ and of God." Ephesians 5:5

Our "greed" is idolatry!

God gets right to the point quickly. Our text is clear, *"No immoral, impure or greedy person … has any inheritance in the kingdom of Christ and of God."* We know that the impure are not bound for Heaven because we need the purity of Christ! But notice, the word *"greedy"* is linked with the *"immoral"* and *"impure."* In the KJV the *"greedy"* one is called a *"covetous man."* We will focus on 3 points.

First, a *"greedy person,"* will not be in Heaven! Three times in our text we see the certainty that a person who holds on to greed won't be in Heaven. We see the words, *"you can be sure."* Eliminate any doubt. *"Has <u>any</u> inheritance,"* none, not even a greedy doorkeeper will be in Heaven. Culture may call *"greed"* successful. God guarantees it is not profitable eternally.

Second, a *"greedy person"* will not be on earth long. How foolish to lose our health to try get more money. Then we lose our money to get our health back! What a waste of God's time and ours!

Third, a *"greedy person"* is an *"idolater."* An idol is what we worship more than God. A *"greedy person"* worships material things more than God. We chant to our Greed Idol, "More! More!" And when the "more" is in the hand it is adored! But, since Greed is like its brother Lust, it soon wants more once again! The *"greedy person"* is more in love with <u>created</u> things than the <u>Creator</u>. That is what makes greed an idol problem! When greed is our idol, there is little time left to work on our relationship with God. A rich person is not the one who has the most money. It's the one who needs the least and is satisfied with little.

Prayer: Lord expose our idols, all of them! We want to worship You alone. Convict us where we need conviction. Change us where we need changing. For the Heavens and the earth and everything in it belongs to You. And as Christians, we are the temple of the living God. Lord, may we not desecrate Your temple. In Christ's name we pray. Amen.

July 7

"Can a man scoop fire into his lap without his clothes being burned? Can a man walk on hot coals without his feet being scorched? So is he who sleeps with another man's wife; no one who touches her will go unpunished." Proverbs 6:27-29

Our "lust" is burning us!

Lust is a giant we need to slay! If we are going to defeat it, we need to use divine weapons like David ended up doing! Let us see what makes lust, pornography and impurity such a strong idol to prevent us from having a proper life.

God did not give us sexual desires to be used the wrong way. He gave us sexual desires to be used in the covenant of marriage. God loves His children intimately and covenantally. Part of the cleaving process in developing a one flesh relationship, between a man and a woman, in marriage involves sexual intimacy. God designed us to find joy and pleasure in each other, just as He wants us to find our joy in Him.

Lust and porn are from the devil, designed to steal the joy out of a close relationship with God and our spouse. Like all addictions, porn promises fulfillment, but delivers death. Porn is a lie! If we are so "fulfilled" with porn, why are we so "unsatisfied"? Why do we only want more?

Lust and porn will burn us up as we *"scoop fire into our lap."* Our spiritual clothes are being *"burned."* The result, we are *"burned,"* both in this life and in eternity! God asks, *"Do you not know that the wicked will not inherit the kingdom of God?"* 1 Corinthians 6:9a. The *"sexually immoral"* are included in the list of the *"wicked."* Perhaps you say, "This porn idol has me in chains. I just can't seem to break its control over me!" Yes, lust and porn enslaves, but Christ sets us free. The proof is 1 Corinthians 6:11! It says, *"that is what some of you <u>were</u>. But you <u>were</u> washed, you <u>were</u> sanctified, you <u>were</u> justified in the name of the Lord Jesus Christ and by the Spirit of our God."* Will we go to Him to be delivered from this idol?

Prayer: Dear Lord, we want a closer relationship with You! You are stronger than any idol or addiction. Set us all completely free by Your Almighty power. In Jesus' name we pray. Amen.

July 8

"With the tongue we praise our Lord and Father, and with it we curse men, who have been made in God's likeness. Out of the same mouth come praise and cursing. My brothers, this should not be."
James 3:9-10

Is our mouth praising or cursing?

The question before us is one of the biggest tests of the Christian life! God gave us a mouth to use it properly, not to abuse it. God has given us many good things to use for His glory, yet how quickly we can use them for evil. We have blessings of sight and hearing, but we look at or listen to things we should not. We have blessings of medicine for pain, suffering, and disease, yet how often these same drugs are abused. Even computers and the Internet are blessings, if used properly.

God is asking each of us in our text to examine our mouth. He knows something eternally important. What comes out of our mouth points directly to the condition of our hearts. *"The good man brings good things out of the good stored up in his heart, and the evil man brings evil things out of the evil stored up in his heart. For out of the overflow of his heart his mouth speaks,"* Luke 6:45. If we want to tame our tongue we need to tame our heart first.

God asks us a question in James 3:11: *"Can both fresh water and salt water flow from the same spring?"* The answer of course is, "No." God is very concerned about our speech because it points to whether Jesus or Satan lives in our hearts!

Parents teach about God and pray to Him in the home. A teacher teaches the Word of God in Sunday school. Pastors teach and explain the Word of God in church. These are all good ways to use our tongue. Then what do we do the rest of the day? It is far easier to listen to ten sermons than it is to live one! May we remember that a sharp tongue can cut our own throats just as easy as it can speak good things.

Prayer: O Lord, our hearts need to be transformed, changed into a heart like Jesus had. Forgive us for using bad words. Lord, we have a problem. We cannot change our own hearts! We need Your Spirit to get more of us, to convict us, to empower us! Lord use our mouths for Your glory and praise. We ask this in Jesus' name. Amen.

July 9

"Create in me a clean heart, O God, and renew a steadfast spirit within me. Do not cast me away from Your presence, and do not take Your Holy Spirit from me." Psalm 51:10-11 NKJV

Where to go with our burden of sin?

The first word of our text sets the tone for the next group of verses. To *"create"* is to make something out of nothing, absolutely nothing. God created when He spoke this world into existence! David here realizes nothing good is in his own heart, and how unable he is to correct his very dead situation. David cries out to God to come to his rescue! He cries out to God to remove the coldness of his heart. He cries out to God with his heavy burden of sin. He pleads with God to take the burden of sin away that he can no longer bear. David knows that it is only by God's power that he can be made alive spiritually. David would agree with the words of the song, "Nothing in my hand I bring, simply to Thy cross I cling." Where do we go with our burden of sin?

Think of the ways we try to soothe our consciences and deaden our guilt. We get super busy doing things instead of being quiet before God. We go places to add excitement instead of going to God. We watch mindless T.V. that pulls us away from God as it literally puts us in a hypnotic state. The drunkard tries to drown his sorrows. The sexual sinner looks for fulfillment in an unlawful intimate experience. The drug abuser wants to be high without a clear mind or an honest conscience. All this mindless activity is practicing spiritual yoga!

In addition to all this, we buy things we don't actually need just to feel good and then we have to take care of these things until we are too tired to seriously seek God. We have idols that steal our hearts and keep us captive! Only God can correct us. May we realize how totally ruined we are spiritually without God!

Prayer: Lord, we can't carry our burden of sin anymore than David could. Forgive us for going to so many wrong places or people to try to quiet our guilty conscience. Lord, You are our only hope! When our hearts don't desire You, create in us hearts that do! Lord, we are born children of Adam, dirty. Make us clean. Make us Your child through Your Son. In Jesus' name we pray. Amen.

July 10

"But the fruit of the Spirit is love, joy, peace, patience, kindness goodness, faithfulness, gentleness and self-control."
Galatians 5:22-23a

The Fruit of the Spirit

We should be able to tell if someone becomes a Christian. When God the Father, Son, and Spirit is alive in a heart, there is going to be a noticeable change in that life. He makes us new by reforming our mind and our conscience. God's Spirit fully gives us a new nature. With that new nature, we are given a new power source, His power! Our spiritual battery now has new cells and it's fully recharged. More than that the Holy Spirit now convicts us when we still sin, pressing us into holy living. Our old pattern of sinning, the deeds of the flesh, is going away, being replaced by new living habits. Like a productive fruit tree, there will be beautiful fruit seen. It is particularly the work of the Holy Spirit that is producing these new changes in us. The grace of God coming out of us is, *"The fruit of the Spirit."*

The first fruit of the Spirit listed is *"love."* Paul confessed as he began the love chapter, if I *"have not love, I am only a resounding gong or a clanging cymbal,"* 1 Corinthians 13:1b. Paul is saying that without love he was nothing. Without love he gained nothing. So then, the Spirit of God makes us into something! He makes us precious to God and precious to others! The love of God is the first character trait of God's Spirit in us, making it the first visible fruit. It is significant that the *"love"* of the Spirit that is now visible in us, is not selfish love, but an overflowing love for God and others, in that order. That is the perfect love in 1 John 4: 7 & 18 and the love expressed in the Ten Commandments.

Prayer: Lord, how thankful we are that You are in us. We know that we only love because You first loved us! Now we can finally be consistent in serving You and others, instead of being so selfish. We thank You for taking the deeds of the flesh out of us. We praise You for replacing it with loving graces, namely the fruit of Your Holy Spirit. In Jesus' name we pray. Amen.

July 11

"I have heard the grumbling of the Israelites. Tell them, 'At twilight you will eat meat, and in the morning you will be filled with bread. Then you will know that I am the LORD your God.'" Exodus 16:12

God can give us a feast in the desert

1. *"I have heard the grumbling."* Israel's *"grumbling"* exposed their anger, bitterness, worry, envy and greed! They forgot what God did for them. God <u>delivered</u> them from their captivity to sin. God <u>plagued the enemies</u> of Israel so completely that they even gave God's people their gold and silver. God <u>led</u> the people; they did not know where they were going. He even led them through the sea on dry ground to safety. But soon after this, the people began to grumble. It was not easy to go through the desert. But then, <u>it wasn't supposed to be easy.</u> God was testing them to see if they would follow Him obediently and trust Him in the trials of life. Our God still does the exact same things for us!

Now we are in the desert! We have some "trust issues" to deal with. Are we grumbling or thankful? Do we <u>trust</u> Him to lead us? Do we have <u>faith</u> in Him who says He *"will not let you be tempted beyond what you can bear"*? Do we <u>believe</u> the One who will *"provide a way out so that you can stand,"* 1 Corinthians 10:13b? If not, why not? *"Grumbling,"* fails a major test in life. *"Grumbling"* accuses God of not doing what is best for us. Our grumbling foolishly says that we are smarter than God.

2. *"At twilight you will eat meat."* A time of blessing is coming. God our provider is never late with His provision. But neither is He early with it either! God supplies us, *"in our time of need,"* according to Hebrews 4:16b. To the *"grumbling"* Israelites God said, *"In the morning you will be filled with bread."* It does not matter what century, year, month, day or hour it is, God promises to provide for His children. We need to start acting like His children!

Prayer: Gracious Lord what a beautiful God You are! We see our grumbling displeases You much. Forgive us for doubting Your ability to fully care for us. Thank You for giving us what we need, when we need it! Help us to see that You still make a feast in the desert. Build our faith and trust in Your precious love. In Christ's name we pray. Amen.

July 12

"He will guard the feet of His saints, but the wicked will be silenced in darkness." 1 Samuel 2:9a

God's powerful protection again

Hannah had an intimate faith with the living God. She poured out her heart in prayer and in praise for God's loving protection. She learned by faith and experience what we must desperately learn. The God of the Bible is dependable. Hannah had no doubt that God in all of His perfect attributes would be with her. This is the kind of living faith God delights in. We are on the other side of the Cross. We have seen the crucified, risen, and ascended Christ more fully than Hannah ever did. We have a full Old Testament and a complete New Testament!

<u>Hannah knew that God took great delight in protecting her, His precious child!</u> That is something to meditate on. An earthly father delights in wrapping his strong arms around his child when they are scared. Well, that father's delight pales in comparison to how much God delights and is especially honored to protect His children. It is every father's responsibility to protect their children. By covenant, it is also God's responsibility to protect us.

"He will guard the feet of His saints." "Feet," in Israel's culture were untouchable. No one touched another person's foot! Feet were nasty. They stepped in all kinds of vile things! Yet God even notices and protects dirty feet! Our text promises it. Jesus washed the feet of His disciples in John 13. We are disciples of this same God!

The transformed, bold and wandering Peter also wrote about his absolute confidence in God's protection. May Peter's statement of faith be ours! We list it here as our prayer.

Prayer: *"Praise be to the God and Father of our Lord Jesus Christ! In His great mercy He has given us new birth into a living hope through the resurrection of Jesus Christ from the dead, and into an inheritance that can never perish, spoil or fade — kept in Heaven for you, who through faith are shielded by God's power until the coming of the salvation that is ready to be revealed in the last time,"* 1 Peter 1:3-5. In Jesus, our Savior's name we pray. Amen.

July 13

"What do righteous and wickedness have in common? Or what fellowship can light have with darkness? What harmony is there between Christ and Belial?" 2 Corinthians 6:14b-15a

Mrs. Church must divorce Mr. Psychology

The church is the bride of Christ! But the bride has not been very faithful. Mr. Psychology has come along and has successfully sweet-talked her into having an intimate affair! The problem is, Mrs. Church does not think the affair is all that serious. Well, Jesus Christ, her Husband sees her hand-holding with Mr. Psychology. As a jealous God, He is not happy about it! You may think that this is not an accurate picture of the relationship the Church has with psychology. I believe the situation is even more serious and there is adultery going on! May Christ and God's Word speak to you about this relationship because it is killing us and our Christian brothers and sisters too!

Psychology is basically about man's way of living. The many psychologists do not agree with each other, yet their agenda has a common theme. Elevate man. Love yourself more. Then we will be well!

The Bible is God's way of living. The consistent message is: love God the Father, the Son, and the Spirit, and secondly love others. Deny yourself. How radically different from man's way of living!

In the course of history, the church has recognized many intrusions that try to rob her of true worship and holy loving. Yet she sleeps on this issue! To even speak negatively about psychology is to be treated as if you're a racist or ignorant. In fact, psychology has so invaded the church that it is even fashionable for a Christian to get a degree in it! Dear friends, psychology's goal is to make the Bible's truth irrelevant! Pastors and church leaders, please beware, these false prophets are working to replace you! They think they must minister to the souls of men. The next 14 devotions help to show us God's help for our sick souls.

Prayer: Lord please open our eyes we pray. You clearly said, *"There is a way that seems right to a man, but in the end it leads to death,"* Proverbs 14:12. Lord give us the heart to live Your way. Then teach us to live Your way! For we want to grow in holiness and be a blessing to Your eternal kingdom. In Christ's name we pray. Amen.

July 14

"'For My thoughts are not your thoughts, neither are your ways My ways,' declares the LORD. 'As the Heavens are higher than the earth, so are My ways higher than your ways and My thoughts than your thoughts.'" Isaiah 55:8-9

How selfish man failed Biblically

We will compare what psychology has to offer and then what Christ and the Bible has to offer. To do so, we need a clear picture of exactly how far man has fallen. We need to know what Adam's sin did to each of us. Then we can understand what must be fixed!

1. Man failed spiritually. God told Adam, *"For when you eat of it you shall surely die,"* Genesis 2:17b. Man separated from God spiritually.

2. Man failed physically. When man ate from the tree, he physically gave into self-gratification and self-exaltation, Genesis 3:6-7.

3. Man failed mentally. Man hid in the garden and was afraid in Genesis 3:8-10. Fear, worry and anxiety are now in man forever!

4. Man failed socially. The man blamed the woman and the woman blamed the serpent in Genesis 3:12-13. Social problems are here!

5. The environment failed! God said to man, *"cursed is the ground because of you,"* in Genesis 3:17-19. And it will keep failing!

6. Man failed interpersonally. Cain kills Abel in a fit of anger in Genesis 4:4-5 & 8. To this day man fails to love his brother!

7. Man failed personally. Cain refuses to repent in Genesis 4:9-12 and forever wanders in the wilderness of sin.

8. Man failed universally. Adam, *"had a son in his own likeness, in his own image,"* Genesis 5:3b. Adam's sin passes on to all as Romans 5:12 clearly expresses. Man is no longer holy. He can't be in the presence of a holy God. So God drives man out of the Garden of Eden, out of Heaven itself! God places *"a flaming sword flashing back and forth to guard the way to the tree of life,"* Genesis 3:24b.

Can psychology restore man to God? No but Christ can!

Prayer: Lord, You have the answers to life and death. Jesus said, *"I am the way and the truth and the life. No one comes to the Father except through Me,"* John 14:6. Lord, what man can't possibly do, You did in the person of Your Son! In His name we pray. Amen.

July 15

"Jesus replied: 'Love the Lord your God with all of your heart and with all of your soul and with all of your mind. This is the first and greatest commandment. And the second is like it: Love your neighbor as yourself. All the Law and the Prophets hang on these two commandments.'" Matthew 22:37-40

Man's way of living exposed! Part 1

There are a number of critical points in which the Bible shows how man is on the wrong road. We will look at these.

1. The love of self must be last, not first. Anyone who says that we must love self more to solve our personal problems is wrong. Self-esteem, self-exaltation, self-gratification, self-worth, self-assurance, self-assertiveness, self-confidence and self-righteousness kill us spiritually. Does anyone really hate themselves? The Bible says, *"No one ever hated his own body, but he feeds and cares for it, just as Christ does the church,"* Ephesians 5:29.

Adam's first sin was to please self and it has not stopped! Try telling a drunkard, an adulterer, a thief, even a depressed person, that they need to love themselves more. That is their problem. And it's ours too. This theology permeates our schools and churches. I was in an adult Sunday School class in a conservative church. When asked, 25 out of 30 people believed that you needed to love yourself more and first, before you can possibly love God and others! Dear friends, that is the Bible completely upside down!

Jesus Christ, the Wonderful Counselor, is very clear in our text. Loving God first and others second is the order of the Ten Commandments, the whole Old Testament, and taught here in the New. In fact, our text is a basic summary of the whole Bible. We are to love God first, others second, and this puts self in the last position!

Prayer: Merciful Lord, You told us many times to beware of those men who will creep into the church to destroy it. Lord, we are being assaulted with thoughts that are not Yours. Open our eyes to every error because Your Truth alone sets us free! In Christ's name we pray. Amen.

July 16

"Why do you look at the speck of sawdust in your brother's eye and pay no attention to the plank in your own eye? How can you say to your brother, 'Let me take the speck out of your eye,' when all the time there is a plank in your own eye? You hypocrite, first take the plank out of your own eye, and then you will see clearly to remove the speck from your brother's eye." Matthew 7:3-5

"Hypocrites" try to change others, not self! Part 2

After evangelism, discipleship must begin with this verse. If we miss Jesus' point here, all discipleship will go in the wrong direction! See a picture of the truth. We have a log in our own eye. A log is 6 to 20 feet long. We cannot reach our brother from this distance to remove a *"speck"* from his eye. We can't even see him to *"remove the speck."* So, we must judge our own life. Change ourself first. This is 100% true for every counselor, counselee, pastor, teacher student, worker or parent.

2. Some say our problems are from what others have done to us, so change them first. Our parents or children are the problem. Society is the problem. Classmates, workers, bosses are the problem. Even demons are the problem! Notice, how some think our problems are basically outside of us! In Ezekiel 18:2 there was a psychological saying going around that said the fathers were drunks, so the children were not able to live a proper life! The implication is: leave the children alone, they're victims. Don't even expect them to change! God hated this theology so much that He said: *"As surely as I live, declares the Sovereign LORD, you will no longer quote this proverb in Israel,"* Ezekiel 18:3. Today, even the church has embraced this proverb!

God knows our problems are in us, in our hearts. God says, "Don't try change your wife, husband, child, father, or mother without first changing yourself." That girl did not cause our lust. Our hearts did! Others did not make us angry. Our hearts did. Difficult conditions did not cause our fear. Our hearts are bitter. Our depression is not because our spouse cheated. Our hearts are bitter. God in His love shows us that our hearts are the bigger problem. This Biblical principle is so critical in true Biblical discipleship. The "victim mentality" prevents change!

Prayer: Almighty Lord, we need Your wisdom to change from man's way to Your way. Fill us with Your Spirit. In Jesus' name we pray. Amen.

July 17

"God... commands all people everywhere to repent." Acts 17:30b

Change yes, but into what?

We will get little argument when we say that people need to change! Because as we look around, almost everyone is involved in the change process in one way or another! The disagreement comes when we discuss what we should be changed into! The drunk and addict have another opinion! *"Repent"* is God's idea, also called Biblical change.

To understand repentance we need to go back to the beginning of created man, to Adam! God made man good, in His own image. But then "good" man sinned and became bad! Why? Because man was initially created with a free will! But he used that free will to sin! Already in Genesis 6:5 we read, *"The Lord saw how great man's wickedness on the earth had become, and that every inclination of the thoughts of his heart was only evil all the time."* Now that is quite a statement! Man's free will is no longer free. Man's will now is only to sin, all the time! What needs to change then is man's will to sin! Christ alone changes that will by giving us a new heart. That is the Gospel message!

We reviewed this brief history of creation and our fall into sin because it is essential to see the truth of what our real problem is, and what we all need to change into. In the next few devotions we will look closely at what Biblical change looks like. Christ alone changes us in justification, that one time salvation event. There is a specific process outlined for us in the Bible that explains our ongoing sanctification, our day-to-day repentance.

We are looking at God's process of change because it is so little understood and practiced, even in the church! That is exactly why people continue to struggle with serious "issues." This is also why church leaders in frustration hand over the souls of church members to those who do not teach Biblically.

Prayer: Dear Lord, we look forward to examining Your ordained process for Your children to change and grow in grace! Help us to understand and apply this knowledge to our hearts. In Jesus' name we pray. Amen.

July 18

"The heart is deceitful above all things and beyond cure. Who can understand it? I the LORD search the heart and examine the mind, to reward a man according to his conduct, according to what his deeds deserve." Jeremiah 17:9-10

Three things that need to change

Many verses teach about repentance, which is Biblical change. Our text highlights the number one thing that must always change, the heart! However, three things in all must change: 1. Our heart, 2. Our thoughts, words, and actions, and 3. Our feelings must change. This is a basic outline of repentance. This outline is just as true for Christians as it is for non-Christians. This means it is just as true for evangelism as it is for discipleship. Learning how to help someone move from the least important feeling level, to the most important heart level is critical!

Preachers and teachers speak much about the condition of the heart! But a problem quickly comes when we fail to teach how the heart relates to what we do, and then, to how we feel! Such an omission is out of touch with our daily life and normally not very friendly! Other teachers focus on the 3rd level, the feelings. They never get to the 1st level, the heart issues. They are friendly, but lack sound doctrine!

The truth is: the condition of 1. our hearts, leads to 2. our thoughts, words, and actions. These in turn lead to 3. how we feel. All three levels are connected! Sinners that are concerned about how they feel and want only to change their feelings, can easily get into drugs, alcohol and other serious issues.

God in Trinity, teaches us that our feelings or emotions can only change Biblically when our thoughts, words and actions change first! God counseled Cain, *"Why is your face downcast?* (feelings) *If you do what is right,* (actions) *will you not be accepted?"* Genesis 4:6b-7a. Cain was depressed! To change his feelings, God pointed to what he did, his wrong thoughts, words and actions! God started with Cain's feelings and worked towards the condition of his heart.

Prayer: Dear Lord, You know our hearts are sinful and beyond cure without the blood of Jesus Christ! Yet with a new heart, we can change and glorify You! We praise You for Your process of change that is made possible. In Jesus' name we pray. Amen.

July 19

"All Scripture is given by inspiration of God, and is profitable for doctrine, for reproof, for correction, for instruction in righteousness, that the man of God may be complete, thoroughly equipped for every good work." 2 Timothy 3:16-17 NKJV

Four ways God's Word changes us!

God works through His Word and Spirit to change our hearts. He gives us the direction and power we need, to be what He created us to be. The Bible is like a manual for living. Our text lists four distinct ways the Scriptures must be applied to our lives.

1. *"Doctrine"* – The Bible teaches about man's fall into sin and God's divine redemption to restore us once again. We learn that we are all born sinners, under the wrath of God! Adam knew this after one sin! He tried to work his way back to God, but couldn't. God saved him by shedding innocent blood to cover his sin and made him righteous.

2. *"Reproof"* – The Bible reproves or convicts us! It tells us what is wrong in our life! The Bible calls sin by its right name! The world increasingly tries to rename sin as a disease, disorder, stress, tension, anything but sin, anything but confessing it. Thus, there is very little *"reproof"* resulting in very little change! If we are not willing to use the Word of God to convict, do not expect to see much change!

3. *"Correction"* – The Bible corrects us. God not only tells us what is wrong, He also tells us what is right! God's Holy Spirit gives us guilt when we are wrong, joy when a Biblical correction is made! A change in behavior apart from the Bible is not freedom but is a continued slavery to sin problem. Christ gives us His wisdom and power to change!

4. *"Instruction in righteousness"* – This righteousness is a new pattern of living God's way. God's good *"doctrine,"* His right *"reproof,"* His perfect *"correction,"* moves us to the center of His will for our lives so that we stay on the path of righteousness!

Prayer: Lord, we praise You for being the Author and the Perfecter of our faith. You tell us the truth. You gently rebuke us when we are wrong. You graciously change our hearts. You set us straight again. You continue to move our feet to Your paths of righteousness. How great You are! How blessed we are! In Jesus' name we pray. Amen.

July 20

"Then the Lord said to Cain, 'Why are you angry? Why is your face downcast? If you do what is right, will you not be accepted? But if you do not do what is right, sin is crouching at your door; it desires to have you, but you must master it.'" Genesis 4:6-7

Can depressed people change?

I'm shocked! Even many "church people" think depression is some kind of disease! You hear, "She has some real issues, but she suffers from depression. Meaning, she has a disease and cannot help herself! But, if she takes her three medications on time, she is okay! Then from time to time, her doctor has to "adjust her chemicals," and use different medication. From the world's view, depression has little to do with a pattern of living that needs to change!

The person has periods of "mood swings" between mania highs and the depression lows that are often abrupt. This should bring up a question! What is a "mood swing"? Is it not a description of how we feel? Where does a feeling come from? It comes from how we think, speak or act! "Moods" are a direct response to a thought, word or action. Why do we try to change someone's mood with medication? Would it not be wiser to change the thoughts, words or actions instead of drugging a person to be in a "better mood"? The argument that some can't help what "mood" they are in, is twisted logic that God doesn't accept.

Cain's *"face was downcast."* He was in a depressed mood. Why? We know he was *"very angry."* God said to him, *"If you do what is right will you not be accepted?"* God knew if Cain did right, his mood would change. God knew Cain's angry actions caused a reaction in how he felt. God held Cain accountable for his thoughts, words and actions. Why don't we? How did we get to the point where we excuse so much behavior by calling it a disorder or a disease. There are legitimate diseases! But how we live is still important.

Prayer: Lord, we think we are not being judgmental when we call some behaviors diseases or disorders. But by doing so we have judged You to be a liar about what is sinful, and about what You want to change in us. Help us to see that our wrong actions have consequences that need to change. In Jesus' name we pray. Amen.

July 21

"Then he who had received the one talent came and said, 'Lord, I knew you to be a hard man...' 'And I was afraid, and went and hid your talent in the ground. Look, there you have what is yours.' But his lord answered and said to him, 'You wicked and lazy servant.'"
Matthew 25:24-26a NKJV

He was not in the "mood" to be faithful!

Because of it's importance, we continue yesterday's discussion. Jesus gives us two pictures or parables in Matthew 25 to show us the need of working wisely for the kingdom of God. In the first parable we see five *"foolish"* virgins and five who were *"wise."* The wise were disciplined in their preparation to meet the bridegroom, Jesus. Their faithful living habits grew out of their true faith! The *"foolish"* five claimed a true faith, but they refused to exercise it! They were simply, "not in the mood" to be faithful, and lived accordingly to how they felt!

In this second parable there were three servants. Two were faithful, exercising true faith in preparation for the Master's sure return! The third servant was not faithful! Why? What was his problem? He knew the Master! He knew the Master was coming back again! He knew he was required to exercise his faith! His reason in our text for not being faithful was his fearful and worried "mood." He didn't "feel" like working, so he didn't. He thought, "life is too hard" and "I can't." Like the foolish virgins, he sat on his hands! And this is exactly why, when the Master returned, He called this unfaithful servant, *"wicked and lazy."*

Fast forward to today. This "not in the mood" man gets some pills to feel better. Some say this man will now faithfully do his duties in life. Will he? Does the drunk who regularly "fixes his feelings" become a better worker? What if our "bad moods," are feelings of guilt, given by the Holy Spirit for some sin? Will not the pills to some extent, just cover up the feelings of guilt? So then we still sin, but we just feel better about it. Is the depressed person who is now on the heavy meds, suddenly faithful in his relationships and responsibilities? Pills are not wrong, but a lack of repentance is.

Prayer: Lord, in verse 30, You *"cast the unprofitable servant into outer darkness."* Lord, we don't want to go there. Make us love You with all of our heart. Help us change. In Jesus' name we pray. Amen.

July 22

"You were taught, with regard to your former way of life, to <u>put off</u> your old self, which is being corrupted by its deceitful desires; to be made new in the attitude of your minds; and to <u>put on</u> the new self, created to be like God in true righteousness and holiness." Ephesians 4:22-24

God's process of Biblical change

Notice that the first three chapters of Ephesians are all about how we have been saved by the grace of God. Grace specifically means that God moved to us while we were dead and sinning! By grace, God gave us a new heart along with a new power to change. Now, with His grace in us, here in chapter 4, God demands that His grace flows out of us, as we live differently!

Immediately after telling us that we need to put off the old nature and put on the new one, God gives us some examples. In verse 25, telling lies are put off, speaking the truth is put on. In verse 28 stealing must be put off; getting a job and giving to those in need must be put on. And finally all anger and bitterness must be put off, kindness and forgiveness must be put on in verses 31-32.

As simple as this process is, this is exactly where people fail and many even in the church just don't get it. What is needed is to see that God's process of "put-off and put-on" is for every sin, for every sinner. We do not need to understand how to overcome every sin individually. We must understand the <u>process</u> to overcome every sin! We are looking at that process.

The put-off must happen first. Sins like lying, cheating, stealing, anger, fear, and worry are areas that need to be confessed specifically. We must tell God in detail what we have done wrong. Not to inform God, but to tell God that we now agree with Him about what is sin. Forgiven of in the past, we must now change in the future! If we do not confess and put off the old sinful habits first, it is as foolish as putting perfume on a stinking garbage pile. We must remove the sin garbage, then replace it with God's sweet-smelling change.

Prayer: Lord, convict us by Your Holy Word. Empower us by Your Holy Spirit. Make us able and willing to change into Your holy people. Forgive us where we have failed. In Jesus' name we pray. Amen.

July 23

"Be made new in the attitude of your minds; and to <u>put on</u> the new self, created to be like God in true righteousness and holiness."

Ephesians 4:23-24

Putting on the new self God's way

After putting off the old sin habit, focus on the Biblical *"put on,"* then we will change! This means putting all our attention on the new thoughts, words and actions! Why? <u>Focusing on the put-off prevents change!</u> For example, don't say, "I am an alcoholic, I'll always be an alcoholic." Don't focus on anger and bitter thoughts. We don't have a right to be angry just because someone hurt us. That is a victim mentality and self-pity! If I asked you to fix a picture of a lion firmly in your mind, and then said, "Don't think of the lion anymore," yet I keep saying "lion, lion!" You can't put the lion out of your mind! But, if you replace the lion with a cow and concentrated on that, you would have replaced it! This is a huge principle for all.

A friend was a deep-sea diver/welder. Before going down in the water to work, the team needed to plan their dive, and then dive their plan. In that way, in the confusion that will come, they would focus on what needs to be done. This is what each of us must do in our daily relationships and responsibilities. Focus on living out God's plan for our life.

A former drunk or drug user must not concentrate on how good it would feel to do the sin. They must <u>replace it</u> by focusing on what must be done to live God's way. Follow that plan no matter what! We all have many choices. We either focus on what we should not do, or on what we must do. For example, turn off the T. V. and instead concentrate on our school work or house work, <u>and do it with the right attitude also</u>. Thank God for the relationships we have and then work to improve them. Be a blessing to others. Plan how we are going to be a blessing, then do it, regardless of how we feel. That is how to change.

Prayer: O gracious Lord, Your wisdom shows us the right path of real Biblical change. You give us a relationship in Christ. By Your Spirit, You give us joy and peace when we walk Your way. You give guilt and sadness when we don't walk Your right paths. You are truly the Author and Perfecter of our faith. We praise and thank You! In Christ's name we pray. Amen.

July 24

"When He comes, He will convict the world of guilt in regard to sin and righteousness and judgment: in regard to sin, because men do not believe in Me." John 16:8-9

From evangelism to discipleship, Part 1

God created man perfect. Adam with his free will sinned and started to experience serious problems. God in His grace provided a way for man to be restored. We still need a Biblical approach to solve our problems.

When people seek help, their first words often are: "Please help me, I'm feeling terrible!" Notice how they are focused on their feelings! To do evangelism, we must keep in mind that how a person feels is directly related to what they are doing! We will present three counseling examples. First, an unbelieving man was filled with guilt, and he knows why! The second is a lady filled with guilt but won't admit it. She is a church member, but probably not a Christian. Third, we will look at a pastor who doesn't quite get it. We must lead them all to the Cross! For our use here, this is greatly summarized.

The Man: "I have horrible suicidal feelings that keep coming. Please help me. What can I do?" This is a forty-year old Hindu man.

Counselor: "What did you <u>do</u> that caused you to feel so bad?" Notice that we did not dwell on his feelings but immediately moved the discussion to a deeper level by seeking out what he did.

Man: "I have done a very foolish thing. I am a doctor. Years back, I put a 17 year old girl under sedation, then I abused her. She didn't know, but the next day her mom saw her health condition. I ran from that place! Now because of guilt and fear, I cannot hold a job. After one month I get afraid and run. My wife has also left me."

Counselor: "What did you <u>do</u> to your wife?"

Man: "I beat her and smashed the T.V. her dad gave as a gift."

Counselor: "Yes, you are guilty and you know it! You have "smashed" a lot of people, and things! Did you know that your heavy guilt is from God's Spirit that is chasing you? His Spirit is after your spirit! You are running from God. But God's Spirit is leading you to the Lord Jesus Christ where your guilt can be taken away, then your healing begins."

Prayer: Lord, thank You for Your Holy Spirit who convicts us of our sin and leads us to the Great Physician! In Jesus' name we pray. Amen.

July 25

"Why is your face downcast? If you do what is right, will you not be accepted? But if you do not do what is right, sin is crouching at your door; it desires to have you, but you must master it." Genesis 4:6b-7

So lost, and they don't know it, Part 2

We are moving a man from how he <u>feels</u>, to his <u>thoughts, words and actions</u>, then finally to the <u>condition of his heart</u>. If the heart changes, the thoughts, words and actions will change. Then finally, the feelings will start to change.

Man: "I know I am very guilty, very angry, and have done bad things. I have ruined others. I want to change, but I can't."

Counselor: "Correct! You can't change your heart because you are a <u>slave</u> to sin. You need a new heart. If God gives you a new heart, you will be able to walk His way and change how you live."

Man: "Can I buy a new T.V. and fix the problem with my wife?"

Counselor: "If you were perfect the rest of your life you couldn't make things right with your wife or this girl that you hurt. You need forgiveness for what you did! You have a far bigger problem than your wife and this girl. You have sinned against a holy God who holds you accountable!"

Man: "What can I do?" This man's solution is the Gospel message, which is in the middle of the next story as their need is the same!

Church Lady: "My headaches are killing me. I can't take it anymore. Please help!" (This lady of 40 thinks her pain is her biggest problem).

Counselor: "Why are you so miserable?" (Digging for what she's doing).

Lady: "I have so much tension in my life." (She stays on her feelings).

Counselor: "Why do you have all this tension?"

Lady: She finally admits she is not living with her husband...

Counselor: (He thinks to himself, "She believes she is a Christian. If I ask her if she is, she will say 'Yes.' So I will ask a question.") "If you should die today, why should God let you into Heaven?"

Lady: "Because I have been a good mother to my two children."

Counselor: "Great, but God will not let you into Heaven for that!"

Counselor: "Let me show you a few verses so you may know why."

Lady: "Yes, please tell me."

Prayer: Lord, we thank You for Your Word and Spirit who work to bring people to the Cross. In Jesus, our Savior's name, we pray. Amen.

July 26

"For Adam and his wife the LORD God made tunics of skin, and clothed them." Genesis 3:21 NKJV

The way to the abundant life, Part 3
No one can change their thoughts, words or actions without a change of heart first. That is why we tell the Gospel message now.

Counselor: "In the beginning there was a perfect world. There was no sin of any kind. Man walked and talked with God in sweet fellowship. God gave one command to man: *'And the LORD God commanded the man, saying, "Of every tree of the garden you may freely eat; but of the tree of the knowledge of good and evil you shall not eat, for in the day that you eat of it you shall surely die,"'* Genesis 2:16,17 NKJV."

Hindu man: "What happened, did they eat of that tree?"

Counselor: *"'When the woman saw that the tree was good for food, that it was pleasant to the eyes, and a tree desirable to make one wise, she took of its fruit and ate. She also gave to her husband with her, and he ate,'* Genesis 3:6 NKJV. This was the first sin in the world. Man is now separated from the presence of a holy God. Since then, as children of Adam, we are all born sinners. The Bible says, *'Therefore, just as through one man sin entered the world, and death through sin, and thus death spread to all men, because all sinned,'* Romans 5:12 NKJV."

Counselor: "Do you know what Adam and Eve did when they realized they were sinners and God had left them?" **Lady:** "Yes, they hid."

Counselor: "Correct, but before that the Bible says, *'Then the eyes of both of them were opened, and they knew that they were naked; and they sewed fig leaves together and made themselves coverings,'* Genesis 3:7 NKJV. They tried to cover their own sin! Dear lady, you've been doing the same thing. Adam picked a leaf. You think, raising your children well can cover your sin. God could not accept Adam's work payment for sin, nor can He accept yours. But now see the love and mercy of God for Adam and Eve, and for us too. Since Adam could not cover his sin, God in grace covered it for him. *'For Adam and his wife the LORD God made tunics of skin, and clothed them,'* Genesis 3:21 NKJV."

Prayer: O Lord, You shed the blood of an innocent animal to cover the sin of Adam and Eve. How gracious You were to them and to us in Christ Jesus. We worship You. In Jesus' name we pray. Amen.

July 27

"For the life of the flesh is in the blood, and I have given it to you upon the altar to make atonement for your souls; for it is the blood that makes atonement for the soul." Leviticus 17:11 NKJV

To Jesus, the only way, Part 4

God killed an animal. It was the first death of any kind in the world and the first sacrifice for the sin of man! By this we also know why evolution is not true! There was no death after death for millions of years! *"Just as through one man sin entered the world, and* <u>death through sin</u>*, and thus death spread to all men, because all sinned,"* Romans 5:12 NKJV.

Sacrifices for sin covered the whole Old Testament period. God accepted the blood of an innocent animal as a covering for man's sin. **Man:** "How could an animal's blood forgive sin?" **Lady:** "Why did God have to shed blood and kill an innocent animal?" **Counselor:** "Those are good questions. Everything in the Old Testament points to Christ. God explains it this way: 'For the life of the flesh is in the blood, and I have given it to you upon the altar to make atonement for your souls; for it is the blood that makes atonement for the soul,' Leviticus 17:11 NKJV. Remember it is God that we sin against. Thus only God can approve the payment for sin. He accepted innocent blood to pay for guilty blood! And please remember, you too have sinned against God and your sin must be paid for! God's not cruel. He's holy!"

"One day after thousands of years of animal sacrifices, God said, 'My only Son, Jesus, will shed His own blood and become the perfect Lamb of God who will take away the sin of the world.' Jesus lived a perfect life. He was killed on the Cross even though He was innocent. His blood was poured out as a sacrifice for those who believe. *'John saw Jesus coming toward him, and said, "Behold! The Lamb of God who takes away the sin of the world!"'* John 1:29 NKJV."

Man: "But why is Jesus the Lamb of God?"

Prayer: Merciful Lord, we have a sin problem. We need Jesus. We need a Mediator who is a true and righteous man. We need blood stronger than the animals. We need a man who is perfectly just to do what the first Adam did not do, and what we can't do. Only God can stand in the gap to bear the awful burden of His holy wrath against our sin. Thank You Jesus, for being our Lamb! In Your name we pray. Amen.

July 28

"Everyone who calls on the name of the Lord will be saved."
Romans 10:13

Why works won't save us! Part 5

Man: "Does God know all our sins?"

Counselor: "Yes sir, *'God will bring* <u>every</u> *work into judgment, including every hidden thing, whether it is good or evil,'* Ecclesiastes 12:14 NKJV. God made us and knows everything about us. Since we cannot hide from God we need to confess our sins and ask Him to forgive our sin and replace it with Christ's righteousness. Then we will be clean!

"Dear lady, just one verse to see that even as a church member, we must still cry out to God for the blood of Jesus. This is also why, our 'being good' will not erase our guilt. God's view is: *'We are all like an unclean thing, and all our righteousnesses are like filthy rags,'* Isaiah 64:6 NKJV. *'Our righteousnesses'* here are the good works we do, to try earn salvation or favor with God. The *'filthy rags'* are a woman's bloody cloth, not a pretty picture! Our works to earn our salvation is like saying to God, 'My own blood will save me.' 'I don't need Your Son's blood.'"

"Lady, do you see what you have done? You said your good job in raising your kids will earn you a place in Heaven. God will not accept a bribe as payment for your sin. He is a Righteous Judge. You are still carrying your guilt around. You are not forgiven. You are feeling awful because your spirit aches to be reconciled with God."

Lady: "I have done that! It's true! What can I do?"

Counselor: "God was gracious to Adam and He is willing to be gracious to us. But we must ask God for His mercy and grace. He will not refuse any request."

Lady: "Do I need to go to God in prayer?" **Counselor:** "Yes, God never turns a repentant sinner away. Jesus said, *'Come to Me, all you who are weary and burdened, and I will give you rest,'* Matthew 11:28. Also, *'If we confess our sins, He is faithful and just and will forgive us our sins and purify us from all unrighteousness,'* 1 John 1:9."

Prayer: O Lord, we thank You for taking our sin and giving us new clean hearts along with the power to change. Now our thoughts, words and actions will change and our feelings too. How wonderful to have a new heart. In Jesus' name, accept our praise and prayer. Amen.

July 29

"For I tell you that unless your righteousness surpasses that of the Pharisees and the teachers of the law, you will certainly not enter the kingdom of Heaven." Matthew 5:20

A leaf picking pastor, Part 6

Something happened that really surprised me. It sheds a light on a big problem. A retired pastor came to my office in Chennai. He wanted a job. He was a decent guy. I really did not know what to ask him about his qualifications. So I just asked him that evangelism question we mentioned before. "If you should die today, why should God let you into Heaven?"

I was curious to hear why he considered himself a Christian. He quickly responded, "When I was 20 years old I went to Bible school, then seminary. By the age of 24 I started my first church. When I was 30 I already had 4 churches." At this point I stopped him. I asked him if he understood the question. He said "Yes" and then added, "By age 40, I started a school and 2 more churches."

You may remember from three devotionals back, Adam picked a few fig leaves to try cover his sin and earn his righteousness. Well, this pastor picked every leaf off the tree to cover his! He never once made reference to Christ taking his sin and receiving Christ's righteousness.

Now I can't say this man was not a Christian, but I have my doubts. He didn't give any evidence by his words that his sin was covered by Christ. Instead, by bringing up his own works he thought that he covered his own sin. The self-righteous Pharisees did the same!

What about us? Do we try to do "good things," so that God will like us and allow us into Heaven? The problem is we can't be good enough! We have sins that need to be forgiven! We are guilty. We cannot forgive our own sins by doing good! God the judge must forgive us. Paul wrote, *"For it is by grace you have been saved, through faith – and this not from yourselves, it is the gift of God – not by works, so that no one can boast,"* Ephesians 2:8-9.

Prayer: O gracious Lord examine our hearts. See if there is any self-righteousness in us. For Christ earned our righteousness by paying a big price. We praise You for Your grace to us. We serve You because of Your grace, not to earn it. In Jesus' name we pray. Amen.

July 30

"Whoever loves money never has money enough; whoever loves wealth is never satisfied with his income." Ecclesiastes 5:10a

"Whoever loves wealth is never satisfied"

We all need money to survive. We need money to tithe to God and to bless our families. The problem is with "whoever *loves* money" and "wealth." If we love money more than God, it is our god. This is a matter of the heart! When such affections fill our heart, there is no room for God. "No one can serve two masters. Either he will hate the one and love the other, or he will be devoted to the one and despise the other. You cannot serve both God and money," Matthew 6:24. When we love money, we can't serve our fellow man either. How can we serve others if we want to use them to get more?

We often hear that a poor man steals because he needs the money! Then why does the rich man steal? Why does the wealthy businessman cheat? We do so because we are sinners! "People who want to get rich fall into temptation and a trap and into many foolish and harmful desires that plunge men into ruin and destruction. For *the love of money is a root of all kinds of evil*. Some people, eager for money, have wandered from the faith and pierced themselves with many griefs," 1 Timothy 6:9-10.

We need a good test to see if we have a money problem. Do we faithfully tithe? If not, we are robbing God! God asks, "Will a man rob God? Yet you rob Me. But you ask, 'How do we rob You?' In tithes and in offerings" Malachi 3:8. God requires His children to give back to Him 10% of their wages for His work. God promises in Malachi 3:10-12 to bless His children abundantly, to protect them, and to give them a good reputation if they tithe.

A rich man gave a man just out of prison $900.00 of the $1000.00 he had. When the rich man left, the former prisoner forcefully took the last $100.00 from his pocket. We do this to God when we do not tithe!

Prayer: Lord, we have loved money too much. Forgive us for not being satisfied with what You give us! We know that Satan is the father of all greed! We do not want to worship him in any way. Lord, help us to love You more. In Christ's name we pray. Amen.

July 31

"Remember now your Creator in the days of your youth, before the difficult days come, and the years draw near when you say, 'I have no pleasure in them.'" Ecclesiastes 12:1 NKJV

Procrastination, thief of time and eternity!

Solomon begins the last chapter of his book with a summary and also a warning to the *"youth."* We can tell a *"youth"* that life here on earth is short, but they don't understand. They have anxiously waited to grow up to experience some of the "adult privileges." They do not think much about life being short. Solomon warns them and all of us!

"Remember now," is the warning. Don't put off knowing God and having a close relationship with Him. Solomon knew that *"youth"* have a passion for seeking out worldly pleasures instead of God. Many are skipping church. God's warning here is: don't wait for six strong men to take you to church in a coffin! Remember your Creator *"now,"* today! The devil's day is tomorrow! If you keep putting off getting serious with God, your tomorrows will suddenly end. Get going. One thing you can't recycle is wasted time.

Solomon knew the passion for life that youth have will <u>soon</u> slow down as they age. Their mental process will slow down <u>soon</u>. Every strong man's muscles will turn to flab <u>soon</u>. Every woman's soft and beautiful skin will turn to wrinkles <u>soon</u>. Your strength and beauty will <u>soon</u> fly away, so use them <u>now</u> for the glory of God!

Solomon pursued pleasures more than anyone. He was the richest, the smartest and had more women. But in the end, worldly pleasures did not satisfy him. It was his relationship with God that gave him lasting pleasure! That's why Solomon is urging his readers to live in the light of eternity. His book ends, *"Here is the conclusion of the matter: Fear God and keep His commandments, for this is the whole duty of man. For God will bring every deed into judgment, including every hidden thing, whether it is good or evil,"* Ecclesiastes 12:13b-14.

Prayer: Dear Lord, move us closer to Yourself, even when we don't desire You. Move us to that old rugged Cross! Lord may we use our strength and what beauty we have, for You! In Jesus' name we pray. Amen.

AUGUST

*"But those who hope in the Lord
will renew their strength.
They will soar on wings like eagles;
they will run and not grow weary,
they will walk and not be faint."*
Isaiah 40:31

August 1

"The evil deeds of a wicked man ensnare him; the cords of his sin hold him fast." Proverbs 5:22

What the Bible says about addictions

Addictions hurt us personally and are destroying our families. They plague the church. Addictions have greatly weakened the very structure of our society. We know that we have a problem! But what is the nature of the problem? How do addictions develop? How can we overcome addictions? We know that the Bible, *"is God-breathed and is useful for teaching, rebuking, correcting and training in righteousness,"* 2 Timothy 3:16b. But the word "addiction," is not even in the Bible.

The Bible uses a different language to describe "addictions." The Bible says an addiction is a pattern of <u>sin</u> we can't stop because it has enslaved us! Addictions start with a <u>self-imposed</u> slavery to alcohol, sex, food, money, shopping, gambling, drugs, even the Internet, and so on. After we chain ourself to the addiction, it finally rules over us and controls us. The words of our text, *"The cords of his <u>sin</u> hold him fast,"* are words that explain all addictions. Again the "sin" word is there. The closest word to "addiction" in the Bible is <u>slavery to sin</u> in Romans 6:6-7. In the coming devotions we will also see that addictions are 1. a worship problem, 2. an idol problem, and 3. demonic forces are involved.

The problem with even using the word "addiction" in our society, is to suggest that it is a disease. Then, of course, we can quickly take the next wrong step, when we claim to be a victim to that "disease." The loud implication then is, that we are not directly responsible for our behavior. Exactly what Satan and the world wants! Yet the Bible is clear. Every thought, word or action is a spiritual matter.

Prayer: Most holy God, as we look into this important subject of addictions, make us see this as You do. For You warn us in Proverbs, *"<u>There is a way that seems right to a man, but in the end it leads to death</u>."* Lord, we need Your wisdom because addictions are killing us mentally, spiritually, physically, emotionally, financially, socially and more. Lord, help us understand. In Jesus' name we pray. Amen.

August 2

"They exchanged the truth of God for a lie, <u>and worshiped and served created things rather than the Creator,</u> who is forever praised. Amen."
Romans 1:25

The "addicted" have a worship problem

All addictions are a worship disorder! God created us to worship Him alone. Let us then see the addiction problem as God and the Bible does.

1. A "drunkard" worships alcohol. Proverbs describes the behavior of a drunkard, such as in our text. The drunkard offers his or her mind, body and soul in worship to this idol god.

2. An "adulteress" worships sex. In Proverbs 5 and 7 she keeps cheating on her husband sexually and she passionately chases after other men to worship the sex idol within her.

3. A "sluggard" worships comfort. He is not interested in putting out a real effort to work in a faithful way. The life of the sluggard in the Bible is lazy, unproductive and a waste of God's gift of time.

4. A "greedy" person worships material things, including money. Their material possessions are their main security and comfort. A greedy person does not believe that God is their help and strength!

5. A "glutton" worships food. They worship food for satisfaction, for security and for companionship. God and His spiritual food are not nearly as important as their physical food!

What great pride is shown in all these worship acts. It is all about what I want. It's about what I feel like doing. How ungrateful not to love the "God" who made us. How inconsiderate not to love those in the world that God put in our lives to care about.

Prayer: O Lord, You are the Almighty Creator and lovingly care that our addictions are a worship problem. In Romans 1, You tell us that we *"exchange the truth of God for a lie, and worship and serve created things rather than the Creator."* Lord, convict us to worship You. Strengthen us to love You more than anything else in this world! In Jesus' name we pray. Amen.

August 3

"This is what the Sovereign LORD says: When any Israelite <u>sets up idols in his heart</u> and puts a wicked stumbling block before his face and then goes to a prophet, I the LORD will answer him Myself in keeping with his great idolatry. I will do this to <u>recapture the hearts</u> of the people of Israel, who have all deserted Me for their idols." Ezekiel 14:4b-5

The "addicted" have an idol problem

Underneath all addiction and sin is idolatry. We think we don't have idols because we don't bow down to some image as the pagans do. But idols are not so much what we have in our hand, but what we hold in our heart! See our text. <u>God sees idolatry when our heart clings to someone or something other than Him</u>. Idols of the heart are the worship of food, money, sex, power, fame, glory, and the list goes on. In time, these idols rule over us. That's why we hear: "I can't stop gambling, drinking, or eating." How does it happen?

By nature we are very selfish. We quickly want something more exciting. People start with cheap drugs to worship the idol and that idol takes over their life. Soon they lie, cheat and steal to keep that idol. With sex, it's the same pattern. It begins with self-sex, often combined with porn. After time, experiments turn into even wilder things. Now lust has a hold on us, but get this, <u>no lust in ever satisfied</u>! Like a fire, it only wants more fuel. Any person who has sex for an idol, makes a terrible marriage partner! Many of our youth today are enslaved in lust to the sex idol, already by the age of 15. They get married at age 25. After 10 years of being addicted to the sex god, marriage will not fix their sexual addiction! We take our idol into marriage, just like Rachel carried her idols into hers! Even our spouse becomes sort of an idol because we now expect them to please us! We do not realize by truth or experience that love is a sacrificial giving of ourself to others, for their good. And then we ask, "Why is my marriage failing?" Idols, that's why! If we start loving God with all of our hearts, we would quickly find that the truth of God is the best mind-altering drug that exists.

Prayer: Dear Lord, *"recapture our hearts."* We have not loved You as we should. We want to be a blessing to Your kingdom and to every relationship we have. Help us! In Jesus' name we pray. Amen.

August 4

"Jesus said to them, 'If God were your Father, you would love Me... You belong to your father, the devil, and you want to carry out your father's desire. He was a murderer from the beginning, not holding to the truth, for there is no truth in him. When he lies, he speaks his native language, for he is a liar and the father of lies.'" John 8:42a & 44

Demonic deception goes with the idol

By using this title, I'm not suggesting all people with addictions are demon-possessed. Only an unbeliever can be demon-possessed! But even then, demons are never the <u>cause</u> of a bad heart or life. Satan <u>tempts,</u> not <u>causes,</u> any heart to go astray. He is called the father of this sinful world. That is what our text is teaching. Satan uses various idols to deceive us into living *"worldly."* 1 John 2:16-17 is also useful to see how.

When non-Christians give into the deception, they quickly have enslavement. When Christians give in to demonic deception through idols, the Holy Spirit will surely go after them and begin to convict them of their guilt. But be careful here! We must not think all those who go to church are believers! If we think that, then we will be confused when someone in the church is demon-possessed.

It is the work of the Holy Spirit to make a person holy. That is why He is called The Holy Spirit! Until Christians are surrendered to Christ in a particular area in their life, they will struggle with idols. Is not struggling for the Christian, basically delayed obedience? That is why repentance is what is needed to forsake any idol. Christ alone sets us free! So, <u>Christians are tempted by idols to derail them from being what God wants them to be. And behind these temptations there are demonic deceptions to get us to serve these idols.</u> How does Satan do it?

Satan hangs whatever bait on a hook we will find tempting! Food, money, sex, power, fame, glory, pleasures, all get put on the hook. Then he dangles these temptations before us like a fisherman. If we go for the bait, he will try set the hook to reel us in. The Bible shows us how demonic deception presents itself through idols.

Prayer: Dear Almighty Lord, we thank You that in Trinity You deliver us from Satan and all of his schemes to destroy us. If You were not our God, this struggle would be hopeless! In Jesus' name we pray. Amen.

August 5

"For the lips of an adulteress drip honey, and her speech is smoother than oil; but in the end she is bitter as gall, sharp as a double-edged sword. Her feet go down to death; her steps lead straight to the grave."
Proverbs 5:3-5

How demons use idols to lie

Starting in the Garden of Eden, Satan used demonic deception to get Adam and Eve to believe him instead of God. Our text shows his same crafty deception with the sex idol. *"For the lips of an adulteress drip honey."* What is on the hook? *"Honey."* What is the lie? It will taste good, be sweet and will satisfy you. How does she do it? *"Her speech is smoother than oil."* She is beautiful. She is seductive. She is aggressive. She is alluring. And she looks like *"honey."* But, it's all a lie! The truth is, that idol *"is bitter as gall, sharp as a double-edged sword."* It will take us to our death and to Hell. It will rob us of wealth and freedom. We may get a venereal disease and die. Fools believe the lies of idols!

If we are a youth, thinking it would be exciting to sleep around, consider what the sex idol wants to do with you in the rest of Proverbs 5. The sex idol will talk sweet things, kiss, and have sex. And the idol makes false promises! Things like: "My husband won't know," and "It will be a fun time," are both lies! The idol promises a good time in the sack, but will give death in the grave. That is a cold, dead bed, not a hot one!

The alcohol idol lies also! These are some of the lies in Proverbs 23:29, "Are we stressed out and having trouble sleeping? I, the alcohol idol, will help you relax and sleep!" Proverbs 23:31b-32 says, *"It goes down smoothly! In the end it bites like a snake and poisons like a viper."* And guess what? Now the alcohol idol owns you and you can't live without it. You awake hung over. Even then, the idol volunteers to fix you. "Take another drink. You will feel better!" The drunkard believes and gets more addicted! Why do the addicted lie so much? Because Satan is the father of lies and idols. God said, *"Those who make them (idols) will be like them, and so will all who trust in them,"* Psalm 115:8.

Prayer. O Lord, how foolish we are to put our faith in idols of any kind! Forgive us. Deliver us. Change us. You are the only way, the only truth, and the only life. In Jesus' name we pray. Amen.

August 6

"Little children, keep yourself from idols."
1 John 5:21

Turn to God, not to demons or idols!

The big question is: how does anyone stop being a sex addict, porn addict, drug addict, gambling addict, spending addict, alcohol addict, or glutton addict? The answer is; turn to God and worship Him alone. Know this for sure, all sinful habits need to be <u>replaced</u>! We can't change any addiction unless we replace the idol with something else. The world understands this to a degree. But they just exchange one idol for another. When they make an effort to get a drunk to stop drinking they end up with a <u>proud glutton</u> or one who is addicted to <u>pills</u>. That's trading in one idol for another! The Bible deals with a change of heart, because that is the problem. In the heart, we need the worship of God, by itself.

This "idol subject" is critical for evangelism and discipleship. That's why we are spending a lot of time here. Apart from God's Word and Spirit, we don't realize how idols are our undoing spiritually. We must see our idol problem from God's eyes. He sees our idol marriage as adultery, like a married couple who suddenly agrees to have an intimate affair with others. God sees our sinful love affairs as worship affairs! God is a jealous God who created us to worship Him alone. He made us for Himself.

Idols on the other hand, are not jealous! They are willing to share our soul with other idols. "Anything but Jesus" is the idol's death chant. The reason is that idols love death. Death to family. Death to friends. Death to every good thing that God created.

In review, please remember that behind addictions are idols. Behind those idols are worship acts. And behind those worship acts are demonic forces seeking our destruction. Jesus' disciple John knew this clearly. He ended his letter which focused on true religion and false teachers by saying, *"Dear children, keep yourselves from idols,"* 1 John 5:21.

Prayer: Dear Lord, we thank and praise You for telling us about such important truths in Your Holy Word. We also thank you for delivering us from idols and that You continue to hold us in Your loving arms. May we worship You alone! In Jesus' name we pray. Amen.

August 7

"If we confess our sins, He is faithful and just and will forgive us our sins and purify us from all unrighteousness." 1 John 1:9

How do we turn from idols to God?

When addicted, we want to know, "How can I live differently?" "How can I change?" "How do I get over my addiction problem?" "I don't know how to do it." If these are our thoughts, God had us in mind when He inspired the book of 1 John. We need forgiveness for what we have done wrong. We need the guilt, the penalty of our sin removed. <u>We need a new heart</u> to live differently! Jesus will forgive our sin and give us a new heart. Both are needed. Then we can rebuild our life on the solid Rock, which is Christ Jesus.

John is very direct in his solution. *"If we confess our sins, He is faithful and just and will forgive us our sins and purify us from all unrighteousness,"* 1 John 1:9. This means, we must get on our knees in private. Get serious with God in prayer. Openly admit how we have not loved Him. We must be specific in what we have done wrong. We must resist the temptation to blame others for our addictions. Pray and pray some more about how we personally have given in to temptation. Amazingly, God is always willing to forgive us.

Our sin is never too big. David was forgiven the sin of adultery and murder. Paul was forgiven for killing Christians. When Paul gave his testimony in Acts 26, he shared how Christ appeared to him, forgave him, then gave him a specific command. *"I now send you, to open their eyes, in order to turn them from darkness to light, and from the power of Satan to God, that they may receive forgiveness of sins and an inheritance among those who are sanctified by faith in Me,"* Acts 26:17b-18 NKJV. This is also God's will for our life: that we turn to Him, then work to turn others to Him. It is God's normal pattern to use weak things like us to do His will. May God strengthen us all to be an ambassador for His glory!

Prayer: O Lord, we have all had idols. Some of us more than others. We need Your forgiveness. We need Your power. We want to serve and love You alone. Please help us to learn and grow. In Jesus' name we pray. Amen.

August 8

"Do you not know that your body is the temple of the Holy Spirit who is in you, whom you have from God, and you are not your own? For you were bought with a price; therefore glorify God with your body and in your spirit, which are God's." 1 Corinthians 6:19-20 NKJV

Our body is now God's holy "temple"

In the verse before our text, we were told to *"flee sexual immorality."* We must flee all sin, but this one more than any other. Why? *"Every sin that a man does is outside the body, but he who commits sexual immorality sins against his own body,"* 1 Corinthians 6:18b. In our text God tells us why this is so important! We need to know this to help stop our sexual sin, including lustful thoughts.

In the Old Testament this subject of *"God's temple,"* was far more impersonal. We first see the *"cloud"* leading the people out of Egypt. This was God's presence. Then later in the Old Testament, the people went to the temple. *"When the priests came out of the holy place,... the cloud filled the house of the Lord,"* 1 Kings 8:10b NKJV. This *"cloud"* is the holy presence of God, inside the temple building. Today, His presence is far more personal.

In the New Testament, *"your body is the temple of the Holy Spirit who is in you."* Wow! What a beautiful change from our personal Lord. God told us to *"flee sexual immorality,"* because He lives in us. Our body is His. But there's more! Jesus bought us personally. He owns us. He paid a huge price for us, shedding His precious blood. He experienced our hell. He came alive from death, our death to sin. He intercedes for us now in Heaven. From there, He sent His Spirit to live in us. So when Satan knocks on the door of our heart, don't open the door. We must not disrupt our intimate love relationship with Jesus Christ!

"What agreement is there between the temple of God and idols? For we are the temple of the living God. As God has said: 'I will live with them and walk among them, and I will be their God, and they will be My people,'" 2 Corinthians 6:16. May we live like we are God's *"temple."*

Prayer: O most holy Lord, You claimed us by shedding Your own blood for our sin. May we not mock You like those who killed You. Instead, may we love You like You loved us! In Jesus' name we pray. Amen.

August 9

"You cannot drink the cup of the Lord and the cup of demons; you cannot partake of the Lord's table and the table of demons."
1 Corinthians 10:21 NKJV

Idols, demons, and the Lord's Supper

Since we have just studied demons and idols let us make one more application. Think of what communion or the Lord's Supper is all about. It is a real picture form of the Gospel that Jesus came to proclaim. We are literally at the table with Jesus, just like the twelve disciples were. They were one with Him, except for Judas. He gave them the bread and wine, His very own life. There was a <u>common union</u> between them, or communion. That union, that holy glue that held them together, was Christ's body and blood. And we are saved by that blood alone!

Jesus was specific in the sacrament of communion. *"Do this in remembrance of Me,"* 1 Corinthians 11:24b. He doesn't want us to forget Him, who never forgets us! By giving us this communion warning or plea, it should be obvious that it is possible to forget our union with Christ. We actually forget it every time we sin!

<u>Satan also has a cup and some bread to offer us!</u> But it is not a cup of blessing! It is a cup of curses! He wants us to dine with him, to partake with him in all that is evil. He got Old Testament Israel to dine with him again and again. He now offers us his cup of poison! He wants us to take idol bread into our hearts. He wants us to love anyone and anything more than we love God. That is the bread from Satan.

May God open our eyes to Satan's communion meals. May the Holy Spirit convict us of coveting Satan's ways. May we go to the Table with Christ, aware that He is the Bread of life. May we take communion remembering Samuel's message to the sinning Saul: *"To obey is better than sacrifice and to heed is better than the fat of rams. For rebellion is like the sin of divination, and arrogance like the evil of idolatry,"* 1 Samuel 15:22b-23a.

Prayer: Dear Lord forgive us for our love affair with the things of this world. We have provoked You to jealousy! We have acted as if our will is more important than Your holy will. We too have been *"rebellious."* Cleanse us, we pray. In Jesus' name we pray. Amen.

August 10

"In due time their foot will slip." Deuteronomy 32:35b

Sinners in the hands of an angry God

This title is one of the most famous sermons ever preached. Jonathan Edwards gave this message 275 years ago. I will quote part of it so we can see what God used to stir so many.

> "God holds you over the pit of Hell, much as one holds a spider, or some loathsome insect, over the fire, abhors you, and is dreadfully provoked: His wrath towards you burns like fire; He looks upon you as worthy of nothing else, but to be cast into the fire; He is of purer eyes than to bear to have you in His sight; you are ten thousand times more abominable in His eyes, than the most hateful venomous serpent is in ours... And yet, it is nothing but His hand that holds you from falling into the fire every moment... There is nothing to be given as a reason why you do not this very moment drop down into Hell."

> "O sinner! Consider the fearful danger you are in: It is a great furnace of wrath, a wide and bottomless pit, full of the fire of wrath, that you are held over, by the hand of that God. His wrath is provoked and incensed as much against you, as against many of the damned in Hell. You hang by a slender thread, with the flames of divine wrath flashing about, ready for the string to burn through. And you have no interest in a Mediator, nothing to lay hold of to save yourself, nothing to keep off the flames of wrath, nothing of your own, nothing that you have ever done, nothing you can do to induce God to spare you..."

> "Almost every sinful man that hears of Hell, flatters himself that he shall escape it, depends upon himself for his own security, flatters himself on what he has done, is now doing, or what he intends to do. Every one lays out matters in his own mind how he shall avoid damnation."

God is still just and holy. He must punish sinners in Hell. His holiness demands it. Knowledge of this still moves many to repentance. Jesus still saves us from the wrath of God in Hell. May we lovingly preach the truth!

Prayer: Loving Lord, convict those who do not believe Hell is real. We thank You for warning us and giving us a perfect Mediator, Your Son., Jesus. He is willing to spare us Hell's fire. May You be eternally praised for Your grace and mercy to us sinners! In Jesus' name we pray. Amen.

August 11

"Does not the potter have the right to make out of the same lump of clay some pottery for noble purposes and some for common use?"
Romans 9:21

God the Potter

This verse tests our faith! God Himself asks us this question to see if we believe in His sovereign will. *"Does not the potter (God) have the right to make out of the same lump of clay some pottery for noble purposes (Christians for Heaven) and some for common use, (non-Christians not for Heaven)?"* The question is hard! We don't like it. But then, God is the one who is asking it. The point is: He can give His grace to whom He wants. After all, He is God and we are dust, clay dust.

Let's be honest. Many of us object to the way Paul gets to the root of sovereign grace in Romans 9. In the verse after our text, we see the wrath of God, so that we see His grace more clearly! *"What if God, choosing to show His wrath and make His power known, bore with great patience the objects of His wrath – prepared for destructions?"* Romans 9:22. God's point is that one person is prepared *"for noble purposes,"* and one is *"prepared for destruction."* The example, *"Jacob I loved, but Esau I hated"* in Romans 9:13, is just part of a wider truth!

We still don't like it. Why? We don't fully accept that we all deserve death. We would rather believe that we all deserve life. Yet this truth is written for us to glorify God and thank Him for the depths of His grace to us. It's important for understanding how we must worship God.

Spurgeon said it well. "If I was asked, 'Why is a man damned?' I should answer as an Armenian answers, 'He destroys himself.' I should not dare lay a man's ruin at the door of divine sovereignty. On the other hand, if I were asked, 'Why is a man saved?' I could only give the Calvinist answer, 'He is saved through the sovereign grace of God, and not at all of himself.' I should not dream of ascribing man's salvation in any measure to himself."

Prayer: O gracious Lord, You taught us in Romans 6:23 that we all deserve death because of our sin. But You mercifully pardoned some with an executive pardon for all eternity. We worship You and sing about Your amazing grace! In Jesus' name we pray. Amen.

August 12

"Do not fret because of evil men or be envious of those who do wrong; for like the grass they will soon wither, like green plants they will soon die away." Psalm 37:1-2

The secret of contentment, Part 1

We want contentment! We strive for it. But so few people have it! Why? Part of the reason is, it is not what we <u>do</u> to get it, but what God does in giving it! Psalm 37 is instructive and has five key thoughts that show us contentment is *"in the LORD,"* and *"to the LORD."*

1. Don't worry or envy as the world does. 2. *"Trust in the LORD."* 3. *"Delight yourself in the LORD."* 4. *"Commit your way to the LORD."* 5. *"Rest in the LORD."* All are *"in the LORD,"* because it is through His Spirit that *"rest"* or contentment finally comes! But we have a problem. We can't *"rest in the LORD,"* in number 5, until we *"commit our way to the LORD."* And we can't *"commit our way to the LORD"* until we *"delight in the LORD."* We can't *"delight in the LORD"* until we *"trust in the LORD."* And finally, we will never *"trust in the LORD"* until we put off worry and envy! So then, let's first address the problem of worry and envy.

Worry is a misplaced trust, because it's not trusting in God. Worry trusts in our own ability to solve our greatest needs. The problem is that we are not self-sufficient. The Christian who thinks he or she is self-sufficient will be shown by God that He is their sufficiency! Biblical trust is about the sufficiency of God. The misplaced trust of worry and envy will never bring contentment.

Jesus called worry, *"little faith"* in Matthew 6:30. God shows us envy is a deed of the flesh, not a spirit-filled life as seen in Galatians 5. In fact, envy indicates a depraved mind in Romans 1:29. If we really want to be content, we first need to be convicted that our worry and envy are wrong. In the process of change (repentance), we must put off sin and the love of things (idols), before the love of God can be put on. We then need to confess it and put it off. Then we can *"trust in the LORD!"*

Prayer: Almighty Lord, we want to trust in You, to delight in You, to commit our ways to You, and finally to rest in You! But some bad habits need to go first, in order to receive Your contentment! Lord, forgive and help us to stop our envy and worry. In Jesus' name we pray. Amen.

August 13

"Trust in the LORD and do good; dwell in the land and enjoy safe pasture." Psalm 37:3

"Trust in the LORD," Part 2

Trusting in God is all about having faith in His ability to do what He says He will do. To trust God, we must know something about the character of God. *"Faith is being sure of what we hope for and certain of what we do not see,"* Hebrews 11:1. But faith must be tested to see if it is real. To test us, God allows a difficult situation to come. Can God do what He says He will do? Or, will we trust and have faith in our own ability to get through the trial?

Biblical contentment comes as God in Trinity gets us through the trial. *"I can do everything through Him who gives me strength,"* Philippians 4:13. Paul was content with little or much. Why? He fully trusted in God to give him what he needed, when he needed it. Trust is an intimate and deep relationship with God. So God teaches us contentment when we trust Him for it. That is exactly why Paul could say, *"I have <u>learned</u> to be content whatever the circumstances,"* Philippians 4:11b. God taught him!

Like Paul, David <u>learned</u> contentment. God convicted him and changed him also. He then confessed, *"My heart is not proud, O LORD, my eyes are not haughty; I do not concern myself with great matters,"* Psalm 131:1. <u>David no longer went to God with great demands</u>. Instead, he humbled himself before God saying, *"I have stilled and quieted my soul; like a weaned child with its mother,"* Psalm 131:2a. David finally trusted in God's wise providence and timings for his life. He learned something important, the battle is the Lord's! The big question for us is: "Are we content to belong to the Lord, trusting that He will use us as He so pleases, all the time protecting us?"

Prayer: Dear faithful and gracious Lord, we want to know Christ, to abide in Him, to live for Him! But Lord, we need to trust You more to do that. Our selfish ambition gets in the way! Lord, Paul said in Philippians 2:13, *"It is God who works in you to will and to act according to His good purpose."* So fill us Lord with Your holy presence. In Jesus' name we pray. Amen.

August 14

"Delight yourself in the LORD and He will give you the desires of your heart." Psalm 37:4

"Delight yourself in the LORD," Part 3

We want to *"delight"* in God more, but our hearts and our wills still have so many other "delights" that get in the way. May God help us and convict us. Christ must become our ambition in life. No one can serve two masters. We can't delight in idols and God at the same time. And that is what we try to do. We will not have contentment if we are so preoccupied with what God is not yet willing to give us.

Another problem we have is that we <u>insist</u> on knowing what God is doing in all parts of our life! We <u>demand</u> to know what God plans to do with our future. We just are not ready to *"delight"* in whatever God wants to put us through. When we question God, we elevate ourselves, trying to be equal with God. If we only realized, we deserve nothing from God. We bring nothing to God, to earn anything. We need to get to the point where we can truly say to God, "Nothing in my hand I bring, simply to Thy Cross I cling." That is the kind of *"delight"* in the providence of God we need.

We are like Adam in the Garden when he sinned. Adam and Eve were not content with God. They wanted more. Our hearts need to be satisfied with God if we are going to *"delight"* in Him! Christian contentment comes as a fruit of having no higher ambition than to belong to God and be totally at His disposal. That means, we have to give up our rights. We must do what is good and pleasing in God's eyes. Then, <u>we must leave the results totally up to God</u>. That point too is important. We insult God when we worry and fret about the results of our Christian service after we give it as worship to Him. That is like giving someone a gift, then asking for it back to give them a better one. May we delight in God.

Prayer: Lord, too often we don't *"delight"* in You as our Shepherd. The truth is, we do not yet fully trust in You! Our lack of contentment accuses You of doing something wrong. Lord, change us to *"delight"* in You more. Lord, work in and through us we pray. In Jesus' name we pray. Amen.

August 15

"Commit your way to the LORD; trust in Him and He will do this: He will make your righteousness shine like the dawn, the justice of your cause like the noonday sun." Psalm 37:5-6

"Commit your way to the LORD," Part 4

We have a *"commit"* problem! We don't always do things for God's glory. We do things for our own glory. We are still so in step with the world. Years ago commitment to responsibilities was far more common. Now, we are more concerned with our "rights." We may ask, "Why is there so much pain and suffering in the world?" By doing so we imply God gives out needless pain and suffering. In the back of our minds, we think that what God does for us is too little, and what we do for God is too much! We have negative minds that are selfishly preoccupied with who we are. We have a commitment problem.

What needs to change is our trusting and our depending more fully on Christ! Think of how we came to Christ. We were dependent on Him for forgiveness, for strength and for eternal life. We were so in love with His grace and mercy! What happened? Do we now depend more on "our performance" for contentment, than in "His provision"? I think so. We sing, "His grace will lead us home!" But we live more like our performance will get us there!

We must not lose sight of who God is. That is part of our commitment and worship problem. It is good to keep coming back to the attributes of God and study them. We need to review His character and promises. We need to see that He has not changed over the years. He is the same forever. The way He dealt with the people in the Bible, He deals with us. May God help us see how our pattern of living aligns with the Bible.

Listen to David, *"Commit your way to the LORD; trust in Him and <u>He will do this</u>: He will make your righteousness shine like the dawn, the justice of your cause like the noonday sun."* If something is troubling us, live for Him. Experience Him. May we learn what true happiness is, instead of thinking God is unfair. And He will make us *"shine."*

Prayer: Lord, help us *"commit"* all our ways to You, for Your glory and for Your praise. We want to fully experience what David did when he wrote our text. Fill us with Your presence! In Jesus' name we pray. Amen.

August 16

"Rest in the LORD, and wait patiently for Him; do not fret because of him who prospers in his way." Psalm 37:7a NKJV

"Rest in the Lord," Part 5

Resting in the will of the Lord is the spiritual maturity we need! It is being thankful and content with God. But the resting and waiting are hard lessons to learn. We would rather run like a chicken with its head off than wait! It is not just children that have a hard time waiting! We adults do too. We want answers, now. We want to know what to do. We are filled with tension. We can pray nonstop for a long time, not even waiting for God to speak to us. In the end, God must teach us to *"rest in Him."* for we never learn it on our own.

One of the main things God teaches us concerns our selfishness. His commandments point it out. When self is big and God is small we are ready for a fall. The psychologist Maslow was wrong. Self-actualization is not the apex of the triangle. We may say we don't believe his insane theology, but we sure do live it. We are much like the drunk, the adulterer, gambler, glutton or the greedy who live to please self. Are they content? No! They are far from it. Why? Because it's a relationship with Jesus that satisfies. "My only comfort in life and in death is that I am not my own, but belong to Him, body and soul." That's right! Contentment is a heart and soul issue. As Christians, our body and soul belong to God. He purchased us. Now we need to live like we are His possession.

Contentment and resting in God can't come to us until we realize God owes us nothing! We need our hearts worked on by God to say with David, *"Whom have I in Heaven but You? And earth has nothing I desire besides You,"* Psalm 73:25. God will eventually teach every Christian to rest in Him! God will make sure we learn contentment. He may strip us of our health and possessions just to show us that He is "more" and "better" than anything or anyone. Yes, in the end of all "things," God has something far better for us than more of this world. He wants to give us Himself, to live in us and to live through us. And when He does, we will have contentment!

Prayer: Lord, we want to rest in You and be content. Take my life and let it be consecrated, Lord to Thee. In Jesus' name we pray. Amen.

August 17

"Be joyful always; pray continually; give thanks in all circumstances, for this is God's will for you in Christ Jesus." 1 Thessalonians 5:16-18

Give thanks and pray for God's will

Can we *"be joyful always"*? Can we *"give thanks in all circumstances"*? Can we do these two things and at the same time pray for God's will to be done? These are good questions to meditate on. These are commands that we can keep with God's help. To be joyful always and to give thanks in all circumstances is all about having a right attitude in the trials of life.

We are talking about faith and trust issues! Many of us are fearful and depressed because we are not <u>always</u> *"joyful"* or *"thankful"* in all circumstances. Even though we may know these things are really important, we still have to work through them in the trials of life. So how do we remain *"joyful always"* and still *"give thanks in all circumstances"*?

There is a difference between being *"thankful,"* compared to what it means to *"give thanks"* in our text. We may not always be immediately thankful when something happens. Because we trust that God knows what is best for us, we can still *"give thanks."* That is exercising our faith with confidence in the will of God.

Jesus is our example. He showed his humanity in the Garden of Gethsemane. He said *"Father, if You are willing, take this cup from Me."* But He did not stop there! He added, *"Yet not My will, but Yours be done,"* Luke 22:42. Jesus *"gave thanks"* that the will of God is always best! Jesus knows more of the holy will of God than we do. So He teaches us to have faith in God to the point that we are *"joyful"* and to *"give thanks in all circumstances."* True faith is keeping a trusting attitude. Our great God is in control of all things at all times. And because He <u>always</u> works all things for our good, we can trust He knows best what we need, when we need it.

Prayer: Dear Heavenly Father, we want a more Biblical attitude. Give us hearts that trust You, *"giving thanks in all circumstances."* We know that a heart of grace only comes from You. Do Your holy will in us! We *"give thanks"* that Your kingdom, which includes us, endures forever. How privileged we are to be a part of it. In Jesus' name we pray. Amen.

August 18

"For since the creation of the world God's invisible qualities – His eternal power and divine nature – have been clearly seen, being understood from what has been made, so that men are without excuse."
Romans 1:20

Seeing the Creator through His creation!

God in His mercy still lets people know who He is by *"what has been made."* The creation always points to the Creator, more than a beautiful building points to an architect! Think of how insensitive it is, not to thank the one who prepared a delicious meal! Yet supposedly, "intelligent" people give credit for a beautiful day to the work of "mother nature." How that must anger God! It's worse than swearing. God's labor of love in creating everything was accomplished without ingredients. He spoke it into existence. And now, *"His eternal power and divine nature have been clearly seen."* May we enjoy the creation and praise God for it.

Our text is very useful for evangelism. Most of the world today will not read the Bible or even allow it to be proclaimed in any way. Yet we can still present God to an atheist by pointing to the creation. Ask the atheist some questions. Ask, "Where do fruits, vegetables, grains, fish and other meats come from?" "How does it happen that this variety of food is just what our bodies need?" "Do you really think these things just evolved?" Or, "Is there design and a Creator behind all the things we need for good health?" "How did the sun, moon and stars get there?" "How do we get such a beautiful balance of rain and sun to make crops and trees grow?" "Don't you see, it takes more faith, and a blind faith to believe that things just evolved." "Why do you want to deny there is a Creator?" How can you deny there is a God, yet you hate Him so much? How is that possible? "Is it because if you acknowledge the Creator, you have to be accountable to Him for how you live?"

Prayer: Gracious Lord, we praise You for giving us sufficient information about Yourself in what You created! Even by seeing created things, we can do what you have created us for, that is to glorify and enjoy You! How great You are for showing us part of Your *"eternal power and divine nature."* In Jesus' name we pray. Amen.

August 19

"The Heavens declare the glory of God; and the skies proclaim the work of His hands. Day after day they pour forth speech; night after night they display knowledge. There is no speech or language where their voice is not heard. Their voice goes out into all the earth, their words to the ends of the world." Psalm 19:1-4a

Look at the sun, moon and stars!

God speaks to us *"day"* and *"night"* from the skies. The *"Heavens"* speak every language and dialect on earth. The Bible really is the history book of the universe that God created! But what do *"the skies proclaim"*? We can see something about the character of God. We see endless sky, boundless space, made by an infinite, eternal, omnipotent, omniscient, personal and glorious God! That Someone who caused all of these lights in the Heavens to be there is - God. The <u>Cause</u> was God. The <u>effect</u> is what we see. The Heavens teach us to worship the <u>Cause</u>, not the effect, which is the sun, moon and stars that so many worship.

In verses 5-6, we see the testimony of the sun, God's greatest gift in His physical creation. Through the sun, God provides energy of all kinds to sustain life here on earth. The solar heat that the sun gives out <u>commands</u> the physical world to obey. That unending command is called the laws of thermodynamics. The God who is in absolute command of our physical world, is also completely in charge of our spiritual world! Nothing is hid from the heat of the sun. Nothing is hid from the Son of God either. The sun and the Son expose the darkness!

Think of how small the earth is compared to the solar system. Think of how small the 7 billion people are who live on the earth. Physically, we are like a speck of dust. But spiritually, through a relationship with the Son of God, we shine like stars in the universe.

Prayer: Beautiful Lord, what a gracious and merciful God You are! *"When I consider Your Heavens, the work of Your fingers, the moon and the stars, which You have set in place, what is man that You are mindful of him, the son of man that You care for him?"* How great You are. Thank You Lord for Your beautiful creation. In Jesus' name we pray. Amen.

August 20

"On the last and greatest day of the Feast, Jesus stood and said in a loud voice, 'If anyone is thirsty, let him come to Me and drink. Whoever believes in Me, as the Scripture has said, streams of living water will flow from within him.'" John 7:37-38

Two seas that tell God's message!

In the land of Israel where Jesus walked, there are two seas. There is the Sea of Galilee and the Dead Sea. The Jordan River flows into the Sea of Galilee. These waters are alive with fish. Along the shores there are beautiful trees, flowers and grasses. Animals and people come to drink, swim, wash their clothes and just enjoy the lake. It is here that Jesus fed the 5000 and did many of His miracles. He recruited four of His disciples here.

Then there is the Dead Sea. The Jordan River also flows into this sea. But the water is like its name, dead. In fact, the Hebrew word for the Dead Sea means, "Killer Sea." There is nothing living in it. The salt content is very high. The water is good for nothing. There are no fish in it. The banks are void of anything living. Why is this sea so dead? After all, the Jordan River flows into it, just like it flows into the Sea of Galilee. The difference is: the Jordan flows out of the Sea of Galilee but not out of the Dead Sea. In fact, there is no water flowing out of the Dead Sea! So now let us consider our text.

Jesus said, *"Whoever believes in Me, ... streams of living water will flow from within him."* In other words, if we are really a Christian we will have the grace of God flowing in us and out of us! We will be a blessing to many people. Our selfishness will continue to be on the way out. We will be alive because we not only receive from Jesus, we give back.

"For whoever wants to save his life will lose it, but whoever loses his life for Me will find it," Matthew 16:25. The Sea of Galilee does not try to keep the water of the Jordan, and it lives. The Dead Sea selfishly hangs on to the Jordan and it is dead. Will we selfishly keep Jesus to ourselves or tell others about Him?

Prayer: Dear merciful Lord and Heavenly Father, two seas speak volumes to us. Lord, we believe in You. Help our remaining unbelief. May streams of living water flow out from us! In Jesus' name we pray. Amen.

August 21

"Let all the earth fear the Lord, let all the people of the world revere Him." Psalm 33:8

The Creator's perfect design!

I recently read an article in a farming bulletin that points to our great Creator. It is amazing how our God is such a God of order. His creative genius is seen even in the hatching of eggs. The eggs of a potato bug hatch in 7 days. A canary's eggs hatch in 14 days. A hen's eggs hatch in 21 days. A goose egg hatches in 28 days. A mallard egg hatches in 35 days. The baby parrot comes out of the shell in 42 days. All are divisible by 7. There are 7 days in a week. Seven is a number of completeness. It is God's number!

God's incredible wisdom is seen in the making of an elephant. Its super strong legs all bend forward in the same direction. No other animal with 4 legs is made like this! God gave the elephant four huge legs that act as fulcrums to raise it from the ground easily. How could an elephant evolve from something else?

See God's attention to detail in His arrangement of sections, segments and even the amount of seeds in fruit or in a head of grain. A watermelon has an even number of stripes. An ear of corn has an even number of rows. A head of wheat has an even number of grains. God did all this by just speaking it into existence!

God causes the various flowers to blossom at certain specified times during the day. A botanist said that if he had a controlled growing condition for the flowers he could tell the time of day or night just by the flowers that were open, and by those that were shut.

If God is so particular about eggs, elephants, seeds and flowers, will He not order our lives to carry out His purposes in us? God created us to recognize Him, to love Him, to worship Him and to live for Him. By recognizing who God is, by believing what He says about Himself, we will find our purpose in life!

Prayer: O Almighty Lord, what a majestic God of order and design You are! Truly Your plans do stand firm forever. The purposes of Your heart are in every generation. All things are totally under Your sovereign control. We praise and worship You. In Jesus' name we pray. Amen.

August 22

"The LORD is acting as the witness between you and the wife of your youth, because you have broken faith with her, though she is your partner, the wife of your marriage covenant." Malachi 2:14b

Geese teach us "family commitment"!

Geese put us to shame when it comes to commitment in a relationship! We can learn so much from watching them. At about 3 or 4 years of age, the geese pair up for life. The female actually selects the male that she thinks will best protect her. A number of males will court her and dance for her. But she will select one. After this courtship, the selected male will approach the female with his head down, bowing in submission, totally committed to her for life. God shows us how they take commitment to each other seriously!

Now they begin to mate, after the ceremony. When the eggs are hatching, the female guards the nest carefully. The male protects the larger nesting area. Even before the little ones come out of the egg, they can communicate with the parents. After birth, the adults work together to care for the family of 3 to 8 goslings. They furiously protect the little ones from any danger. The male will even sleep on its feet to keep watch at night. The parents teach the little ones how to fly by running down a hill. The whole family stays together until the little ones are mature and can make it on their own. They are very emotional birds! Even if they are separated for a short time, they will greet each other and show affection.

The geese fly long distances in a V formation. The leader of the V changes every few minutes to share the work load of breaking the wind. When flying, they are constantly honking to encourage one another. If for some reason a goose gets sick or injured and has to drop out of formation, its mate will stay with them! What amazing commitment! In the event of death, the mate will mourn for up to two years. A young widow will normally find another mate.

Prayer: Lord, we learn so much from You, our Creator. You are so committed in Your love for us. May we be like You. May our commitment to a spouse be not just a sign of our love, but the cause of it! We praise You for Your love in and through us! In Jesus' name we pray. Amen.

August 23

"Go to the ant, you sluggard; consider its ways and be wise!"
Proverbs 6:6

The ant teaches us how to work!

A little boy dropped part of his cookie outside. Very soon the ants were all over it. Piece by piece the ants took the cookie to their house that was a few feet away. Soon the cookie was gone, stored by the ants for a time when they would need it. Who told them to do this work? No one! *"It has no commander, no overseer or ruler, yet it stores its provisions in summer and gathers its food at harvest,"* Proverbs 6:7-8.

The ant goes to work to build his dream house. He does not wait for someone to give it to him! If we lack the courage to work and the desire to get going, we are already finished. Our ideas of true success will never work unless we learn from the ant.

We want a good amount of provision, so that we can live comfortably. Accumulating wealth is not a bad thing in God's eyes! It is how we get it that matters. Some cheat and steal to get it. Some wait for the government to hand it to them. Many people do not seem to understand that an abundance of wealth comes from God and a lifetime of hard and smart work. The little ant teaches us not only how to work but what our attitude should be towards work!

God created us to work even more than He created the little ant to work! God was satisfied with His own work in creation. God put Adam in the garden to work. If we are not willing to work, we ultimately have a problem with God. He says, *"How long will you lie there, you sluggard? When will you get up from your sleep?"* Proverbs 6:9. If we want our dreams to come true, we can't oversleep.

Jesus said that if we had faith the size of a mustard seed we could move a mountain. We also need the commitment of the ant! We must not wait for someone to tell us what to do but to go ahead and do what is right. May we be a blessing to others and *"Be wise."*

Prayer: O Lord, You are the Almighty Creator. We have so much to learn from what You created. You also tell us in Ephesians 2:10b, *"We are God's workmanship, created in Christ Jesus to do good works."* Lord give us the strength and ability to work! In Jesus' name we pray. Amen.

August 24

"Look at the birds of the air; they do not sow or reap or store away in barns, and yet your heavenly Father feeds them. Are you not much more valuable than they? Who of you by worrying can add a single hour to his life? See how the lilies of the field grow."
Matthew 6:26-27 & 28b

Birds & flowers teach us not to worry!

The people were consumed with fear and worry about the future. They could not figure out how they were going to "make it in life!" They knew that there would be great expenses coming up. How would they pay for their children's education? How would they pay for marriages? How would they get through the present trial? It was all so overwhelming! Does this sound familiar?

We are Jesus' audience. We can't figure out life on our own any more than a flower can with no brain or a bird can with a little brain. We are blind to our real spiritual and physical condition. God says, *"The heart is deceitful above all things and beyond cure. Who can understand it?"* Jeremiah 17:9. The point is that no one can figure out life without God helping them. That is why we need to look to God. Jesus says *"look"* to the birds, and *"see"* the lily. Isn't it interesting? Part of the reason birds and flowers exist is to teach us to see how God cares for them!

We must not be so selfish. The answer to life is not in our ability to care for ourself. Our growth in our spiritual life will never come by something that is in us. Like the flower that grows, our faces need to look to the Heavens. We need to follow the sun (and Son) like the face of the flower does every day. We must raise our eyes to the source of life, God. Concentrate on Him. That is what Jesus is teaching us here.

Jesus explains how true faith depends on God. It doesn't mean we just sit with our hand out. As we pray *"Give us this day our daily bread,"* we go out. We do our daily responsibilities. It is in the doing and in the coming and going, that God arranges circumstances so that He supplies our every need! By faith and by being dependent on God, we will sing like a bird and radiate like a flower!

Prayer: Lord, You truly love us. May we cast all our anxiety on You because You really do care for us. In Jesus' name we pray. Amen.

August 25

"If a man will not work, he shall not eat." 2 Thessalonians 3:10b

Scratch up your own bugs!

Early this morning I was looking out the window and a rooster was excitedly scratching for bugs. He was pecking furiously. He must have been into a juicy pile of something good! Along comes a hen. Without even scratching once, she tries to get her beak into the bugs! Old Mr. Rooster quickly chased the hen away. Even with his pea-size brain, the rooster is smarter than some of us. We allow many non-scratching birds to eat well, year after year, and then wonder why our economy stinks. Seems this rooster has pretty good theology: *"If a man will not work, he shall not eat."*

What one person receives without working, another person must work for without receiving! What will happen if half the people get the idea they don't have to work, because the other half will support them? Will the half that is working keep pecking away at the same pace? No, not likely. They will chase away the non-scratchers! It's not that they mind sharing, but any able-bodied chicken can do their own scratching! After all, they are not helpless chicks anymore.

If we can't learn from our text or from a rooster that work is important, then may we learn it from a pig. What happens when eight little piglets suck on the mother sow? She soon gets skinny! If the piglets are not weaned by the farmer or by the mother pig herself, she would get so skinny she would die. We need a few more farmers in government. But no, what do we do? We keep adding piglets to the pig. She only has so many faucets. That number has not changed over the years. We can breed pigs to be longer and more efficient, but who can add more faucets to a pig? Unless we can grow more faucets, the piglets need to be weaned and fend for themselves. Oink, oink.

Prayer: Lord, bless those who are diligently working. Protect them! Convict those who are lazy. May they see that their unwillingness to work is a pattern of serious sin! You put man *"in the Garden of Eden to work,"* Genesis 2:15. You even show us this same principle in the way birds and animals all labor to survive. Lord, help us to understand and change. In Jesus' name we pray. Amen.

August 26

"God thunders marvelously with His voice; He does great things which we cannot comprehend. For He says to the snow, 'Fall on the earth.'"
Job 37:5-6a NKJV

Every snowflake is different in design!

Most of us have heard the saying, "You need to slow down and smell the roses." It is just as true that "we need to take the time to watch the snow fall." We need to see our Creator's hand in making every snowflake beautiful. Every single one is designed differently! Just seeing the snow softly falling is so peaceful. To see the countryside become white and clean is breathtaking! If you have not had the privilege of seeing the snow like that in person, you are missing something.

If we were to make snowflakes out of white paper, how many different designs could we come up with? Yet God makes every snowflake interestingly different in its intricate design. Perhaps that is some of what Job had in mind when he talked about the great things that God does in sending the snow.

David also talked about snow. He compared the white and clean snow to his dirty sinful life! David said, *"I know my transgressions, and my sin is always before me,"* Psalm 51:3. Our sin is always before us and before our holy God. Our sin keeps us from God's holy presence, until we confess it. That is what David did in Psalm 51.

God wants us to meditate on the clean snow to see that we too can be white and pure if we are forgiven by Him. God invites us, *"'Come now, let us reason together,' says the Lord. 'Though your sins are like scarlet, they shall be as white as snow,'"* Isaiah 1:18a. What a beautiful reality to be accepted by God, totally forgiven, 100% pure! Think too how God uniquely designs each and every child of His, just like He does each snowflake. We are designed to bring glory and honor to our God, just like the snowflake!

Prayer: Dear Lord God who makes us beautiful, we cry out to You like David did in Psalm 51, *"Cleanse me... Wash me, and I will be whiter than snow... Save me from blood guilt, O God, the God who saves me, and my tongue will sing of Your righteousness."* In Jesus' name we pray. Amen.

August 27

"For although they knew God, they neither glorified Him as God nor gave thanks to Him, but their thinking became futile and their foolish hearts were darkened." Romans 1:21

All unbelievers reject God! Part 1

Some wonder, how can God send people to Hell when they never heard of Him? The Bible says all have *"heard"* or *"seen."* The Bible says man willfully rejects God. Then, God responds by doing something. See man's total rejection of God in the following points today and tomorrow:

1. *"The wrath of God is being revealed from heaven against all the godlessness and wickedness,"* Romans 1:18a. This *"is being revealed,"* warns us today of God's present displeasure. Let's see why.

2. *"Men who suppress the truth by their wickedness,"* Romans 1:18b. Instead of heeding God's warning, unbelievers work hard to push God's truths aside. That's what *"suppress"* means.

3. *"What may be known about God is plain to them,"* Romans 1:19a. Unbelievers have God's truth in plain sight. He is not hiding it in any way. The imprint of God and who He is, is everywhere!

4. *"Men are without excuse,"* Romans 1:20b. Even by seeing God's creation, all of us can know Him and His *"eternal power and divine nature,"* Romans 1:20b. God's creation preaches the glory of God. So every person is without excuse.

5. *"They knew God,"* Romans 1:21a. Unbeliever's clearly know who God is! Even though they do not know all there is to know about God, they know enough to see that He is God. An unbelievers problem is that they reject the knowledge of God.

6. *"They neither glorified Him as God, nor gave thanks to Him,"* Romans 1:21b. Here we see choices being exercised. Unbelievers chose not to glorify God. They also chose not to give God thanks. Unbelievers chose not to seek God and have a relationship with Him.

Prayer: O Almighty God, the Creator of the world, we see here that each one of us understands right from wrong. You gave us each a conscience. Our problem is we purposefully reject You the living God. Lord, draw us to Yourself we pray. Take our wills captive to do Your will. Make us repent and believe! In Jesus' name we pray. Amen.

August 28

"They exchanged the truth of God for a lie, and worshiped and served created things rather than the Creator – who is forever praised. Amen."
Romans 1:25

All unbelievers exchange the truth, Part 2

7. "*Exchanged* the glory of the immortal God for images," Romans 1:23a. Unbelievers trade in God for an image! Unbelievers do not want a God that lives in their hearts, to go where they go, to see what they do, to hear what they say, to know what they think. So they willingly trade the true God in, for a god they can put on a shelf to worship when it is convenient!

8. "They *exchanged* the truth of God for a lie," Romans 1:25a. The word "exchange" shows a willful transaction taking place between an unbeliever and God. Unbelievers have the imprint of God in them, but prefer the lie over the truth so they can do what they want to do, which is to willfully sin.

9. "*Worshiped and served* created things rather than the Creator," Romans 1:25b. Unbelievers bow down and serve "*created things,*" rather than the Maker of those things! But, are unbelievers alone in this? How often do we as Christians prefer the blessings of the "*created things*" God can give, more than a relationship with God Himself?

10. "They *did not think* it worthwhile to retain the knowledge of God," Romans 1:28a. With a heart of pride, an unbeliever does not think God's knowledge or wisdom is worth very much. Unbelievers actually prefer the world's wisdom, and then worship it.

11. "*They know* God's righteous decree," Romans 1:32a. Unbelievers are fully aware that even death is the ultimate punishment for wrong living habits. But still, they refuse to turn from their love of evil and of those who do evil. Unbelievers have a problem called rebellion. They want to do things their own way, not God's way.

Prayer: O forgiving Lord, Your Word reveals how completely the wicked reject You. Lord may we be bold, yet loving, in calling people to repentance. We see they are "*without excuse*" because "*they know.*" Lord, we praise You for Your mercy to those who come to You for it. In Jesus' name we pray. Amen.

August 29

"In a desert land He found him, in a barren and howling waste. He shielded him and cared for him; He guarded him as the apple of His eye, like an eagle that stirs up its nest and hovers over its young, that spreads its wings to catch them and carries them on its pinions. The LORD alone led him." Deuteronomy 32:10-12a

Stirred like the eagle, Part 1

The habits of an eagle are beautiful pictures of what good parents should look like. The eagle's love and protection of its chicks is patterned after how God loves and protects us and how parents must raise their children. The way an eagle prepares and trains their chicks to live a good life, often follows what God does for us. An eagle truly is a majestic bird and how blessed an eagle chick is to have such a devoted parent. How blessed we are to have such a majestic and devoted God!

Eagle parents stay together and use the same nest for life. They build their huge dwelling place high in the trees or on a cliff. They mind their own business. When the babies are ready to fly, the mother goes into the nest and with much commotion pushes a chick out of the nest. The chick tries to fly, but slowly falls towards the ground, too weak yet. Before the little bird flutters to the ground and hurts itself, the mother flies beneath it. She catches the chick on her huge wing span and returns the baby to the safety of the nest. This must shout to parents who do nothing to prepare their children to leave home someday! The mother bird keeps pushing them out, yet keeps catching them until they finally learn to fly alone. Now that is a good discipleship pattern, exactly what God does to each one of us!

Is God stirring our comfortable nest? What do we think? Is it okay if God pushes us out of our comfort zone to help us fly better on this wicked earth? Is it okay if He prepares us to soar with Him in the Heavens? Are we learning to trust His heart when He stirs our nest?

Prayer: O Lord, You said, *"You yourselves have seen what I did to Egypt, and how I carried you on eagles' wings and brought you to Myself,"* Exodus 19:4. Lord, You deliver us from sin. You lead us through the desert of life. You bring us to Heaven. All on Your back! May we trust You more for how You accomplish this! In Jesus' name we pray. Amen.

August 30

"Who satisfies your desires with good things so that your youth is renewed like the eagle's." Psalm 103:5

Renewed like the eagle, Part 2

Six hundred years ago Ponce de Leon looked for the fountain of youth. He didn't find it! Many are still looking, doing foolish things! It is so amazing how young kids can't wait to grow up. Then when they do, they want to be young again. Middle age adults often go through a mid-life crisis. When they do, they are really seeking to find a new meaning to their existence. They think: "Is this all there is to life?" No, sir. No madam, there is more! But we have to look in the right place. God is the one who makes our life new. God uses an eagle in our text to show us what He does for us.

Like us, an eagle commonly lives to the age of 60. But in order to do so the eagle must go through a time of renewal at about age 30. If they don't, they will not make it to old age. So an eagle goes off to a quiet place high on the mountain. There they begin to claw at their face and tear out their damaged feathers. It is bloody and painful! Yet by doing so, they get new healthy feathers and are good to go for another 30 years. This is what God is telling us in our text. He can give us a spiritual renewal that will also have physical benefits! For when God makes a heart more beautiful, the face and the rest of the body will radiate the joy also. Real beauty comes from the heart!

Psalm 103 calls us to *"forget not all His benefits."* Then five benefits on how God *"renews"* us are listed! 1. He, *"forgives all your sins."* 2. He *"heals all your diseases."* 3. He *"redeems your life from the pit."* 4. He *"crowns you with love and compassion."* 5. He *"satisfies your desires with good things."* God faithfully does these things for His child! Why? *"So that your youth is renewed like the eagle's"*!

Prayer: O Lord, may we not forget all Your benefits, but praise Your holy name! May our minds be transformed from crawling like a worm, to soaring like an eagle! How amazing You are. As You renew the eagle, so too You renew us when we need a lift physically and spiritually. We thank You for making us fly again and again. We worship You. In Jesus' name we pray. Amen.

August 31

"But those who hope in the LORD will renew their strength. They will soar on wings like eagles; they will run and not grow weary, they will walk and not be faint." Isaiah 40:31

Soaring like the eagle, Part 3

An eagle was created by God to soar! So were we for all eternity, and in this life too! The problem is that with our sinful nature, we put our hope in just about everything but in God! We've not yet fully learned to live above all of our problems because we've not yet learned to fully trust in God. Our fears ground us. There are many uncertainties. Yes, but then, there are supposed to be uncertainties. The question is not that we have them, but what we do with them. God tells us here, to put our hope in Him. God says, "I will *renew* you." Meaning, He will make us new again. His eye is always upon us. He may let us fall a little, but His power will catch us, every time. His wisdom will guide us.

Our text says, His people *"will soar."* It does not say maybe, might, or possibly. It says *"will soar."* In the same way Psalm 23 says, the Good Shepherd *"makes"* His sheep to lie down in the green pastures. These soaring promises of God are true. May we put our *"hope in the LORD."*

We were not made by God to be captive to sin, any more than an eagle was made by God to be a captive in a zoo! In captivity, an eagle is a dirty bird! Free, they are clean, and they soar. Let us then not be a captive in the dirt of sin and be a dirty bird. May we go to God, confess our sin and get washed in the blood of the Lamb. He will clean us. He wants to clean us. By His Spirit He wants to train us in righteousness so we too can soar and be above it all. Our load in life is light according to God. It is because all God wants from us is for us to love Him and others. But that means we must first get rid of our dirty selfishness and be renewed by Him. Then, after we are faithful in whom we love, we will soar!

Prayer: Dear Lord God our healer, help us to copy the habits of the eagle. What a majestic bird You created! How majestic we are also when we live as You created us to live. Lord help us. Make the promise about soaring come true in our lives. Make us *"to soar on wings like eagles."* In Jesus' name we pray. Amen.

SEPTEMBER

*"Be still, and know that I am God;
I will be exalted among the nations,
I will be exalted in the earth."*
Psalm 46:10

September 1

"Why do the wicked live on, growing old and increasing in power?
They spend their years in prosperity and go down to the grave in
peace. Yet they say to God, 'Leave us alone! We have no desire to
know Your ways. Who is the Almighty that we should serve Him? What
would we gain by praying to Him?'" Job 21:7 &13-15

Why do bad things happen to good people?

In one day Job lost both his family and all his material goods. And Job was very righteous. Still he lost everything in one day! Job also saw unrighteous people prospering. He too thought, "Why do bad things happen to good people?" After thinking more, he wisely asked, *"Is my complaint directed to man?"* Job 21:4. Job was not sure. Ultimately Job's questioning and ours really is directed at God. Job's real question was, "Does God have the right to take everything away from me?" Or, "Did Satan do this to me?" We know from a closer study of Job that Satan approached God, noticing how God protected Job. Satan needed permission to touch Job and us also.

Job thought much about the ways of God. *"When I think about this,* (the unrighteous getting blessings) *I am terrified; trembling seizes my body."* Job 21:6. Job further asked, *"Why do the wicked live on, growing old and increasing in power? They see their children established around them, their offspring before their eyes. Their houses are safe and free from fear; the rod of God is not upon them,"* Job 21:7-9. *"They spend their years in prosperity and go down to the grave in peace. Yet they say to God, 'Leave us alone! We have no desire to know Your ways. Who is the Almighty, that we should serve Him? What would we gain by praying to Him?'"* Job 21:13-15.

Job was not saying that all the wicked prosper! Why some do was the puzzle to him. Like Job we have these questions. In the end, Job trusted in the sovereignty of God and so must we!

Prayer: Dear Almighty God, we are so much like Job. We question why some people seem to have more of Your blessings than we do. We in turn, face so many difficulties. Lord forgive us for judging what is a blessing and what is not. You know what we need. Help us to trust Your wisdom when we cannot trace Your hand! In Jesus' name we pray. Amen.

September 2

"The LORD gave and the LORD has taken away; may the name of the LORD be praised." Job 1:21b

Praising God in good times and bad

Job answered his own question about God's sovereignty. *"The LORD gave and the LORD has taken away; may the name of the LORD be praised,"* Job 1:21b. Job recognized it was the hand of God that afflicted him, testing him. Do we? We all love *"the LORD gave"* part! It is *"the LORD has taken away"* part, that we have a problem with. Yet both are fully from the Lord, for God's glory, and for our good!

In Psalm 37 David said almost the same thing as Job, quickly reaching a conclusion. *"Do not fret because of evil men, (great advice) or be envious of those who do wrong; for like the grass they will soon wither, like green plants they will soon die away,"* Psalm 37:1-2. David is saying, we need to get an eternal perspective of our worldview. This life is not the end! An eternity of blessings await the believer, later on!

Solomon said, *"In this meaningless life of mine I have seen both of these: a righteous man perishing in his righteousness, and a wicked man living long in his wickedness,"* Ecclesiastes 7:15. Jeremiah complained; *"You are always righteous, O Lord, when I bring a case before You. Yet I would speak to You about Your justice: Why does the way of the wicked prosper? Why do all the faithless live at ease?"* Jeremiah 12:1. We see bullies, drug lords and thieves living like kings, yet many who are faithful are having a tough time of it! Why Lord?

Satan accused Job for praising God because God *"gave"* Job so much. But Satan could not begin to accuse Job of being a hypocrite when he praised God in his affliction! The question we are left with is: Will we pass the test like Job when we lose material blessings and sweet relationships? When our faces are pushed into the dust, will we worship God as Job did? Or, will we be bitter? It is human nature to ask, "Why do the unrighteous prosper?" But in the end, we must agree with the righteous Job. God knows what He is doing!

Prayer: Most righteous Lord, forgive us for glorifying Satan by accusing You for not blessing us more. You know what is best for us. May we rejoice in that. In Jesus' name we pray. Amen.

September 3

"This is what the LORD says: 'Maintain justice and do what is right, for My salvation is close at hand and My righteousness will soon be revealed. Blessed is the man who does this, the man who holds it fast, who keeps the Sabbath without desecrating it, and keeps his hand from doing evil.'" Isaiah 56:1-2

True Sabbath worship

God put us on earth to worship Him. Right Sabbath observance is a need of the hour. We can understand Biblical worship in three points.

The pattern of true worship. *"By the seventh day God had finished the work He had been doing; so on the seventh day He rested from all His work. And God blessed the seventh day and made it holy, because on it He rested from all the work of creating that He had done,"* Genesis 2:2-3. God created the world in six days and then rested on the seventh. God here set the pattern for our week, for all generations! God did not rest because He was tired, but to set the pattern for our worship. God loved us and knew what would be good for us and for His kingdom.

The commandment for true worship. *"Remember the Sabbath day by keeping it holy. Six days you shall labor and do all your work, but the seventh day is a Sabbath to the LORD your God. On it you shall not do any work, neither you, nor your son or daughter, nor your manservant or maidservant, nor your animals, nor the alien within your gates. For in six days the LORD made the Heavens and the earth, the sea, and all that is in them, but He rested on the seventh day. Therefore the LORD blessed the Sabbath day and made it holy,"* Exodus 20:8-11.

The blessings of true worship. *"'If you call the Sabbath a delight and the LORD's holy day honorable, and <u>if you honor it by not going your own way and not doing as you please</u> or speaking idle words, then you will find your joy in the LORD, and <u>I will cause you to ride on the heights of the land and to feast on the inheritance of your father Jacob</u>.' The mouth of the LORD has spoken,"* Isaiah 58:13b-14. God keeps His promises!

Prayer: O holy Lord, forgive us for loving our pattern of living more than Yours, and then expect to be blessed. Thank You for clearly setting a pattern of worship and even promising to bless us if we keep the Sabbath day holy. In Christ's name we pray. Amen.

September 4

"If you <u>do well</u>, will you not be accepted?" Genesis 4:7a NKJV

The Bible on suicide, Part 1

People range in the opinion that suicide is the unpardonable sin, all the way to those who think that suicide is an okay way to end one's life. It would be helpful to spend some time looking at this topic according to the Word of God. We will first look at what leads up to suicide. Then we see why suicide and the depression that preceded it is not the unpardonable sin. So then, how do suicidal thoughts develop, and what can we do to prevent it?

Suicide is sin. The 6th commandment says, *"Thou shall not kill."* We are not to kill others, or self. Granted, suicidal people are often depressed, but that does not excuse it. Psalms 38 and 88 describe the sadness and the pain of the depressed/suicidal. The pain associated with these feelings is great. A person may contemplate suicide but a <u>temptation</u> to sin is not wrong. Jesus was tempted just as we are! Giving into that temptation is the problem. It is the yielding to sin that is wrong. Know this: The same trial that is a temptation from Satan to end a life, is also a test from God to overcome our problems! We can pass the test in God's strength, and then encourage others to do the same.

The fall of Adam and Eve touches every aspect of our lives. In the first family, already murder happened. The depressed Cain killed Abel. It was a sin, not a sickness or a disease. Previously, God had asked Cain, *"Why is your face <u>downcast</u>?"* (depressed). God told unbelieving Cain, *"If you <u>do well</u> will you not be accepted?"* Cain did not do well because his heart was cold to God, and to his brother.

Believer David was also depressed, <u>after</u> he committed murder and adultery and did not confess it! David was filled with feelings of guilt, <u>after he sinned</u>! Guilt itself, cannot be sinful, for it comes from the Holy Spirit according to John 16:7-10. Pain also follows sin. God in His mercy and blessing intended guilt and pain <u>to help us stop sinning</u>! All pain is not from sin, but all guilt is.

Prayer: Lord, You tell us the truth because that is what sets us free. Lord help us to learn about depression and suicide so we can be more of a blessing to You and others. In Jesus' name we pray. Amen.

September 5

"Your arrows pierce me deeply, Your hand presses me down."
Psalm 38:2 NKJV

The Bible on suicide, Part 2

In Psalm 32 & 38, David records both his depression and his way to a victory over it. He starts the discussion with our text, admitting his selfish living caused God's hand to press him down. The Ten Commandments and the whole Bible teaches us to love God first and others second. A depressed person is filled with self-pity. That's a "me first" theology. The words "I" and "me" dominate their life. That is backwards to how God wants us to live. The way out of depressed and suicidal thoughts is not to crawl into a hole and hide in self-pity. Instead meditate on who God is, His attributes. Forgive others and reach out to them. Never think we have the right to feel sorry for self because of what someone did to us. That is a bitter response to someone who wronged us. Read Hebrews 12:15, James 1:20, and 3:14-16. An angry or bitter response to anyone about anything is not a *"righteous life."* It is *"of the devil,"* *"misses the grace of God,"* and it *"defiles many."* So, if we want to justify our self-pity, God does not agree. We must learn better habits instead. We must trade in our anger for more of Christ's grace and start giving it to others. And may we keep our eyes on Christ, not on our difficult trial.

How can we get our eyes on Christ and hope again? We can think about what Christ went through, so we won't think we have it so bad. Think of how Christ will never leave us or forsake us. Think of how no one can take us from Jesus' hands. Christ is far bigger than our problem. He will give us the power to gain the victory. Our problem is just a common one to Him. God told us, *"No temptation has seized you except what is common to man,"* 1 Corinthians 10:13a. God understands our trial and has a promise for us.

Prayer: Dear Lord, Your promises are precious! Help us believe *them.* You will not let us be tempted beyond what we can bear. That promise, based on Your faithfulness, never fails! You never give us a stronger trial than we can bear. What You allow us to go through, only strengthens us. May we be like David with the giant and get our eyes off from our big trials and on to You. In Jesus' name we pray. Amen.

September 6

"For it is by grace you have been saved, through faith – and this not from yourselves, it is the gift of God – not by works, so that no one can boast." Ephesians 2:8-9

When suicide does happen, Part 3

Too often we stand in judgment, wanting to fix the blame for a suicide! Could the family have done more? Could the church have done more? Could the spouse, parent, teacher or child have done more? Of course, we all could have done more. Maybe a greater problem is that we expected too much of the one who did the suicide. Whatever the problem is, the answers are in Christ and His atoning blood! God forgives sinners of all kinds. We need to also according to Ephesians 4:32. It is far more important to be driven to Christ, than to explanations. We cannot fix the suicide situation, but Jesus will not fail anyone.

Think of how our own performance falls short every day! And some days more than others. Are we still accepted by God through Christ? Are we going to Heaven based on our performance? No! Then why do so many want to condemn the suicide person to Hell because their performance failed? Is there even one person who will get to Heaven based on their performance? If we think so, we have a problem. If we attach performance to earning Heaven, we are lost.

What we do will not even get us into Heaven, even as a gatekeeper. Therefore, what we do will not get us out of Heaven either. God accepts the work of Christ on the Cross for our sin. *"It is finished"*! The *"good work"* has been done. In salvation, Christ gets our every single, sinful work. We get His perfect work. We also get His perfect righteousness. It is His work and righteousness that gets us in, and keeps us in. Salvation is by grace alone, never by works. So if we think a suicide person cannot go to Heaven based on some "bad work," we have a significant Gospel problem! I say it strongly, because it needs to be said.

Prayer: O Lord, help us to remember grace theology when a suicide happens. Forgive us for finding fault. Help us to encourage those who need encouragement! And Lord, may the brokenhearted come to You for comfort! In Jesus' name we pray. Amen.

September 7

"Everything is possible for him who believes." Mark 9:23b

But the suicide never repented! Part 4

Our title is a reason people give for why they think a person who commits suicide can't go to Heaven. Truly, God does save sinners that repent. Mark 1:15 says, *"Repent and believe."* But what about the title question? It is an honest concern. Let me ask some questions to answer it.

What about us? We are all "confessed up" this morning in our private devotions. Then, on our way to work we swore at a person who cut us off in traffic. Moments later we are hit by a truck and die. Will we go to Heaven? Did we confess our last sin? When God forgives us at the time of salvation, He forgave all our past, present, and the future sins! We are already seated with Christ in Heaven. Our spot is that reserved, that guaranteed! Our salvation is not based on our future performance to stay saved. Nor is it based on our performance to get saved. We will be in Heaven because of Christ's merit, period.

Jesus was looking for faith in an *"unbelieving generation,"* Mark 9:19a. He arranged for a man to meet Him who had a mute son, demon-possessed from birth. The father wanted help! Jesus then told the father of the mute boy, *"everything is possible for him who believes,"* Mark 9:23b. The man knowing his own weakness, cries out to Jesus in verse 24, *"I do believe; help me overcome my unbelief!"* Even with his small faith, he was saved and his son was healed! Why? Because he trusted in Jesus! Next to perfect Jesus, we all have "small faith." It's never the bigness of our faith that saves us. It is the object of our faith, Jesus, and the quality of His perfect blood. We must remember that always.

Why did a gracious God let this suicide happen? We may never know. Let us not judge the character of God. We know His ways are higher than ours. If we want proof of God's love, then look to the Cross. Look to His suffering Son. Look what God did to restore us to Himself for all eternity. Look to Him!

Prayer: Dear gracious Lord, when we fix our eyes on You, "Then the things of earth will grow strangely dim, in the light of Your glorious grace!" In Jesus' perfect name we pray. Amen.

September 8

"Two blind men were sitting by the roadside, and when they heard that Jesus was going by, they shouted, 'Lord, Son of David, have mercy on us!'" Matthew 20:30

Lord, "have mercy on us!"

This subject of God's *"mercy"* is our greatest need! Two blind men were crying out to Jesus for *"mercy"* in Matthew 20:29-34. It is a powerful sermon in just a few words. Imagine the noisy crowd following Jesus as He leaves Jericho with His disciples. Yet He hears two beggars cry for His mercy. The crowd tells the two men to *"be quiet,"* but Jesus listens to them! He asks, *"What do you want Me to do for you?"* In the midst of all the noise in this world, Jesus still hears a whisper for mercy!

This particular moment is arranged by God, for a specific teaching purpose! First, we see two men with a joint prayer request. Jesus loves to answer heartfelt prayer from humble believers. Second, the two beggars know exactly who Jesus is. They recognize and worship Him as the *"Son of David,"* the promised Messiah. Third, the two blind men looked to God and sought *"mercy"* from Him. Each of these points are far beyond what the religious leaders knew who filled with their own self-righteousness, did not seek the righteousness of Christ! Thus they did not cry for the *"mercy"* of God. Have we cried to Jesus?

From this meeting with the blind men we must learn that Jesus' ways are much different than man's. Earlier in Matthew 19, Jesus' disciples did not want the children to be by Jesus. Here the crowd does not want the blind men to be by Jesus. Yet, Jesus had compassion on both! Is it possible that we spend too much of our evangelism efforts on the high and mighty, those not likely to believe? So often, the ones we think should believe, don't. And those who we think will never believe, do. This must speak to us about how we must reach out to all with the compassion of Christ!

Prayer: Dear soverign Lord, there are so many who want to be first, yet are last. There are others who seem to be last, yet are first in Your eyes. Lord, that reality makes us prayerfully consider, "Where are we in Your eyes?" Are we so full of self that we do not seek Your mercy? Lord, be merciful to us sinners! In Christ's name we pray. Amen.

September 9

"I will not leave you as orphans; I will come to you." John 14:18

"I will not leave you as orphans"

Jesus was about to return to Heaven and leave His disciples. He knew they would be lonely, confused, and in need of comfort! So He clearly tells them, *"I will not leave you comfortless,"* which is what the KJV uses instead of the word *"orphans."* The comfort that Jesus gives is for all of His children! Let us see what that comfort is. Let us enjoy His comfort. And then let us thank God for the comfort He gives!

The *"I,"* in our text is He who is alive in Heaven, the Lord Jesus Christ, the King of kings and Lord of lords. He, the One who is always faithful, is the One who is making this promise of comfort.

"Will not," absolutely never, will He leave you or forsake you! He will always be faithful to you! Life will be difficult. You will be in many trying situations. But, Jesus will be with you in your trials. You will be like David who could say, *"I walk <u>through</u> the valley of the shadow of death."* *"Through"* it because Jesus, the "Good" Shepherd, *"<u>will not</u> leave you."*

"Orphans." To be an orphan in most of the world is to be without hope, without a solid future, almost dead. And we were this before salvation! But now, by the grace of God through Jesus Christ, we are in His immediate family! He adopted us! God the Father <u>made us</u> joint heirs with Jesus Christ. Now an heir has to be living to collect on the inheritance. And we will live, because He lives!

The principle here is: no disciple of Jesus Christ can be an orphan! That simply is not possible. Even when we as Christians walk away from God, and we do every time we sin, He will not walk away from us! Instead, He sends His Spirit to catch us, to bring us back to the Cross, back to a closeness with Him. Yes, by sinning we try to become an orphan again, but the Holy Spirit convicts us. Christ forgives us. God the Father holds on to us!

Prayer: O Lord what a beautiful reality! You promise, *"I will not leave you as orphans."* What a comfort it is that, in body and in soul, in life and in death, we are not our own, but belong to our faithful Savior Jesus Christ. Every part of sin is gone. We are perfectly holy! We love You Jesus, because you first loved us! In His beautiful name we pray. Amen.

September 10

"Beyond all question, the mystery of godliness is great."
1 Timothy 3:16a

What is the *"mystery"*?

Christianity really is a huge *"mystery."* You can't buy it. You can't sell it. You can't go to school to get it. You can't work for it. The *"false teachers"* thought they could do all four of these. They were blind to the *"mystery,"* as are many today! Only in Christ, is the *"mystery"* understood. Meditate on the rest of the verse from our text. See the six ways or six critical doctrines that solve *"the mystery of godliness"* that is in Christ.

1. Christ *"appeared in a body."* How can God appear in a body, in flesh and blood like us? God made Himself known! *"The Word became flesh and made His dwelling among us,"* John 1:14a. When people do not see Christ as fully man, they do not know the *"mystery."* Here we see the miracle of Jesus' <u>incarnation</u>.

2. Christ *"was vindicated by the Spirit."* Jesus did not stay in the grave. The Spirit raised Him just as the Spirit will someday raise us. Here we see the power of God in the mystery of Jesus' <u>resurrection</u>.

3. Christ *"was seen by angels."* Angels were present at Jesus' birth, at Jesus' wilderness temptations. They saw His agony on the Cross, witnessed His resurrection and ascension! The angels honored Jesus, ministered to Him, yet what a *"mystery."* Jesus is Lord of the angels.

4. Christ *"was preached among the nations."* The Gentiles, even we ourselves, are included in God's family. What a *"mystery"* that we have The Great Commission. Sinners, redeemed then going out for God.

5. Christ *"was believed on in the world."* Jesus' name is not just preached, but believed in! What a *"mystery"* to see believers in the universal church of the Lord Jesus Christ coming from all over the world!

6. Christ *"was taken up to glory."* By faith we know that our Lord Jesus Christ is reigning in Heaven. What a *"mystery"* that He is sitting on a throne, our Mediator, bringing our prayers to God and answering us!

Prayer: Dear Father in Heaven, we praise You that You solve so many spiritual mysteries in the person of Jesus Christ, our Lord and Savior. In His name we pray. Amen.

September 11

"There was a man who had two sons. The younger one said to his father, 'Father, give me my share of the estate.' So he divided his property between them." Luke 15:11-12

A Father and two sons, Part 1

Recently I was with 5 pastors who were arguing about the grace of God, again. Later I was reading this parable of Jesus in Luke 15 and realized these pastors needed to adjust their "grace theology" to these illustrations. Jesus tells the same parable three ways. First, the lost sheep. Next, the lost coin. Finally, the lost son. In each case, something was lost, something was found, showing the grace of God!

In Luke 15:1-2, *"the tax collectors and sinners,"* along with the *"Pharisees and the teachers of the law"* who *"muttered"* are the audience. With these two sons, Jesus is showing two kinds of people in the church. We have a father, God Himself. Covenantly, God was Father to all the Jews. The elder son with a bad attitude describes the complaining and self-righteous Pharisees. He is pictured here as "Mr. Goody Two Shoes," who in his own eyes was a loyal son who perfectly kept the old covenant of works! Then we also have a second son. He represents the sinners that Jesus is adding into the kingdom of the Father, through the covenant of grace! This parable is an important message for us today! For this is exactly the problem we have in our churches.

Through our father Adam, we all have a prodigal problem! The Pharisees just didn't recognize it! *"For all have sinned and fall short of the glory of God,"* Romans 3:23. We are all sinners, born that way and still sinning. As we study this parable, it is rather plain that we need to examine our own spiritual journey to see which son best describes who we are. Are we a Pharisee trying to work our way to the Father by doing some good things? Or, are we the sinner who comes to the Father, with empty hands, looking for His grace and mercy?

Prayer: Dear Heavenly Father, we thank and praise You for Your mercy in giving us a clear picture of the two kinds of people in the church today. And if we are not the prodigal going to You the Father for forgiveness and grace, then please Lord, push us there! In Jesus' name we pray. Amen.

September 12

"The younger son got together all he had, set off for a distant country and there squandered his wealth in wild living." Luke 15:13b

The prodigal son *"squanders,"* Part 2

The prodigal son first said, *"Father, give me my share of the estate,"* Luke 15:11b. Now that is a very demanding boy who wants to do his own thing and he wants it all, right now! He is bent on getting far away from the father! It is a picture of our own depravity, rotten to the core, dead spiritually. Watch how he, and we also, fall further from the Father.

"Wild living" was his passion. Forget about study. Do no work. Just play. Life is all about personal pleasure. And since Father God doesn't know what is best, get away from Him. I will do life, my way! See how selfish pride is the road to destruction, the devil's agenda.

He *"squandered"* his riches. Yes, he became poor. But this is really a spiritual poverty! He spent his money. He spent his time and talents. But what he really spent was all the Lord's. He wasted the Lord's provision for him. He did not worship God and he became dirt poor!

He *"hired himself out,"* Luke 15:15b. He became a slave. Leaving God the Father is to willingly become a slave to sin. Think of all the various lusts, drinking, porn, adultery, gambling, drugs... They have a hold on us. We become a slave to them and these sins are a cruel master! The prodigal left Master God who was kind, for master Devil who had him feeding pigs! Then he became a slave to pigs! He ate with pigs. How much lower can one go away from God? Much lower!

"No one gave him anything," Luke 15:16b. He became a hopeless beggar! Relief, none! No one would or could help him, for he had willingly left the father. More than that, the prodigal became like a dead man. He couldn't even help himself. This is the eternal picture of a man apart from the living God. We really are this pathetic, both physically and spiritually! Only a living God can restore us!

Prayer: Dear gracious Lord, how our sin and rebellion is a one way street away from You. Without You there is no hope for today, no hope for the future. When we see a picture of our lost condition, we can see how hopeless we really are apart from You! How great is Your grace in comparison! We praise You for it. In Jesus' name we pray. Amen.

September 13

"'I will set out and go back to my father and say to him: Father, I have sinned against Heaven and against you. I am no longer worthy to be called your son; make me like one of your hired men.' So he got up and went to his father." Luke 15:18-20a

The Spirit convicts the prodigal, Part 3

What we have now is a turning point. Literally the beginning of the prodigal son's conversion. In verse 17 it says, *"when he came to his senses."* Now how can a dead man, a slave to sin, suddenly come to his senses? Where does a starving slave of a pig, who only eats what the pigs don't want, suddenly get his wisdom from? It will take God to wake him up, and that is exactly what happens!

Jesus said *"No one can come to Me unless the Father who sent Me draws him,"* John 6:44a. So the prodigal is now, on the way to the Father, through Jesus. But the Spirit also is involved in waking this dead guy up, like He does to every dead sinner He calls! *"He will convict the world of guilt in regard to sin and righteousness and judgment,"* John 16:8b. When the Trinity calls, every sinner must go!

How wonderful it is that Jesus tells the story of the prodigal to help us understand some of the mystery of His grace to us dead sinners! At another time Jesus said, *"I tell you the truth, a time is coming and has now come when the dead will hear the voice of the Son of God and those who hear will live,"* John 5:25. This is not just in the resurrection, but in the salvation of every prodigal son and daughter. If you doubt this truth, read Ephesians 2:1-10, especially verses 4-5. It says, *"But because of His great love for us, God, who is rich in mercy, made us alive with Christ even when we were dead in transgressions — it is by grace you have been saved,"* Ephesians 2:4-5.

Where there's life, there's hope! Pray for your lost loved ones! The grace of God can soften the hardest heart! The prodigal and the Apostle Paul aren't the only hard hearts that were turned. The Bible gives us these pictures so that we may see the truth. Praise God for His grace!

Prayer: O Lord, what a beautiful picture the prodigal son is of Your grace to us dead sinners. We can only begin to understand Your grace when we see it. We praise You for it! In Jesus' name we pray. Amen.

September 14

"But while he was still a long way off, his father saw him and was filled with compassion for him." Luke 15:20b

A Father sees the son coming! Part 4

What a beautiful truth we have set before us! *"While he was still a long way off, his father saw him."* The story of the prodigal is mainly about the love of the Father! Why was the father so lovingly looking down the road? It was because the Father knew exactly when the prodigal would come! It was the Father's irresistible grace at work! Still another grace point that puts a knife into the free will of man choosing God!

Think of the history of the soul of the prodigal and of the soul of every single believer that will come to the Father! The prodigal's name, as a son of the Father, was written on God's hand even before the world was made! God tells us, *"He chose us in Him <u>before</u> the creation of the world to be holy and blameless <u>in His sight</u>,"* Ephesians 1:4. And don't miss the last three words, *"in His sight."* God not only planned every salvation, but each one is always, *"in His sight."* Today, if we are a believer we are *"in His sight."* What a privilege! God is not in Heaven wringing His hands to see if people will accept His salvation!

The truth is that God is busy moving world events, governments, and people, all from here to there, to finally bring each and every child of His into a *"holy and blameless"* relationship with Him! After all, *"He predestined us to be adopted as His sons through Jesus Christ, in accordance with His pleasure and will,"* Ephesians 1:5. *"Predestined"* means God preplanned the prodigal's and our Christian destiny!

Why do so many hate the doctrine of predestination? Is it because we want to claim to have something to do with our own salvation? How can that be possible when God is actively *"with His pleasure,"* working out His *"will,"* doing His *"adoptions"*?

Prayer: O gracious Lord, we can see from Ephesians 1:6 that You planned the prodigal's salvation. You planned ours also for *"the praise of"* Your *"glorious grace, which"* You have *"freely given us."* Forgive us for trying to take some responsibility for our salvation! We praise You for Your amazing grace! In Jesus' name we pray. Amen.

September 15

"His father saw him and was filled with compassion for him; he ran to his son, threw his arms around him and kissed him." Luke 15:20c

A loving reunion with the Father, Part 5

Another beautiful scene is set before us! The father, *"ran to his son, threw his arms around him and kissed him."* His gracious atonement is limited to those He kisses! Note that the father *"kissed"* the son, even before the son opened his mouth to say, *"Father, I have sinned against Heaven and against you."* Why? Because salvation is all about God the Father, *"kissing"* the sinner! It's not about the sinner kissing the Father. Plus, the sinner was for all practical purposes, already forgiven! He was actually forgiven before the foundation of the world, when God *"chose us in Him before the creation of the world to be holy and blameless in His sight."* All God had to do was work out the final details to His gracious plan for each adopted child. We are so privileged to see His grace plan in a drama like parable!

After the son's confession, God teaches us yet another grace point! *"The father said to his servants, 'Quick! Bring the best robe and put it on him. Put a ring on his finger and sandals on his feet. Bring the fattened calf and kill it. Let's have a feast and celebrate,'"* Luke 15:22-23. No one can ever take this son's salvation away. He will persevere because of the gracious love of the Father! A sign of God's persevering grace is His giving the *"best robe,"* *"the ring,"* and *"the sandals"*! Since the son is now a permanent member of God's family, there is a celebration in Heaven itself. The rags of the prodigal are replaced with the *"best robe,"* the righteous, white robe of Jesus Christ. The former sin is fully covered. Even the feet are covered. Every part of the prodigal is fully righteous. For each child of God it is, *"Quick! Bring the best robe."*

"Bring the fatted calf." Suddenly the prodigal who was formerly eating husks with the pigs, is now dining with the King of Heaven. Believer, that is our privileged position by grace alone! Surely this fattened calf was grown for this very reason! It was properly fattened at just the right time, just for this celebration!

Prayer: Dear loving Lord, Your grace just gets more amazing and wonderful. How privileged we believers really are! Accept our praise and worship! In Jesus' name we pray. Amen.

September 16

"Meanwhile, the older son was in the field. When he came near the house, he heard the music and dancing." "The older brother became angry and refused to go in." Luke 15:25 & 28a

But look who is not celebrating! Part 6

The older son representing the Pharisees and scribes is upset! Remember that Luke 15 began with Jesus describing how the Pharisees *"muttered,"* because Jesus *"welcomes sinners and eats with them."* What was their problem? The Pharisees were trying to work their way into the Father's good graces by their keeping of the Law. The older son here was not just trying to earn his righteousness, he was proud of his efforts! At another time the rich young ruler asked, *"What good thing can I do to inherit eternal life?"* The older son here, thought he was already doing it! He angrily said to the father, *"Look! All these years I've been slaving for you and never disobeyed your orders,"* Luke 15:29b. Do you see it? Here he not only claims to be righteous, but perfectly righteous, all by his own efforts! He didn't need the forgiveness and the love of the Father. He didn't see the need to love his brother either! (Reminds us of Cain, another older brother.) And then he refused to come to the celebration. This is so huge. He refused the Father in Heaven! He missed the whole point of needing the grace of God!

So now this parable begs the question! Which son are you? Are you trying to do many good things to earn your way to the Father's favor? Are you trying to bribe God to let you into Heaven by your good deeds? It is not just Hindus who do this, but many in the church!

Or, are you this younger brother who comes to the Father with empty hands begging for forgiveness? Can you see why it is so important to understand what the grace of God means, and the need of it? If you come to the Father confessing your sin, know this, there is already a celebration in Heaven! Your name was written on God's hand. And you have finally come! Praise God for His grace!

Prayer: Dear Father, we know from Your Word that each one of us is in the shoes of one of these two sons! May we be the one seeking Your pardoning grace; thankful to be eating with You; welcoming others who come to Your table. In Jesus' name we pray. Amen.

September 17

"Surely I was sinful at birth, sinful from the time my mother conceived me." Psalm 51:5

Why do we sin?

We are not sinners because we sin. We sin, because we are born sinners! Every person in this world was born with a nature that is completely 100% a slave to sin! This is exactly what it means to be born with "original sin." This is also what David is teaching in our text. David had that "sin gene" in him already at the time of conception. This means that the very first cell in David's body had sin written all over it!

The reason we have original sin is because our father Adam is the father of every human being. When Adam sinned, he was our representative man, so he sinned for all of us. A well known verse that explains this is: *"Just as sin entered the world through one man, and death through sin, and in this way death came to all men, because all sinned,"* Romans 5:12. Later in verse 18, the same point is again presented to help us understand the salvation message: *"Just as the result of one trespass was condemnation for all men, so also the result of one act of righteousness was justification that brings life for all men."* The first Adam condemned us, the Second Adam, Jesus, pardons us! The first Adam made us like him, morally and spiritually, totally depraved. The Second Adam, Jesus, makes us like Him, totally righteous, just as if we never sinned!

Why do we need to know we were born sinners? So we seek Christ. So we don't get the wrong idea that we might have been born Christian. So we understand what the root of our spiritual problem is. So we can see how lost we really are. So we can fully understand, *"There is none righteous, not even one;"* Romans 3:10b. So we can see how important the grace and mercy of God is. The grace and mercy of God makes no sense if we are not sinners through and through!

Prayer: O God of all grace, we praise You for helping us see what complete sinners we really are. We needed to know how hopelessly separated we are from You with our sinful nature. Lord, be merciful to us sinners. Cleanse us Lord, because as slaves to sin, we cannot cleanse ourselves. In Jesus' name we pray. Amen.

September 18

"Give the reason for the hope that you have. But do this with gentleness and respect." 1 Peter 3:15b

A temple prostitute hangs herself

This true story really shouts to us of a need in the church today. At age 5, Rani was given to the temple. Her mother brought her to become a temple "worker." Her mother worked in the temple like this for 25 years, until she was too old for this work. She was expected to bring her daughter. So little Rani now became a slave to the lusts of men.

Fifteen years later, a young 28 year old man we will call Raju, visited the city. He went to the famous temple. Raju was not a Hindu, but he was interested in seeing the temple. The priest there asked him, "Where are you staying in the city?" Raju said, "I have no place yet." So the priest invited him to stay in one of the temple rooms. That night the priest sent 20 year old Rani to his room to "serve" him.

Raju talked to the girl for some time, but did not have any "relations" with her. But she suggested showing him an enjoyable time before he left the next day. Raju was shocked at what she had in mind, and that she normally did this every day. Raju then shouted at her! Even though he was not a Christian, he believed in Heaven and Hell. He told her she was going to Hell for her wicked actions! In 15 years, Rani had never heard this. She left the room crying, and Raju left the city. A week later Raju returned to the temple to see Rani. But, he found out she had hung herself the day before!

Raju did convict Rani that she was wrong. But he took all the hope she presently had for life, without telling her how to live differently. She finally knew she had to change, but this was the only life she knew! With no hope, crushed with guilt, she ended her life.

How often do we as Christians tell someone how wrong they are, but do we give them hope? We don't set before them Jesus who died for their sins. We don't clearly tell them how Jesus can give them a new heart and new power to live. May the Lord help us in our weakness!

Prayer: O Lord, we cannot live without hope! No one can live without hope. May we make sure we give real Biblical hope to those who are in need. Lord help us to help the hurting! In Jesus' name we pray. Amen.

September 19

"Above all, you must understand that no prophesy of Scripture came about by the prophet's own interpretation. For prophesy never had its origin in the will of man, but men spoke from God as they were carried along by the Holy Spirit." 2 Peter 1:20-21

Is the Bible inspired?

The words of our text show that the Bible is inspired, meaning it comes from a supernatural source, God Himself. He put His thoughts into the heads of the men who wrote them down. The different men had their various styles, yet the words written were God's words. This is exactly why we call the Bible, the Word of God. The implication is: the words are without error, without even the possibility of error. But what if someone does not believe that? What can we say to prove that the Bible is inspired? Four things:

1. The Bible is not just one book. It is collection of 66 books.

2. The Bible's 66 books are written by 40 different authors including doctors, kings, shepherds, and prophets. Most of these authors never knew each other personally.

3. The 66 books of the Bible were written over a period of 1500 years in ancient Aramaic, Greek and Hebrew. Included in the books is the historical content of the world.

4. The 66 books were written in the continents of Asia, Africa and Europe and all have the same theme. It tells of the creation, the fall into sin, God's love and redemption of man.

If anyone does not believe that the Bible is inspired, just ask them a question. "Where else can you find a large book that contains 40 authors, living over 1500 years, who never knew each other, who wrote in three languages, who lived on three continents, and have the same interactive theme without any contradictions?" You must admit that is impossible! Yes it is. No one could do such a task. But God did it, to tell the old, old story of Jesus and His love! And that is why we know that even apart from faith, we can see that the Bible is inspired.

Prayer: O loving Lord, what care You took to give us Your Word, the only inspired set of books we will ever read. We thank and praise You for Your mercy in giving this to us! In Jesus' name we pray. Amen.

September 20

"Come and see." John 1:39b NKJV

Do we point our family to Jesus? Part 1

John the Baptist knew he was in this world to point others to Jesus and that is exactly what he did. The background to our text is John telling some of the people who were following him, to take notice of Jesus. He clearly wanted them to follow Jesus. He said, *"Behold the Lamb of God,"* John 1:36b NKJV. John knew that Christ was the Son of God, the Savior, and that He was eternally God. John knew that in contrast, he himself was a mere mortal man. But is this not true for all of us? None of us are here on this earth for long. The Bible describes our lives as a flower that is here one day and gone the next. Yet we have an even bigger problem! We are all born into this world pointing to ourselves. We want people to see us!

Next in our text is Andrew, the first disciple to come to Jesus. He spent just one day with Jesus and was overwhelmed. It was the best day of his life! *"The first thing Andrew did was to find his brother Simon and tell him, 'We have found the Messiah (that is, the Christ),'"* John 1:41. So, first he tells a member of his family, his brother Peter. He found the Lamb of God that took away the sin of the world, and he could not keep it to himself. He went to his family first.

Today it is common that people point to Jesus as a Sunday School teacher, a deacon, an elder, and even as a pastor. But in their own home and family they have nothing to say. Andrew, whom we hear very little about after this, accuses us. He went to his brother who became a main leader in the church. How many future church leaders do we have sitting in our homes?

There is another issue. We need to first *"come and see"* Jesus personally, before we can help others see Him. We need Jesus in our hearts. We need our sins forgiven. We need to love Jesus more than anything else. We do need to point others to Him. If we don't, then our actions will point to things that don't matter.

Prayer: Eternal and almighty God, our text accuses us of being two-faced. Lord, You are more precious than gold! May we point others to *"come and see"* who You are! In Jesus' name we pray. Amen.

September 21

"Fathers, do not exasperate your children; instead bring them up in the training and instruction of the Lord." Ephesians 6:4

Do we have the right to be critical? Part 2

There was a child who was honest. She worked hard and was willing to do things her brothers and sisters would not do. She helped clean the house, cut the vegetables, and wash the cooking utensils. She did her school work sincerely. She just wanted to be a blessing and she was. But her father <u>never</u> said a kind word to her! Then one day she scolded her brother for being mean to her and her father beat her severely. Did this father have the right to discipline her so severely when he never even once praised her for her good points?

There was a church member who was very sick. He suffered for more than a year but the pastor never came to his house to visit him. The sick man was not able to go to church but his "pastor" still did not visit him, did not give him encouragement, and did not pray with him even once! In the meantime, this pastor would visit the popular and influential church members and inquire about their families regularly. If they missed a church service he called them. But now, a member of this sick man's family makes a small mistake. Finally the pastor goes to his house and blasts him and his wife for that mistake! Does that pastor have the right to be critical after failing to show any concern for such a long time?

There was a hard working common man, plain in appearance, but sincere. He went to work every day, doing whatever was needed to make the company a success. But the boss never seemed to notice him or encourage him in spite of his dedicated service! Yet this same boss brought in new people and promoted them because they were more "polished" in their appearance, with a more "formal" education. One day this hard working man did a job that did not turn out well. The boss man came down on him hard, even in the presence of others. Does this boss have the right to be so critical after never praising this worker's good points? Do we have the right to be critical?

Prayer: Dear Lord, forgive us for our horrible discipleship practices! Give us new hearts so that we can live a life of grace. In Jesus' name we pray. Amen.

September 22

"Fathers do not provoke your children to wrath, but bring them up in the training and admonition of the Lord." Ephesians 6:4 NKJV

Do we protect our child's emotions? Part 3

I was asked to talk to teenage kids about serious issues that will affect them now and into adulthood. As we talk more on this topic, there are concerns that parents should be more aware of to help prepare their children for the adult years. We will do it in story form.

Father was so busy at work. He worked late. When it came to money he provided very well for his family. He was also often gone on the weekends. His wife did her best to bring up the family, but it was not possible for her to be the father as well as the mother. The two boys and two girls basically grew up without a father. They longed for his affection and approval. The children knew their father had to work, but if he would just notice them a little! They tried everything they could think of to get his attention. The two boys were very naughty, extra naughty! When they were naughty the other kids noticed them, but still not dad. The girls were extra good! They got great marks in school. But daddy never seemed to notice, never came to a school function, rarely hugged them, seldom told them they were special or beautiful. They were emotionally starved!

By the time the girls were teenagers, some of the boys noticed that they were cute, and told them so. How great it was to finally be noticed. Since their emotional tanks were so empty, they sought to fill them up on the sweet words of the boys and girls in their school!

In time the children found ways to meet other kids. They started some handholding, advancing to more touching, and kisses in time. It made them feel so loved and accepted. They thought they were finally at peace, not realizing that it was a false peace. They did not yet realize how weak and unprotected their emotional foundation was, and they got into trouble because of it. The truth is that the children's mother is also emotionally affected for the very same reasons!

Prayer: Lord, You call fathers to love their children and families. Forgive us where we have failed. Help us to see all the needs in our families and how we can protect them emotionally. In Jesus' name we pray. Amen.

September 23

"Children, obey your parents in the Lord, for this is right. 'Honor your father and mother,' - which is the first commandment with a promise — that it may go well with you and that you may enjoy long life on the earth." Ephesians 6:1-3

Child, your *"honor"* will protect you! Part 4

This word *"honor,"* is important. God wants to protect children. So He appeals to that truth in the fifth commandment. To *"honor"* a parent should have been learned by the child before the age of one. But many children don't learn *"honor,"* because some parents don't enforce it. I recently was in a home where an 11 month old boy was there. I purposely left my plate of snacks where he could reach them because we were discussing the discipline of children. The child reached for my plate and I said no, and hit his hand very slightly. I did this 4 times. Ever so slightly was all that was needed at this age for this boy. He listened, without crying! He looked right into my eyes. He knew he had to *"honor"* the "No." Some kids aren't disciplined and parents wonder why their "No" reaches deaf ears in the teenage years!

"Children, obey your parents," is not just a command to children, but to parents first. It is our responsibility to instill in our kids, to give honor. If we are faithful in this early on, our children will more quickly follow our yes's and no's later on. However, as parents, we are far from perfect ourselves! We make lots of mistakes. By the time our children are grown up, we see our mistakes quite clearly. But that's a little late. This is exactly why we need to listen to God, so we can get it right the first time.

However, if we are that child who never heard the "no" word, then our parents have basically given us whatever we wanted. At times, we got in trouble for it. What will we do now at age 15? We get angry when things don't go our way. We are not even interested in honoring our parents or those in authority. We need to listen and obey God. Know that the truth of our text, "honor" will protect you.

Prayer: Gracious Lord, please help each child to see how important this is! Help them to love their parents by forgiving them, with an attitude that gives *"honor."* For in the end, we want our children to honor You. In Jesus' name we pray. Amen.

September 24

"His master replied, 'Well done, good and faithful servant! You have been faithful with a few things; I will put you in charge of many things. Come and share your master's happiness!'" Matthew 25:21

Faithfulness before privileges, Part 1

This is a huge Biblical principle for discipling a child, student, worker or church member. More than that, this is a big principle for every life, as it comes from the Parable of the Talents. In this parable, Jesus as Master rewards the *"faithful"* in The Judgment. The point is that the Master only gives privileges to the *"faithful servant!"* That is why our title is, "Faithfulness before privileges."

If we give privileges freely to anyone before faithfulness is shown in their relationships and responsibilities, we will have a proud and a hard to live with person! God warns us: Don't make a *"recent convert"* a leader, lest they *"become conceited and fall under the same judgment as the devil,"* 1 Timothy 3:6. A church member must first be *"above reproach"* before they are given a position in leadership! They must be *"self-controlled, respectable, hospitable, able to teach, not given to drunkenness, not violent but gentle, not quarrelsome, not a lover of money. He must manage his own family well and see that his children obey him with proper respect,"* 1 Timothy 3:2b-4. This describes what *"faithful"* should look like in the church. How does our lack of faithfulness begin?

There are many little children who have egos the size of an elephant! Their parents have treated them like Rajas (kings) from birth! They are given what they want without first being faithful in any duties, responsibilities or by respecting their parents. If a child will not listen to a parent or be responsible, then pouring privileges on them will not correct them! God shows us how to live a disciplined life. God then blesses us after we are faithful, as a reward to encourage us to keep being faithful.

Prayer: Lord, we have a problem. We have failed at discipleship at ground level. Little children are becoming out of control because we as parents have neglected Your principles for living. We have brought them up our way instead of Your way. Forgive us and help us to adjust to Your way. In Jesus' name we pray. Amen.

September 25

"His master replied, 'Well done, good and faithful servant! You have been faithful with a few things; I will put you in charge of many things. Come and share your master's happiness!'" Matthew 25:21

Faithfulness before privileges, Part 2

Yesterday's topic is so important it needs further study. If a child is raised by giving them privileges without first demonstrating any faithfulness, do not expect him or her to change their pattern of living when they get older! In fact, many young children demand the privileges up front, without even the slightest hint that they will be faithful. After five years of permissive nonsense, the spoiled child now goes to school.

Suddenly, the child is expected to behave in an orderly way. After all, there are 50 kids in the classroom. But the child cannot handle being told to sit still and listen. So the child acts up. Then the parent blames the school for not being able to handle their kid. If only the parent could understand that their lack of discipline in giving five years of privileges without expecting the child to be faithful, is the real problem.

Dear parent, what do you think would happen if the school gave your child high marks in their classes, without your child faithfully giving the right answers? Would your child ever study faithfully? No way! Why should they? Really, if the school followed the pattern of many undisciplined homes, they would give a 100% grade for a blank test paper! They would give the child a high score just for showing up in school. The whole system of building up faithful workers would be destroyed in just one generation!

Carry this a little further. What if a government program gave a monthly payment to a physically and mentally able man or woman, without being required to work faithfully in any way? Would such a person want to get a job and be faithful? Again, no way. How important it is to expect labor before honor, and faithfulness before privileges!

Prayer: Lord, we have ignored Your principle of faithfulness before privileges to the ruin of our families, churches and even our country. Forgive us we pray. May we have a change of heart and follow Your principles for living. In Jesus' name we pray. Amen.

September 26

"If your brother sins against you, go and show him his fault, just between the two of you." Matthew 18:15a

Communicating when it is difficult, Part 1

A husband and wife loudly complain to their friends about their son or daughter who is out of control. They announce that they are going to have a family meeting to get to the bottom of the "issues." Of course, their friends tell them, "We don't know how this could happen, you are such great parents!" Isn't that exactly why the couple leaked this information? They are embarrassed. Their pride and "good name" has been stepped on. They are worried.

Dear embarrassed parents: Grace and peace may not happen so quickly. There may be a bigger problem than an out of control child. When these things happen, it is not all about our reputation. We start on the wrong foot to fix a serious relationship problem when we tell others about our private family problems. Why didn't we talk to our child first about what they did wrong? How would we like it if our child went to their "friends" and told about all the mistakes we made as parents? We would be quite angry! But this is what we often do.

Our text is quite clear, *"If your brother sins against you, go and show him his fault, just between the two of you."* Private matters need private discussions! This is true for immediate family, and also true for church brothers and sisters! Perhaps there is a time coming when our circle for friends can help. But for now, be careful when we ask them to pray. Because when we say that, we can selfishly be looking for their pity and try to get out of the blame for the current situation. May we instead, humble ourselves, pray, and go privately to our child. This is an important first step. There are other important things God wants us to do. But for now, may we keep it private and pray.

Prayer: Dear Heavenly Father, forgive us for not talking about problems openly in our families, and with You also. O what needless pain we bear, all because we do not carry, everything to You in prayer. Help us to personally change, so that we can build up strong families that honor You. In Jesus' name we pray. Amen.

September 27

"Reckless words pierce like a sword, but the tongue of the wise brings healing." Proverbs 12:18

Communicating healing words, Part 2

Our line of communication with someone is broken. We know some things need to change. We know that faithfulness must be more evident. But how do we get into a good discussion without getting into a big fight?

It would be wise to begin our "talk" by quietly admitting the mistakes we as a parent (if it's your child) have made. We do share in the communication breakdown. When our child sees we are serious about changing our life, they may get serious in fixing theirs! Besides, God holds us responsible to change anyway, even if our child doesn't.

We could say, "I have done a lot of wrong things. I have hurt you, and others also. I have used people to benefit myself instead of trying to be a friend to them. Let me tell you about a mistake I learned as a boy. I found some bad pictures and then gave them to the other boys. Soon the boys in my class were seeing who could get the "best" bad pictures. Then we got caught and the principal beat on us. When we got home our dads disciplined us again. Some learned, others did not!"

As a parent, we still make many mistakes. We say we're too busy to go to a school program. We should have found the time. We do not encourage like we should. At times we shout so loudly that the neighbors can hear every angry word! As parents we have been wrong in how we responded. Forgive us! You are important to us.

We have a personal discipleship problem when we directly dig into the garbage can of someone else's sins, and are not willing to put a lid on our own! When others see that we are serious about confessing our sins and changing, it will be much easier to communicate concern for their "issues." *"The tongue of the wise brings healing."* Let us be wise.

Prayer: Dear Lord, how true it is that our words bring either healing or hurt. You have told us that out of the same mouth comes blessings and cursings, and that it should not be like this. Forgive us Lord. Help us to communicate Your way. In Jesus' name we pray. Amen.

September 28

"Be still, and know that I am God; I will be exalted among the nations, I will be exalted in the earth." Psalm 46:10

Be quiet!

Satan just loves how our world is racing faster and louder every day. We try three tasks at once. We are told that is good! We work into the evening hours. We plop into a chair or the bed exhausted. We are too tired to read the Bible and pray! The noise level is intense and doesn't quit! People are talking loud on their phones in public, sometimes on two of them. The music is turned way up to drown out any other competing sound! The husband comes home from work and his wife has the T. V. serial on loud and she is talking with a friend. Not only is she not talking to her husband, she is not talking to God. But then, the husband eats dinner, watches sports, reads the newspaper and regularly checks his cell, all at the same time. And he calls this "family time." His wife, children and God are not able to put their nose into his busy world. One of the great needs in our homes today is to slow down and *"be still."*

"Be still and <u>know</u> that I am God." How much we need to take the time to meditate on God, to know Him. Even in prayer, how often we speak to God as soon as we shut our eyes. We must learn from young Samuel who said, *"Speak, for your servant is listening,"* 1 Samuel 3:10b. How often we say something to God in prayer, wanting His will to fit into what we want, instead of the other way around. God wants to speak to us also! He is very interested in us becoming more like Christ. He wants to speak to our hearts. We sometimes say God is not listening to our prayers. But are we listening to God? It would do us much good if we would learn how to *"be still."*

"Meditate within your heart on your bed, and be still," Psalm 4:4b NKJV. Let us leave our shopping list of wants in the kitchen. May we find a more intimate relationship with God as we learn to *"be still."* May we learn about what is on God's heart. May we learn to listen.

Prayer: O Lord, You are God; we are not. Help us to put our hand over our mouth like the righteous Job did. Move us into the quiet room, seeking You in a private way. In Jesus' name we pray. Amen.

September 29

"So in everything, do to others what you would have them do to you, for this sums up the Law and the Prophets." Matthew 7:12

She did it to me!

Something happened that opened my eyes to how insensitive I have been. A few days ago my wife was gone all day doing this and that, important things really! But when she came home in the afternoon I had a number of things I needed to talk about. But her mother also called during the day. So I told her about that, and so she immediately called her mom. She talked for what I thought was a rather long time. Any other time it would not have mattered. But I had five things that I wanted to talk about! The truth is: I wanted to talk so I could get out of the house. I admit, I was frustrated! So I wrote all five things down on paper and then impatiently waited!

My wife noticed that I was sitting in a chair (not too normal when there is work to do) and my eyes were saying, "You need to talk to me!" So she said good-bye to her mother. Then she asked, "I take it you are waiting to talk to me?" I said, "Yes." Then I went over the things I had written down. I was greatly relieved. Then it hit me! I said to her, "How many times have I done this to you over the years? How many times did I get home from work and then head outside to do other things?" She got this big smile that said, "You finally understand." Yes, years too late!

She had finally done to me just once, what I had often done to her! I should have cared more. The verse, *"In everything, do to others what you would have them do to you,"* Matthew 7:12a, was meant to include *"everything"*! And if the word, *"everything"* was not inclusive enough of all things, the Bible adds, *"for this sums up the Law and the Prophets,"* Matthew 7:12b. The whole Old Testament teaches this in its entirety, and it was also said by Jesus in the New Testament.

Prayer: Gracious Lord, how we hurt people because of our selfishness. Lord, even when we are unavailable to others, You are so available to listen to us, day or night! We have so much to learn. We have so little time to learn it. Help us to see that *"listening"* is an important task. Maybe we can even ask others, "How was your day?" instead of being so focused on our own issues. In Jesus' name we pray. Amen.

September 30

"The earth is the LORD's, and everything in it, the world, and all who live in it; for He founded it upon the seas and established it upon the waters." Psalm 24:1-2

This is my Father's world

With all the turmoil that is going on in the world today, we know this world is becoming harder to live in. We know suffering will increase. We know there will not only be more earthquakes, but *"great earthquakes,"* Luke 21:11. We know there will not only be false prophets, but *"many false prophets,"* Matthew 24:11. Persecution will be more intense. It is so easy for us to get worried and fear these coming difficult events. May we remember, this is our Father's world!

"The earth is the LORD's, and everything in it." Our God is in total control of what is going on today. Not only that, God will always be in total control of the world's calendar of events. And better yet, God is our Father! He will always be our Father. He calls us by name. He gave us the name Christian and adopted us to be His son or daughter. Yes, this is our Father's world. To help us meditate Biblically on some of the ways that this is our Father's world, we will use two verses of a most beautiful song.

This is my Father's world, and to my listening ears
All nature sings, and round me rings the music of the spheres.

This is my Father's world! I rest me in the thought,
Of rocks and trees, of skies and seas, His hand the wonders wrought.

This is my Father's world, O let me ne'er forget
That though the wrong seems oft so strong God is the ruler yet.

This is my Father's world! The battle is not done;
Jesus who died shall be satisfied, and earth and Heaven be one.

Prayer: Lord, may we rest in the fact that this is our personal, loving Heavenly Father's world! As a good Father, You always have Your eye on us. May this cause us to keep our eyes on You in love, in hope, and in true faith. In Jesus' name we pray. Amen.

OCTOBER

*"And we know that in all things God works
for the good of those who love Him, who have
been called according to His purpose."*
Romans 8:28

October 1

"Contend for the faith that was once for all entrusted to the saints. For certain men whose condemnation was written about long ago have secretly slipped in among you. They are godless men, who change the grace of our God into a license for immorality and deny Jesus Christ our only Sovereign and Lord." Jude 3b-4

Satan's gospel message, Part 1

Satan's main deceptive message is this! "People are bad because the evil that is in them is from their parents, neighbors, friends and others who have not loved them enough. If we would just look for the good that is in people and then nurture it, they would come around. It is not possible for people to love God or others, because they do not even love themselves. People first need to learn to love themselves. They need better self-esteem. When their love for self is overflowing, then they will finally be able to love God and others." Does that short message from Satan sound a little familiar? We will only fall for such terrible theology, when we are not very sure of the truth!

Satan, the leader of all that is evil, deceives people by replacing the prophet's and apostle's teachings in Scripture that were *"once and for all entrusted to the saints."* He sends out pretend prophets and apostles. He does some miracles and healings through them to try convince people! He does everything in his power to divert people's attention away from that which makes them holy, the grace of God through Jesus Christ. Plus, Satan will give an experience that is out of the ordinary, to really win us over. Satan really does just that!

Already in the early church, imposters had *"slipped in,"* *"godless men,"* whose whole purpose was to change the Gospel message into something it was not. These godless men, (false prophets) did not preach about the one true God in a right way. They perverted the Gospel. Salvation in Christ by grace alone, was replaced with the grace of Christ plus something else. We will look at their errors in the coming devotions.

Prayer: Merciful Father, in almost every book in the New Testament, You warn us about false teachers. Here You tell us to *"contend for the faith."* Lord, help us to see the truth so we can also see the errors! Give us a burden to teach it. In Jesus' name we pray. Amen.

October 2

"Let <u>Us</u> make man in <u>Our</u> image, in <u>Our</u> likeness." Genesis 1:26a

The war in the spirit world, Part 2

Before we look at what Satan and his angels are doing, let us review what the Bible teaches about the Holy Spirit and His work!

1. God the Holy Spirit always existed. The Holy Spirit as God was <u>not</u> <u>created</u> but has eternally existed. The first word in the Hebrew Bible is God - meaning our covenant-keeping Trinitarian God. This includes the Father, Son and Holy Spirit, three persons, yet one God.

2. The Holy Spirit as God created the world. We know from Genesis 1:1-2 that the Holy Spirit was involved in the creation process. The words, *"the Spirit of God was hovering over the waters"* is speaking of the Holy Spirit. What God then made was declared *"good."* See how the Holy Spirit creates, and Satan and his spirit demons destroy.

3. The Holy Spirit as God created man. *"Then God said, 'Let <u>Us</u> make man in <u>Our</u> image, in <u>Our</u> likeness,'"* Genesis 1:26a. The plural words of *"Us"* and *"Our"* are speaking of the Father, Son, and the Holy Spirit.

4. The Holy Spirit puts His Spirit into man. We are both physical and spiritual. *"The Lord God formed the man from the dust of the ground* (physical part) *and breathed into his nostrils the breath of life* (the spiritual part), *and the man became a living being,"* Genesis 2:7.

5. Man sins and the Holy Spirit must leave him. Why? Because now man, like Satan, is under the wrath of God. This is clear in John 3:36 and Romans 1:18. Satan was removed from the presence of God when he fell. Man is removed from the presence of God because man is no longer holy! This is the story of the fall of man in the Garden of Eden in Genesis 2 and 3.

6. God the Father, Son and Spirit defeat Satan at the Cross. Jesus said on the way to the Cross, *"Now is the time for judgment on this world; now the prince of this world will be driven out,"* John 12:31.

Prayer: Almighty Lord, we see some of the history of Your Holy Spirit and the war for the souls of men. You call sinners to make them holy. Satan works to deceive them! We are thankful that You are stronger than Satan. He can't stop our salvation, or our becoming more holy. We praise You for Your Spirit who makes and keeps us holy! In Jesus' name we pray. Amen.

October 3

"Having believed, you were marked in Him with a seal, the promised Holy Spirit, who is a deposit guaranteeing our inheritance until the redemption of those who are God's possession." Ephesians 1:13b-14a

Must we go & get an anointing? Part 3

After becoming believers, must we "get" more of the Spirit by our own effort as some teach? Or, does the desire to get more of the Spirit, on our own, insult the grace of God? If we are going to worship God in spirit and in truth, we must know the truth!

1. God in Trinity *"chose us in Him before the creation of the world to be holy and blameless in His sight,"* Ephesians 1:4. God "got us" as Christians, *"before the creation of the world to be holy."* That is grace! God *"chose"* us! That's also grace. *"He predestined us to be adopted"* in verse 5. That's more grace! The "getting" is all God, all of grace! Now, some say we need to get more of God. How can we do that? We didn't get any of God on our own so far!

2. After salvation the Holy Spirit *"marks"* **and** *"seals"* **us in the faith!** By grace alone the real Holy Spirit gets more of us again! *"Having believed, you were marked in Him with a seal, the promised Holy Spirit,"* Ephesians 1:13b. We don't mark Him. He marks us! *"You were marked."* These words show that the Holy Spirit continues to get more of us. Some try to sweep God's grace under the rug by saying this is an external sealing and not internal. Our hearts are quite internal. See how next.

3. The Holy Spirit *"is a deposit guaranteeing our inheritance until the redemption of those who are God's possession,"* Ephesians 1:14. Do you see how the grace of the Spirit continues? Grace is not just in the salvation process. God's grace is completely in sanctification too! He gives us, *"the will and to do for His good pleasure."* And, God's grace is *"until the redemption."* God's grace "gets us" all the way to Heaven. All of it is a gift. All is given by God! None is gotten by us!

Prayer: Our Triune and gracious God, we praise You for Your grace in buying our souls with Jesus' precious blood for all eternity. Even, *"guaranteeing our inheritance until the redemption."* In Jesus' name we pray. Amen.

October 4

"Dear friends, do not believe every spirit, but test the spirits to see whether they are from God, because many false prophets have gone out into the world." 1 John 4:1

Mediator vs. mediums, Part 4

1. What is the work of the Mediator? Jesus Christ is the only God-appointed representative to connect us to God the Master of all that is good and holy. We cannot get connected to God on our own because we are sinners and God is holy. We need help. We need a Mediator. Jesus alone is that Mediator!

2. What is the work of *"mediums"* in the spirit world? A medium is a go-between that directs people to Satan, the master of all that is evil and profane. The word *"mediums"* is much like the word Mediator. Just as mediums connect us to Satan, Jesus our Mediator connects us to God! People chant the name of a god in a pagan temple to "get connected" and get the power. Keep this in mind.

3. Who is the medium in "slaying in the spirit" "worship"? It is a false prophet! *"Dear friends, do not believe every spirit, but test the spirits to see whether they are from God, because many <u>false prophets</u> have gone out into the world,"* 1 John 4:1. See a detailed report of this in my experiences in the November 8 and 9 devotions.

4. Is real repentance seen where "slaying in the spirit" is practiced? No! I have been in many churches and very little change of life for the better is evident. Instead, there is a greater interest in money, power, adultery, and just plain evil.

5. What about laughing and barking in the spirit? What spirit would bark like a dog, or laugh in a "worship" service? A preacher was teaching on the subject of Hell when an epidemic of "laughter in the spirit" broke out. What spirit would laugh at Hell?

Prayer: O holy God, You command us, *"test the spirits to see whether they are from God."* Lord give us wisdom to know which Spirits are holy and which ones are wicked. Help us to worship You in a way that pleases You. For Your Spirit is called Holy, because another spirit isn't! We thank You for warning us. In Jesus' name we pray. Amen.

October 5

"And when you pray, do not use vain repetitions as the heathen do. For they think that they will be heard for their many words."
Matthew 6:7 NKJV

Worship, but to what deity? Part 5

I was teaching at a meeting. Five pastors from mega churches were leading the singing, "worship time" they called it. Before each class, one of these "pastors" would "do their thing!" The songs got louder and faster, saying the same words over and over. More women than men were jumping, rapidly clapping, hysterical, often ending on the floor. They said the Holy Spirit was moving them. Was it? If this "spirit" was Holy, why were the other four pastors in the back telling jokes? This "worship" scene was repeated by the different pastors, while the four in the back had their own party. Which spirit teaches us in Galatians 5:23a, that *"gentleness and self-control"* are *"the fruit of the Spirit."*

I was invited to eat with the "big" pastors in a separate air-conditioned hotel, with "special" food, on big soft chairs. The "common people" sat on the floor in the big hall, eating tomato rice! Who would Jesus eat with? What kind of a pastor would consider himself "too good" to eat with the people. What an eye opener!

I questioned three of these pastors about the "holiness" of the singing time. Knowing they would not listen to Scripture, I told this story: "I was on the train last week and saw a Hindu priest playing a drum with three Hindu ladies facing him, swaying to the music. The priest chanted some mantra while working the drums. The three ladies passed "out," fully hypnotized! What "spirit" did this?" Two of the pastors said, "It was the Holy Spirit." I asked them, "How can the spirit be God's, if a Hindu priest is leading them?" The other pastor said, "The spirit was not holy." So I said to him, "I don't understand, you do the same thing. You play a few notes again and again until you move a person into a hypnotic state! Even in prayer, you repetitively chant instead of talking to God in intelligent prayer. You say things like 'sha da ba ba ba' again and again with a few hallelujahs thrown in."

Prayer: Lord, open our eyes to what is holy and what is not. May we worship You in spirit and in truth. In Jesus' name we pray. Amen.

October 6

"Casting down arguments and every high thing that exalts itself against the knowledge of God, bringing every thought into captivity to the obedience of Christ." 2 Corinthians 10:5 NKJV

Prophets, with which spirit? Part 6

Years ago, Satan got a hold of Franz Anton Mesmer. He was a French physician who lived from 1734-1815. From his name we get mesmerism. He has also been called the father of psychotherapy (another religion) as well as Christian Science (a cult). He was the discoverer of hypnosis, the forefather of clairvoyance, and communication with the dead. This man was a radical theologian! He did so much damage! In his day, Mesmer was considered a money hungry magician who had sold his soul to the devil. A counterfeit revival began, where enlightenment is sought through a personal "experience." Religion, it is. Holy, it is not!

Many churches now mentally manipulate people using hypnotics and mesmerism. A main focus of a "false priest" in some churches today is to try convince the people that the "power" or "feeling" in their "experience" is the real Holy Spirit. I have personally seen so much of this and it is ugly! People are now going to such "churches" to get a personal experience, to feel good. Such "worship" is man-centered, not God-centered. The real Biblical goal of "giving worship to God" has been exchanged for getting an altered state of consciousness, to "get the feeling." Once someone is under or mesmerised, the power of suggestion and peer pressure can create an experience that is literally out of this world. That is what "worshipers" now crave each Sunday! The objective of this altered state of consciousness is to dull the critical thinking process! Why? Because a clear mind is a huge obstacle in selling satanic "theology."

In worship, God wants us to *"take captive every thought to make it obedient to Christ,"* 2 Corinthians 10:5. We are not to empty our minds but to fill our minds with the presence of the Lord, with His Spirit. Then we will not believe or do sinful things in worship and in life!

Prayer: Lord, You tell us that Your Word enters our hearts through the ear! Your Word says *faith comes by hearing, and hearing by the Word of God."* Thank You for Your Word, Lord. In Jesus' name we pray. Amen.

October 7

"Dear friends, do not believe every spirit, but test the spirits to see whether they are from God." 1 John 4:1a

Which Spirit/spirit is in us? Part 7

1. Do we have assurance of salvation? *"The Spirit Himself testifies with our spirit that we are God's children,"* Romans 8:16. Satan's *"spirit"* can never give us an assurance of salvation. Do we have assurance?

2. Do we have guilt for our sins? The Holy Spirit *"will convict the world of guilt in regard to sin,"* John 16:8b. Satan's *"spirit"* will never help us be sensitive to our sin. Are we convicted that we are sinners?

3. Are we growing in holiness? *"Live by the Spirit, and you will not gratify the desires of the sinful nature,"* Galatians 5:16b. The question is not, "Do we feel more holy," but are we growing in holiness?

4. Do we keep the Sabbath Day holy? One *"spirit"* teaches us to do what we want on Sunday. God's Spirit teaches us to worship the LORD. *"'If you keep your feet from breaking the Sabbath and from doing as you please on My holy day, if you call the Sabbath a delight and the LORD's holy day honorable, and if you honor it by not going your own way and not doing as you please or speaking idle words, then you will find your joy in the LORD, and I will cause you to ride on the heights of the land and to feast on the inheritance of your father Jacob.' The mouth of the LORD has spoken,"* Isaiah 58:13-14. What are our Sunday habits?

5. Do our prayers reflect an increasing friendship with God? Do we use many different words that reflect a deep relationship with God? Or, do we use the same words over and over, and *"keep on babbling like pagans,"* Matthew 6:7?

6. Are we loving others more? The Holy Spirit said, *"If anyone says, 'I love God,' yet hates his brother, he is a liar,"* 1 John 4:20a. Satan's *"spirit"* tells us to love self more. Who are we following?

7. Are we growing in humility? One Spirit teaches humility. One *"spirit"* teaches pride! Who are we listening to? We either grow in pride, united to Satan. Or, we are growing in humility, united to Christ.

Prayer: Lord, put Your Spirit in us more and more. That is what we need. We need You to fill and complete us. In Jesus' name we pray. Amen.

October 8

"Let no one be found among you who sacrifices his son or daughter in the fire, who practices divination or sorcery, interprets omens, engages in witchcraft, or casts spells, or who is a medium or spiritist or <u>who consults the dead</u>. Anyone who does these things is detestable to the LORD, and because of these detestable practices the LORD your God will drive out those nations before you." Deuteronomy 18:10-12

Why is consulting the dead "detestable"?

God tells us here about a pagan practice He hates! His people were going into Canaan. The evil ways of consulting the dead were common there. God did not want His people to copy these habits. So He uses strong words to show them and us, what consulting the dead was connected to. God wants us to understand the spiritual war that is going on for the souls of men. In this war there are mediums to Satan, and there is a Mediator to God. God is telling His people, "don't fall for a medium to Satan! It is *'detestable'* to Me."

The souls of those in Heaven or in Hell cannot see or hear us! If we try to call them, Satan will answer the phone! He will use this opportunity to speak lies and to deceive us. Consulting the dead quickly becomes a demonic invasion into our spiritual life. In Leviticus 20:7-8, the words, *"I am the LORD your God"* and *"I am the LORD who makes you holy,"* shout to us! Evil mediums cannot make us holy and cannot give us peace. Instead, they will do the opposite, defile and torment us!

"We have a great High Priest who has gone through the Heavens, Jesus the Son of God." He can *"sympathize with our weaknesses."* *"Approach the throne of grace with confidence, so that we may receive mercy and find grace to help us in our time of need,"* Hebrews 4:14-16.

Job said about the dead, *"If his sons are honored, he does not know it; if they are brought low, he does not see it,"* Job 14:21. Our loved ones who died can't see or hear us, so why call out to them?

Prayer: Dear Lord, it is good that You instruct us from Your Holy Word. David was right when he said in Psalm 73:25, *"Whom have I in Heaven but You?"* We thank You that we can freely speak to You anytime, anyplace, on any subject and You hear us. May Your name be praised. In Christ's name we pray. Amen.

October 9

"To slander no one, to be peaceable and considerate, and to show true humility toward all men." Titus 3:2

Why are we "slandered"?

We are to do good to all men. *"Slander"* does not do good. *"Slander"* is different than gossip. A gossip tells many people things about others that are true, but not always nice. A person who is into *"slander"* tells nasty things about others that are not true. *"Slander"* tries to ruin a person's reputation. Everyone involved in *"slander"* gets hurt. But what must we do when *"slander"* hurts us? There are 3 things we can do.

1. Expect slander from others! People have jealous hearts. Christians do also! If we happen to be alive to God, in a church or community that wants to sleep, we will be slandered. The main reason is that people try to cover up their own shortcomings! Expect slander as it will happen. If we do not expect it, we will have a far greater temptation to become angry and bitter when it does happen. That is a big mistake on our part.

2. Think of how Jesus was slandered! Jesus was perfect. We are not. Even though God's Son had no faults, people still found fault with Him. Jesus was even charged with having a demon. God the Father who is perfect and holy, was slandered by Satan in the courts of Heaven. We are privileged to suffer with Christ. May we act like it.

3. Follow Paul's example. Don't bite back! Do not retaliate in any way to slander. The temptation is there, but don't do it. The safest way to defend our character is to say nothing about it. Paul said, *"When we are cursed, we bless; when we are persecuted, we endure it; when we are slandered, we answer kindly,"* 1 Corinthians 4:12b-13a. God's ways are higher than the world's ways. May we learn to respond as our Lord and Savior instructs us to react.

Prayer: Father of compassion, how much it hurts when others throw stones at us for being salt and light. We are grateful that You personally understand. Lord help us to live out our text, to *"be peaceable and considerate, and to show true humility toward all men."* In Jesus' name we pray. Amen.

"They get into the habit of being idle and going about from house to house. And not only do they become idlers, but also gossips and busybodies, saying things they aught not to." 1 Timothy 5:13

Why do we gossip about others?

In our text God is specifically warning widows about the sin of *"gossip."* Yet this is a big problem for more than just widows!

1. What is wrong with *"gossips"*? As *"gossips"* we proudly pretend to show how informed we are about what is going on. Our *"gossip"* pulls others down by speaking about their mistakes/problems, to those who have <u>no need to know</u>! Where in the Bible are we ever told to pull others down? In Luke 9:23, Jesus says to *"deny"* self. Gossip doesn't do that. Instead, it grumbles about others, to others. We can also do this in our minds, without speaking it. From God's eyes, this is a form of *"bitterness"* and *"of the devil,"* James 3:15. The Israelites grumbled to others about how God was treating them. But ultimately, this was a big dissatisfaction with God. So is our *"gossip."*

2. What must we do instead? We must have a heart cleaning! Jesus will do it if we would just ask Him. *"The good man (or woman) brings good things out of the good stored up in his heart, and the evil man brings evil things out of the evil stored up in his heart. <u>For out of the overflow of his heart his mouth speaks</u>,"* Luke 6:45. What is in our hearts comes out. If a lot of gossip is coming out of our mouths there is a lot of evil in our hearts. Evil shows! Our lives here on earth are a test to see if we will give out gracious words, encouragement and loving correction. *"Gossip"* miserably fails the grace test! There's nothing gracious about *"gossip."*

Prayer: Lord, as we look at our own bodies, we can see how every single part beautifully serves our whole body. Our *"gossip"* hurts the body of Christ. We would never intentionally hit our finger with a hammer, but we purposely hit others with our words. We do need a heart cleaning on this issue. O Lord, full of grace and love, forgive us of our sin. Help us to speak the truth, with love! In Jesus' name we pray. Amen.

October 11

"We wait in hope for the LORD; He is our help and our shield."
Psalm 33:20

"He is our help and our shield"
Psalm 33 is a beautiful call to worship God, who is *"our help and our shield."* It is our Creator, not created things, that is our help and shield! The Psalm begins by calling us to worship God. Verses 4-5 praises God for His love, faithfulness, righteousness, and justice. Verses 6-7 praises the wisdom and the sovereign power of God. Verse 6 reminds us that God spoke and the world was created. With all of these facts about the amazing attributes of God, the Psalm now states:

"The LORD <u>foils</u> the plans of nations; He thwarts the purposes of the peoples," Psalm 33:10. God does this because the world is moving according to His agenda. *"The plans of the LORD stand firm forever, the purposes of His heart through all generations,"* Psalm 33:11.

God *"<u>blesses</u>"* all who belong to Him. His eye *"sees all mankind,"* Psalm 33:13b. He *"watches all who live on earth,"* Psalm 33:14b. He *"considers everything they do,"* Psalm 33:15b. God specifically pours out His blessings on those who are His.

God *"<u>helps</u>"* His own. He gives them exactly what they need, when they need it. His mercy is never early so that our faith is exercised. Yet God's mercy is not so late that we would lose hope! *"Let us then approach the throne of grace with confidence, so that we may receive mercy and find grace to help us in our time of need,"* Hebrews 4:16. God is our helper, so we need not fear what man can do to us!

God *"<u>shields</u>"* His own, both physically and spiritually. Satan cannot afflict us without God's permission as Job 1 teaches. Jesus taught us to pray, *"Deliver us from the evil one."* God can and will do it! *"The eyes of the LORD are on those who fear Him, on those whose hope is in His unfailing love,"* Psalm 33:18. *"The Lord will rescue me from every evil attack and will bring me safely to His heavenly kingdom. To Him be the glory for ever and ever. Amen,"* 2 Timothy 4:18.

Prayer: Dear Father in Heaven, Your goodness is our need! *"May Your unfailing love rest upon us, O LORD, even as we put our hope in You,"* Psalm 33:22. In Jesus' name we pray. Amen.

October 12

"From one man He (God) made every nation of men; that they should inhabit the whole earth; and He determined the times set for them and the exact places where they should live; God did this so that men would seek Him and perhaps reach out for Him and find Him, though He is not far from each one of us. For in Him we live and move and have our being." Acts 17:26-28a

Are we personally seeking God?

The next 7 lessons are a study on the important topic of evangelism. We are going to ask some questions, starting with personal ones. Why were we born? Why do we have the parents that we do? Why do we live where we do? Our text tells us. Everyone is here completely by the will of God, born and placed exactly when and where God wanted us to be. Why did God do this? *"God did this so that men would seek Him and perhaps reach out for Him and find Him."* We are here to find God, to know Him, and to enjoy Him forever. Are we seeking Him?

If our life presently has very little meaning, a most likely reason is that we are not *"seeking"* God. If He put us here for that reason, how can our life have meaning apart from Him? Our text is so clear. We have a personal responsibility to *"find Him." "Seek and you will find"* we read in Matthew 7:7b. Jesus also said, "Seek first His kingdom and His righteousness," in Matthew 6:33a. Then our life will have meaning! As we come to God in prayer we will use a beautiful prayer from 1000 years ago. Author unknown.

Prayer: "Lord Jesus Christ, let me seek You by desiring You, and let me desire You, by seeking You. Let me find You by loving You, and love You in finding You. I confess Lord, with thanksgiving, that You have made me in Your image, so that I can remember You, think of You, and love You. But that image is so worn and blotted out by fault, darkened by the smoke of sin that I cannot do that for which I was made unless You renew and refashion me. Lord, I desire to understand more of Your truth, which my heart already believes and loves. I do not seek to understand so that I can believe. But I believe so that I may understand. Help my weakness Lord." In Jesus' name we pray. Amen.

October 13

"'Zacchaeus, come down immediately. I must stay at your house today.'
So he came down at once and welcomed Him gladly." Luke 19:5b-6

Do we love the lost? Part 1

We move into the important subject of the evangelism of others. There are six main points. 1. Do we love the lost? 2. Do we weep over the lost? 3. Do we seek the lost? 4. Am I my brother's keeper? 5. Am I my neighbor's keeper? 6. Do we pray for the lost?

1. Do we love the lost? Jesus hated sin, yet He loved the sinner deeply! Because of this, sinners *"welcomed Him gladly."* Jesus was comfortable mingling with them, and they were in turn, comfortable being with Jesus. In other words, those who were sick spiritually, enjoyed the presence of their spiritual healer! Jesus enjoyed ministering to their needs in a most gracious, gentle, and tender way. We too are called to help others spiritually. They must come into fellowship with the body of Christ!

Jesus did not have something better to do. We may labor in the Word and in prayer to help someone. But even when we do help, we can so easily think of other things we would rather be doing. Jesus knew the importance of spending time with His disciples. He spent that time with a right attitude, for He came to earth to redeem and guide lost sinners! Jesus was <u>with</u> His disciples.

Jesus was not bothered by those who thought He should not love sinners. The religious leaders accused Jesus by saying, *"Here is a glutton and a drunkard, a friend of tax collectors and 'sinners,'"* Matthew 11:19b. They did not understand what ministry was. After all of Jesus' warnings, this is still a problem today! It is not a mark of Biblical righteousness to keep sinners away from us, our homes, and our churches! Corporate worship and our private lives must be places where sinners can come and be welcomed and encouraged!

Prayer: Lord, You love the lost and go to them! Forgive us for the many times we have been so hard in our condemnation of sinners who need Your love! Help us to point those who are still <u>slaves to sin,</u> to a relationship with You. For with You living in a heart, we sinners change and become <u>slaves to righteousness.</u> Lord, thank You for making that kind of change in us and in others. In Jesus' name we pray. Amen.

October 14

"As He approached Jerusalem and saw the city, He wept over it and said, 'If you, even you, had only known on this day what would bring you peace.'" Luke 19:41-42a

Do we weep over the lost? Part 2

In today's text, God's Ambassador from Heaven weeps for lost souls. Jesus saw so many lost opportunities from those who heard the Gospel but did not respond. Jesus is not weeping over pagans here, but covenant Israel. In the context of our text, Jesus is approaching Jerusalem with a great view of the city. He can see into the future. He can see the Roman commander Titus approach the city. Jesus can see him digging a big trench and building a big wall all around Jerusalem, to seal it off. He sees the murdering Romans going into the city, leveling it. Not one stone was left upon another. No one could escape. So great is the coming destruction.

Why is this great destruction coming? *"Because you did not recognize the time of God's coming to you,"* Luke 19:44b. The people did not seek a peace with God! They wanted relief from the persecuting Romans. They did not understand that God allowed the Romans to trouble them because they rejected a real relationship with Him. Israel broke covenant again and again! God laid the blame of His rejection on the cold hearts of the people. Such rejection of the Holy Spirit is unforgivable, if we ignore the conviction of sin that He brings. The people of Jerusalem were brought up for generations to know the Law. They knew right from wrong! Yet they persisted in doing the wrong. God strives and pleads with them, and us also, to change our wicked patterns of living. Israel refused God's many admonitions. He even sent His own Son in the flesh to warn them. What will we do with this Jesus? Is Jesus rejoicing over us? Or, is Jesus weeping over us and our children?

Prayer: O holy and loving Lord, so many are lost and Your Judgment is coming! Help us to understand the importance of being ready personally, and move us to seek the lost who are not yet ready to meet You. Help us to see that You made us, not so much for this world, but for eternity. Help us to live our short life with eternity in mind. Lord, save us and use us for Your glory! In Jesus' name we pray. Amen.

October 15

"For the Son of Man came to seek and to save what was lost."
Luke 19:10

Do we "seek" the lost? Part 3

Earlier we saw that sinners loved to be with Jesus, and Jesus loved to be with them. If we do not love sinners in point one, we will not weep over them in point two, nor will we "seek" them here in point three! And this is exactly why we are not effective in doing evangelism! The real mission of Christ was to "seek and to save the lost." That is the commission that Jesus gave to each of His disciples, and to us personally. This will take much of our time and energy.

For too many, their main idea of evangelism is to put a sign out in front of their church listing their worship times. They think that if a lost sinner has a spiritual problem, they will see the sign and come in. Once in a while this may be true, but not often. This kind is thinking is about as ridiculous as a hunter sitting in his easy chair at home, expecting the deer to come right to his window! No, the hunter must go into the woods or into the field to see the deer. A fisherman must go out on the lake to catch a fish. And even then, the fish will not jump into the boat. The net must be cast. A line must be put out. Jesus said, *"I will make you fishers of men."* We need to go into the world and fish for sinners.

One of the reasons we need to "seek" out sinners is because they really are "lost." They are suffering. They are perplexed as to what their real problem is. They don't realize that if their hearts changed, their thoughts, words and actions would change. And then their emotions would change also! They need someone willing to be God's messenger and "seek" them out, to lead them to the Savior! If we are willing to be used by God in this way, we must also be willing to leave our comfort zone. Are we willing?

Prayer: Dear Lord, You said in Your Word, *"How beautiful are the feet of those who bring good news!"* If their feet are beautiful, the rest of their person is even more beautiful to You! Lord, may we get uncomfortable for Your kingdom. We know that will bring glory and praise to You, and also bless us. In Jesus' name we pray. Amen.

October 16

"Am I my brother's keeper?" Genesis 4:9b

Are we our brother's keeper? Part 4

The world was created, man was formed and children were born. Cain was the first baby. Then Eve, *"gave birth to his brother Abel,"* Genesis 4:2a. Cain became angry and jealous of Abel. God confronted Cain and told him to change his attitude but Cain would not listen. *"Cain attacked his brother Abel and killed him,"* Genesis 4:8b. *"Then the LORD said to Cain, 'Where is your brother Abel?' 'I don't know,' he replied. 'Am I my brother's keeper?'"* Genesis 4:9. God's question is not for Cain alone! It is a question for us also. God knew Abel was dead, for his blood was crying out to God. Cain's answer, *"I don't know,"* showed his indifference to God and for his dead brother.

Did Abel do something wrong for Cain to hate him? Did God do something wrong? No, the problem was in Cain's hard heart. Cain cared too <u>much for himself,</u> too <u>little for others</u>. And that is exactly why we do not do evangelism! So the question, "Are we our brother's keeper?" is a serious evangelism question. It is just as important for discipleship as it is for evangelism. If we are a silent Christian who has yet to make known to others what God has made plain to us, then we are worse than not being our *"<u>brother's keeper</u>"*! We have actually had a hand in his death! If we have not blessed our brother, then by our neglect we have tried to destroy him. We can't be neutral concerning evangelism!

The point of God's question to Cain about his brother's whereabouts shows Cain had a covenant responsibility to love him and be a blessing to him. Remember what God said in 1 John. If we don't love our brother, we don't love God. Even today, most of the persecution we face is from within the church. That is not loving our brother! May we examine our hearts today to answer God's important question, *"Am I my brother's keeper?"*

Prayer: O merciful Lord, we are no better than Cain. We are guilty. We have been indifferent to a fellow brother. We have been indifferent to those who are dead in their trespasses and sins. Lord, forgive us! Use us to encourage others. Loosen our tongues to advance Your kingdom. Then bless our efforts for You. In Jesus' name we pray. Amen.

October 17

"A man who lacks judgment derides his neighbor, but a man of understanding holds his tongue." Proverbs 11:12

Are we our neighbor's keeper? Part 5

God says that our attitude to our neighbor is important to Him. Our text gives the meaning that a man who runs his neighbor down with his mouth *"lacks judgment."* But who is my neighbor? It's the office person who sits near me. It's a student at my school. It's a person from my church. It's the one who lives next door. But my closest neighbor of all, is my immediate family. Are their mistakes leaping off my tongue? *"A man of understanding holds his tongue."*

No doubt our *"neighbor"* has many sins and bad habits. But are we called to tell <u>others</u> about them? If we have anything to say, it should be to our *"neighbor"* only! We would not like it if our *"neighbor"* told others about our mistakes. And even if they did, we must not do the same thing. That kind of behavior quickly stops evangelism.

"Blessed are the peacemakers," Matthew 5:9a. More than that, *"Blessed are you when people insult you, persecute you and falsely say all kinds of evil against you because of Me,"* Matthew 5:11. God sees the testimony of our life! He will somehow turn their hurting words into a blessing for us. So let us not copy our neighbor's evil ways but *"in everything, do to others what you would have them do to you, for this sums up the Law and the Prophets,"* Matthew 7:12.

If we want to discuss our neighbor's annoying sin problem, go to him or her privately, as Matthew 18:15 teaches! Why? Because a gossip makes a poor evangelist! We must be more concerned about our own mistakes to be useful in the work of evangelism. If we tell pagans that Jesus changes us, and then we ourselves are not changed, it will be evident. We are a hypocrite when we point out the sins of others without dealing with our own. This doesn't mean we need to be perfect before we go to others, but we do need to be working on our own sins.

Prayer: Lord, we have openly confessed the failings of others, to those who have no reason to know. You tell us a true believer confesses his or her own sins. Forgive us for our lack of love and concern for our *"neighbor."* In Jesus' name we pray. Amen.

October 18

"I do not pray for these alone, (Jesus' disciples) but also for those who will believe in Me through their word; that they all may be one, as You, Father, are in Me, and I in You; that they also may be one in Us, that the world may believe that You sent Me." John 17:20-21 NKJV

Do we pray for the lost? Part 6

John 17 is a prayer of Jesus. He prays for the glory of God. Jesus prays for Himself in verses 1-5; for His disciples in verses 6-19; then for every disciple of His disciples in verses 20–26. In these final verses He is praying for us, for every single sheep that will ever come to Him before His Second Coming! This is a prayer of evangelism because Jesus prays, *"that they may become one in Us,"* one with the Trinity.

Jesus prayed more for others than He did for Himself, and His betrayal was less than an hour away! His trial, His suffering on the Cross, His death will all happen in the next couple of days. Still, Jesus prays for lost souls to come to God! His selfless prayers accuse us of our selfish ones. Lord help us be more like You.

Jesus prayed for the disciples of His disciples! Are we doing that? Are we concerned how our children, students, church members are doing in their discipleship efforts? Or are we too selfish to think of such things? Jesus, the perfect man, was focused on discipleship and evangelism. What interest in us is seen by how much He prays for us.

Jesus' prayer here does far more than direct us to pray. It accuses us for not praying more! We need God's forgiveness for this omission of praying for His kingdom to come specifically. We should not wait for our deathbed to remind our loved ones to follow Jesus. We need to do that today. The prayer of a righteous man avails much. Righteous people pray for the souls of others. James 5:16b tells us to, *"pray for each other so that you may be healed."* This is true for both a physical and a spiritual healing.

Prayer: Dear Lord, we thank You for instructing us to pray for lost souls. Forgive us for being so preoccupied with less important things. May Your eternal kingdom come! In Jesus' name we pray. Amen.

"From there he went on toward the hills east of Bethel and <u>pitched his tent</u>, with Bethel on the west and Ai on the east. There he <u>built an altar</u> to the LORD and called on the name of the LORD." Genesis 12:8

Whose kingdom are we building?

What a gem of a verse! Grasp how Abram *"<u>built</u> an altar,"* but he *"<u>pitched his tent</u>."* Abram knew what would last throughout eternity! What will our legacy be? Are we more interested in building our buildings, or in building God's *"altar,"* His kingdom? We should know that <u>God's "altar,"</u> His <u>place of worship</u>, and <u>His priest</u> in the Old Testament are all fulfilled in Jesus Christ.

We who are in the church need to clearly see what God called Abram to. He called Abram to *"leave"* something in 12:1. If Abram refused to *"leave,"* how could he possibly build God's *"altar"* out in the world? A main reason we are not as effective as we should be in the area of evangelism and missions is because we are not willing to *"leave."* We are more inclined to do the opposite of Abram, to *"<u>build</u> our tents,"* and *"pitch God's altar."* God wants us to labor for His kingdom.

What possession will we take with us when we leave this world? Will we take any part of our *"tent"* with us? No, even our body will return to dust. Eventually every possession, both great and small, will become ashes. We were told that which is done for Christ will last. So in the light of eternity, it is wiser to *"build an altar,"* and seek His kingdom more. Salvation is free, but discipleship is costly! May we count the cost and *"leave"* with the right attitude!

Jim Elliot had the right idea. He said, "He is no fool who gives up what he cannot keep, to gain what he cannot lose"!

Prayer: O merciful Father, please forgive our gross idolatry. We have been more interested in building our own kingdoms than in Yours. You told us that we cannot love You and our possessions at the same time. Like Abram, we too need to leave so that we can cleave to You. Lord help us to be more like Abram. Help us to be like Your Son who left Heaven itself, to build Your kingdom. May we say with Jesus, *"Lord, not My will but Thine be done."* In Jesus' name we pray. Amen.

October 20

"Into Your hands I commit my spirit; redeem me, O LORD,
the God of truth." Psalm 31:5

Do we trust our soul to God?

These words of the psalmist were also the last words Jesus spoke before He died. It would be most fitting if these were ours also. Jesus did not say the last part, *"redeem me..."*, for He had no sin, yet He is our personal <u>Redeemer</u>! That is exactly why we can trust God's Son. A redeemer buys! Jesus bought us with His blood, which is more precious than gold. The redemption cost Him everything, and us nothing! Only through the eyes of faith can we say the words of this text. Wouldn't it be great if these were our last words here on this earth!

The words, *"Into Your hands I commit my spirit"*, were true for Jesus because no one took His Spirit from Him! They took His body away, but not His Spirit. No one could possibly take it because He is God, and as God, His Spirit belongs to no one else. If Christ has redeemed us, no one can take our spirit/soul from us either, for we belong to Him. Jesus clearly said about His sheep, *"No one can snatch them out of My hand. My Father, who has given them to Me, is greater than all; no one can snatch them out of My Father's hand,"* John 10:28b-29. Our soul is safe with God, if we are His child! Are we comfortable with the fact that God has complete control of our soul, now and in eternity? Can we trust our soul to God for all eternity? If we say "Yes," that brings another question. Can we also trust our soul to God for today's living? These are trust and faith questions that have everything to do with our attitude.

The first question of the Heidelberg Catechism is a great one. "<u>What is your only comfort in life and in death</u>?" The answer is: "That I am not my own, but belong - body and soul, in life and in death - to my faithful Savior Jesus Christ. He has fully paid for all my sins with His precious blood, and has set me free from the tyranny of the devil." That is the first part of the answer. How comforting that the King of the universe bought us!

Prayer: O Lord, what a benefit, what a joy divine, leaning on Your everlasting arms! Lord, what a privilege that in Christ we can truly say, into Your hands we commit our spirits. In Jesus' name we pray. Amen.

October 21

"When that year was over, they came to him the following year and said, 'We cannot hide from our lord the fact that since our money is gone and our livestock belongs to you, there is nothing left for our lord except our bodies and our land.'" Genesis 47:18

A government can take everything!

We must learn from history. Four thousand years ago, economic hard times fell upon Egypt and the countries that surrounded it. Suddenly there was a giant government stimulus package! One of the greatest tax increases the world has ever seen was dropped on the people. In the end, see who ended up with what. <u>At the same time, see how God protected His people</u>!

<u>In the first year</u> of economic ruin, *"Joseph collected all the money that was to be found in Egypt and Canaan in payment for the grain they were buying, and he brought it to Pharaoh's palace,"* Genesis 47:14.

<u>In the second year</u> of economic ruin, the government said, *"I will sell you food in exchange for your livestock, since your money is gone,"* Genesis 47:16b. Now the government has all the money and all the businesses in its possession. But this is not the end

<u>In the third year</u>, *"When that year was over, (the second year) they came to him the following year and said, 'We cannot hide from our lord the fact that since our money is gone and our livestock belongs to you, there is nothing left for our lord except our bodies and our land,'"* Genesis 47:18. So now the government gets the people's land! *"The Egyptians, one and all, sold their fields,"* Genesis 47:20b. The people surely did not receive a fair price since no one had any money! More than that, the government *"reduced the people to servitude, from one end of Egypt to the other,"* Genesis 47:21. In three short years the people became slaves to the government. Do not blame Joseph. He worked for the government! We must learn that turning to the government instead of to God to be our provider in hard times only leads to slavery!

Prayer: O Lord, You are our Master. We rely on You to protect us, just as you protected the people of Israel in the land of Goshen. May we put our trust in You. May Your name be praised! In Jesus' name we pray. Amen.

October 22

"But now that he is dead, why should I fast? Can I bring him back again? I will go to him, but he will not return to me." 2 Samuel 12:23

Where is my baby?

Believers ask, "Is my child who died in Heaven?" Unbelievers ask the same question. I wish I could say yes, but there are theological difficulties. For example, some think all infants, born or unborn, are automatically in Heaven. If this were true, we should be for abortion! Then evangelism by abortion would be 100% effective. It makes no sense.

Some think that the children of Christians are Christian, until the age of "accountability," which is age 7 or so. But that would mean that a child who was a Christian early in life, could lose their salvation. This is an impossibility according to John 10:28-29 and other passages. It ignores the reality of original sin of Adam that we all share in. *"I was sinful at birth, sinful from the time my mother conceived me,"* Psalm 51:5b.

The Armenian especially has a problem here. Small children do not have the opportunity to choose God and exercise their free will. The Bible teaches that all those who were elect before the foundation of the world are saved by the mercy of God, not anyone's ability to choose. We don't know who all the elect are. But we do know that our God who loves His sheep (Christians), also loves their lambs! The small child born to David and Bathsheba died after being sick for seven days. David's words were written to be a comfort to us in our loss. *"I will go to him,"* can only mean that David looked forward to seeing this child in Heaven some day! David surely was relying on the pure mercy of God and His sovereign pleasure, which is how we are all saved.

We don't know all the reasons God takes a child home to Himself early. But even saying "early" is a problem, because that is our perspective. Luke said it is God who, *"determined the times set for them and the exact places they should live,"* Acts 17:26b. Personally, I was born a twin. But the twin never lived. That was God's purpose, which is perfect. God ordains for some to live a long life, some a short one.

Prayer: O soverign Lord, surely Your election and grace are key to infant salvation. Lord, You said for our comfort, *"I will have mercy upon whom I will have mercy."* We rely on that! In Jesus' name we pray. Amen.

October 23

"But godliness with contentment is great gain." 1 Timothy 6:6

Godliness with contentment = Great Gain

"Godliness with contentment," is far too rare in the Christian community! There is a reason for that. The act of growing up in Christ (sanctification), is a lifelong process. But that does not mean it must take a lifetime to learn *"contentment."* We all need to grow up. Sooner is far better than later. *"Contentment"* is not only good for us, it is good for God's kingdom that we mature in the faith. There are three faith points based on Paul's explanation which follow our text.

1. We leave this world with either *"godliness"* or godlessness! *"For we brought nothing into this world, and we can take nothing out of it,"* 1 Timothy 6:7. We came with little hair, no teeth, no clothes, no money. We leave the same way! We take either *"godliness"* or godlessness with us into eternity. May we live in the light of it.

2. *"People who want to get rich fall into temptation and a trap and into many foolish and harmful desires that plunge men into ruin and destruction,"* 1 Timothy 6:9. This is not for only the *"rich."* It says, *"people who want to get rich."* God gives wealth to some for the building of His church. This verse concerns those who make money their god. Their problem is that they cannot work on godliness because they are too busy working on getting money. We see it all around us. We fight it ourselves. Paul says, *"Be content with having food and clothing."* Most of what is beyond that is materialism. It will *"plunge men into ruin and destruction."*

3. *"For the love of money is a root of all kinds of evil,"* 1 Timothy 6:10a. Paul basically repeats his earlier words, giving Timothy and us a warning. Paul saw that some, *"have wandered from the faith and pierced themselves with many griefs,"* 1 Timothy 6:10b. They do not have contentment!

Prayer: Lord, Paul's words to Timothy (in verse 11) are our benediction and prayer also. *"But you, man of God, flee from all this, and pursue righteousness, godliness, faith, love, endurance, and gentleness. Fight the good fight of faith. Take hold of eternal life to which you were called."* Lord help us to do this! In Jesus' name we pray. Amen.

October 24

"God also said to Moses, 'Say to the Israelites, '"The LORD, the God of your fathers — the God of Abraham, the God of Isaac and the God of Jacob — has sent me to you.'" This is My name forever, the name by which I am to be remembered from generation to generation.'" Exodus 3:15

The ten plagues and the Lamb

Ten plagues covered all of Egypt. But in the land of Goshen where God's people lived, they were free from some of the plagues and others were less painful. God showed the people that He was able to protect them. They learned to trust in God as He revealed Himself more fully to them. This God is our God!

Finally, the last plague comes. A lamb had to be slain and its blood put on the doorpost. If the house had this blood on its doorpost when the Angel of Death came, the family would be spared. The Angel (God Himself), came. The firstborn sons of Egypt died along with their firstborn animals. Why? Because they were not covered by the blood of the Lamb!

The most important animal of Egypt was the ram, the male sheep. This ram was their biggest god who was believed by the people to be at the very peak of his power on the night the Angel of Death came to rescue God's people. Interestingly, the people of Egypt were not even allowed to touch the ram, nor were they ever allowed to bring it in their house. When Moses told the Israelites to each select a _male_ lamb and bring it into their homes for a week, this was quite something. But since they had learned to fear God during the other plagues, they faithfully obeyed. God's people killed the lamb as directed that night.

Can you imagine that Passover scene as the people of Egypt watched? The "I AM that I AM," spared His people as He passed over them. God did this because *"the life of the flesh is in the blood,"* and the Lamb gives life! So, the firstborn of the unbelieving Egyptians and their firstborn animals are dead. There are dead rams all over the place. Not only were the people of Egypt devastated, their most important god was dead.

Prayer: O Almighty Lord, You delivered Israel from the Egyptian people and the gods that enslaved them! May we see that You deliver us from slavery to sin today by that same blood! In Jesus' name we pray. Amen.

October 25

"For the wages of sin is death, but the gift of God is eternal life in Christ Jesus our Lord." Romans 6:23

Do we want God's justice or His grace?

We have been hurt! The pain has been great for years now. We don't know what to do. We have screamed to God for His justice, but we have felt no real sense of peace or His close presence. Is it possible we are asking for the wrong thing? If we were to demand God's justice for our personal life, we would be instantly dead! *"For the wages of sin is death."* That is a hard but accurate truth. Our greatest need is not for God's justice.

May God help us to see that we are in far greater need of His grace and mercy. So are all the "others" in our lives! They need our grace and mercy. Or do we give them justice alone? We cry to God for His grace also. Others cry to us for our grace! The two go together! His grace frees us. So Lord, do not give us the justice that we deserve. Give us the grace that we need. Give us Your forgiving grace that is greater than all our sin!

Paul said, *"I urge you, brothers, <u>in view of God's mercy</u>, to offer your bodies as living sacrifices, holy and pleasing to God — this is your spiritual act of worship,"* Romans 12:1. Because of God's mercy to us, we are now merciful to others. That's what it means to keep our minds on the mercy and the grace of God. The rest of Romans 12 teaches how.

Verse three teaches us, don't be proud. Verse six reminds us that every person has different gifts. We are to serve others in verse seven. Love sincerely in verse nine. *"Be devoted to one another"* in verse ten. Practice hospitality in verse thirteen, *"Bless those who persecute you,"* in verse fourteen. Finally in the end, *"Do not be overcome by evil but overcome evil with good,"* Romans 12:21.

God's Word is clear. Pray for His grace to us in abundance, giving His grace to others in the same way. *"Leave room for God's wrath,"* in verse nineteen, for justice is more God's business, than ours.

Prayer: O Lord God of grace, we have been bitter to those who have hurt us. We have not lived graciously. Fill us with Your grace so that Your grace flows out of us. In Jesus' name we pray. Amen.

October 26

"And we know that in all things God works for the good of those who love Him, who have been called according to His purpose."
Romans 8:28

"We know... God works"

This whole verse is really a strong statement of faith by Paul concerning the character of God. It also must be a statement of faith that we experience. By saying the words, *"we know,"* show our <u>absolute</u> assurance of His faithfulness in all circumstances. The godly Job was an *"I know"* man. He said, *"I know that my Redeemer lives,"* Job 19:25a. What personally is it, that *"we know"* by faith?

"We know" that *"all things,"* every part of our lives is completely in God's hands. *"We know"* God is working everything *"for the good."* He never even once does anything that would harm any believer. But I must make a confession. There is a big piece of this verse that I have overlooked. That truth is the fact that *"God works."* So then, part of our statement of faith is: *"We know... God works."* That is a huge comfort!

It is a great thing when a husband or father works. It is a great thing when a wife or mother works. It is a great thing when children do their school work and other work for the good of family and friends. But none of us ever works perfectly. Think about how *"God works."* He never slumbers or sleeps. *"God works"* 100% of the time perfectly. *"God works"* His eye perfectly to see everything in the world, great and small. *"God works"* His ear to hear every sound. *"God works"* His wisdom to know every secret thought anyone presently has, or will ever have. No one can possibly plan anything that God is unaware of.

"God works" His grace to perfection in us. *"It is God who works in you to will and to act according to His good purpose,"* Philippians 2:13. God works at giving us the will and the desire to be obedient, all for His good pleasure. Now that should teach us how to pray!

Prayer: Dear hard working and lovng Lord, You truly are our everything, our all. You even give us "the will," or the motivation to do anything. We can only pray that You "work us" to love You more. In Jesus' name we pray. Amen.

October 27

"Therefore, as we have opportunity, let us do good to all people, especially to those who belong to the family of believers." Galatians 6:10

Do good works for God's people!

To understand our text we have to know the context. Paul ended Galatians 5, by teaching us to live in the Spirit. Now in chapter 6, he shows us what "living in the Spirit" looks like in practical living.

1. "Restore" others. This is the work of evangelism and discipleship. *"You who are spiritual should restore him <u>gently</u>,"* Galatians 6:1b. Spirit-filled living is restoring others to God and to man. *"But watch yourselves."* Great advise! While we are taking the sliver out of someone else's eye, make sure a log is not in our own! How much this is needed today. Nothing is worse than trying to do ministry by getting others to change, but not changing our self. Our message will then be irrelevant. The blind cannot lead the blind.

2. "Carry each other's burdens." This is so important that it *"fulfills the law of Christ."* How? Well, half of the law is to love others. How can we do that if we are not willing to *"carry each other's burdens"*? Love is not just a feeling. It has legs and arms. It is a sacrificial action for others. "Worship" and "serving" is the same word in the Bible.

3. Test our actions. It is far easier to tell what we personally believe based on what we do. If we say one thing and do another, what do we truly believe? *"Each one should test his own actions,"* Galatians 6:4a. We must be an action figure for God.

4. Do good, "especially to those who belong to the family of believers." Our text, in verse 10 is really a summary of the last couple of chapters. It is not enough for us to "be good," we also must "do good." "Do good" not only to everybody but especially to our fellow brothers and sisters who need our help and encouragement to be fruitful. In this verse we are held accountable for how we live with other Christians. A good way to be faithful is to live humbly with those who will cry at our funeral!

Prayer: Dear Lord, we thank You for the serious instructions You give us so that we might get a good view of what it means to live a Spirit-filled life. Lord, strengthen us to be servants. In Jesus' name we pray. Amen.

October 28

"Your attitude should be the same as that of Christ Jesus."
Philippians 2:5

Obedient, because God elected us to be!

Throughout Philippians 2, Paul is telling us how to live as children of God. He shows us what Jesus' attitude was, and why it was like that. First, He tells us that even though Jesus was God, He took *"the very nature of a servant,"* in verse 7. He *"became obedient to death,"* in verse 8. Then Paul applies the argument of the greater to the lesser. If God elected or planned for "Jesus as God" to live as an "obedient servant," then how much more should we do the same! After Jesus lived faithfully, *"God exalted Him."* Jesus lived humbly and was glorified. So will we be!

Paul says in Philippians 2:12 to the Philippian believers, *"Therefore, my dear friends, as you have always obeyed - not only in my presence, but now much more in my absence - continue to work out your salvation with fear and trembling."* This is not a verse to go and earn our salvation, but to live as God elected us to live the Christian life!

Peter says, God elected or planned for Jesus to live like one of us. So that, we can live like Him, to be partakers of His divine nature! *"His divine power has given us everything we need for life and godliness through our knowledge of Him who called us by His own glory and goodness,"* 2 Peter 1:3. Why did God do this? So *"you may participate in the divine nature and escape the corruption in the world caused by evil desires,"* 2 Peter 1:4b. The message is: live like you are saved!

"Your attitude should be the same as that of Christ Jesus." Jesus lived for the Father! He didn't give in to self-interest, self-exaltation or self-pity! When we are preoccupied in loving self, God is not on the throne of our hearts. God allows adversity to test us, to see if our attitude is the same as Christ Jesus. May God help us to live like His perfect Son!

Prayer: Dear Heavenly Father, may we keep in mind that You planned for us to be obedient and faithful, even before the world was made. You caused us to come to Christ to live like Him and live for Him. You have even given us His name! Correct our attitude when it is wrong. In Jesus' name we pray. Amen.

October 29

"But because of His great love for us, God, who is rich in mercy, made us alive with Christ even when we were dead in transgressions – it is by grace you have been saved." Ephesians 2:4-5

What is justification?

This is one of the most important questions ever! The answer may be shocking if we have not thought this through as the Bible teaches. These truths must sink into our hearts.

Our repentance does not save us. Repentance happens because of what God has done for us through Jesus Christ and the Holy Spirit. *"Therefore, if anyone is in Christ, he is a new creation; the old has gone, the new has come,"* 2 Corinthians 5:17. This turning from the old pattern of loving evil, to the new pattern of loving God comes because of justification, the one time salvation event! Let's understand justification better through the truths in our text.

We are not really saved by our believing either! Justification is not all about you or I believing. It's not about what we do. We only believe because of three grace justification points on God's part. These three reasons are all in our text. Justification starts with God's *"great love for us,"* not our great love for God. Then His love moves Him to have *"mercy"* on us. After that God *"made us alive with Christ."* Then finally, after we are alive, we believe.

How can anyone who is *"dead in transgressions"* believe, if God did not wake him up? How can anyone who is God's *"enemy"* (Romans 5:10) suddenly love God? Justification is God directed, grace driven, and nothing to do with man making a decision to believe! In our pride, we have a bad habit of getting the cause of justification, which is; 1. *"God's great love for us;"* 2. His *"mercy"* on us; and 3. How He *"made us alive with Christ,"* mixed up with the effect, which is our believing.

Prayer: O gracious and merciful God, *"since we have been justified through faith, we have peace with God through our Lord Jesus Christ,"* Romans 5:1. Open our hearts to the amazing truth of Your grace! We have peace with You our God because You justified us. We worship You. In Jesus' name we pray. Amen.

October 30

"When Abram came to Egypt, the Egyptians saw that she was a very beautiful woman. And when Pharaoh's officials saw her, they praised her to Pharaoh, and she was taken into his palace." Genesis 12:14-15

God's grace preserves Abram and Sarai

Genesis 12 begins with God's call to Abram, *"Leave your country, your people and your father's household and go to the land I will show you,"* Genesis 12:1b. So Abram obediently *"set out for the land of Canaan and they arrived there,"* Genesis 12:5b. In verse 8, Abram built an altar. So far, so good! Now comes a faith test, <u>recorded for us to examine our faith journey</u>! *"Now there was a famine in the land,"* verse 10. Abram's response was that he *"went down to Egypt to live there for a while because the famine was severe,"* Genesis 12:10b.

Abram decides to lie about his beautiful wife Sarai. He was thinking "God can't protect me, so I must protect myself." But in the end, God protects him anyway. King Pharaoh, with all his power doesn't touch Sarai and doesn't harm Abram either. So great is the perseverance of the saints because of God's amazing grace!

Note that Abram was called to be a blessing and he was, as long as he followed God! But in Egypt (a symbol for sin) he quickly became a curse as *"the Lord inflicted serious diseases on Pharaoh and his household because of Abram's wife Sarai,"* Genesis 12:17. The chapter closes with Abram being sent on his way.

Jesus also had a faith test. He was baptized as Matthew 3 ends. Matthew 4 begins with the Spirit leading Him into a place of famine! Why? His faith had to be tested. In Genesis 12 Abram's faith was tested. Ours will likewise be tested! When God allowed Abram to leave Canaan, it was to teach us. Even though Abram had the faith to <u>leave</u> his family years before, he didn't have the faith to cleave to God in his first *"famine"* trial. And we do the same thing.

Prayer: O gracious Lord, like Abram, we fall into sin. But You restore us and bless us once more, even though we don't deserve it. Then You quickly send other tests to help us examine our faith. Lord, help us to pass Your tests and sustain us in the faith. In Jesus' name we pray. Amen.

October 31

"Simon Peter climbed aboard and dragged the net ashore. It was full of large fish, 153, but even with so many the net was not torn."
John 21:11

Not one fish was lost!

John 20 ends with a beautiful testimony about the life of Jesus. It seems like the book of John is over. But suddenly, we have another chapter, like an exclamation point to Jesus' ministry! His disciples are now fishing all night, the normal fishing time. Soon after daylight comes, the fishing is poor. The disciples had fished all night and caught nothing. A man on the shore calls to them, "Lads, put *'your net on the right side of the boat.'*" So the disciples throw the net on the other side. They suddenly realize they have a net full. In the meantime, disciple John recognizes Jesus' authoritative voice, and he tells Peter that it is Jesus. How common this pattern was. John is the first to know. Peter is the first to go. And Peter jumps in the water to go to Jesus.

Normally they caught a few big fish, but it's usually the smaller ones caught in the net. There were 153 *"large fish."* Personally I do not know why there were 153. Some say that is how many countries there were who needed to hear the Gospel. Others say there were 153 different kinds of fish, again representing the different nations.

In spite of the number of large fish, *"the net was not torn."* When Jesus catches a person they are never lost again either! Every believer will make it to Heaven's shore! No one can snatch a single fish out of His hand! Every saint makes it because Jesus has an unbreakable net around them! And that net holds a lot of "big fish."

On the shore, Jesus waits with fish and bread over a fire. It's fast food at its best! Jesus miraculously feeds seven of His disciples with that food, including some fish they caught. Jesus can provide a fish dinner when we can't catch one! Jesus can still provide for us today, when our work is not going well.

Prayer: Dear Soverign Lord, You not only catch us, You clean us up for Heaven. We believers will be in Heaven because, we cannot escape Your grace net. Hallelujah! What a Savior. In Jesus' name we pray. Amen.

NOVEMBER

*"Cast all your anxiety on Him
because He cares for you."*
1 Peter 5:7

November 1

"Then Gideon said to God, 'Do not be angry with me. Let me make just one more request. Allow me one more test with the fleece.'"
Judges 6:39a

Is it okay to lay a fleece before God?

"Again the Israelites did evil in the eyes of the LORD," Judges 6:1a. In response, God sent oppressors to humble and plunder His people. The children of Israel cried for God's mercy. God heard their cries and sent His servant Gideon to help them turn back to Him. This is the history of Israel and the history of evangelism. This is our history!

Gideon was a lowly farmer. So he wanted to be sure God was calling him specifically to this service, for surely the people would not think him qualified! So, Gideon lays a fleece before God. That night God made the fleece wet with dew and the ground dry. Again Gideon asked for one more sign to be sure that God was calling him to this task. This time, God made the fleece dry and the ground wet. Gideon knew! What about us? Is God calling us into some service for Him? Are we willing to plead with God to make it even clearer? This would be profitable for us and for God's kingdom.

This is very personal for me. I was asked to go to India, so I pleaded, "Please Lord, I'll go, but only if You really want me to!" While I continued to pray, I went to the church library to look for books on India. There was a book on Mother Teresa. I read it. The next week I asked if there were more books on India. The librarian said, "No." So I continued to pray. Again I returned to the library a week later. While talking to a friend I took a book off the shelf without looking at the title, then scanned the back page. The first line said, "If you are interested in missions you need to read this book." I was shocked. The second line said, "If you are interested in India this book is a must!" I thought with tears, "Lord, You didn't have to put it in writing." I was personally grateful for the Lord's confirmation. A few weeks later that confirmation was essential!

Prayer: Lord, thank You for making things so clear, that we might boldly go ahead with Your work, even in the face of many obstacles. We are grateful that You call people from all stations in life and then equip them. We worship You. In Jesus' name we pray. Amen.

November 2

"Do not be afraid of those who kill the body but cannot kill the soul."
Matthew 10:28a

God's amazing protection!

By nature I am fearful. I trust that you have times when you are fearful also. Within a few weeks of knowing that I was supposed to go to India, I received a phone call from there saying, "Don't come." Some terrorists were demanding a bribe. The Christian leader would not pay. So the terrorist threatened him and his family, saying they would be back. The phone call said, "It's not safe." I replied, "I'm coming because I know that's what God wants. So pray." And they did. We were in India for about three weeks. The prayers continued. Nothing happened!

The following was told to me later. I was not there to see it. As soon as we reached home again, the prayers stopped. Immediately the terrorists returned. They took a child by knifepoint, demanding a ransom. The police caught the terrorists. When on trial, there was a Hindu judge, a Hindu lawyer and the terrorists could have denied the charges and been relased. But the lead terrorist said to the judge, "Sir, we did it. We are more afraid of the Christian's God, than we are of you and a jail cell. They admitted that they saw Mr. David and others and wanted to harm them, but their God prevented us!" They were convicted. To this day, I do not know what God did! Somehow His angels surrounded us.

Even more amazing, the pastor's wife brought a Christmas dinner to the men in jail. They wept. They could not understand why anyone would do this. The terrorist leader became a Christian. Shortly after that, the other terrorists killed him. He was *"not afraid of those who kill the body but cannot kill the soul."* Our God is soverign and He is in complete control.

Prayer: O Almighty Lord, Your ways are far higher than ours! You amaze us with Your mercy and grace. We do not deserve Your precious blessings or protection. Lord, when we were Your enemies, we were reconciled to You through the death of Your Son. The terrorist You saved by Your grace was like each of us! We praise and worship You for Your goodness to us in Christ. In His name we pray. Amen.

November 3

"As one of them was cutting down a tree, the iron axhead fell into the water. 'Oh, my lord,' he cried out, 'it was borrowed!'" 2 Kings 6:5

God floats an axhead and a car!

In our text, God floated the axhead so that it was not lost. He who created the force of gravity can alter it at any time. God was teaching Elijah and us that our lives are that completely under His sovereign control. For if God can protect us in small things, He can in the bigger things also. I would like to share another of my experiences.

My wife and I borrowed a nice new car. We had taken a trip to another state along with another couple and some youth from church. They sent us away for the evening to a nice place to eat because it was our 25th wedding anniversary. After dinner we went up a mountain road to a lookout over the city. We spent time in prayer. We thanked God for our family, for His presence, and for His protection over the last 25 years. We thanked God for allowing us to serve Him. We prayed to God for His continued protection. We didn't have to wait long!

It had just quit raining, and it had rained a lot! Unknown to us, the state had just filled in a big section of road that had washed out, then they put new tar down. We started back down the mountain road. We met a car and had to move over. We stopped instantly! With the car on a serious angle, we looked straight down for 200 feet. My wife yelled, "Get out, it could go down!" We got out and walked to the back of the car; the tire was one foot off the road, hanging in space. There was no dirt ahead of the tire for 10 feet or behind it for 30. We went to the front. There was a single 6 foot column of dirt. Our front tire was in the middle of it! Empty space was in front of the column and behind it. What happened? The tar broke because the new sand washed away from under the road. The car instantly moved over, but the rear axle dug into the tar road. Why didn't this car go over? One reason! God. Why? To show us beyond any doubt that He could and would protect us.

Prayer: Dear Lord, You are such a big God! You still see our problems and help us at just the right time. You build our weak faith. Lord, we don't deserve such protection, yet You faithfully give it. We thank You. In Jesus' name we pray. Amen.

November 4

"Do not be afraid nor dismayed because of this great multitude, for the battle is not yours, but God's." 2 Chronicles 20:15b NKJV

God sends us with His blessing!

This verse is a main one God used to encourage and press me to move forward boldly for Him. I must admit, I was fearful. I knew for sure that God was calling me to teach, but still, I was shaking in my boots! My problem was a lack of faith and obedience. It is true that some of the people who should have been the most encouraging, were often the most discouraging. But God is not like that. He tenderly pushes us at just the right rate of speed so we do not run ahead of Him.

My third day in India, was also my first Sunday in Madras. Twice in the same day God used our text to encourage me. The evening speaker began his sermon by saying he did not understand why, but God impressed him strongly all week to preach the same text that was used by the morning preacher. Again I heard, *"Do not be afraid nor dismayed because of this great multitude, for the battle is not yours, but God's."* Again, I knew God was speaking to me clearly!

The evening pastor ended by suddenly jumping way ahead in the text to this verse; *"And on the <u>fourth</u> day they assembled in the Valley of Berachah, for there they blessed the LORD; therefore the name of that place was called The Valley of Berachah until this day,"* 2 Chronicles 20:26 NKJV. When I heard this I was shocked, yet comforted! On Monday, my my fourth day in Madras, I needed to speak at a place on Berachah Road. Berachah also means "blessing" in Hebrew.

My extreme worry was that I did not have a college education or a seminary degree. Now I had to teach many who did, for a week. I was so encouraged by the Word of the Lord. He went to great lengths to take the fear out of my heart, and to move me forward in His name. What a comfort and strength our God is, in our time of need!

Prayer: Lord, You are an amazing God. Your protection, promises and blessings are pure gold. Even Your very last words before You left this earth were, *"Surely I am with you always, to the very end of the age,"* Matthew 28:20b. Lord, thank You for making us trust in You. May Your name be praised! In Jesus' name we pray. Amen.

November 5

"He called out to them, 'Friends, haven't you any fish?' 'No,' they answered. He said, 'Throw your net on the right side of the boat and you will find some.' When they did, they were unable to haul the net in because of the large number of fish." John 21:5-6

Can God still catch fish?

My wife and I visited a minister friend and his family in Visak, in Andhra Pradesh, India. In the morning my friend and I walked to the sea to see some Hindu fishermen. We asked, "How is the fishing?" They said, "Not good." I asked them, "Can we ride along and can we pray and read something from God's Bible?" They said, "Yes." So we read John 21 in the Telugu language, explaining how Jesus put fish in the net. After tying a rope to a post on the shore, we rowed out a quarter mile, across another 100 yards, then back to shore again. Ten of us on each rope, began hauling the drag net in. A man patroling the outside edge of the net, began yelling excitedly! He beat the water with a stick to keep the big fish from jumping over the net. When the net finally got close to shore, *"they were unable to haul the net in because of the large number of fish."* The fishermen took the fish out, with the net still in the water, so it wouldn't break! What an enormous amount of fish, baskets full. They even gave me a big fish!

Back from a teaching assignment in Orissa, I again visited the fishermen. They begged me to go fishing with them. We prayed and repeated the process, and were once again shocked! There wasn't enough fish in the net to buy everyone a cup of tea! Why? If God had filled the net again, they would have added Him to their list of gods. They learned, the Creator God could give much, or little!

That afternoon, my wife and the pastor and his wife were standing on the roof of his house looking at the sea. An eagle flying hundreds of feet above us released a foot long fish and it hit the pastor right on the head! I said to him, "Do you think God wants you to teach these pagan fishermen about the one true God?"

Prayer: Lord, You who created everything, also control everything for Your glory! Teach us more and more to trust in You, for You hold the whole world in Your hands. In Jesus' name we pray. Amen.

November 6

"Cast all your anxiety on Him because He cares for you." 1 Peter 5:7

Lord, this is Your problem!

By the spring of 1999, I had traveled all over in India teaching. Now there was a need to set up an office to start printing discipleship materials. We needed to reach the same people again, as well as others. I was back in the USA for about a month and had already purchased an airline ticket to return to India. But I had basically just 20% of the needed funds to get things going! Worse yet I had just a week or so left before I had to leave. It was Saturday afternoon. Totally discouraged, I placed my hand on the phone, ready to call the airline to cancel my ticket.

Then I thought, "Lord, I have been faithful in what You wanted me to do. You called. I went. I have prayed about this urgent need but still, I do not have the funds. Lord, this is Your problem, not mine. You have to do something." So, I put the phone down. The next day we had a visitor at church, a man I knew. After the service he said, "I heard you are going back to India." I said, "Yes." He asked, "Do you have enough money to go." I said, "No." He asked, "How much do you still need?" I named the number. He said, "What are you going to do if you don't get it?" I said, "I have already discussed this with God and it is His problem." Later he asked, "Is it okay if I go with you?" I said, "I would love that!" Problem over! Plus, a day before leaving, I was treated for a serious case of blood poisoning by this man's nephew, a caring doctor. Our office/home in India was beautifully set up in just three very hot summer weeks. What a blessed time. God is so good!

Was God late in showing His faithfulness? No, He tells us, *"cast all your anxiety on Him because He cares for you,"* 1 Peter 5:7. Plus, *"We are God's workmanship, created in Christ Jesus to do good works, which God prepared in advance for us to do,"* Ephesians 2:10. The battle is the Lord's. He has everything under His sovereign control!

Prayer: Dear Almighty Lord, when we look back at Your faithfulness we marvel at Your merciful timings. You truly do give us mercy, not so much when we want it, but exactly, *"in our time of need."* You truly build our faith, one trial at a time. Help us to trust in You, more and more! In Jesus' name we pray. Amen.

November 7

"Do not crave his delicacies." Proverbs 23:3a

A ladder for a rat

I had been traveling all over India teaching. It was three days here, five days there, for months. It was hot. The food was even hotter. The mosquitoes were hungry. I was alone and exhausted. I was really hoping for a nicer place to stay. At the next teaching assignment, the pastor did not have sufficient room in his house so he arranged for me to stay with a rich man in the neighborhood! I was so happy about that. I was ready for a little comfort. I thought I had "arrived" when I got to this house.

About four in the morning I was sitting up in bed, no shirt on, praying. Suddenly a huge rat jumped right on top of my shoulder. If I was not already fully awake, I was then! I turned the light on but I could not find that four-legged terrorist. So I turned the light off and went back to sleep, for five minutes. The rat knocked my glass of water over that was right by my head! That rat had no manners and it was time for him to go on a holiday. I finally found him, and he went up to the ledge above my head and exited out a 10 inch fan hole in the wall. It did not take me long to turn that little fan on! He would be rat burger if he tried to get in now! The next night, the power went off. Guess who visited? No respect!

I think God was teaching me something. I had grumbled to Him about the difficult conditions. I wanted more comforts. He provided them, with surprises. He was teaching me that His grace is sufficient! Why does it take us so long to be content with what we have? Our text tells us not to crave the rich man's delicacies. The rest of that verse says, *"for that food is deceptive."* It really is as it can come with rats embeded!

The Lord has very effective ways of teaching us to be more content! We read that His ways are higher than ours. Without a word He can get our attention. He humbles us in very effective ways. He corrects our attitudes. He conforms us to the image of His Son. He makes us His servants. We worship God for all of this!

Prayer: Dearest Lord, John the Baptist was right. *"He must become greater; I must become less."* Lord, thanks for making us live in a way that is pleasing to You. In Jesus' name we pray. Amen.

November 8

"You shall keep My Sabbaths and reverence My sanctuary: I am the LORD. Give no regard to mediums and <u>familiar spirits</u>; do not seek after them, to be defiled by them: I am the LORD your God."

Leviticus 19:30-31 NKJV

Holy Spirit or *"familiar spirit,"* Part 1

There are two spirits at work for the souls of men. There is the Holy Spirit, God Himself. The other one is a *"familiar spirit"* who is not God, but is still powerful. Of course that is Satan and all of his followers.

I heard of "slaying in the spirit" and wondered if this was really the Holy Spirit as some claimed. In 1997, while in Madurai, South India, I clearly found the answer. I gave a midweek message at a church. Then "missionaries" from Australia took over. Soon they were "slaying" people, one at a time by putting their hands on the people's heads. All but three of us fell to the floor, down and out. I stood near the back, watching. Then the "missionary" man stood in front of me. He said, "You need to be slain in the spirit." I said, "I have the Spirit." He insisted, "You need to be slain in the spirit." Finally, but still skeptical, I put his hand on my head and said; "Do it." But then, I prayed, "Lord, if this is really Your Spirit knock me down. But if this is not Your Spirit, protect me with your angels." Somehow he knew I was praying and he said to me, "DON'T PRAY!" This is the first warning. A *"familiar spirit"* was at work!

It was interesting to watch. One man did the slaying. The other would catch and set them down so they wouldn't get hurt. I wonder now, would God's Spirit hurt one of His children? Also, the one doing the "slaying" would often take two fingers and open one eye of the person he wanted to "slay." He was looking to see if the pupil was fixed on him, (still with it) or if the eye was rolled back into the head, fully hypnotized. Was he doing this to see how much he needed to push? More tomorrow.

Prayer: O Creator of all, You warn us about *"the person who turns to mediums and <u>familiar spirits</u>, to prostitute himself with them."* You tell us that You will set Your face against us if we do that. You are the only God and the only One who makes us holy. Lord, holiness is what we need! We are so grateful that You are our God and that You sanctify us and You make us holy! In Jesus' name we pray. Amen.

November 9

"Dear friends, do not believe every spirit, but <u>test the spirits</u> to see whether they are from God, because many false prophets have gone out into the world." 1 John 4:1

Holy Spirit or *"familiar spirit,"* Part 2

Let's "test the spirits" as God commands us to. After the "slayings," the "missionaries" asked a man to give his testimony concerning these things. His exact words were, "This has happened many times to my wife. I have been praying for it to happen to me. All I can say is that IT FELT SO GOOD." <u>This is the second warning that a *"familiar spirit"* is at work.</u>

At dinner that night, around the "privileged" table, I asked the two "missionaries" from Australia, "How is a person really slain in the spirit?" They told me, "You think too much. Just empty your mind of all thought. DON'T THINK, JUST LET IT HAPPEN!" <u>This is the third warning that a *"familiar spirit"* is at work.</u> Now, who in the spirit world would tell you; 1. "Don't pray," 2. "Don't think," and 3. "Do what feels good"?

First, the real Holy Spirit who is God said, *"<u>Pray without ceasing</u>"* in 1 Thessalonians 5:17 NKJV. **Second,** the Holy Spirit wrote, *"We demolish arguments and every pretension that sets itself up against the knowledge of God, and we take captive <u>every</u> <u>thought</u> to make it obedient to Christ,"* 2 Corinthians 10:5. **Third,** Jesus said, *"If anyone desires to come after Me, let him <u>deny himself</u>, and take up his cross daily, and follow Me,"* Luke 9:23b NKJV. Jesus did not say, "If it feels good do it!"

What would Satan say if he wanted us to get drunk or into some sexual sin? Satan's three point sermon would be; 1. "Don't pray." 2. "Don't think about it." 3. And, "It will feel so good." He would say the very same things the *"false prophet"* missionary was saying! A *"familiar spirit"* was working with *"false prophets,"* who were doing this "slaying in the spirit." John the disciple said, *"Dear friends, do not believe every spirit, but <u>test the spirits</u> to see whether they are from God, because many false prophets have gone out into the world,"* 1 John 4:1.

Prayer: O Lord, we see Satan wants us to "feel holy," but not "be holy." We praise You for showing us how Satan wants us to base our holiness on an "experience" he can give, instead of a relationship with You! Lord, You alone sanctify us. Thank You! In Jesus' name we pray. Amen.

November 10

"Just then a man in their synagogue who was possessed by an evil spirit cried out." Mark 1:23

A demoniac stops worship, Part 1

About ten years ago, twice in a short time, the same thing happened. The first time I was teaching at a missionary conference for young people. About 200 youth were assembled. I was teaching on the difference between love and lust and of the specific evil practices that needed to stop. We were openly discussing the horrible practices among the youth of viewing pornography in magazines and on the Internet. We explained how these evil practices were worshiping Satan, not God. We discussed the great need of missionaries to live a holy life!

It was so quiet you could hear a pin drop. Youth involved in these sinful practices could only look down in shame. We began to pray. And then it happened, right in the middle of our prayer. Suddenly a young man leaped forward, jumping up and down screaming nonsense! This man leaped right into the ladies' section! What spirit would move a man to stop prayer, stop the confession of sin, and jump in by the ladies? Not a man under the influence of the Holy Spirit! At the time I did not fully understand this, so I searched the Scriptures.

In Mark 1, Jesus was going around teaching. He had just called His first disciples. *"They went to Capernaum, and when the Sabbath came, Jesus went into the synagogue and began to teach. The people were amazed at His teaching."* "Amazed," because the Holy Spirit was impressing the truth of the Word on their hearts! *"Just then a man in their synagogue who was possessed by an evil spirit cried out,"* Mark 1:23. He *"cried out"* because he was exposed by the Word of God! He *"cried out"* because he hated God. He *"cried out"* to try stop the truth. He hated the Holy Spirit teaching the truth!

We still have that *"amazing"* Word of God! It says, *"He taught them as one who had authority, not as the teachers of the law,"* Mark 1:21-22. We have Jesus' authority to teach the truth in the Great Commission.

Prayer: O merciful Lord, how Satan still hates Your message and tries to stop it! We are so grateful that You are more powerful than Satan, and so are we when we are in Christ. In Jesus' name we pray. Amen.

November 11

"Each one should use whatever gift he has received to serve others, faithfully administering God's grace in its various forms." 1 Peter 4:10

A demoniac stops worship, Part 2

One Sunday in India, I was preaching from Acts 2. We taught how the Holy Spirit gave the ability to speak in different "known languages" so that the Gospel could go quickly to the Gentiles. "Tongues" were initially important! But, already there was a problem in the church of Corinth. Paul addressed it in 1 Corinthians, chapters 12-14. The point is: there are *"various"* gifts, given by the Holy Spirit to *"serve others"* in the church, to build them up in the Lord. The Corinthian church focused too much on this showy *"tongues"* gift, which Paul listed as least important. Paul said, *"Eagerly desire the greater gifts,"* 1 Corinthians 12:31. In 14:4 we see why the gift of tongues was listed last. The other gifts built up others, but *"He who speaks in a tongue <u>edifies himself</u>."*

God gives all Christians a gift to serve the church! Some have the gift of music, others administration, prayer, compassion, some of wealth, others the teaching and preaching gifts! And yes, there was the gift of tongues also. So I asked these church members, "Why do you emphasize the tongues gift so much? Why do you say this gift is the greatest, when Paul doesn't agree?"

I asked them, "Look at your own bodies. You have toes, feet, knees, arms, fingers, eyes, ears, teeth, noses, and a tongues, just to name a few. All these members *"serve"* our bodies! What if your toes and fingers were tongues? What if your ears, noses, and eyes were tongues? Would you have a healthy body? Well, your church is like this!" The people were very quiet. The pastor's wife respectfully said, "Amen." The people were understanding something was wrong. At this exact time, a man jumped up and began to scream like a mad man! He carried on for two minutes, stopping everything. What "spirit" would stop the teaching of God about the gifts that the Holy Spirit gives? What "spirit" doesn't want God's people built up? The serious answer is: a demonic spirit.

Prayer: Lord, we thank You for these chapters in Corinthians that show us true love is serving others sacrificially. May You make our gifts clear, and bless the use of them. In Jesus' name we pray. Amen.

November 12

"The LORD is my rock, my fortress and my deliverer; my God is my rock, in whom I take refuge. He is my shield and the horn of my salvation, my stronghold." Psalm 18:2

God's amazing providence, again!

David cries out in praise to God for all of His most wonderful protection. So must we! Our God still protects us today. The examples of David and others in the Bible, were people just like us. God tells us these things to give us hope, as Romans 15:4 teaches. Why? So that we might keep our eyes on God as we move boldly in His name.

It was summertime in South India. I had to go on a fourteen hour journey on the train to teach for a week. It was very hot. I asked a staff member to get me a ticket in an air-conditioned car, of which there are usually two. When I got to the train station, I suddenly realized that the ticket I had was S-6. That is not an air-conditioned car! I was upset that the staff could make such a mistake in this heat. I needed my strength and sleep for the days ahead. As I began the overnight journey I was feeling very sorry for myself. I was so hot. I did not sleep because I had a top bunk that was even hotter than the lower ones!

Suddenly, at four in the morning, in the middle of a dense forest, the train came to a sudden stop! There was a security guard in our car who sat by the open door. I asked him, "What's wrong? Why has the train stopped here, in the middle of nowhere?" I noticed that he did not want to go out and see. He was afraid. The number one air-conditioned coach had just been robbed. The terrorists took all the money, gold, jewels and watches, then hit the emergency stop, and escaped into the jungle.

One hour later, again the train stopped quickly! A/C coach number two was robbed! Grateful, is not nearly a strong enough word to express my thanksgiving to God! And this is where David is at in our text. The king of the most powerful country, could not catch David, even in his own country! Our God is such an awesome God! How He protects us!

Prayer: Lord, with David, we praise You for Your amazing grace and power! Truly, if You in all of Your perfect attributes are for us, who can possibly be against us? In Jesus' name we pray. Amen.

November 13

"Call the Sabbath a delight and the LORD's holy day honorable... by not going your own way and not doing as you please." Isaiah 58:13b

Monkeys in church

I was teaching in a rural village on Sunday. The floor of the church was dirt. The roof was thatched with big poles holding it all up. The sides of this church were open. Cats and dogs were wandering into the worship service. A chicken or two that were given as an offering were tied to the table up front by the pulpit. Birds flew in from time to time. But now a monkey pays a visit. That was a new one!

I was in the middle of giving a message. The monkey came down the center pole and sat on a lady's shoulder. He was looking for a snack. The monkey tried to pick the flowers out of this lady's hair. But she quickly pulled her head scarf up over her head. The monkey pulled it down again. This struggle for the possession of the flowers went on for a few more ups and downs of the head covering. Finally, the lady handed the monkey the flowers. He grabbed them, and quickly ran back up the center pole just a chattering! But the people in the church paid no attention to this monkey! Perhaps it was a frequent visitor.

Are there monkeys (distractions) in our church? What do we think about when the pastor is teaching? Are we thinking of what we are going to do after church? Are we thinking of this or that person sitting in church? Where is our mind? How many different monkeys can the devil throw at us to stop our worship of God? This is an important question, because we do go to church to worship God. He calls us to worship Him! Is He the main object of our worship?

The first day of the week is a joy for redeemed Christians. It is a day of peace and resting in the goodness of the Lord and thanking Him for all that He is, and for all that He does! It is a day for bringing our prayers and offerings to worship Him. The point is that we need to drive out all distractions. We need to give up our flower gardens, our favorite sports and come to Him in true worship! He will hear our cry for mercy and our words of praise!

Prayer: Dear Lord, forgive us for letting the "Sunday monkeys" steal our worship of You. We have not honored You as we should! Help us to delight in You! In Jesus' name we pray. Amen.

November 14

"Enter by the narrow gate; for wide is the gate and broad is the way that leads to destruction, and there are many who go in by it. Because narrow is the gate and difficult is the way which leads to life, and there are few who find it." Matthew 7:13-14 NKJV

The Narrow Gate

The Sermon on the Mount, the greatest sermon ever, is almost over. Now Jesus speaks about two gates in verses 13-14; two trees in 16-20; two responses in 21-23, and two different kinds of builders in verses 24-27. Jesus speaks to win the souls of those He is talking to. Jesus sees the hunger in the people's eyes as He opens up Heaven to them. He describes the radical righteousness they need to enter Heaven. Knowing it's not easy to enter the kingdom of Heaven, Jesus describes the dangers and the difficult climb.

There is a gate, but the problem is, there is more than one gate. There are false prophets trying to direct us away from the narrow gate that leads to Heaven. On top of that, the narrow gate is really narrow. The wide one is really wide. And there are paths beyond these gates. Looking past the wide gate, we see the way is very easy! Beyond the narrow gate, the way is very *"difficult."* The small gate is so narrow that we need to squeeeeeeze through it. We suddenly realize that we can't take anything or anyone with us! Our sin baggage won't fit through the gate either! Our comforts in life won't fit. We need to leave the "fun" baggage behind to squeeze through! And if that were not enough, the other side of the gate is also *"difficult."* All we can see is a steep and dangerous path. We see suffering, persecution, and trials galore! We see ten signs. Ten "Thou shalt not" commandments we can't keep perfectly. This narrow path looks so hard, so difficult, and so few are on it. On our own, we would never choose that one.

Prayer: Gracious and loving Lord, we would never choose the right path if You didn't open our eyes to it. Even ten of the twelve spies Moses sent, said Canaan/Heaven was too difficult. Lord, You not only show us the narrow path, You give us the strength to walk it. We are so blessed by Your mercy and grace. In Christ's name we pray. Amen.

November 15

"Enter by the narrow gate; for wide is the gate and broad is the way that leads to destruction, and there are many who go in by it. Because narrow is the gate and difficult is the way which leads to life, and there are few who find it." Matthew 7:13-14 NKJV

The Wide Gate

How beautiful the *"wide gate"* is! Never has there been such an awesome gate! We can walk right through this gate without slowing down. We can keep on doing what we want to do. We can bring all the possessions we have. That wide gate tolerates everyone and everything! It is so accepting! The wide gate is so easy. There's no uphill climb. There's no hazards. There is not even one *"Thou shalt not"* on this wide road. In fact everybody seems to be writing their own truth about themselves. There is no absolute truth except for the fact that we can write our own truth. It's called perfect tolerance. So what is the problem?

Tolerant paths that do not believe in anything become a flamboyant lifestyle. But the no restrictions, and the no "thou shalt nots," soon are at the end of the road. Sickness and death comes very quickly! Then another huge shock! "Tolerance" on earth, is now "despair" in a place called Hell! That is exactly where that wide road leads to. And that is what Jesus is warning us about.

The point is, the wide road is not what we think. May we listen to God! That which believes in nothing, interferes with nothing, hates nothing, finds its purpose in nothing, lives for nothing, <u>never dies in Hell</u>! At the end of the wide road of careless living is an eternity of despair!

Prayer: Dear precious Lord, the wide gate is so appealing now! It looks so good and so inviting. Every pleasure this world offers is there. There are so many people enjoying life on this road. It is so popular and fun. Some are even laughing about those who are traveling on the narrow road. Lord, our sinful nature wants this road, for we are but rebellious and dead sinners. You Lord, are a merciful and sin-forgiving God. So Lord, please, make us take the road that is less traveled, but leads to You. In Jesus' name we pray. Amen.

November 16

"Enter by the narrow gate; for wide is the gate and broad is the way that leads to destruction, and there are many who go in by it. Because narrow is the gate and difficult is the way which leads to life, and there are few who find it." Matthew 7:13-14 NKJV

Which gate will we enter?

Which road do we want to be on? Do we want the narrow road, with the difficult path, with few on it? Let us not give the Sunday School answer and say yes so easily. An hour from now the world and all of its glamour will call out to us! Jesus Christ also calls out, *"Enter by the narrow gate."* Jesus knows the destination of both paths! He can see further than we can! He knows that even though the gate is narrow and difficult, it leads to eternal life. The wide gate and easy road leads to destruction. The Greek word is "Apollyon," meaning "to the devil and Hell"!

We can't see either destination from the gate. From the entrance to the wide gate, everything looks so perfect. But Jesus warns us, that road is deceptive! The most deceiving part is that the road is so smooth and so easy. The further we go down that path we reach the point that even if we want to return, we can't! It's too smooth. There is no traction. The surest road to Hell is the gradual one, the gentle slope, without sudden turnings, without milestones.

What can we do? There is no way, in our own wisdom that we will ever choose the right road! We will always be just like Lot. We will choose the green valley of Sodom and Gomorroh! <u>When Jesus taught this He knew we could not choose Him!</u> How can a dead sinner choose anything anyway? If God requires us, who are dead in sin, to take the first step to get back to Him, then salvation is still impossible, even in the New Testament! Man is equally just as unable to believe as he is to obey! <u>May God move us</u> to the right gate which is Jesus.

Prayer: Merciful Lord, we cry to You! Before telling us about this *"narrow"* and *"wide gate,"* You said, *"Ask, and it will be given to you; seek, and you will find; knock, and it will be opened to you. For everyone who asks receives, and he who seeks finds, and to him who knocks it will be opened,"* Matthew 7:7-8 NKJV. Lord, You are that Narrow Gate! Only Your grace calls us into it! We praise You for that! In Your name we pray. Amen.

"Watch out for false prophets. They come to you in sheep's clothing, but inwardly they are ferocious wolves." Matthew 7:15

"Watch out"!

As Jesus ends the Sermon on the Mount, He gives us a "heads up" to a real danger! *"Watch out for false prophets."* Interestingly, the word *"watch out"* is a sailing term in the original. Jesus is saying, "Beware, this is a serious danger." These fake *"prophets,"* (plural), do not speak for God. *"Watch out... they come to you."* They don't wait for you to come to them, they are coming to you full of deception. *"They come to you in sheep's clothing, but inwardly they are ferocious wolves."* They appear to be one thing, but beneath the surface they are something else. They want to tear you apart. *"Watch out,"* because they look just like us and *"care nothing for the sheep,"* John 10:13b. They are coming!

Where do these false prophets come from? Paul writes, *"Such men are false apostles, deceitful workmen, masquerading (disguised) as apostles of Christ. And no wonder, for Satan himself masquerades as an angel of light. It is not surprising, then, if his servants masquerade as servants of righteousness,"* 2 Corinthians 11:13-15a. Later Jesus again warns us, *"Many false prophets will appear and deceive many people,"* Matthew 24:11. *"False prophets will appear and perform great signs and miracles to deceive even the elect — if that were possible. See, I have told you ahead of time,"* Matthew 24:24b-25. Jesus told us these things because it is important for us to know so that we will *"Watch out."*

Peter warned that these false teachers are *"among you."* And, *"They will secretly introduce destructive heresies,"* 2 Peter 2:1b. Do not look for a messenger of Satan carrying a pitchfork! They have *"sheep's clothing."* Paul warned the Ephesians, *"Even from your own number men will arise and distort the truth in order to draw away disciples after them. So be on your guard!"* Acts 20:30-31b. False prophets are in churches and dressed like sheep. There are pastors and teachers with a deceptive agenda!

Prayer. Dear Lord, You have warned us time after time in the Bible about *"false prophets."* Help us to recognize them, to run from them and instead, run to Christ! In Jesus' name we pray. Amen.

November 18

"Watch out for false prophets. They come to you in sheep's clothing, but inwardly they are ferocious wolves." Matthew 7:15

The *"false prophets"* problem historically

Church history teaches us what to look for in a *"false prophet."*

<u>Paul saw the problem</u>! Paul said, *"The time will come when men will not put up with sound doctrine. Instead, to suit their own desires, they will gather around them a great number of teachers to say what their itching ears want to hear. They will turn their ears away from the truth and turn aside to myths,"* 2 Timothy 4:3-4. When those in the pew do not want to hear the Word or repent, they will welcome a false teacher!

<u>Jeremiah saw the problem</u>! God said, *"Woe to the shepherds who destroy and scatter the sheep of My pasture!"* Jeremiah 23:1a NKJV. False prophets were preaching a false peace, giving a false hope. They were not teaching the Word of God, not feeding the sheep. They were simply unconverted loudmouths pretending to be the mouth of God. God said, *"If they had stood in My counsel, and had caused My people to hear My words, then they would have turned them from their evil way and from the evil of their doings,"* Jeremiah 23:22 NKJV. *"False prophets"* do not preach about practical day-to-day repentance.

<u>Ezekiel saw the problem</u>! *"This is what the Sovereign LORD says: Woe to the shepherds of Israel who only take care of themselves! Should not shepherds take care of the flock? You eat the curds, clothe yourselves with the wool and slaughter the choice animals, but you do not take care of the flock,"* Ezekiel 34:2b-3. Who is in the ministry for a fat salary instead of caring about feeding the sheep? If those in the pew do nothing, God will act! He is not blind. God says, *"I will remove them from tending the flock so that the shepherds can no longer feed themselves. I will rescue My flock from their mouths,"* Ezekiel 34:10b. God will protect His church. Don't be part of a cover-up for a false shepherd.

Prayer: O Almighty God, we pray for boldness. Paul <u>named</u> *"Hymenaeus and Philetus"* who were *"destroying the faith of some."* John <u>exposed</u> *"Diotrephes, who loves to be first."* Lord, You see the *"false prophets"* today. Please remove them from us and from Your holy presence. We want to be true to You and to Your Word. In Jesus' name we pray. Amen.

November 19

"By their fruit you will recognize them." Matthew 7:16a

What does a *"false shepherd"* look like?

Jesus gave the command *"beware"* in verse 15, NKJV. He then said, *"By their fruit <u>you will recognize them</u>."* We will recognize false shepherds by the *"fruit"* of their lives. By the way they treat people, we will be able to recognize them. *"Do people pick grapes from thornbushes, or figs from thistles?"* Matthew 7:16b. We can tell the difference from a grape that grows on a grapevine from a berry that grows on a bush! A child knows the difference. The ways of false teachers will be that clear!

At first, a false teacher may sound great and even be entertaining! But over time, it becomes clear, he is really a thornbush! Why? Because, *"Every good tree bears good fruit, but a bad tree bears bad fruit. A good tree cannot bear bad fruit, and a bad tree cannot bear good fruit,"* Matthew 7:17-18. The Spirit of God opens our eyes!

A false teacher's message today is fully Satan's agenda! Satan teaches, *"It's all about us. Man is at the center! God wants us to be happy! We need to please self and love self more. We have problems because we hate ourselves. Real happiness will come when self is satisfied!"* They redefine the object of faith, and the content of faith.

How can we tell a drunk, a sex addict or a thief that they must love themselves more? Love of self is their problem, not their solution. The false shepherd believes Peter could not walk on water because he lost faith in himself, not in God! Real joy to the *"false shepherd"* is you first, others second, God last.

Shepherd Jesus tells us He is the way, the truth and the life! Joy in life is about God, a relationship with Christ, and obedience to the Word and Spirit of God. It's all about God's glory. God's goal for our life is holiness, just like Christ. If we deny self and follow Christ we are on the right road! Peter sank in the water because he took his eyes off Christ. Contentment comes when we keep our eyes fixed on Jesus and are satisfied with Him.

Prayer: Dear Heavenly Father, You expose the false prophets by Your Word and Spirit! We thank You for that. Draw us to Your holy presence more and more we pray. In Jesus' name we pray. Amen.

November 20

"Not everyone who says to Me, 'Lord, Lord,' will enter the kingdom of Heaven, but only he who does the will of My Father who is in Heaven."
Matthew 7:21

Walking in obedience

Jesus here compared those who <u>said</u> they lived a holy life to those who actually <u>did</u>! He contrasted the <u>words</u> they spoke with the <u>way</u> they walked. Some people were not allowed into Heaven who had <u>said</u> in worship, "Lord, Lord," to show their passion! By saying "Lord, Lord" again and again they were trying to leap into Heaven with their <u>words</u>! Jesus is saying, that we are going to need more than that to get into the kingdom of Heaven. We will need to act on the will of God.

Words of love to God without obedience is a dead faith! Jesus knows the difference! That's why He said, "<u>Many</u> will say to Me on that day, 'Lord, Lord, did we not prophesy in Your name, and in Your name drive out demons and perform many miracles?'" Matthew 7:22. This is personal! If we say, "Lord, we love You," but our actions tell a different story, we have an eternity problem! Jesus could see the people over the years who would be involved with "driving out demons" and working "miracles." Yet not all belonged to Him. Their lives were not surrendered or obedient to Him.

Our text is not an angry message from Jesus. It is a loving warning. People heard His Sermon on the Mount and listened carefully. They understood it was not enough to just say, "Lord, Lord," or "Jesus, Jesus." It was not enough to sing songs over and over again. The name of Jesus is not a password to Heaven. What Jesus said in Mark 1:15b helps us to understand this even better. "The kingdom of God is near. <u>Repent</u> and <u>believe</u> the good news!"

Prayer: Lord, it is good to hear Your warning. You openly tell us that our words of lifting up Your name is not the truth of our convictions, if we live as if we don't know You. Lord, forgive us. Help us to walk with You as Enoch did. Help us to love You as Your disciple John did. Create in us clean hearts O God. In Jesus' name we pray. Amen.

November 21

"Many will say to Me on that day, 'Lord, Lord, did not we prophesy in Your name, and in Your name drive out demons and perform many miracles?' Then I will tell them plainly, 'I never knew you. Away from Me, you evildoers!'" Matthew 7:22-23

"I never knew you"

Before Jesus spoke the shocking words, *"I never knew you,"* He told us about false prophets. They were in churches saying *"Lord, Lord,"* very solemnly. This is still happening. I hear these words just across the street from me here in Chennai. Every week it is <u>exactly</u> the same songs and prayers. "Lord, Lord" and "Praise the Lord" is shouted over and over. Jesus' name is clearly on their lips! But is Jesus in their hearts? That is what will matter in The Judgment! In our text, the false prophets did *"prophesy."* They did *"drive out demons."* They did *"perform many miracles."* <u>They thought they knew Jesus, but the problem was Jesus did not know them.</u>

Do the false prophets know they are ravenous wolves? I think the wolf has worn the sheep's clothing so long, they really think they are a sheep. He is going to stand before the Lord not knowing that he is a wolf, trying to pull one last trick over on the Lord. He is going to be absolutely stunned to hear what Jesus will say. The finality of Jesus' words are beyond comprehension!

Do we ever consider that Jesus has other people besides false prophets who are going to be surprised? "Could I be fooled myself, and be one of the many who will give the wrong answer on Judgment Day?" When I sing songs and pray, do I really mean them? Yes, but so did the *"false prophets."* The problem was they were *"evildoers,"* not Jesus followers. Jesus said, *"Away from Me, you evildoers!"* They lied, cheated, stole, committed adultery and did many other evils all week long and then in worship told Jesus that they loved Him! Jesus is saying that "our Sunday experience in church" means zero if we do not really love Him and want to be obedient.

Prayer: O Lord and Savior, we plead for Your mercy! Cover us with Your perfect blood. Fill us with Your holy presence. Make us obey Your Father's perfect will. In Your name we pray. Amen.

November 22

"I never knew you. Away from Me, you evildoers!" Matthew 7:23b

How can Jesus know me?

Jesus said, *"I am the Good Shepherd; I know My sheep and My sheep know Me,"* John 10:14. He also said, *"My sheep listen to My voice, I know them, and they follow Me,"* John 10:27. That is how salvation works! The Good Shepherd *"knows"* His sheep and because of that they *"listen"* to His voice. Because they listen, they *"follow"* Him! Paul wrote, *"It does not, therefore, depend on man's desire or effort, but on God's mercy,"* Romans 9:16.

If there is a knowing, loving, caring <u>relationship</u> established between Jesus and us, it was established even before we were born, before we had done any good or evil! Our faith is a relationship based on grace and mercy, not on our works. We cannot deny the sovereignty of God. But we also have a personal responsibility to come to Jesus! For Jesus said, *"Whoever comes to Me I will never drive away,"* John 6:37b. So, have we thrown ourself on the mercy of God? Have we pleaded for His grace and mercy? He loves to give it! Who can stop the will of the Father and the Son from giving it? *"For My Father's will is that everyone who looks to the Son and believes in Him shall have eternal life, I will raise him up at the last day,"* John 6:40.

Can we have confidence today, that we will stand boldly before our Savior in that day? Yes, if we stand as a beggar now, if we go as a leper, or as a blind man today. May we never stand before Jesus and tell him about all the good things we have done for Him! We will only be in Heaven because of what He has done for us. If we remember that, our worship and daily living will stay sweet!

Prayer: Lord, we praise and thank You that You are showing us that since we cannot do our works perfectly, we must come to You looking for Your grace and mercy. We also thank You for that invitation to come to You. Move us Lord. Make us come! Because You told us in the Sermon on the Mount, *"Be therefore perfect as your Heavenly Father is perfect."* Lord, we can only be perfect when You make us come and when You forgive us and clothe us with Jesus' righteousness! In Jesus' name we pray. Amen.

November 23

*"Have mercy on me, O God, according to Your unfailing love;
according to Your great compassion blot out my transgressions."*
Psalm 51:1

Those who cried for *"mercy"*

Think of the people in the Scriptures who cried for mercy! David here in Psalm 51 cries, Lord *"have mercy on me."* The Canaanite woman said, *"Have mercy on me, O Lord."* Blind Bartimaeus said, *"Jesus, Son of David, have mercy on me."* An anonymous beggar on the road to Jericho said, *"Have mercy on me."* If we cry out like that to God, we will receive mercy! We will receive a love relationship between us and God. And even our crying out, *"Lord have mercy on me, a sinner,"* is only because in an eternity past, before the world was even created, before we were even born, the Triune God had already established that relationship with us! It happened when the Father gave His sheep to His Son! Christ knew us and loved us already then. In fact, that is exactly why Christ came to this wicked and sinful world. He came to rescue His sheep who were not only lost, but were written on His hand.

If we have not cried out, "Lord have mercy on me, a sinner," do it today. Then, on the Judgment Day we will not even think of bringing up anything that we have done to earn our salvation! It will be because of His mercy that we loved Him. Christ Himself will bring up all the fruit and the works and deeds we have done because of our relationship with Him! All we need to say is, "Lord, here am I, a sinner, upon whom You had mercy and grace." "Lord, who am I that the Lord of the earth would care to know my name?" How great is our God. Please let us pray.

Prayer: Father, how priviliged we are to cry out to You, the One who is the way, the truth, and the life! How wonderful that You are eternally God and Lord, eternally holy and eternally all-knowing. You will not only know us today, but on that great day You will still know us. How wonderful it will be to be with You eternally, along with characters in the Bible. How wonderful it will be to see friends and loved ones, all there because You loved them. We praise You. We pray in Jesus' name. Amen.

November 24

"And I - in righteousness I will see Your face; when I awake, I will be satisfied with seeing Your likeness." Psalm 17:15

Touching the face of God

Did you ever watch a one year old baby try to communicate with an adult that they want to get to know? As the adult holds them, the baby touches the face, especially the eyes and the mouth. The baby knows that those senses are speaking to them, trying to establish a relationship with them. So they focus intently on the face, probing into the one that is interested in them. What a beautiful picture of how the Christian must seek God, to try understand Him, to develop a close relationship.

Here in Psalm 17, David's heart is to know God and for God to know him. See how clearly that is expressed when David said, *"Keep me as the apple of Your eye; hide me in the shadow of Your wings,"* Psalm 17:8. David wants to be very close to God. That must be the ultimate longing of our hearts too! We will not find rest, until we rest in Him. David ends the Psalm with the words of our text.

We know that no one has ever seen God, because God is a Spirit. Yet these words are said in a way we can understand what our longing for God must be. We were created to know God and to seek Him. Paul instructed idol worshiping people that God did not live in temples as they believed but that His dwelling was in the hearts of men. God specifically put each one of us on this earth for one specific reason. *"God did this so that men would seek Him and perhaps reach out for Him and find Him,"* Acts 17:27a. We will study this topic more tomorrow.

Prayer: Dear Father, we have not sought Your face as we must for our spiritual good and for Your glory. We wander from the shelter of Your wings. We wander from being close to You where we can touch You and learn to know You better. We so quickly cuddle up to the things of this world and then wonder why our relationship with You is not what it should be. Lord forgive us once again. Lord, we want to touch Your face to know You better, to serve You more faithfully. Lord help us to do this because we are weak. In Christ's name we pray. Amen.

November 25

"From one man He made every nation of men, that they should inhabit the whole earth; and He determined the times set for them and the <u>exact places</u> where they should live. God did this so that men would <u>seek Him and perhaps reach out for Him and find Him</u>, though He is not far from each one of us." Acts 17:26-27

Children, why are you here? Part 1

Dear child, if you are trying to understand why you are here in this world, look to our text. It gives you God's thoughts. Ultimately, you belong to God. He gave you to your parents to bring you up. God wants your parents to teach you many things, but especially for you to know God. One thing you must be aware of. God put you exactly where He wanted you to be! God planned the country you should live in and where you should live in that country. He planned the exact year, the month, and the day you would be born. He carefully selected your parents. Not one of these things are by accident, or by chance.

Notice that one of the main reasons you are here in the world is to *"find Him,"* that is God. But, you cannot see God. He is a Spirit. He does not have a body that you can touch. But God is everywhere in Spirit form. We can find Him, especially through prayer and reading the Bible where He tells us what He is like.

In love, God gave you Ten Commandments, in Deuteronomy 5:6-21. The first four commandments are to love God more than anything else in the world, including people. God then gave the next six commandments to love other people. Four plus six equals ten. You can do the math. The problem we all have is that we are selfish. Already at birth, we all began to love self more than anything else, more than God, and more than others. A big part of our parent's responsibility is to train us to be aware of the fact that we are selfish. At times they will need to use painful discipline to train us not to be so self serving. God demands our parents do this. We must know this and accept this to keep a right attitude all the days of our lives!

Prayer: O Lord, it is wonderful to know that You have a definite plan for our lives. We need to know that we are right where You want us to be. Lord, teach us what we need know. In Jesus' name we pray. Amen.

November 26

"If anyone says, 'I love God,' yet hates his brother, he is a liar. For anyone who does not love his brother, whom he has seen, cannot love God, whom he has not seen. And He has given us this command: Whoever loves God must also love his brother." 1 John 4:20-21

Children, why are you here? Part 2

There is an important connection between loving God in the first four commandments and loving other people next. This means it is really critical that we love our brother, sister, and all other people including our parents. We are going to talk about this in a way that is easy to understand. Remember that by loving others, we will also be respecting the reason God put us in the world.

Children, look at your own body. You have fingers, toes, ears, eyes, teeth, feet, a nose, a heart that pumps blood. Lungs help you breathe. There are many other parts of your body also. God gave you all of these body parts for a good reason. <u>It is the purpose of the parts of your body to serve the rest of your body</u>. Your fingers pick up food and feed your body. Your fingers help to put on clothes to cover your body. Your fingers write so you can do your schoolwork, and other work too. If you were to list all of the things that your fingers do to serve your body, there would be a very long list.

What if one day your finger said to your body, "I will no longer serve you"? What would happen to your body? What if your foot said, "I am no longer going to serve you by carrying you everywhere"? Why, you would be miserable! When a body becomes much older, some of the body parts do stop working! When they do, the body gets sick and after a while the body will even die. We can understand these things by just looking at our body.

God made us part of this world for the same reason; to help others. May we not have a bad attitude when God expects us to do it.

Prayer: Dear Lord, we can see that You also created us to be a blessing to others, especially to our families. Forgive us for all the times we have been selfish and did not do this. We thank You that You even use our own body parts to teach us how to serve others! In Jesus' name we pray. Amen.

"Honor your father and your mother, as the LORD your God has commanded you, so that you may live long and that it may go well with you in the land the LORD your God is giving you." Deuteronomy 5:16

Children, why are you here? Part 3

Dear children, you can clearly see that it is God's design first to serve others by obeying your parents. That is exactly why God gave you the 5th commandment. Did you notice the promise that God gives, if you obey this commandment? He promises, *"You may live long and that it may go well with you."* That is a pretty good reason to obey your parents!

Surely you want a good life! But that will not be easy. It will require discipline on your part as well as on your parents' part. The natural selfishness in you does not feel like obeying your parents. In these specific times, God reminds your parents, *"Do not withhold correction from a child,* Proverbs 23:13a NKJV. God says this because discipline is the loving thing to do. Do you know why? *"He who spares the rod hates his son, but he who loves him is careful to discipline him,"* Proverbs 13:24.

You may be a bit surprised, but God tells us these things so that we all learn how to obey and live God's way. After all, *"Foolishness is bound up in the heart of a child; the rod of correction will drive it far from him,"* Proverbs 22:15 NKJV. Your foolishness, is mostly all of the ways you are selfish. God wants this driven out of all of His children, both young and old alike. That is why God says, *"Discipline your son, for in that there is hope; do not be a willing party to his death,"* Proverbs 19:18. As parents, and grandparents too, we want you to live as a child of God.

By now you surely know that life has two roads. The easy, selfish road leads to a place we do not want to spend eternity. The harder road is more sacrificial and not very popular road. It leads to Heaven. We hope that through your training, you *"would seek Him and perhaps reach out for Him and find Him."* You are on earth for this purpose!

Prayer: Dear Lord, bless our children, and grandchildren too! We thank You for them. We pray that You know them personally, for then they will know You! In Jesus' name we pray. Amen.

November 28

"His sons did not walk in his ways. They turned aside after dishonest gain and accepted bribes and perverted justice." 1 Samuel 8:3

Samuel's sons were not Christians!

This third verse in 1 Samuel 8 is a huge warning to children who have Christian parents. No child is a Christian just because his or her parents are! Surely Samuel's boys were at many sacrifices and prayers. But did all that religious activity affect their hearts? No. Their hearts did not have the love of God in them. That truth is simply stated in our text, *"His sons did not walk in his ways."* What was the problem? It is not recorded that Samuel was a bad father like Eli was.

True religion is more than having knowledge about God and the Bible. After all, even Satan knows more about the Bible than we ever will. True religion starts with the knowledge of how God is holy and we are sinners apart from Him. But this knowledge must drive us to our knees in prayer for God's mercy and His forgiveness for our personal sin. Samuel's sons did not humble themselves before God, and therefore were not humble before man either!

It was because their hearts were not changed that they, *"turned aside after dishonest gain and accepted bribes and perverted justice,"* 1 Samuel 8:3b. Samuel's sons <u>rejected</u> God. They deliberately made the choice to <u>exchange</u> the truth and justice of God for *"dishonest gain."* They *"accepted bribes."* Satan's many appeals to better themselves through cheating appeared more glamorous to Samuel's sons!

Dear child, Satan has many schemes to steal your soul. *"Dishonest gain"* or *"bribes"* are just a couple of his attractions. Sin *"blinds those who see and twists the words of the righteous,"* Exodus 23:8b. Don't let Satan pluck your spiritual eyes out. Don't walk into his traps and ensnare your soul, like Samuel's sons did. Listen to God's advice. *"Above all else, guard your heart, for it is the wellspring of life,"* Proverbs 4:23.

Prayer: Dear Lord, You purposely give us many warnings in Scripture to walk in Your ways. We know that Satan will tempt us with his delicacies and hide his traps where we cannot see them! Lord, we thank You for warning us and our children. Make us and our families choose Your righteous ways. In Jesus' name we plead and pray. Amen.

November 29

"For God so loved the world that He gave His one and only Son, that whoever believes in Him shall not perish but have eternal life."
John 3:16

Child, do you *"believe"* in Jesus?

John 3:16 is one verse you can easily understand! *"Whoever believes in Him (Jesus) shall not perish."* The question is: Do you *"believe"* in Jesus? That is the issue. God's love here is to *"whoever believes."* Our text tells us about the love of God for <u>believers</u> *"from every tribe and language and people and nation,"* Revelation 5:9b. This text cannot possibly mean that God loves all the people in the world. Because, already in John 3:18, (which explains verse 16) we read, *"Whoever believes in Him <u>is</u> <u>not condemned</u>, but whoever does not believe stands <u>condemned already</u> because he has not believed in the name of God's one and only Son."*

Do you see the words *"condemned already"*? These are strong and serious words. Why are some people *"condemned already"*? It is because they have sin that is not covered, not forgiven by God! You see, God can only love you personally, because of Jesus. The reason is, God is perfectly holy, without any sin. He cannot have sweet communion with you until you are also holy and without sin. You can only be holy when Jesus takes your sin away. Then Jesus gives you His righteous, clean clothes in exchange for your sinful rags. After that God loves you fully, because you are personally forgiven, personally accepted, personally reconciled!

The best way to tell if Jesus' love is in you is to ask a simple question. Do you love Jesus? Do you love Jesus more than any other person or thing? If you do, there can only be one reason. *"We love because He first loved us,"* 1 John 4:19.

Prayer: Dear Lord, we thank You that You poured out Your love on us sinners *"from every tribe and language and people and nation."* You took our sin and gave us Jesus' clean clothes. You loved us personally so we can love You fully! Fill us with Jesus, the Bread of Life, because we, dead sinners, need You above all else. We who deserve Your wrath, need more and more of Your mercy! In Jesus' name we pray. Amen.

November 30

"Nevertheless, God was not pleased with <u>most</u> of them; their bodies were scattered over the desert." 1 Corinthians 10:5

Christian privileges are not salvation!

The early Corinthian church was a real mess. The people were living any way they wanted to. They thought that since Christ's blood covered any sin, their old pattern of sinning could continue. We are not immune from this "covenant presumption!" The people of Corinth were playing around with some serious sins, including sexual ones. Paul reminded them and us too about the children who came out of Egypt. He said in 1 Corinthians 10:2a, *"<u>They were all baptized</u>"* in the sea. *"<u>They all ate the same spiritual food,</u>"* in verse 3a. But, *"God was not pleased with <u>most</u> of them; their bodies were scattered over the desert,"* 1 Corinthians 10:5. They wasted their one and only life. They didn't make it to the promised land, meaning Heaven. What a shock! What if at the end of our life Christ said to us, *"I never knew you."* There would be no greater tragedy!

Dear child, please wake up! It requires more than privileges to be saved. Joab was David's captain. Gehazi was Elisha's servant. Judas was Christ's disciple. All three died in their sins! All three had the right knowledge. All three had serious warnings. All three had a lifetime to repent. Yet all three were lost for all eternity. Child, value your religious privileges, but never rest upon them! It is great to be a child of a godly father and mother. It is great to be brought up in the midst of many prayers. It is blessed to be taught the Gospel from infancy. It is essential to hear of sin, Jesus, the Holy Spirit, holiness, and Heaven! BUT, take heed that you personally turn to Christ!

Not one of us can enter the kingdom of God on the coattails of our parent's religion. We must take in *"The Bread of life,"* Jesus. We must repent on our own. Our faith in Christ's atoning blood, must be ours. Do we have the grace of God in us? If we do, it will show by how we are gracious and kind to others!

Prayer: Gracious Lord, search our hearts! If Jesus is not there, move Him from our heads to our hearts! Cover us with His sinless blood. Then Lord, may Your grace flow out of us so we become increasingly more loving and kind. In Jesus' name we pray. Amen.

DECEMBER

*"Now may the Lord of peace Himself
give you peace at all times
and in every way.
The Lord be with all of you."*
2 Thessalonians 3:16

December 1

"All who were appointed for eternal life believed." Acts 13:48b

"All"

I cannot get this text out of my mind. Paul is teaching. Some are believing. But, why are they believing? Paul explains, *"The God of the people of Israel chose our fathers; He made the people prosper ..., with mighty power He led them out of that country. He endured their conduct for about forty years,"* Acts 13:17-18a. The truth is that this is our lives as Christians. What noteworthy thing did any of the people of Israel do on their own? This message in Acts and elsewhere is about what God did!

Paul is tracing the finger of God's amazing and life-changing grace! This fact must melt our hearts to worship God. We did not believe in God and in the truths of the Gospel because we were so wise. We did not believe in Christ because our parents taught us the right way to live. We did not believe because we made a decision for Christ. We believed because we were *"appointed"* to believe! The provision of our *"eternal life"* has its source in God's eternal plan! *"All who were appointed for eternal life believed,"* Acts 13:48b. Meditate on the underlined words. We were selected by God to be pardoned to *"eternal life."* It is the age-old story of amazing grace!

What is our problem in understanding, *"All who were appointed for eternal life believed"*? Do we somehow think that *"all"* or everyone deserves to be saved? Is it not true, *"The wages of sin is death,"* Romans 6:23a? That is what every sinner really does deserve. Nor do we believe the second half of the verse, *"but the gift of God is eternal life in Christ Jesus,"* Romans 6:23b. Grace is a *"gift."* Do we have a problem with God giving a gift? After all, *"We are God's workmanship, created in Christ Jesus,"* Ephesians 2:10a. To *"create"* is to make something out of nothing. If by grace we are something that God made from nothing, we can only say, "Thanks!"

Prayer: Dear Lord, this single word *"all"* blows us away. Every single Christian is a Christian, only because You *"appointed"* them to be so! Our gratitude for Your divine appointment *"for eternal life"* is beyond words! Lord, may the truth of our appointment, melt our hearts and increase our devotion to You. In Christ's name we pray. Amen!

December 2

"For to me, to live is Christ and to die is gain. If I am to go on living in the body, this will mean fruitful labor for me. Yet what shall I choose? I do not know! I am torn between the two: I desire to depart and be with Christ, which is better by far." Philippians 1:21-23

Living in the light of eternity

Nothing is more important for us on this earth than living in the light of eternity. This life is a preparation for something else! We need to know what that something else is, if we are going to live for it! Paul knew something. He knew that going to Heaven was *"better by far"* than being on this earth. What did Paul know? What can we know? We know that God made a perfect world and placed a perfect Adam in it. Adam sinned and then the perfect man and the perfect world became totally corrupt. We know this from Genesis.

We know there is a Heaven and a Hell. Many do not want to talk about Hell because it is not a pretty reality. But many are traveling on the wide road that goes there. To live in the light of eternity we can't deny the reality of Hell. We will first talk about Heaven. As we study these topics in the coming devotions, we quickly see God never gave up on having a perfect man living in a perfect world. In fact, at the end of this world, God will remake this world. And then we will have a resurrected world, filled with resurrected people, living with a resurrected Jesus. As Christians, we need to get a clearer <u>Biblical</u> picture of Heaven, because we do need to live in the light of eternity!

You may be thinking, how can we know much about Heaven? After all, *"No eye has seen, no ear has heard, no mind has conceived what God has prepared for those who love Him."* 1 Corinthians 2:9. Don't stop reading. The next verse says, *"But God has revealed it to us by His Spirit,"* 1 Corinthians 2:10a. What we want to do is search the Scriptures to try understand what God has *"revealed"* about Heaven for His glory and for our good!

Prayer: Dear Heavenly Father, we rely on You to enlighten us about the subject of Heaven. We know that it is important to keep our eyes on You, keeping Heaven in mind by how we live. Help us dear Lord to live in the light of eternity. In Christ's name we pray. Amen.

December 3

"Set your hearts on things above, where Christ is seated at the right hand of God." Colossians 3:1b

Be more Heavenly minded!

We are commanded to set our hearts on *"things above,"* on Heaven and on Christ. The Greek word for *"set your hearts"* is to search or seek earnestly for these things. God wants us to think more about *"things above"* so we are more earthly good! The problem we have is that we think too much of worldly "things." We love our material things. We buy "things." We enjoy them. We spend time with them. We fix them. Basically, we have idols. We spend more time seeking other "things," than *"setting our hearts on things above."*

Paul warns us in Philippians 3 not to live to please the flesh. He used words like *"press on… take hold of that for which Christ Jesus took hold of me,"* Philippians 3:12b. Words like *"set your hearts"* are words of urgency. The easiest thing to do for the kindgom of God is nothing. God's point is: Get busy! Get on track! Stay focused! That is what is important. May we not let unimportant things rob us of what we were created for. May we seek God and a relationship with Him!

Only those things that are done for Christ and in Christ will last! Our children, our grandchildren, all those we disciple, will come to Heaven with us if they are Christian. Our text comes as a warning! *"Set your hearts on things above,"* because we, our children and all those we have a privilege to witness too, will not go to Heaven automatically or naturally! We need to say that openly because Hell is the place people go automatically! For all have sinned and fall short of the glory of God! Unless our hearts are changed, we are under the curse, not under the cure! Not everyone who hopes that they are going to Heaven will do so. Only those who have been redeemed by the blood of the Lamb will be in Heaven. *"Set your hearts on things above."* May we aspire to inspire before we expire!

Prayer: Lord, Your warning is so needed. Forgive us for setting our hearts on the things of this world. A relationship with You is what is eternal. Lord, strengthen us to look for that as we *"set our hearts on things above."* In Jesus' name we pray. Amen.

December 4

"I cry aloud to the LORD; I lift up my voice to the LORD for mercy."
Psalm 142:1

David teaches us to cry to God for help!

We may complain to others in times of trouble, but are we crying to God for His mercy? After all, God allows difficult trials in our lives to build up our weak faith. He wants to show us that He is capable of turning difficult events into victories and build our trust in Him. Why don't we go to God in prayer with the eyes of faith like David did here?

A man has work problems and family problems. He is greatly stressed out. Instead of going to God in prayer, he goes to the bar to try find comfort in a bottle and from others. A woman has been greatly hurt by her family's poor relationships and she holds a bitter grudge as she goes to pills to get some relief from all her tension. A young girl eats, or doesn't eat, because she is so tensed about her relationships or the lack of them. And then there is the young man who pursues his "fun" with all the gusto of a mad man to find satisfaction!

God sees an idol problem! God wants us to come to Him. In this psalm, David teaches us to go to God. David says, *"I pour out my complaint before Him, before Him I tell my trouble,"* Psalm 142:2. David is in a wilderness cave. His back is against the wall, literally. It is dark. His life and livelihood are in great danger. He is separated from his close relationships. He is greatly threatened. He realizes how weak he really is and he tells us what to do in our dark situations!

"When my spirit grows faint within me, it is You who know my way," Psalm 142:3a. He knows through many "faith experiences" that God is his help and shield. But now, David is in a new trial. He cries, *"No one is concerned for me. I have no refuge; no one cares for my life,"* Psalm 142:4b. David knows, if God is for us who can be against us!

See how David ends his prayer request from this cave. *"Set me free from my prison."* Why? *"That I may praise Your name."* And, that *"the righteous will gather about me because of Your goodness to me,"* Psalm 142:7. David is concerned for God's glory, that others know God's mercy.

Prayer: Almighty Lord, You are our hope and our hearts' desire. Shower us with Your mercy! It is what we need. In Jesus' name we pray. Amen.

December 5

"We hear that some among you are idle. They are not busy; they are busybodies. Such people we command and urge in the Lord Jesus Christ to settle down and earn the bread they eat. And as for you, brothers, never tire of doing what is right." 2 Thessalonians 3:11-13

Get busy!

The Apostle Paul is finished with a serious discussion on the second coming of Christ. He now shares a couple of prayer requests with the Thessalonian church. He also boldly chews out some of the people for not working. Listen to Paul's inspired reasoning.

"In the name of the Lord Jesus Christ, we command you, brothers, to keep away from every brother who is idle and does not live according to the teaching you received from us," 2 Thessalonians 3:6. That is strong language and easy to understand. Paul clearly says keep away from a Christian Brother or Sister who is lazy and talks too much about others! People do this two ways. They <u>gossip</u> or say things that are true to people who do not need to know. They <u>slander</u> others by saying things that are not true. Slander is punishable by law in many places, while gossip is not. Yet God hates both.

The problem is what these people are not doing! *"They are <u>not busy</u>, they are busybodies."* They work little and talk much! *"Such people we <u>command</u> and urge in the Lord Jesus Christ to settle down and earn the bread they eat."* Work, is not a suggestion. It is clearly a command! Since the beginning of time, God put people in the world to work. God thought so strongly about this that He had Paul write, *"If a man will not work, he shall not eat,"* 2 Thessalonians 3:10b. People come up with such lame excuses for not working. The real issue is, they would rather just sit and talk. It is wrong. In the Parable of the Talents, in Matthew 25:26-30, the Master (Jesus), sent a person to Hell for being *"wicked and lazy."* Good workers build God's kingdom. Good workers sleep better and are more healthy. Good workers are a blessing!

Prayer: O Lord, what a practical God You are. You cut through the excuses we have for not working. You tell us hard things for our good. We praise You for the ability to work. Please provide work for those who are having a hard time finding it. In Jesus' name we pray. Amen.

December 6

"I beg you, father, send Lazarus to my father's house, for I have five brothers. Let him warn them, so that they will not also come to this place of torment." Luke 16:27b-28

What those in Hell would love!

Imagine a person in the torments of Hell who has already experienced the wrath of God for a few thousand years! Imagine what would happen if suddenly repentance was made possible again! What if they could hear one more sermon at a church service? Imagine what the response to that message would be? The people would think nothing of crawling for a thousand miles to get there! The people would come from every part of Hell just to be able to look to the blood of Christ that covers all sin and frees them from the wrath of God! Every word preached, would be grasped quicker than a bar of gold here on earth!

Sad to say, there will never be an opportunity to repent in Hell. The day of salvation is today only! Today we can flee from the wrath of God and have forgiveness in Christ! But this illustration is given so that the ministry worker and the one who sits in the church can grasp the huge privilege we have in hearing the Word of God today!

Jesus used the strong language to warn us about the reality of Hell. Jesus knew first hand how absolutely terrible Hell is! After all, He not only created it, but He personally spent time there to pay for the sins of the redeemed. Jesus never joked about Hell, because there is nothing funny about it. What a pity that so many people laugh about the reality of Hell. Sad to say, a person can laugh their way into Hell, but they will never be able to laugh their way out of it.

The problem with those who do not believe in a real Hell is that they do not believe in a real Heaven. They do not believe that Jesus died to shed His perfect blood to atone for their sin! They do not believe that Jesus can give them His perfect righteousness so that they can stand before God, completely holy! The example of the rich man and Lazarus shows us the eternal reality of both Heaven and Hell.

Prayer: O merciful Lord, keep the reality of Heaven and Hell in the forefront of our minds. May we be serious about the importance of evangelism, living in the light of eternity. In Jesus' name we pray. Amen.

December 7

"Teach us to number our days aright, that we may gain a heart of wisdom." Psalm 90:12

Three views about the end of the world

The term millennium is a Latin word that means "one thousand." It concerns the thousand-year period described in Revelation 20. There are three main views concerning what will happen to believers in this time period. The three views are as follows:

Premillennialists believe the thousand years in Revelation represents a literal time of a worldwide kingdom of peace and righteousness on earth that will be established by Christ after His second coming. So, the "pre" means that Christ will return before this actual 1000-year reign. They also believe there will be 7 years of trouble here on earth called the tribulation period. In the last 3.5 years of that, a dominant antichrist emerges. Christians are raptured out prior to these last 3.5 years.

Amillennialists believe the thousand years in Revelation represents a large period of time we are now currently in. It is also called the Gospel Age and the "Gentile Age." It began at Pentecost and ends with Christ's second coming. They believe in a spiritual kingdom of Christ's rule, not a political kingdom. Running alongside the Gospel Age, is another 1000-year period (also symbolic) in which Satan is bound, so the Gospel can go out to all the Gentiles. At the end of this time, Satan is let loose for 3.5 years and a dominant antichrist appears. After this horrible time, the world ends when Christ comes.

Postmillennialists believe the thousand years in Revelation is a figurative period in which peace and righteousness will be established by the worldwide spread of the Gospel. They also believe the world will get better before the end and that there will be a great spiritual and political awakening. National Israel will be restored again.

Prayer: Dear eternal Lord, help us to understand what is correct, so we know how to respond to changing times! We praise You Lord that as the end of the world nears, it is You alone that keeps our souls safe so that we do not fall away! We look forward to praising You in eternity. In Jesus' name we pray. Amen.

December 8

"And this Gospel of the kingdom will be preached in the whole world as a testimony to all nations, and then the end will come." Matthew 24:14

When will the end come?

As this world becomes more corrupt, more violent and more difficult to live in, we question, "When will Jesus come again?" Jesus' disciples asked Him this question one day. The occasion and the question happened like this: "*As Jesus was sitting on the Mount of Olives, His disciples came to Him privately. 'Tell us,' they said, 'when will <u>this</u> happen, and what will be the sign of <u>Your coming</u> and of the end of the age?'"* Matthew 24:3.

First of all, "<u>*this*</u>" refers to Jerusalem falling. That's clear from the connection to the first two verses of Matthew 24. This is when Nero would completely end the Jewish age in about 70 AD. Secondly, the words, "*Your coming"* is "parousia" in the Greek. It means the end of the world when Jesus comes again. So, the disciples thought that Jerusalem falling and Jesus coming again were the same event. Of course they are not. Yet the end of the Jewish age and the end of the present Gentile age we are now in, are similar in how they end. But first, some terms need to be understood.

About 35 years before the Jewish Age ended, the Gentile Age began. This was at Pentecost, also called the Gospel Age, the thousand-year reign of Christ, or the Millennium on earth. During this time, the Gospel will go to all people. Before Jesus comes again, the "*Gospel of the kingdom will be preached in the whole world as a testimony to all nations, and then the end will come,"* Matthew 24:14.

The Gentile Age is now almost 2000 years old. Many Gentiles have come to Christ. For years I wondered about whether missions could be conducted in the time of the great tribulation that we will speak of in the coming devotionals. I now understand the answer is right in front of us. When that number of Gentiles is <u>complete</u>, "*then the end will come."* So yes, until Christ returns, there will be new Christians.

Prayer: Dear Lord, You know it is getting much harder for us to openly do Your work. Lord, we kindly ask You to help us. Strengthen us and protect us! We want to stand firm and complete the job You gave us in the Great Commission. In Christ Jesus' name we pray. Amen.

December 9

"Don't let anyone deceive you in any way, for that day (Jesus' 2nd coming) will not come, until the rebellion occurs and the man of lawlessness is revealed, the man doomed to destruction."
2 Thessalonians 2:3

The coming of the antichrist, Part 1

As we begin to understand chapter two of 2nd Thessalonians, many of the things going on in some churches makes more sense. This chapter describes things that must take place in the church, before Jesus returns. Follow the points of Paul here. Compare them to the overall condition of the church today. Keep in mind, this is God's outline for the coming of the antichrist and Jesus' own Second Coming.

First, Paul says to the Thessalonians that Christ's return to earth (second coming) will not happen *"until the rebellion occurs and the man of lawlessness is revealed,"* 2 Thessalonians 2:3b. There were some in Paul's day saying that Christ would come back any day. Paul corrects them saying that there first needs to be a great falling away from the faith. That is the *"rebellion"* spoken of here. Plus, *"the man of lawlessness will be revealed."* This is the antichrist. There have always been types of antichrists, like Hitler, Stalin, etc. But at the end of this world, a single, evil leader will emerge. I don't know who this is, nor do I think you do. But, it is helpful to know who this person will be working with to deceive people.

"He will oppose and will exalt himself over everything that is called God or is worshiped, so that he sets himself up in God's temple, proclaiming himself to be God," 2 Thessalonians 2:4. He will have no respect for God's laws, meaning the Ten Commandments! Law and order will become a huge problem in the church and in society. This evil man will even think he is God and set his own rules for living. It will be worse than nasty! There will be much corruption and violence!

Prayer: Dear merciful and gracious Lord, we thank You for telling us what will happen. You also comfort us! The lawless one will be <u>revealed</u> and then the Lord Jesus will overthrow him, *"<u>with the breath of His mouth.</u>"* Lord, the victory is Yours, and ours too in Christ. In Jesus' name we rejoice! And in His name we pray. Amen.

December 10

"The coming of the lawless one will be in accordance with the work of Satan displayed in all kinds of counterfeit miracles, signs and wonders, and in every sort of evil that deceives those who are perishing. They perish because they refused to love the truth and so be saved."
2 Thessalonians 2:9-10

The coming of the antichrist, Part 2

Before the world ends, Satan will display, *"all kinds of counterfeit miracles, signs and wonders, and in every sort of evil that deceives."* Satan can only do "counterfeit miracles," working through somebody, because Satan is a spirit! Who will this somebody (person) be? Jesus taught, *"False prophets will appear and perform great signs and miracles to deceive even the elect - if that were possible,"* Matthew 24:24b. What is a *"false prophet"*? Moses said, *"If what a prophet proclaims in the name of the LORD does not take place or come true, that is a message the LORD has not spoken,"* Deut. 18:22a. Are these *"false prophets,"* here now? Do any churches claim to have real *"prophets"* and claim *"great signs and miracles"*? A real prophet is right 100% of the time, or he is a fake!

When Jesus and his disciples healed people, they stayed healed. When the apostles did a miracle they also preached the Gospel message. In Acts 3, Peter healed a man *"crippled from birth."* Peter claimed no credit for this healing. Why? Because it is not about a leader's performance, but it's about Christ! No apostle in the Bible ever announced ahead of time he was going to have a healing service! Even when the Jews did ask for a *"miraculous sign,"* Jesus gave them a message! *"Destroy this temple, and I will raise it again in three days,"* John 2:19b. In John 6:30-31, the Jews again asked for a *"miraculous sign,"* like *"bread from heaven."* Jesus responded telling them that He is the Bread from Heaven. Jesus never gave a sign to unbelievers. Why? Because a message was needed. Do you see a problem today?

Prayer: O Lord, You are the most holy one. How sad that people still come to see a miracle or to have faith in a speaker. Then the speaker falls from some scandal, and the people leave the church. They had no faith in the fact that You are the living Christ! Lord, *"sanctify them by the truth; Your word is truth."* In Jesus' name we pray. Amen.

December 11

"Man is destined to die once, and after that to face judgment."
Hebrews 9:27b

Why will there be a Judgment?

The Bible warns us again and again that The Judgment is coming. It is called *"The,"* because there is only one Judgment. It will be the biggest courtroom ever! It is called *"Judgment"* because *"God will bring every deed into judgment, including every hidden thing, whether it is good or evil,"* Ecclesiastes 12:14. It will be one big test on how we had lived.

Why judgment? First, there are those living on earth who need to be judged. Second, there are souls in Heaven and in Hell now, that must be judged also. Their matching bodies are on earth, sleeping in the ground. <u>We will be judged in body and soul</u>. Both will need to be put together again, to be judged together. In The Judgment, every person, body and soul, will be eternally sent to Heaven or to Hell. How we do in God's courthouse on Judgment Day is far bigger than life. That's why the Bible warns us again and again.

It is so sad that so many people are deceived into thinking that they will simply cease to exist when they die. They do not understand that this life on earth is but a test for what comes after it. So they live as if they will never die! Our text is clear. A judgment is coming.

Many in the church think the purpose of The Judgment is simply to see who is Christian and who is not, and then separate them. The Judgment has to be more than that. Jesus knew who were His, even before the foundation of the world according to Romans 8:29-30.

More than anything, the guilt of sin must be judged. God's holiness and justice demands it! Plus, Jesus Christ must be publicly glorified. Jesus was publicly disgraced on the Cross as a criminal. Those who have unrighteously judged Jesus will now be judged by Him. Jesus will be publicly honored as the righteous Judge of Heaven and of Earth!

Prayer: Lord, what a solemn event is coming soon! How wonderful that we can go through The Judgment with hope and confidence! For You Lord, would never allow Your Son to be our substitute in vain. Because You accept His perfect sacrifice, we pass the test. May the name of our Savior be praised! In Jesus' name we pray. Amen.

December 12

"I tell you the truth, a time is coming and has now come when the dead will hear the voice of the Son of God and those who hear will live. For as the Father has life in Himself, so He has granted the Son to have life in Himself. And He has given Him authority to judge because He is the Son of Man." John 5:25-27

Who will the Judge be?

Jesus is the Judge. Our text explains that God gave this honorable position to Jesus, *"because He is the Son of Man."* Because of the redeeming work that Jesus did in coming to earth and dying on the Cross, God the Father gave this honor to the Son. The Apostle Paul also taught the same thing. *"Therefore God exalted Him to the highest place and gave Him the name that is above every name, that at the name of Jesus every knee should bow, in Heaven and on earth and under the earth, and every tongue confess that Jesus Christ is Lord, to the glory of God the Father,"* Philippians 2:9-11.

Jesus will have help in The Judgment. Angels will work with the Lord. Jesus said, *"He will send His angels with a loud trumpet call, and they will gather His elect from the four winds, from one end of the Heavens to the other,"* Matthew 24:31. Paul also said surely The Judgment will come and angels will be involved. *"God is just: He will pay back trouble to those who trouble you and give relief to you who are troubled, and to us as well. This will happen when the Lord Jesus Christ is revealed from Heaven in blazing fire with His powerful angels,"* 2 Thessalonians 1:6-7.

It seems the saints will also help Jesus in judging. Paul made a comment to the Corinthians about their bad practice of bringing another Christian to court before unbelievers. He asked them, *"How dare you do this? Can't you settle matters between Christians without going before those who do not even know why they are here on this earth?"* Then, arguing from the lesser to the greater, Paul adds, *"Do you not know that the saints will judge the world?"* He also adds, *"Do you not know that we will judge angels? How much more the things of this life!"* 1 Cor. 6:2a &3.

Prayer: O Lord, we thank You that You who are all merciful, gracious, wise, loving and just will be the great judge on the Judgement Day. In Jesus' name we pray. Amen.

December 13

"Man is destined to die once, and after that to face judgment,"
Hebrews 9:27b

Who will be judged?

In our text we can plainly see that every man will surely be judged. However, demonic angels know they are also going to be judged by a holy God, to an eternal Hell. When Jesus approached two violent demon-possessed men, they said to Him, *"'What do You want with us, Son of God?' they shouted. 'Have You come here to torture us before the appointed time?'"* Matthew 8:29. God has set an *"appointed time"* (singular) for a Judgment Day!

It seems other fallen angels despised their <u>God-given place in life</u> along with their <u>God-given responsibilities</u>. Jude 6 shouts to us! *"Angels who did not keep their positions of authority but abandoned their own homes — these He has kept in darkness, bound with everlasting chains for judgment on the great Day."* God is telling this so we will not fail like these angels did! We should not complain about our need to be faithful. We must not run from our relationships and responsibilities! Created man will not escape what created angels must face!

Some people think that Christians will escape The Judgment because of Christ's atoning blood. If you think this applies only to the unbelieving, then listen to Paul. He said to a fellow Christian, *"Why do you judge your brother? Or why do you look down on your brother? <u>For we will all stand before God's judgment seat</u>. It is written: 'As surely as I live,' says the Lord, 'every knee will bow before Me; every tongue will confess to God.' So then, each of us will give an account of himself to God,"* Romans 14:10b-12.

At another time, Paul said to the Corinthian church, *"For we must all appear before the judgment seat of Christ, that each one may receive what is due him for the things done while in the body, whether good or bad,"* 2 Corinthians 5:10.

Prayer: O holy Lord, Your Word is clear. We will all stand before Your judgment seat. Lord prepare us today for that solemn event. Convict us of our sin. Forgive us in Jesus' name. For You will be forever praised. May we praise You now! In Christ's name we pray. Amen.

December 14

"The hour is coming in which all who are in the graves will hear His voice and come forth — those who have done good, to the resurrection of life, and those who have done evil, to the resurrection of condemnation." John 5:28b-29 NKJV

Why only one Resurrection and Judgment?

Some people believe there will be more than one resurrection and judgment. They believe one will happen at Jesus' Second Coming, another, 3.5 or 7 years later, and yet another 1000 years after that. In a way there will be two resurrections, one for the just, one for the unjust, but they happen the same "*hour.*" Jesus said in our text, "*The hour is coming.*" The NIV says "*A time is coming.*" "A" means one time. How many times was Jesus raised from the dead? The Bible has talked many times about a resurrection day, and The Judgment day. Paul clearly said, "*He has set a day when He will judge the world with justice by the Man (Jesus) He has appointed. He has given proof of this to all men by raising Him from the dead,*" Acts 17:31. These are singular words!

But you might argue that these verses only speak of the dead. There are also the living; Paul clearly taught about that! "*Brothers, we do not want you to be ignorant about those who have fallen asleep, or to grieve like the rest of men, who have no hope. We believe that Jesus died and rose again and so we believe that God will bring with Jesus those who have fallen asleep in Him. According to the Lord's own word, we tell you that we who are still alive, who are left till the coming of the Lord, will certainly not precede those who fall asleep. For the Lord Himself will come down from Heaven, with a loud command, with the voice of the archangel and with the trumpet call of God, and the dead in Christ will rise first. After that, we who are still alive and are left will be caught up together with them in the clouds to meet the Lord in the air. And so we will be with the Lord forever. Therefore encourage each other with these words,*" 1 Thessalonians 4:13-18. Paul is very clear. Jesus is not going back to Heaven and later coming to gather the souls for another resurrection.

Prayer: Lord, Your Word is truth. We can see that the events of the coming resurrection and judgment will be quick. You say in an hour. May we not argue, but be ready! In Jesus' name we pray. Amen.

December 15

"Then I saw a great white throne and Him who was seated on it. Earth and sky fled from His presence, and there was no place for them."
Revelation 20:11

When and where will The Judgment be?

God's eternal timetable for the world stays right on schedule. The elect are now all saved! The devil, Satan, and all his host are completely destroyed in the verse before this. They are out of the way. Jesus is watching all this happen. More than that, He is making it happen! John sees a *"great"* throne. He sees a throne that is majestic beyond description, one befitting the King of the universe. Judge Jesus is on that throne! John notices that the throne is a *"white"* one. *"White,"* because it is perfectly holy and just.

"Earth and sky fled from His presence." Suddenly the earth is no more. Everything on it is burned up with fire, totally cleansing it! Every effect of sin upon the earth is burned up. This is all necessary for it to be remade perfectly. The old has to go. So the earth is no longer habitable. What happened to the people? John tells us.

"And there was no place for them." There is more than one meaning here. First, no one can possibly escape The Judgment, anymore than the people could escape the Genesis flood! There is *"no place"* for them to go to! In fact, *"the great white throne"* will come down to everyone! The Judgment couldn't be in Heaven, because no sinner can go there. It couldn't be on earth, because the perfect souls that Jesus brought with Him from Heaven can't go back to a sinful earth. So, the earth *"fled from His presence."* What is left? Only that distance which is inbetween. It appears that the judgment of both the just and the unjust is right now in the air.

Prayer: Dear holy Lord, what a huge and solemn moment The Judgment will be. Truly every knee will bow before You. Suddenly, Your words in Ecclesiastes 12:14 come into focus. *"God will bring every deed into judgment, including every hidden thing, whether it be good or evil."* Lord, if it wasn't for Your grace and mercy, we would all be judged severely! We bow to You King Jesus, our Lord and Savior. Accept our praise and worship. In Jesus' name we pray. Amen.

December 16

"Come to Me, all you who labor and are heavy laden, and I will give you rest. Take My yoke upon you and learn from Me."
Matthew 11:28-29a NKJV

"Come" to Jesus today!

In saying, *"Take My yoke upon you and learn from Me,"* Jesus was saying, "Let Me be your teacher and you will find rest for your souls." His original hearers would have had no difficulty in understanding this language. Everybody in those days was speaking of the yoke of Torah, the yoke of the Law of Moses that the hand of God laid on them. They felt like they were under bondage to it. So Jesus is now setting up His own teaching in which He both endorsed the Law of Moses and is now transcending it. He is teaching a new yoke to which His disciples must submit to, literally a new covenant! Then later Jesus commissioned His disciples to pass on to their converts everything that He had taught and commanded them! And later still, the Apostle Paul wrote of the need to bring every thought of our minds into captivity to the obedience of Christ. So, *"Take My yoke upon you and learn from Me,"* is the new yoke Jesus is teaching.

Many people were paralyzed by fear. They tried so hard to keep the law but they couldn't do it. They knew something was wrong. They knew something was missing. This is still true for unbelievers today! Jesus is saying rest in Me. Don't think that your good deeds will somehow overshadow your bad ones, and thus you will enter Heaven. Rest in Me, in Christ! He has accomplished the perfect work for us.

There are also believers, those who were saved by His grace alone, that are still paralyzed by fears! How can this be if the very things which we are afraid of, are under the feet of Jesus? *"Jesus is Lord,"* what are we afraid of? How can we dread death if we are buried with Christ in His death? He was raised. So will we! Let us not fear then, but go to the One who removes our fears!

Prayer: O Lord, how wonderful it is that You destroyed death and him who has the power of death, that is the devil! By Your victory, we have the victory! Thank You Jesus! In His name we pray. Amen.

December 17

"I have been young, and now am old; yet I have not seen the righteous forsaken, nor his descendants begging bread." Psalm 37:25 NKJV

A testimony about God's faithfulness

This verse is David's true testimony about what he had seen in his own personal life. It is a testimony about the care that the Heavenly Father has for all His children. It is a precious verse about the amazing attributes of God, especially His faithfulness! What an amazing comfort for us. David experienced difficult living conditions. Remember how he was hunted down like a dog by the king of the land? Yet David survived by the hand of God and writes about God's amazing care.

Why does God bless the righteous? Does God bless us just because we are living righteously? That is part of it. Jesus did say, *"Blessed are the merciful, for they shall obtain mercy,"* Matthew 5:7 NKJV. But there is far more to it than this. A question needs to be asked. Why is anyone even righteous? The best answer is in a couple of verses before our text. *"The steps of a good man are <u>ordered</u> by the LORD,"* Psalm 37:23a NKJV. His grace and mercy never leaves us! *"We are His workmanship, created in Christ Jesus for good works, which God <u>prepared</u> beforehand that we should walk in them,"* Ephesians 2:10 NKJV. God created us for His own pleasure! So when God blesses the righteous, He is also praising Himself. He is praising His own works!

We must humble ourselves! The good that we do, we do only because God ordained it. He gave us the will to do it. Then He helped us do it! *"For it is God who works in you both to will and to do for His good pleasure,"* Philippians 2:13 NKJV. So the fact that we are righteous and not *"begging bread,"* is a testimony to the wonderful grace of God.

What's the point of knowing this? We must keep doing our good works, our righteous acts with the right attitude. We must not become proud. The true source of our righteousness, in every part, is from God and His strength.

Prayer: Dear gracious and merciful Lord, You are the author and perfecter of our faith! You not only make us righteous, You make us do righteous acts. To You belongs the praise. Keep us humble, productive and blessed for Your honor and praise! In Jesus' name we pray. Amen.

December 18

"The LORD said to Moses, 'Tell Aaron and his sons, 'This is how you are to bless the Israelites. Say to them: 'The LORD bless you and keep you; the LORD make His face shine upon you, and be gracious to you; the LORD turn His face toward you and give you peace.'" Num. 6:22-26

God's blessing on His people

This is perhaps one of the most used benediction (blessing) in the Bible. God gave these words to Moses, <u>commanding</u> him to use them. The priests were appointed by God to bless the people in His name. These words of God then, come with His enduring promise! Just think, these words of blessing were already true in the Old Testament. The people of Israel knew that because the name of the Lord was mentioned three times, there was something special in this blessing! Having the New Testament, we know more about why it is so special.

Paul's closing words to the Corinthians is the same benediction in more clarity. *"May the grace of the Lord Jesus Christ, and the love of God, and the fellowship of the Holy Spirit be with you all,"* 2 Corinthians 13:14. It is our God in Trinity, giving us His blessing!

Note who God's blessing is to in particular. It is personal. Even though this blessing is given in group functions, it is for us personally! Meditate on what our promises are! We have the beautiful and needed *"grace of the Lord Jesus Christ"* given to us, in the place of our sin. We have *"the love of God"* we need, instead of His wrath that we deserve! We have *"the fellowship of the Holy Spirit"* to guide us, comfort us, and protect us in every way, every day. All of these blessings are in the place of Satan controlling us.

God's three-fold blessing is not a maybe. It is a guarantee. God confirmed His promised blessing in the verse that follows our text. *"So they shall put My Name upon the children of Israel; and I will bless them,"* Numbers 6:27 NKJV. Are we looking for God's blessing? Are we thankful for it? God's blessing is important for our worship of God.

Prayer: *"The LORD bless you and keep you. The LORD make His face to shine upon you and be gracious to you. The LORD turn His face toward you and give you peace."* In Jesus' name we pray. Amen.

December 19

"So likewise you, when you have done all those things which you are commanded, say, 'We are unprofitable servants. We have done what was our duty to do.'" Luke 17:10 NKJV

Christian duty, an obligation to be faithful

Jesus begins Luke 17 by giving us an example of how it is our *"duty"* not to offend a child or new believer. He warns us that if we do this, we might better tie a stone around our neck and jump into the sea. Jesus is showing us that true faith involves a real sense of *"duty."* By using another story, Jesus shows how *"duty"* is a moral obligation to be faithful to our Master and Lord!

Jesus uses the subject of forgiveness, (a prime ingredient to make all relationships work), to drive home His point on the importance of Christian duty. In verses 6-10, a servant is working all day in the field. After all this, the master (Jesus) asks the servant to fix him something to eat. The servant (every believer) prepares the food. Then the master does not even thank the servant. Do you know why? It was the servant's *"duty"* to obey and be faithful in doing what he was told to do!

The principle here in Luke 17, is much bigger than just forgiveness. Duty is more important than any other selfish interest we might have! It is for all of the Christian life. Christians must be the best students, the best workers and the best people to do business with. If Jesus is our Master, our Christian duty compels us to be faithful in everything.

So how are our daily *"duties"* going? Sad to say, overall, the concept of *"duty"* is slipping from our vocabulary because it is slipping from our practice! Jesus said to His Father, *"not My will but Yours be done."* That is a model of duty! Our selfishness kills our duty. *"Unless a kernel of wheat falls to the ground and dies, it remains only a single seed. But if it dies, it produces many seeds,"* John 12:24.

Prayer: Dear Lord, You are our Savior and King. What a serious subject You give to us here. We must admit, our selfishness affects our *"duty"* to You and to our fellow man. Please forgive us and help us love You more than ourselves. Give us a real sense of *"duty"* regardless of how we feel about it. In Jesus' name we pray. Amen.

December 20

"On the outside you appear to people as righteous but on the inside you are full of hypocrisy and wickedness." Matthew 23:28b

Hypocritical perfectionism

The scribes and Pharisees demanded perfection in others, but they themselves were *"full of hypocrisy and wickedness."* We also point out faults of others, yet fail to look at our own hearts. It is easy to be a hypocritical perfectionist! No matter what others do, we still see faults! If we are a perfectionist, we will see the mistakes of our child clearly, but ignore their good points! Our child then cries inwardly for love and encouragement! A child wants to please a negative perfectionist parent, but can't. No one is harder to live with than such a person.

In the church, a perfectionist thinks he or she is in the will of God. They see God's justice so clearly, but know so little of God's love, little about Jesus that would not break a bruised reed or let a smoking flax go out! A perfectionist is big on law (no problem), but small in being gracious to others. Law without grace crushes spirits! Truly God's law must guide a Christian's home, church, and business, but God's grace must govern it also!

The perfectionist thinks he is showing the world how neat, clean, and orderly the case for Christianity really is. However in the process, in his stubborn ignorance, he unknowingly shuts out God's love. A perfectionist is a loveless creatures, living in a loveless home, doing a loveless ministry! When we walk into a perfectionist home we would think someone just died. It is a tense place! Joy is simply not allowed!

I know a "Christian" man who had brilliant children. He made them recite the pastor's sermon when they got home from church. Yet, 40 years later, it seems only one of his six children is serving the Lord. His wife lived a very hard and loveless life. He saw all of her bad points! And he let her know about them! If a person is all law and no grace they are so frustrating and not easy to live with!

Prayer: Gracious Lord, too often we also point out other people's mistakes without looking at their good points! Forgive us; correct us and make us more gracious. In Jesus' name we pray. Amen.

December 21

"But as for you, continue in what you have learned and have become convinced of." 2 Timothy 3:14a

Help through every hardship

The early church is in transition! Christ has departed this earth. Now the apostles, including Paul, are leaving this world one by one. Paul is concerned for young Timothy, but he is also concerned about those whom Timothy will disciple! This is discipleship at its best. If we are not personally concerned about how well our disciple's students are doing, we miss a main point of discipleship. It is about passing on the faith! Jesus' passion for discipleship is seen in His farewell prayer in John 17. We are privileged to see here how God leads Paul to instruct Timothy. Paul is writing his last letter.

Paul recounts the way he has instructed Timothy over the years in verses 10-11. He reminds Timothy of the many persecutions and how God delivered them! Paul reminds Timothy that, *"everyone who wants to live a godly life in Christ Jesus will be persecuted,"* 2 Timothy 3:12. And Timothy, it's going to get worse! *"Evil men and imposters will go from bad to worse, deceiving and being deceived,"* 2 Timothy 3:13. This is also true for our day. It is getting worse quickly. How will we all survive and persevere in our world that is becoming more violent and corrupt? How is the church that is named after Christ going to prosper?

The persecuted church will now make it in the present Gospel age for one reason. *"All Scripture is God-breathed and is useful for teaching, rebuking, correcting and training in righteousness, so that the man of God may be thoroughly equipped for every good work,"* 2 Timothy 3:16-17. Like Timothy, we are personally going to make it because we have the Bible, the holy Word of God to guide us through life, to help us endure every hardship. Jesus has not left us. The Spirit will not leave us. God the Father will not leave us. The gates of Hell cannot prevail against us! Greater is He that is in us than He that is in the world.

Prayer: O Sovereign Lord, You took great care to have Your promises and Your will written down for us. May we value it! Thank You for the promise that You will never leave us or forsake us! In Jesus' name we pray. Amen.

"But the people who live there are powerful, and the cities are fortified and very large. We even saw descendants of Anak there." Numbers 13:28

"But," the big little word

The context here is Moses sending 12 spies to check out the Land of Canaan. This event was specifically designed by God to examine the faith of the children of Israel. <u>Were they ready to enter the Promised Land?</u> Are we? Our faith will also be tested to see if we are ready to enter Heaven. It happened like this:

The Lord instructed Moses, *"Send some men to explore the land of Canaan, which I am giving to the Israelites. From each ancestral tribe send one of its leaders,"* Numbers 13:2. Note that these were not 12 "flunkies," but *"leaders"* of the 12 tribes! For forty days they took a sneak preview of the land God was giving them. They saw huge grapes and beautiful fruit! The land was fertile. They were well fed in this land! *"BUT,"* the spies also saw something else that alarmed them! What a big lack of faith this *"but"* word is! *"<u>But</u> the people who live there are powerful, and the cities are fortified and very large. We even saw descendants of Anak there,"* Numbers 13:28. *"Anak"* was a family of giants.

The twelve spies reported back to Moses and the children of Israel. They mentioned the good things, but focused on the obstacles! The cities were not only huge but well defended. They had no weapons to even break down the walls. And the giants would surely step on them like they were a bug. The bottom line was, "<u>But it's too difficult.</u>" After all that God had done for them, they still did not see the size of their God! Their faith was weak. The people disregard the report of Caleb and Joshua. It was simply easier to not have faith! *"The LORD said to Moses, 'How long will these people treat Me with <u>contempt</u>? How long will they refuse to believe in Me, in spite of all the miraculous signs I have performed among them?'"* Numbers 14:11.

What about us? Jesus said, *"Follow Me."* What excuses do we give for not following the Lord?

Prayer: O Lord, we can see from the lives of the spies that it's easier not to have a strong faith. Lord, strengthen our weak faith. Give us that solid faith of Joshua and Caleb. In Christ Jesus' name we pray. Amen.

December 23

"But the angel said to them, 'Do not be afraid. I bring you good news of great joy that will be for all the people. Today in the town of David a Savior has been born to you; He is Christ the Lord.'" Luke 2:10-11

The "Good News" of Christmas! Part 1

First, the good news of Christ's birth took the shepherds fear away! Picture them, they are in the field on a dark night taking care of their sheep. Suddenly, *"An angel of the Lord appeared to them, and the glory of the Lord shone around them, and they were terrified,"* Luke 2:9. Can you imagine a bright angel standing in front of you on a dark night? Plus, the glory of the Lord is all around also! They knew something big was up. The news of Jesus' birth calmed them. We too have many fears. Know this: Jesus in us, calms us.

Secondly, the good news of Christ's birth brought the shepherds *"great joy."* The living Jesus does just that. The shepherds were not the first to be joyful either. Mary, the mother of Jesus, visited her Aunt Elizabeth when her aunt was in her sixth month of pregnancy. Elizabeth told Mary, *"As soon as the sound of your greeting reached my ears, the baby in my womb leaped for joy,"* Luke 1:44. Then Mary sang a song to God, *"My soul glorifies the Lord and my spirit rejoices in God my Savior,"* Luke 1:46-47. Jesus not only removes our fears, He fills us with joy!

Thirdly, the good news of Christmas gives us a lasting peace. The joy of the Lord never ends. Jesus' name itself means "Yahweh saves" in Hebrew. The purpose of Jesus' coming to earth is summed up in His name. He came, to *"save His people from their sins."* What a lasting, eternal peace that is!

Jesus' coming into the world is the Gospel message, the good news. He is the second Adam. The first Adam plunged the world into sin and separated us from God, but Jesus takes our sin, gives us His righteousness and restores us back to God. That is Good News!

Prayer: Merciful Lord, we thank and praise You for coming into this sinful world. Your coming takes away our fears and gives us much joy. With You living in our hearts, we have a peace that passes understanding! You humbled Yourself to our earthly world so that we could be elevated to Your heavenly home. In Your precious name we pray. Amen.

December 24

"But the angel said to them, 'Do not be afraid. I bring you good news of great joy that will be for all the people. Today in the town of David a Savior has been born to you; He is Christ the Lord.'" Luke 2:10-11

The "Good News" of Christmas! Part 2

When Jesus became flesh as a little baby He was truly a bundle of joy. Think of how wonderful this angelic announcement of Jesus' birth was to the shepherds. His birth was not what you would expect. Look at our text. It does not say, "Unto you is born this day in the city of David a Savior who is the <u>Lord's Christ</u>." Nor did the angel say, "Unto you is born a Savior who is the Christ, <u>of the Lord</u>!" It clearly says; *"He is Christ, <u>the Lord</u>."* Jesus did not grow up to become the Lord. He was born "The Lord." It is important to see that Jesus did not cease to be God when He became a baby. Jesus was not just the Lord's anointed One, but the Anointed, who is Himself "the Lord." How wonderful it is that Jesus brought "the Lord" title with Him to this earth!

When His earthly mommy and daddy wrapped Him in swaddling clothes, Baby Jesus was declared by the angels to be the Lord, fully man, fully God, our Savior. The kingdom of God has come to earth! Throughout Jesus' ministry He gave much evidence of the fact that He knew Himself to be *"the Lord."* Jesus announced with His coming into the world that the kingdom of God had arrived. God's kingly rule had come. People could now receive it. People could enter into it. People could inherit it. All this, by being related to Him! Jesus' birth ushered in the kingdom of God, making it now a Christ-centered doctrine and a Christ-centered reality. By being related to this Jesus, we are today, already now, in the kingdom of God! The King incarnate, in the flesh, has come. That is good news!

Prayer: Dear Lord, as we celebrate Your birth into the world, we fall down with the angels in worship. We are beginning to understand what the angels and shepherds knew to be true, that the Lord Himself has come into this world. About 4000 years of Old Testament history all pointed to Your coming. Two thousand years now have looked back to Your miraculous birth. Lord, accept our praises and our prayer in Your most holy name. Amen.

December 25

"Whoever believes in the Son has eternal life, but whoever rejects the Son will not see life, for God's wrath <u>remains</u> on him." John 3:36

The "Bad News" of Christmas! Part 3

Many of us have seen Christmas after Christmas. We know about Christmas, but do we know the Christ of Christmas? Believing in the Christ of Christmas is literally a matter of life and death! Not believing the "Good News," of Baby Jesus in the manger, becomes really "Bad News," if we reject Him. It would be better to not have been born, than to reject Jesus who is God. Baby Jesus came to give us eternal life and free us from the wrath of God!

The bad news for unbelievers is that they will not cease to exist, as some believe, but they will experience the eternal wrath of God in Hell forever. That is exactly what we all deserve. God gives us death for our sin, simply because, *"The wages of sin is death,"* Romans 6:23a. God told Adam if he sinned he would surely die. God, as the Maker and righteous Judge of the world, alone determines the penalty for sin. As a holy God, He cannot go against His character. His holiness demands sin must be punished. If Jesus does not take our sin and give us His righteousness, then the bad news of Christmas is ours.

Think of how Jesus fully experienced rejection by God later on when He died on the Cross. If Jesus did that for us personally, that is "Good News." If we reject Him, that is "Bad News." On the Cross, Jesus felt the full force of God's wrath when He cried out, *"My God, My God, why have You forsaken Me?"* Matthew 27:46b. This cry of Jesus was a scream heard around the world. This was 100% the scream of all those who enter Hell. This is our cry if we reject this Baby Jesus! Just think, the *"wrath"* of God against Jesus was so great that rocks split. There was an earthquake, and it was dark at midday. An eternal Hell under the wrath of an unrelenting, offended and holy God is Bad News!

Prayer: Lord Jesus, we learn that You in love experienced our pain on the cross. Now we will sing in Heaven with You. Lord, move us to that Good News of the Baby in the manger, the Lord Jesus Christ. In His name we pray. Amen.

December 26

"A teacher of the law came to Him and said, 'Teacher, I will follow You wherever You go.' Jesus replied, 'Foxes have holes and birds of the air have nests, but the Son of Man has no place to lay His head.'"
Matthew 8:19-20

Jesus builds the faith of His followers!

Jesus told the man in our text that it is not easy to follow Him. Sometimes when we see all the glitter that surrounds Christmas we can easily lose the connection to who Jesus was and how He lived in this world. There have been books written to "Follow in His Steps." But do we really want to walk where Jesus walked? Do we really want to live like Jesus lived? Do we really want to experience the rejection that Jesus faced? Do we want people to look at us and think we are weird, even radical? If we say, "Yes," praise God. That is good! But then we should search out some of the ways Jesus lived! We should examine some of the conditions that Jesus faced. We must particularly see how Jesus responded to the various events that faced Him every day.

1. Our willingness to follow Jesus will soon be tested!

Right after Jesus spoke the words in our text, He got into a boat to cross the sea. Only 12 disciples followed Him. They thought they were willing to cross the dangerous water with Jesus. Immediately, *"without warning a furious storm came up,"* Matthew 8:24a. The disciples faith quickly failed! *"Lord, save us!"* they cried. *"We're going to drown!"* Matthew 8:25b. Jesus' response in verse 26a was, *"You of little faith, why are you so afraid?"* How weak our faith is also! We want to follow Jesus but our faith is so weak. What can we do?

2. We must keep our eyes on Jesus!

Jesus *"Rebuked the winds and the waves, and it was completely calm,"* Matthew 8:26b. The disciples quickly learned that Jesus was the Lord of the winds and the seas, as well as God of the dry land. Their faith grew! As their God grew bigger, their faith grew stronger!

Prayer: Almighty Lord, we have so much to learn about You! How wonderful it is that You build our faith one storm at a time. Build our faith Lord! In Jesus' name we pray. Amen.

December 27

"Still other seed fell on good soil, where it produced a crop."
Matthew 13:8a

Am I prepared for Sabbath worship?

We all know that a preacher should not preach God's Word without first meditating and preparing that message. We criticise a pastor for not being prepared. But are we who sit in the pew prepared for worship? After all, we in the pew should be the *"good soil"* in the parable of the sower that needs to be prepared!

A farmer or sower needs to be prepared to plant. He needs his equipment in good shape. He needs to gather the seed that will be sown. Yet there is much more the farmer must do. The ground must be prepared to receive the seed! The ground needs to be leveled, the clumps of dirt broken up, the fertilizer put on and worked into the soil. All this needs to be done <u>before</u> the seed goes in! So in farming, the ground needs to be prepared to receive the seed. This may take more time than it does to plant a crop!

We believers are the ground that must receive the seed, which is the Word of God. How prepared are we to enter Sunday worship? What are we doing on Saturday night to prepare for worship? Do we stay out late, get to bed late and end up really tired in the morning? Or are we quiet before the Lord and do we have a prayerful expectation of meeting God in worship? If we are not prepared for worship, it is not the pastor's fault! In the parable, some seed fell on hard ground. We are that hard ground if we are not prepared to worship God! That is the main reason the Word of God is not growing in us. Plus, when the ground is hard, the water runs off, not doing any good! Our hearts are hard if we have personal issues with other church members. And then, there is the singing, the tithing, and the prayers. Do we participate in a meaningful way? What about the money in our pocket? Is the note or bill too small for Saturday night's fun, yet way too big to hand over to God on Sunday? We need to be prepared for worship!

Prayer: Merciful Father, forgive us for not being prepared to worship You on Sunday. You know that our hearts are hard. Lord, soften our hearts to receive Your precious Word. In Jesus' name we pray. Amen.

December 28

"Once more Jesus said to them, 'I am going away, and you will look for Me, and you will die in your sin. Where I go; you cannot come.'"
John 8:21

No passport, no ticket, no go!

This morning it was difficult to explain our text and the verses that follow to the orphan children. I could not get them to understand that Jesus was leaving this world, and that the unbelieving Pharisees could not go where He was going. The Pharisees were also confused as to who Jesus was, and where He was going! So Jesus made it clearer. *"He continued..., 'You are of this world; I am not of this world. I told you that you would die in your sins; if you do not believe that I am the one I claim to be, you will indeed die in your sins,"* John 8:23-24.

I told the children I had to go to another country in eight days, and they could not go along. I asked them, "Why can't you go?" One girl said, "I do not have a passport." Another said, "I do not have a ticket." Both were correct. And that's the point. Jesus is the only passport and ticket to Heaven. The Pharisees didn't know these two essential things! They were blind to the truth, even though Jesus had just forgiven a woman they brought to Him, *"caught in the act adultery,"* John 8:4b. This forgiven sinner followed Jesus and heard Him say, *"I am the light of the world. Whoever follows Me will never walk in darkness, but will have the light of life,"* John 8:12b. But, *"The Pharisees challenged Him,"* John 8:13a. They did not believe Him, nor would they follow Jesus.

"The light of the world" was standing in front of them, and they were blind! They thought they were already righteous because they were experts in the Law! They said Moses and Abraham were their fathers! Yet these points condemned them and anyone who doesn't believe in Jesus. Abraham and Moses could see Jesus in the sacrifices, even though He was still thousands of years away! What about us? There is no greater warning in the Bible. Our parents were Christians. They knew Jesus, the Light of the world! They received their passports. Their tickets were purchased. They were ready to travel! Are we?

Prayer: Dear Lord Jesus, You are our passport, our ticket, our only way to Heaven! Help us to see the *"Light."* In Jesus' name we pray. Amen.

December 29

"I consider that our present sufferings are not worth comparing with the glory that will be revealed in us." Romans 8:18

Pain - Big Time Pain

Dorothy was in incredible pain. She lost her husband in the accident. She herself was crushed. The physical and emotional pain was almost unbearable! Her eyes told the story. What can we say to her? We have never had the kind of pain that she is now going through. We are so inadequate to help her, in our own strength. We must point her to Jesus who knows all about her pain!

"Dorothy, we can't help you much, but Jesus can. He understands your hurt! Think about Jesus. Think of Him hanging on that Cross. Think of His broken body. It was beaten to a pulp. He was stripped of all His dignity. He even hung naked on that Cross. Think about His mental condition. His best friends willingly left Him! But, He will not leave you, ever. He is with you. He has invited you to come to Him. So, go to Him. Pour out your heart to Him who can help you. Go to the very throne room of Heaven!" Let us pray for all the "Dorothys" out there.

Prayer: Dear Lord, You know how much it hurts! We need Your help and comfort! Lord there is no need to tell You all about what happened. You have seen it all. Lord, we are so tempted to ask, "Why did this happen?" But then Lord, we don't really need to know all the whys. We just want to trust You because You are the Author and Perfecter of our faith! You said, *"Come to Me, all you who are weary and burdened, and I will give you rest,"* Matthew 11:28. So, Lord, here we are. We kneel as Your child, looking for You to give us the strength and grace that we so desperately need! Lord impress Your promises upon us more and more. Fill us with Your holy presence. Help us to have Your mind and the mind of Paul who suffered much for Your name. Help us to believe, to experience, and to say with Paul, *"I consider that our present sufferings are not worth comparing with the glory that will be revealed in us,"* Romans 8:18. Lord, we trust that somehow You are working all of these things for Your glory and even for our good. We commit our body and soul to Your precious care because You bought us with Your blood. We are Yours Lord. In Jesus' name we do pray. Amen.

December 30

"Before I was afflicted I went astray, but now I obey Your Word."
Psalm 119:67

Affliction, God's obedience prod

Spurgeon said, "It is a most solemn fact that human nature can scarcely bear a long continuance of peace and health. It is almost necessary that we should be every now and then salted with affliction, lest we putrefy with sin!" How true.

There is an old story about a Greek soldier. He had an extremely painful disease. He was sure that he would die soon, yet he managed to live. This soldier was always the first into battle. He went where the fighting was the hardest. He was the bravest man in his company. His pain prompted him to fight so he might forget it. He did not fear to die because he thought he was almost dead anyway! The company commander loved the bravery of this man who was an inspiration to all. So the commander sent this man to the best physician and he was healed. From that day on the soldier was absent from the front of the battle. He now sought a life of ease because he had something to live for. He had health, family, a nice home and many other comforts. Now he would not risk his life as he did before.

We are much like this man! When our troubles are many, grace is right there to make us more courageous for serving God! We are more motivated by the hope of Heaven. We are filled with more zeal for the Lord. We understand our time is short. But then, prosperity comes. The good times and many comforts soon make us soft. The joys and pleasures in abundance make it difficult to think of the world to come. We love our easy chairs. We leave the Lord's battles to someone else. We did our part. We fought the good fight. We are tired of fighting.

We must learn something from trees and fish. A tree that feels no wind is weak. A tree that is not growing is dead! A fish that swims up stream is healthy. A fish that floats down the stream is dead. Are we growing and alive or are we dead?

Prayer: O gracious Lord wake us up. Do not allow us to sleep spiritually! Help us to appreciate Your rod of affliction! We want to be more faithful to You Lord. In Jesus' name we pray. Amen.

December 31

"May the Lord make your love increase and overflow for each other and for everyone else, just as ours does for you. May He strengthen your hearts so that you will be blameless and holy in the presence of our God and Father when our Lord Jesus comes with all His holy ones."
I Thessalonians 3:12-13

A beautiful benediction

Paul is giving a benediction to the Thessalonians. He has just received a report from Timothy. Paul is greatly encouraged by the progress that the Thessalonian church has made in their Biblical living habits. Like a father to this church, Paul longs to see them again, yet can't at this time. So he prays to God for them! All those who teach sincerely, must have these feelings for the ones they are discipling. May this prayer of Paul's bless us as we grow and are a blessing to God's church!

"May the Lord make your love increase." We will never be able to reach deep down inside ourselves for more love for others. Love must come from God. So dependent are we on the grace and power of God! Recognizing God's power, Paul cries out to God for those he is discipling. Are we doing this? If not, this would be a reason we are not seeing much spiritual growth in our personal discipleship efforts. The older we grow in Christ the more we must pray. What else can we do but pray? It is God who changes hearts!

"May He strengthen your hearts so that you may be blameless and holy." Paul again pours his heart out to God. This time he adds a call to holy living. What a great point. Good doctrine must be applied to holy living or our "good doctrine" will crush us! How many people have we already seen that go to church on Sunday but give so little evidence of faith and obediencce in their day to day living? May this not be said of us. Living a holy life is preaching a sermon without words. May we all preach it! God blesses that!

Prayer: O Lord, in Your grace, You have given us good benedictions all over the Bible. Here You lift up Your holy and powerful hand and press it on our hearts. Lord how we need to be impressed by You. Glorify Your name in all the earth! In Jesus' name we pray. Amen

Our first yearly devotional is entitled:
Bind Them Upon Your Heart Forever

Our third yearly devotional is titled:
Bible Characters
The Great And The Not So Great